The Art of Teaching Ballet

Gretchen Ward Warren

The Art of
Teaching Ballet

TEN TWENTIETH-CENTURY MASTERS

UNIVERSITY PRESS OF FLORIDA

Gainesville · Tallahassee · Tampa · Boca Raton · Pensacola · Orlando · Miami · Jacksonville

01   00   99   98   97   96   6   5   4   3   2   1

Library of Congress Cataloging-in-Publication Data
Warren, Gretchen Ward.
The art of teaching ballet: ten twentieth-century masters /
Gretchen Ward Warren.
p. cm.
Includes bibliographical references (p.) and index.
ISBN 0-8130-1459-x (cloth: alk. paper)
1. Ballet—Study and teaching—History—20th century.
2. Dance teachers—Biography. I. Title.
GV1788.5.W27 1996
792.8'07—dc20   96-24408

Book design by Louise OFarrell

Frontispiece: Anne Woolliams teaching at her school in
Zurich in 1991.

The University Press of Florida is the scholarly publishing
agency for the State University System of Florida,
comprised of Florida A & M University, Florida Atlantic
University, Florida International University, Florida State
University, University of Central Florida, University of
Florida, University of North Florida, University of South
Florida, and University of West Florida.

University Press of Florida
15 Northwest 15th Street
Gainesville, FL 32611

Dedicated with love and gratitude to Mila Gibbons

Contents

David Howard in his New York City Studio, working with dancer Fritz Masten.

Foreword

WRITING A FOREWORD to this book about remarkable teachers has most definitely raised important issues for me concerning both the place of the teacher in a dancer's life and the essential qualities that define great teaching.

Often we see teachers who possess great charisma and who have opinions on everything. These are not necessarily the qualities that will do much for the dancer with serious aspirations to be an artist with a masterful technique. I prefer to define the true teacher as someone with an immense knowledge of the body-instrument, intellectual mastery of the ballet vocabulary, and the coordination necessary to perform it in a seemingly harmonious and natural fashion. Add to these a powerful movement sense, a clearly defined discipline, based on love rather than rigidity, and we are almost there. To complete this definition I must mention that difficult-to-describe element, the "eye," which can often instantaneously perceive why something is not working successfully. This eye can be developed to a certain extent, but I think it is a given, something inborn, akin to a dancer's talent.

An ancient proverb attributed to the Chinese, "The teacher opens the door, you walk through it yourself," is an expression of rare profundity with its resonating life message about the taking on of responsibility. It evokes several thought-provoking images for me; one is that of the dancer at the moment of the step and the immeasurable possibilities of it. The other image is of teachers who have opened the door. Questions and hopes fill my mind. How have they opened it? Have they passed on all of the best they know of the past, representing it with honor and dedication? Have they done it without limiting the pupil's curiosity and enthusiasm for the new and unknown? While building the dancer's technique, have they awakened the artist's soul and fanned the flames of inspiration, which must carry the dancer forward through an entire career? What an amazing balancing act, this meshing of body, mind, and soul! It is an incredible challenge, an immense responsibility.

With time and patience, this slow process can expand the life and vision of the dancer, who embraces even the frustrations and the standstills as part of the path that merges career and life.

Being a teacher can be a glorious, lifelong connection to learning, with its wellsprings of curiosity and vitality. Sometimes teaching can even bring the reward of having a pupil stand on one's shoulders to teach everything you have taught, enhanced by the new, vital experiences accorded to him or her. And so it should be.

I know that Gretchen Ward Warren knows all of this. As a dancer, in the time when she worked under my direction in the Pennsylvania Ballet, she impressed me repeatedly with her artistry and her dedication. In her subsequent career as a ballet master, teacher, designer, and writer, she has expanded her skills. Always deep-thinking, curious, and meticulous, she has, in writing about these outstanding teachers, brought them vividly to life. She has recorded them in their maturity as they pass on their legacies, making this book truly an homage to the art of teaching.

Benjamin Harkarvy
Director, Dance Division
The Juilliard School, New York City

Acknowledgments

I WISH TO THANK the following people, each of whom contributed in some special way to making this book a reality: Stella and Will Applebaum, Robin Becker and Peter Galdi, Claude Bessy, Elisabeth Carroll, Terri Charlesworth, Christian Cherry, Susan Danby, Gustav Ecmk and Birgitta Trommler, Fred and Suzanne Endsley, Mila Gibbons, Carol and Peter Gluck, Brenda Gray, Joelle Ingalls, Martin Kravitz, Eugenie Kuffler, Hugette du Lac and Michel Rigal, Deirdre Lee, M. Levinson, Victoria Milton, Helga Nicolas, Eve Pettinger, Sandra Robinson-Waldrop, Emmanuel and Jacqueline Rous, Bonnie and Stephen Simon, Steven and Susan McLain Smith, Arnold Spohr, Hanna and Gottfried Staiger, Margaret Sweet, Violette Verdy, Arthur and Ruth Helen Vogel, Herman and Margery Ward, Jack and Jill Tartar Welch, and Dr. Timothy Wilson, the understanding chairman of the University of South Florida Dance Department. In addition, I am especially grateful for the generous support of the University of South Florida's Division of Sponsored Research. I would also like to offer a special note of thanks to all those dancers who took the time to share with me memories of their teachers. Your tributes proved an invaluable addition to the text. I am deeply grateful to Benjamin Harkarvy for the foreword, and, finally, to the University Press of Florida, in particular Deidre Bryan, Louise OFarrell, and Sharon Damoff.

The Art of Teaching Ballet

Christiane Vaussard teaching class at the Paris Opera Ballet School.

Introduction

"The work of the instructor is an art, and what a great art! The artist creates the role, the teacher molds the personality of the artist into one capable of creating an artistic image ... let us not discuss who is more important. Let us agree that the work of the artist and the work of the teacher are both arts."

GALINA ULANOVA

It has been more than 300 years since Louis XIV of France founded the first ballet school, the Académie Royale de Danse. No doubt, he would be amazed at what has developed from the seed he sowed. Today, ballet enjoys a level of technical virtuosity and stylistic diversity that Louis XIV could never have envisioned. The growth of the art form has been fueled by international popularity on a scale unimaginable even a century ago. To support audience demand, ballet academies and companies flourish in almost every major cosmopolitan center in the world. And it is there, where dancers live, train, and work, that one finds the great ballet teachers. They are the keepers of the flame of an art form that has, regardless of its Eurocentric roots and outmoded aristocratic bloodlines, withstood the test of time. Quite simply, without these remarkable pedagogues, the art of ballet, rooted in tradition, would not survive, nor would its future, forever dependent upon the development of young talent, be ensured.

This book was conceived to showcase the exceptional mastery of several famous ballet teachers and, perhaps, to provoke certain questions about the nature of greatness. I originally embarked on the project as a personal quest. I was at the twenty-five-year mark in my own teaching career. I was looking for inspiration and I was curious. What was it, I wanted to know, that made certain ballet teachers so effective? So beloved? As I watched those profiled in this book, I found that certain common denominators did exist, but the discovery of these did not answer the definitive question: "What was it that made the atmosphere in these teachers' classrooms so magical?" As I began to write, I found my thoughts returning again and again to memories of my own first ballet teacher.

Mila Gibbons, with whom I began training at age ten in Princeton, New Jersey, was the embodiment of the word "dignity." A woman of few words and much mystery, she had impeccable, gracious manners. She floated around the studio, straight-backed and elegant in a simple black dress. The nobility and grace with which she executed even a plain ballet walk clearly communicated that dance was far more than an athletic endeavor. Having been raised in Paris, where she was trained in the 1930s by the great Leo Staats, she spoke fluent French. Her perfectly accented pronunciation, full of luxuriously rolled r's, lent a certain nobility to the French ballet terms.

Mila, with her trim, made-for-ballet physique, had more turn-out and extension than any of us, as well as very firmly developed *derrière* muscles, which she occasionally insisted we feel in order to emphasize how important the gluteal muscles were to a dancer's technique. She had the purest, most beautiful *port de bras* one could imagine and always, wearing the best of French perfume, smelled divine.

Ballet was serious business for Mila; strict professional rules of conduct governed her studio. Children who wished to dress up in sequined tutus and participate in lavishly produced recitals did not flock to study with her. Only classical ballet was taught at the Aparri School of Dance—no toe tap, baton-twirling, or acrobatics—although Mila, a thoroughly independent and cultivated woman, had a sophisticated appreciation of modern dance. At the end of each year, she staged lovely choreographed demonstrations of class work—tailored to our limited technical abilities—which we performed in her studio for our parents. Taste was the name of the game. This was art. And it rubbed off on all of us. We learned that the stage and preparation for being on it were sacred—lessons that served us well throughout our careers.

Once, when I was fourteen and boldly declared my intent to augment my dance studies with jazz classes (having recently discovered, in a local musical production, the joys of pelvic isolations performed to a steady beat), she politely, and unilaterally, decided I should take a hiatus from her studio. I was stunned, but I got the message: the last thing a young ballet dancer needed was to have her placement tampered with by jazz isolations. Plenty of time for that later on when one's ballet technique was solidly under control. Frantic to reinstate myself in Mila's good graces, I begged to be readmitted. Fortunately, she took me back.

Her classes were impeccably structured and accompanied by recordings of classical music. Although it was rarely used, a large black grand piano—polished and waiting, it seemed, for its moment of glory—majestically occupied one corner of the studio. Those of us fortunate enough to study at the Aparri School quickly came to understand that there were definite standards in the professional ballet world, from courteous manners to perfectly slicked hairdos. But the atmosphere in class never seemed rigid or stifling. On the contrary, studying with Mila was more like going to church—pure and exhilarating. She was the most glamorous role model I had, and she fed my dreams. I hung on her every word.

I was never Mila's best student—my body was hardly tailor-made for classical ballet. But I was certainly one of her most devoted. My twice-weekly ballet classes were the highlight of my adolescent years, and, although I'm certain Mila, knowing my physical limitations, had serious reservations about my potential for success in the professional world, she was never anything less than encouraging. Perhaps sensing destiny in the making, my mother saved a school essay from sometime during this period in which I rather pompously declared: "If there is anything I cannot bear it is sloppy teaching." Obviously, I was learning about much more than *tendus* and *pas de chats* from Mila Gibbons. She instilled in me a life-long love of ballet, and, through her example, a great respect for those whose lives are devoted to teaching it well.

I suspect that my desire to write this book had something to do with my wanting to reexamine and put into words what Mila Gibbons, by example, had taught me about the art of teaching. Thus, indirectly, it is as much a tribute to her as it is to the ten world-renowned teachers it profiles. Above all, it is my way of ensuring that the wisdom and methods of these great pedagogues will not be forgotten. Many books have been written about great dancers and choreographers; few have been written about their teachers, most of whose names remain unknown to the majority of the ballet-going public. As one of them so aptly put it, "When we leave the stage to devote our lives to teaching, we must accept that we move from the spotlight into the shadows." Yet teachers are the force and inspiration behind every performance that we, the audience, attend. In fact, without *their* discerning and demanding eyes, no dancer could ever be prepared for *our* eyes.

I have known some of the teachers included in this book for years. Others, I met for the first time when I started the project. The research was pure joy, especially in light of the fact that I was decidedly ready for some mid-career reenergizing. Not only did I watch them teach, but I also spent many hours in conversation with them. With every session, I was further inspired. Observing these teachers—some of whom have spent fifty years in the classroom—was, for me, akin to going to a guru. Each one was extremely generous with both time and information. All seemed delighted, even surprised, that I was interested in writing about them.

Before starting my visits, I had only a general list of teachers I thought I might want to include in the book. It was not a short list. I had been compiling it for some time, asking well-known professional dancers everywhere to suggest names of teachers they held in high esteem. Certain names, I discovered, kept reappearing. I added these names to my own list—those to whom, for years as a young teacher, I had looked for guidance and inspiration. The problems arose when I finally had to narrow the list to ten. There are many distinguished ballet teachers in the world today, profiles of whom could fill several volumes. Would that I were able to pay tribute to all of them! However, in the end, my final selection was influenced by many factors besides reputation.

First, and foremost, was the issue of age. During my lifetime several legendary ballet pedagogues of the twentieth century—people such as Lubov Egorova, Vera Volkova, and Alexander Pushkin—have passed away, leaving behind little or no written documentation of their work. They live only in the memories of those they taught. I was determined not to let this happen to several great elderly teachers living today. Therefore, priority was given to those who were seventy to ninety years old. It was also important to me that all had been teaching for many years and were true pedagogues, in the sense that their extensive knowledge rendered them skilled at teaching all levels of ballet, from beginning to professional, regardless of whether they currently chose to do so.

Second was the issue of language. Obviously, I was concerned about accuracy in conveying the thoughts these teachers shared with me. Although I speak a bit of French and German, I am, unfortunately, fluent only in English. Early in the project, I determined that interviewing non-English-speaking teachers would be difficult, primarily because finding skilled simultaneous translators who were also thoroughly knowledgeable about ballet would not be easy. When I experimented, I found that working through an interpreter in the interview sessions was laborious, but possible. However, in the classroom (where I was particularly curious about the choice of words used to communicate with students), it proved wholly unsatisfactory. First, I felt that the whispering voices of observer and translator, quiet as we tried to be, were probably distracting to the class. More important, though, was the fact that without a ballet teacher's perspective, the interpreter often could not understand, and therefore could not translate, the corrections being given. I found myself missing a lot. The teacher would make a brief comment, the class would laugh, the interpreter would look mystified, and I would be thoroughly frustrated! Therefore, with one exception, I decided to limit myself to writing about teachers who taught in English, although in the case of several it was not their native language.

Also related to the issue of language was the fact that ballet teachers seem to fall into two categories of personalities. Some are very verbal creatures in the classroom; some are not. This does not seem to affect the ability of both types to be equally fine teachers. Several of the most revered master teachers give beautiful classes, make excellent, quiet "hands-on" corrections, but say little. More than anything else, it is their skillfully constructed exercises that seem to teach the dancers. (Baryshnikov's famous Leningrad teacher, Alexander Pushkin, apparently exemplified this approach.) However, I found writing about such taciturn personalities difficult. Therefore, I gravitated toward those who were more colorful communicators, who used a great deal of humor and verbal imagery in the classroom. They simply provided better writing material.

To reflect the international scope of classical ballet, I tried for as wide a geographical distribution of teachers as was possible on my limited travel budget. I chose five teachers from across the United States, one from Australia, and four from Europe. Unfortunately, neither the Far East nor Russia is directly represented. However, four of the teachers included were trained in the former Soviet Union and, I feel, represent the best aspects of the Vaganova-based Russian method. Perhaps my largest regret is the lack of a representative from the Bournonville School.

In the end, the choice was intensely personal. There was no doubt in my mind that those teachers who had been my major mentors for many years must be included. I wanted to share with others, as well as record for posterity, what they had so generously shared with me. With those I had not known prior to beginning the book, the choice was made, finally, because, after watching them teach, I felt a strong desire to study with them at this time in my own development as a teacher. Each had something special that piqued my curiosity, that I wanted to tap.

During the interviews, I asked all the teachers the same questions; however, I did not always receive direct answers. Often, a teacher would steer the conversation toward an alternate subject about which he or she was especially passionate. When this happened, I did not fight it. Interviews, like dances being choreographed, often develop a life of their own! Therefore, each chapter is somewhat unique in content and structure, though all contain biographical material on the teachers, as well as my impressions from watching their classes.

Readers who wish to compare and contrast specific aspects of the teachers' philosophies regarding such areas of ballet technique as proper use of turn-out should be aware that this book was not conceived as a how-to-teach-technique reference text. (Many of these, including my own, *Classical Ballet Technique,* already exist.) Instead, my research in conversation with these teachers, as well as in observing their teaching, focused on the broader philosophical aspects of training dancers, such as class presentation, as well as the important issue of how each teacher has continued to grow and develop over the years. Therefore, I purposely limited myself with regard to writing about strictly technical details.

As the reader will note, many points of view about training dancers are contained in this book—some are contradictory, a few depart from the accepted norm. It was my decision not to comment on which approach might be more valid, or more effective—not only because I feel extremely humble in the presence of these very experienced pedagogues, but also because, as a teacher, experience has taught me that there is never only one way to achieve desired results. Each teacher in this book adheres to a personal system and philosophy that works for him or her at this time in his or her own development. My hope is that the diversity of opinions presented, as well as the similarities, will stimulate teachers reading this book (as they certainly stimulated me) to reflect upon their own methodologies.

One of the most interesting discoveries I made came during interviews with the teachers' former students, now professional dancers. Almost all had difficulty recalling specifics other than the general impact a particular teacher had on them. Their descriptions were always full of superlatives: "She was just incredible, I owe her everything"; or, "He always said such wonderful things in class"; but, surprisingly, few could remember exact words or anecdotes! Therefore, the amount of information provided by former students varies somewhat from chapter to chapter. In no way should a lack of material for one teacher in comparison to another be construed to imply that there was a shortage of former students eager to sing a teacher's praises. There was not. I simply chose to include quotations only from those who provided me with specific material that I felt added a further dimension to my own observations.

Gathered at the end of the book is a selection of exercises culled from the classes I observed. In all cases, these exercises were chosen because I felt they were unique in one way or another to the teacher—signature exercises, one might say. Often, I have noted above an exercise what I felt was particularly unusual or beneficial about it. I have enjoyed using all these exercises at one time or another in my own classes. When I asked one of the teachers, Christiane Vaussard, if she minded if I "stole" some of her *enchaînements* for my own students, she politely corrected me: "Ah, but it's not stealing, dear," she said. "We are obligated as teachers to pass on the good ideas we were given by our own teachers. I do not own this material!" If I had been harboring any misgivings about including the teachers' exercises in this book, they were laid to rest at that moment. Indeed, I found all the teachers as generous as Vaussard. I believe, however, that they would wish me to note that these exercises represent an evolution in their teaching, that they are perhaps different from exercises used by them in the past, and will perhaps not be representative of exercises used in the future. All see themselves as ever-changing in their approaches to teaching ballet.

The reader should also note that the "Order of the Exercises" list at the end of each chapter reflects the structure of only one class from among the many I observed. While I believe this order to be typical of each teacher, the content of individual exercises obviously varies from class to class.

Having now completed the wonderful voyage of writing this book, I find myself, as I suspected, no closer than I was before to being able to describe the exact nature of what it is that elevates a particular teacher to greatness—that intangible quality that produces the classroom atmosphere in which students' natural talent blossoms and flourishes. Obviously, all profiled in *The Art of Teaching Ballet* are skilled and thoroughly schooled in the traditions of classical ballet. Six of them have directed professional ballet companies and seven, their own schools. All had professional careers, although some danced for only a short time. None could be said to have attained in their own dancing the heights of international stardom to which they have led certain students. Most were recognized early in their professional lives as being unusually gifted as teachers, and all of them were themselves students at one time or another of great teachers such as Carlotta Zambelli, Lubov Egorova, or Vera Volkova.

However, among them are some wide differences. Some are stricter disciplinarians in the classroom than others. Some have a wide variety of interests outside dance, some don't. Some are very theoretical in their approach, others very instinctual.

Most common to all, I found, was wonderful musicality, a gift for simplicity (always a mark of greatness) in both exercise construction and communication, complete devotion to the art and teaching of dance, and constant curiosity and desire to discover new ways to teach an old art. All are blessed with remarkable memories and demonstrate an admirable sense of command over material and goals. But these characteristics could also apply to many fine ballet teachers who have not been elevated by reputation to the top ranks of master teachers. So, what is it that differentiates them?

In the end, it seems to boil down to exactly what distinguishes a virtuoso technician from a great artist—personality. A great teacher is one in whose presence students are enchanted. In fact, learning becomes irresistible. A great teacher, like a great chef, is a master at presentation, at making something—even something as painstakingly difficult as the study of classical ballet—so palatable that students swallow without hesitation. And do so joyfully! How exactly these teachers, so full of electricity and physical exhilaration, do this can no more be fully described than imitated. Because much of their magic has to do with personal charisma, it is something that must be seen and felt to be fully appreciated. Even then it remains a bit mysterious, somewhat beyond explanation. One must simply accept the fact (and rejoice in it!) that these special people are born to greatness in teaching—in the same way that artists like Fonteyn and Nureyev were born to greatness in dancing.

To all included here, I owe a great debt of gratitude. I will never forget my time with them. I am keenly aware of their words and example guiding me every day when I teach my own students. They have enriched my life just as they have enriched the lives of so many of the world's best ballet dancers. And they have taught all of us privileged enough to have witnessed their teaching, just as Mila Gibbons so long ago taught me, about far more than the rudiments of classical ballet technique.

1 *Marika Besobrasova*

Marika Besobrasova teaching at her school in Monte Carlo in 1991.

*M*arika Besobrasova is one of Europe's most renowned ballet teachers. She has taught in Monte Carlo since the early 1940s. Her school, L'Ecole de Danse Marika Besobrasova, attracts an international array of students and professionals. Although born in Russia, Besobrasova was raised, and received her dance training, in France. She performed with René Blum's Ballets de Monte Carlo in the 1930s, and, in 1940, while still in her twenties, founded the Ballets de Cannes de Marika Besobrasova. From 1949 to 1950 she worked as ballet mistress and company teacher with the Ballets des Champs-Elysées. Subsequently, in addition to maintaining her own school in Monte Carlo, she also directed the schools of the Ballet de l'Opéra de Zurich, and the Ballet de l'Opéra de Rome (1966–69). She is a frequent guest teacher throughout Europe and, since 1970, has maintained a close relationship with the Stuttgart Ballet. In 1971, she staged Nureyev's *Paquita* for American Ballet Theatre in New York City.

During the 1960s, Besobrasova developed her teaching system into an eleven-year program. Based on Vaganova's Russian syllabus, but heavily influenced by the French School, her system, complete with examinations, is now used by teachers in several countries. Besobrasova is a frequent member of the jury at international dance competitions. She has been decorated on several occasions and is a close friend of Monaco's royal family. Prince Rainier provided her with the lovely villa, Casa Mia, in which her academy in Monte Carlo has been housed since 1974. It was there that I first visited her in 1991.

"You must be

on balance in

the air!"

EACH MORNING, Marika Besobrasova takes a moment to enjoy the view from the balcony of her spacious apartment high in the hills of Monte Carlo. She has already exercised, eaten breakfast, and checked on her many potted plants, including an impressive collection of orchids. As she watches, the pink sun slowly rises through a thick blanket of gray mist over the Mediterranean. Below her, on rocky cliffs descending to the water, the tiny principality of Monaco, a picturesque collage of pastel buildings, flower-filled gardens, and winding streets, sits tightly packed around an azure harbor filled with luxury yachts. Besobrasova has lived here—the city where Diaghilev[1] presented his famous Ballets Russes in the 1920s—for almost sixty years.

Early mornings are the only quiet time in Besobrasova's long days. Yet, even in these calm moments, there is an air of impatience about her. At seventy-three, with her tall, trim figure, she is still a very active woman. Her face, with its aquiline nose and flashing Nordic-blue eyes, reflects a strong, resilient character. Abruptly, she gathers her things, calls for her ever-present Bedlington terrier, Doucy, and descends to the garage for her car. Her first class of the morning begins at 8:30 A.M.

It was only on the five-minute drives to and from her school that I ever saw Besobrasova lose her aristocratic manners. Her performance rivals that of any Parisian taxi driver. Honking and swerving her deluxe sedan through Monaco's narrow streets, she comments colorfully upon the lack of driving ability of all around her. Upon arrival at her academy, Casa Mia, she leaves her car keys with the Italian caretaker, briskly climbs the stone steps to the vestibule, and swirls into her office, casting aside her silk scarf.

In the few minutes before she begins her morning class, Besobrasova may discuss correspondence with her secretary, take international phone calls, answer questions about costumes or music for upcoming performances, or discuss building problems. Perpetually besieged by all the mundane matters of running a large academy (sometimes even in the middle of teaching a class), she somehow manages to remain calm and businesslike.

Surprisingly, in spite of her fame and aristocratic Russian background, Besobrasova has no airs about her. She is neither grandiose nor remote. Polite, efficient, and often wryly humorous, she is simultaneously dignified and down-to-earth. She has a quick, delightful smile that can, in a second, interrupt the determined set of her jaw, causing years to disappear from her face. She moves fast and is by nature a problem solver. One can imagine her rolling up her sleeves without hesitation in order to mop a dance floor or mend costumes.

Her desire to be heavily involved in every aspect of her academy—even if it means, as it usually does, ten-hour work days—is, no doubt, one of the main reasons her school has endured successfully for almost half a century.[2] The intensity of this involvement is reflected in Besobrasova's description of her relationship to her students. "I am not a teacher," she says emphatically in her delightfully accented English, "I am a master—something much more than a teacher." Her statement is not made in an egotistical way. As she explains, "If I'm only a teacher, I will make sure that you begin class on time, finish on time, that you don't miss the next class, and that you know your program. And I will correct your physical and even musical mistakes, but I will not look at your entire life. As a master, I have the right to examine the way a student lives—if, for instance, he is not taking rest at the right moment, or not concentrating insofar as reviewing his day or properly planning for the next. As a master, I have the right to say anything to my pupils. I look further than just teaching—into their souls, not just at the skin."

Elizabeth Hertel, a soloist with the Stuttgart Ballet who trained with Besobrasova for seven years, says: "I'm a very pessimistic person, and she taught me how to be a fighter, to push myself to get through things, to kick myself to go for it, not to waver. One of her favorite sayings is '*Prenez vous par le main*' [Take yourself by the hand]. In other words, don't just stand there and feel sorry for yourself."

Besobrasova feels this kind of personalized teaching is necessary to help students become aware of who they are and how they are acting. "Awareness," she says, "is the key to understanding one's problems. A person makes mistakes until he is aware of making them. A dancer will not correct his 5th position until he corrects his own way of approaching that 5th position." She believes students must be sincere: "They must be willing to be corrected and not pay you just to look at them and admire them, which makes no sense for either you or them."

She readily admits that she or any teacher can make mistakes at various times. "But," she says, "I always know why I have chosen a particular path for the moment. I know, for instance, that even though a mistake may result from my pushing him too fast in a certain area, that this is not as important as another thing I have to make him understand first. But I will always be sincere; if my method doesn't work, I'll say, 'Excuse me. I made a mistake. Let's try something else'."

There is something motherly about Besobrasova. She is charming and earnest as she moves quietly along the barre using her hands to correct the dancers' bodies. Sometimes she leans close to a student, saying something in a low voice, and both will giggle. Often, narrowing her eyes, she will concentrate her gaze on a student across the room for several moments before she speaks. "I try to develop the capacity with myself to penetrate my students," she says. "I stop all my own thoughts and feelings and just go in them. It's a very difficult task because you agree to abdicate yourself, but, in so doing, you start to feel how they feel when they are moving. Then I understand how they are working their machine and what is wrong."

In order to make a student aware of his problems, Besobrasova often uses physical contact. She explains: "I will make him feel my breath, the pulsation of the muscles. I'll make him move my arms, or I'll stand in back of him and make him move." She may jolt a student into awareness by putting him on the spot with a question such as: "Why do you move your shoulders when you start to move your left foot? Can you explain that relationship to me?" One day, when a young lady was having trouble getting her hips into the air on a *failli-assemblé* combination, Besobrasova dragged a chair onto the floor, and, holding the girl's hand, commanded her to step up onto the seat ("*Montez!* Push up!"). Complying, the student immediately felt exactly which muscles must be strongly activated in order to elevate the body from the ground.

Just before 8:30 each morning, Besobrasova breezes hurriedly into the sunny top-floor studio at Casa Mia. It is a lovely, long, pale-pink room with a hardwood floor. A line of partially shuttered, arched, Renaissance-style windows—reminiscent, perhaps, of a set design for *Romeo and Juliet*—stretches along one entire wall above the barre. Through them one sees a vast expanse of blue sky and, on the rocky cliffs across the harbor, the palace of Prince Rainier.

As the students finish stretching and pulling on their shoes, Besobrasova disappears into a small dressing room adjacent to the studio. Quickly, she reappears clad in a dark knee-length skirt, pink tights, and a pretty black-lace leotard. Around her neck are a pair of delicate gold chains. She claps her hands. "*Bon! Allez! Travaillez!* [Good! Let's go! Time to work!]" The students space themselves a few feet away from the barre. Taking a deep breath, they lift their arms to the ceiling. As the music begins, they bend forward, heads dropping toward their knees, in the stretch with which Besobrasova begins all her classes.

Several mornings a week, Besobrasova teaches two classes, working from 8:30 until noon without a break—a very long stretch for anyone, let alone a person in her mid-seventies. Yet she does not seem to tire, perhaps because she paces herself well. She is also well cared for; midway through the morning, her secretary arrives bearing a small tray with biscuits and coffee in a china cup. Besobrasova dispenses with both quickly, almost without thinking and never taking her eyes from the dancers. Although she still has a lovely pair of long, shapely dancer's legs and can move easily and gracefully, she maintains a quiet, rather than demonstrative, presence as she teaches. Her focus is entirely on the students. Only occasionally will she draw attention to herself as a physical example, primarily when making a point about artistry. She is fond of demonstrating (to those who dance with dour faces) how vibrant a dancer's face must be in order to catch an audience's attention. Her students told me that Besobrasova's ability to transform her face momentarily from that of an elderly teacher to a beautiful young ballerina never ceases to amaze them.

Elisabeth Carroll, a former ballerina with the Harkness Ballet who studied with Besobrasova from age fourteen to seventeen, recalls: "When Marika demonstrated, we had to stand perfectly still and watch. Her artistry, coordination, and flow of movement were an inspiration. There was so much to learn by observing the care she gave to small details—the way she used her head and eyes in connection to the tips of her fingers, her feet, and beyond. I watched with my entire being and absorbed in complete trust, hoping to move as gracefully as Marika did. She always told us: 'You must be as expressive with your feet as you are with your hands. Talk with them!'" Another former student, Tamako Akiyama, a soloist with the Stuttgart Ballet, still returns whenever possible to study with Besobrasova and notes that "when Marika demonstrates she seems to extend herself beyond her body."

While Besobrasova can be stern and demanding ("Stop! Stop! Inadmissible!"), she exercises utmost patience in class when explaining things. She stresses that the students must understand exactly *how* to do the exercises. Nothing must be arbitrary. Precise placement of the toe or heel in all positions is essential, as is exact rhythm.

I enjoyed watching the detailed manner in which she worked with students' hands. For those with the tendency to curl their fingers, she had a unique solution. She placed a thin, light-weight stick, about the size of a cocktail straw, between their fingers—over the middle finger and underneath the index and fourth fingers. This forced their fingers to lengthen, producing a correctly shaped balletic hand. At the barre, students would execute one side of an exercise with the stick placed in their outside hand, then quickly change it to the other hand when they turned to the other side.

Besobrasova told me, "The hand is made up of two parts: fingers and palm. The palm must be relaxed—in the center—then you begin shaping the hand from the middle finger. It gives the direction. You lift the index and fourth finger and the little finger highest of all. The thumb moves toward the middle finger." She added that she "hated" the old-fashioned curled hand, which she remembers Balanchine[3] (with whom she had a fine friendship) describing as "like holding an orange." She explained: "If you learn to hold the hand like that, you stay like that forever." (In this, she parted company from Balanchine, who favored such a hand position for students.)

When her students execute an arm preparation beginning with a "breath" *port de bras* outward from 5th *en bas*, Besobrasova tells them not to start the movement from their elbow. "Start it from the middle finger—you have to see your fingernails when you *allongé* your hand. And the opening of the arm happens because of an inhalation. As the ribs expand, the whole arm moves outward. This is involuntary, but the fingers—the nails on top and the tips below—these you must consciously move."

Attention to such detail is not unusual in Besobrasova's teaching. During an allegro combination, she repeatedly stressed the importance of coordinating a small movement of the head and body with the leg action in *temps de cuisse*. As the students did the initial *petit passé,* she wanted them to lean and look down at their working foot. As the foot closed in 5th, she instructed them to lift their chests and chins and look up and out while doing the *sissonne* that followed. "It's so important," she told them, "the movement of the body with the leg."

The breadth of knowledge Besobrasova offers her students has been accumulated during more than fifty years of teaching. "I never had the urge to make a big career for myself as a dancer or choreographer," she says simply. "My wish was always to teach." In Monaco, she is a venerated public figure. Everyone in the Casino plaza where we had dinner one night seemed to know her. The bellboys at the adjoining hotel ran to park her car, and our waiter, with whom she chatted cheerfully, produced steak tartare in a dog dish for Doucy. As we talked, she threw bread crumbs to the tiny sparrows that flitted around our table.

Besobrasova was born to Russian parents in the Crimean city of Yalta in 1918. The event took place, she notes, "in a villa in the garden of the palace where the famous Yalta agreement between Stalin, Churchill, and Roosevelt was later signed." Prior to the Russian Revolution, her grandfather had been a general in command of the Czar's guards, and her grandmother had been a lady-in-waiting to the mother of the Czar. Besobrasova's father fought in the White Army until the last possible moment before escaping with his family (and many others of the Russian aristocracy) to Europe. She was two years old. The family was stopped in Constantinople. "We spent forty days on the pier lying out in the open on our luggage without any protection from the weather," she says. "I got double pneumonia and double pleuritis. Because of this, I have a large scar on my back from the operation I had to have at two-and-a-half." She was bandaged for months after this operation and, as a result, developed skeletal problems that were to plague her much of her life.

After leaving Constantinople, the family stopped briefly in Venice, where Besobrasova notes that, at two-and-a-half, she was taken to see Diaghilev's ballet company. Her family settled first in Denmark. "But my grandfather could not stand the difficult climate there," she says. "He soon left for the south of France, and we followed." During the early part of her childhood, she was educated in a convent where one day a week she spoke English, another French, and the rest of the time Russian. (Since then, she has taught herself Italian and German as well.) From the age of nine, she attended the Russian Lycée in Nice. She began to dance at the age of twelve with Madame Julie Sedova[4] after her parents decided that ballet lessons might correct the weakness in her back, the result of her childhood operation. At fifteen, she started her professional career with the opera ballet on the same stage in Monte Carlo where the Diaghilev company had danced.

When her first opera season finished, Besobrasova completed her academic studies and, in 1934 at the age of sixteen, joined René Blum's Ballets de Monte Carlo.[5] She recalls working with Fokine:[6] "He was a genius—a real genius. You could see it in his eyes. The ballets were always ready in his head when he arrived to begin rehearsals with us."

Besobrasova remembers that when she arrived in Paris, she was told by the other dancers, "Tomorrow we will start *Les Sylphides*." She was very

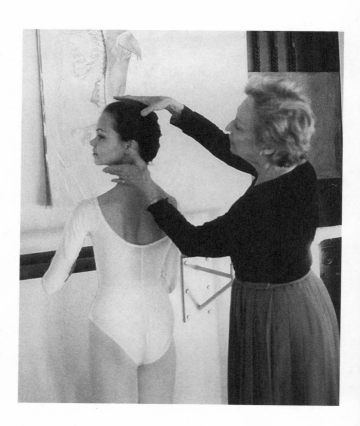

Marika Besobrasova correcting the alignment of a student's head at the barre.

concerned because she seemed to be the only dancer not familiar with the ballet. "So, being sixteen, I had the guts to go to Fokine and say, 'You know, it seems I am the only one who does not know your ballet, *Sylphides*. Would you please forgive me?'" She has never forgotten his reply. "Well," he told her, "you'll be the only one who will know it because the rest all *think* they know it, but they don't!"

She remembers *Les Sylphides* as "lightness and breathing." The movement, she notes, did not come from the arms. It was the arms that reacted to the breath. "Breathing and releasing," she says. "It impressed me so much that in my teaching, there is always a placement of the breath. It is not coming outside the movement; it comes *with* the movement." As she tells her students, "Breath is life. If you don't breathe, you don't live."

Fokine, who was residing in New York City at the time, returned to Europe to accompany the troupe to Monte Carlo, where, Besobrasova recalls, the dancers learned twelve ballets in two months! "We had a season here," she remembers, "and then we went to London. It was a rather peculiar situation because we danced in the old Alhambra Theatre, and the De Basil Ballets Russes was at Covent Garden, so throughout the season there was always this rivalry going on between Blum and De Basil. But we had an enormous success. I remember fifty-six curtain calls after *Scheherazade*."

With the outbreak of war in 1939, Besobrasova, then twenty years old, elected to stay in France rather than follow Blum's company to America. She returned to Monte Carlo and began to give ballet lessons. For a short time, she became involved with staging ballets at the Casino in Monte Carlo, but soon moved to Cannes, where, in 1940, she founded the Ballets de Cannes de Marika Besobrasova. "I was twenty-two," she recalls, "and I really knew nothing, but I took the responsibility of running a company, as well as dancing in it and teaching the dancers." Because it was wartime, many famous dancers came south from Paris to work with her company, among them Janine Charrat, Roland Petit, Serge Golovine, and Jean Babilée.

Babilée, a Paris Opera star, was sent to her by René Blum, who felt it was not safe for the young half-Jewish virtuoso to remain in Nazi-occupied Paris. She remembers the day he arrived. "I understand you are a dancer," she said to him. Without a word, she says, Babilée, then seventeen, assumed a preparatory stance and executed fourteen pirouettes. "Then he threw off his shoes, jumped in the air, and did *entrechat douze*. After that, he looked at me and said in an incredulous tone of voice, 'Do I know how to dance?'"

She says she has known many great dancers. "But Babilée," she says, "did things no one else did. Can you imagine a *grand jeté entrelacé* with a double *tour* in it? And he did a double *manège* of these!" She remembers him as a "fantastic talent," but notes with regret that "he was very naughty, very un-disciplined—a mixture of tiger, monkey, flea, and grasshopper. When I would grumble at him in class, he would do a *jeté* up onto the barre, forcing you to look up at him standing there as you gave the correction. Then, he'd do another fancy *jeté* down. It was very unnerving."

The company in Cannes lasted until 1943. Because of the war, Besobrasova and her dancers endured many hardships, the worst of which was hunger. "There was hardly anything to eat," she recalls, "except olives, mimosa, and carnations." They were saved, she says, by a strange coincidence. The Aga Khan came to a performance one night and, afterward, came backstage. He had recognized the name Besobrasova on the program and wanted to know if she was related in any way to the Besobrasov who had befriended him many years before in St. Petersburg. This man, he told her, had been the president of the balletomanes of the Maryinsky Theatre and, many years ago, had given the Aga Khan, then a young prince, his first tickets to the ballet. The experience had begun his lifelong passion for dance. Besobrasova confirmed that she was indeed related to this man. He was her uncle.

Delighted, the Aga Khan immediately asked what he could do for her, and throughout the war, because his cars had diplomatic immunity, he brought her badly needed supplies from Switzerland: tulle for tutus, chocolate to eat, and vitamins for her dancers. At one point, knowing how exhausted the company was from hunger, he offered to pay for them to take a vacation in the mountains. There it was possible to obtain food, and Besobrasova remembers knitting and mending clothes for the peasants in return for butter and cheese.

In 1943, as the war intensified and the Germans moved south, Besobrasova dissolved her company. She moved to Paris and began studying with two famous teachers: Egorova[7] and Gzovsky.[8] "I worked with her in the morning and him in the afternoon, and between them I had to walk miles and miles because, due to air attacks, there was no public transportation."

She remembers Egorova with particular fondness and believes her greatness as a teacher lay in her wonderful musicality, as well as in her ability to cover in one year all the classical vocabulary. "You wouldn't see it if you only spent a week or two with her," Besobrasova says, "but her classes encompassed a huge amount of material including several steps rarely used in classes today, like *temps de cuisse,* which she'd give with a variety of accents and always with a strong focus on vitality." Besobrasova remembers that Egorova gave a certain *grande pirouette* combination "which was really a man's step" every day in order to build strength in her students. (See "Grande Pirouette Exercise" on p. 286.) Egorova was also, she says, adamant about developing strong backs. "We'd do a stretching exercise with one leg on the barre in which we had to maintain both arms in 5th position above our heads throughout, even when we pivoted to face a new direction. You had to really concentrate on holding your back and keeping your arms aligned with your ears if you wanted to do this without losing your balance."

Besobrasova also notes that when Cecchetti[9] first went to Russia, he invited the young ballerina Egorova to join his master class. (Vaganova,[10] she notes, was not so honored.) "So," she says, "I know from Egorova several early Cecchetti exercises. Later in my life, I met someone who had been one of Cecchetti's last students when he was teaching in London and Milan just before his death. She showed me the same exercises with changes he had made to make them more difficult. So I know two versions that are on either end of a thirty-year time period." Occasionally, Besobrasova inserts some favorite Cecchetti exercises into her classes.

Not only did Besobrasova study with Egorova as a dancer, but she also managed to find a way to have Egorova help train her as a teacher. She tells the following story: "In Paris, I met an American soldier who was a dancer. He wanted ballet lessons, especially because I spoke English, and he found a studio where we could work. I gave him private lessons, but got the idea that instead of paying me, he could pay Madame Egorova to come and watch our sessions in order to give me advice on my teaching. The first lesson came and I was, as usual, correcting his ribs and his back (he pushed his very big stomach out), and Madame Egorova spoke up. 'Leave him alone with that,' she said. 'That's just the way his stomach is.' I replied that I wouldn't dream of letting him go onstage in front of the public like that. 'It's so ugly,' I said. Well, after a while she said, 'By the way, you are right. His stomach is gone now. He has a good position.' So that confirmed my belief that to achieve beauty, the body must be a perfect instrument—not only in technique, but also in placement."

Egorova not only gave her useful advice, but also provided her with a fine opportunity. Once a week she put her classes in Besobrasova's hands. As it happened, that day coincided with the "free" day for the dancers of the Paris Opera Ballet. Therefore, many members of the company came to take Besobrasova's class, including Opera stars, such as Solange Schwartz. "I started to teach," she says, "when I knew nothing. I had to learn myself, but strangely enough I was always interested in sharing whatever I knew and explaining it. Probably I knew instinctively that if I tried to explain it to someone else, I would understand it better myself."

When the war ended, Besobrasova was twenty-six. She was told by her doctors (mistakenly, as it turns out) that she had a bad heart and must stop dancing. "It was a stupid mistake on their part," she says, "but that's when I began to devote myself exclusively to teaching." She returned from Paris to Monte Carlo where, in 1947, she opened her first school. For a short time (1949–50), she divided her time between her students in the south and Paris, where she was company teacher and ballet mistress for the Ballets des Champs-Elysées. In 1952, she finally put down permanent roots in Monte Carlo, founding L'Ecole de Danse Classique de Monte Carlo at the Palais de la Scala.

In the years that followed, Besobrasova became the leading figure in Monte Carlo's dance activities. She was ballet mistress and choreographer for the Monte Carlo Opera. In 1955, she organized an evening of ballet to celebrate the creation of l'Hymne Olympique. In 1956, she was in charge of the gala celebrating the marriage of Prince Rainier and Princess Grace. Repeatedly, at her invitation, major international ballet stars, such as Fracci, Evdokimova, Fonteyn, and Nureyev, came to Monaco to perform with her dancers. As her reputation grew, she was inundated with invitations to work elsewhere. She staged Rudolf Nureyev's *Paquita* for American Ballet Theatre in New York. She guest-taught in Copenhagen, Zurich, Rome, and Paris, and in 1970 was invited to direct the ballet academy of La Scala in Milan. She declined the offer; she had married a Monegasque, and her first loyalty was to her own school in Monte Carlo. She has, however, maintained a part-time affiliation with the Stuttgart Ballet, for whom she has taught on and off since 1970. At the invitation of John Cranko, she toured with them to both the USSR and America. Many dancers trained by her are members of this company. Richard Cragun, principal dancer with the Stuttgart Ballet, told me: "Marika's just tremendous. For years, many of us in Stuttgart ran off to Monte Carlo in the summer to work with her. She has this sort of ageless personality, a kind of beauty in her eyes that always mesmerized me. You feel that she has seen a lot and loves ballet practically more than anyone you've ever known. It's this special quality that comes across, I think, to her students."

Besobrasova waited patiently for more than twenty years for one of her greatest dreams to come true. She wanted a facility in which she could expand her ballet school into a full academy providing both housing and academic classes, as well as dance training. Her dream became a reality in 1974 when Prince Rainier bought for her use the large pink villa Casa Mia, which sits just above Monaco's harbor. This graceful Italianate stucco building of Renaissance columns and arched windows rises steeply on three levels above an elegant terraced garden. Built between 1927 and 1930, it is a vestige of another, more genteel, age in a prime Cote d'Azur real estate location on which most other structures are modern high-rise condominiums and hotels. "I was lucky to get it," Besobrasova says. "Many others wanted it." In gratitude, she named the new facility l'Académie de Danse Classique Princesse Grace after her good friend and benefactor, Rainier's wife.

The first door on the left as one enters Casa Mia's marble vestibule is that of Besobrasova's private office. It is a large, airy room dominated at one end by tall French windows that overlook the harbor. With its high ceiling, ornate furniture, and mirrors, the soft blue-green room seems more drawing room than office. Clustered on the marble fireplace mantle are pieces of dance sculpture and memorabilia. Papers are piled on the coffee table in front of the low, soft-pillowed chaise lounge on which Besobrasova most often sits to work or talk on the telephone. Odd bolts of fabric and stray tutus lie on some of the chairs. Most impressive, however, is the large library of dance books, some quite rare, filling the floor-to-ceiling bookcases. She has been collecting them her entire life.

One of the most important additions to her library was presented to her in 1960 when a friend who was an architect brought a copy of the complete Vaganova syllabus from Russia. Having never before seen a nine-year professional program like this, she became very excited. She was particularly intrigued by the way the Russians developed every movement from its most basic root. Today, she is a strong advocate of the Russian method. "For instance," she says, "they don't work *petit battement* right away. First they work on the position *sur le cou-de-pied,* making the child hold and feel it, and then after that they start to build up the movement toward its final form. Every aspect of each movement is broken down into bits and neatly worked. I realized that every movement could be reduced to a simple, basic form."

After studying the Russian syllabus in great detail, Besobrasova decided to use it as the basis for developing a program of her own. Many teachers, she says, had been asking her for help. Outside the Paris Opera School, no system existed for graded teaching and examinations for the numerous provincial schools throughout France. The arrival of the Russian syllabus provided the impetus she needed. "I started to think," she recalls, "about what we could do for young children (ages six to nine) who should be introduced to all the important basics of ballet training, but who were too young to begin the intensive work contained in the first year of the Russian program. Also, I knew these children would not be training every day, nor were most of them likely to pursue professional careers. In addition, they often came to ballet classes tired, after school." With such students in mind, she created a Preparatory division with two levels, later expanding it to four. To these, she added two other divisions, Elementary (for students aged ten through twelve) with three levels and Superior (for students aged thirteen to seventeen) with five levels. The final four years of this top level, which she termed Excellence I, II, III, and IV, were specifically aimed at students preparing for professional careers in ballet.

In developing her program, Besobrasova says she added a few movements from the French School—*temps de cuisse*, for instance, or the small French *failli* which is like a *glissade* on half-toe—that she feels the Russians had forgotten. "But I found very little that the Russians did not do," she says. "It was a matter of very small details. However, I did have to adjust many of the names they used. They were simply a bad translation of the French. Our teachers here would never have understood them because they were not appropriate." She also mentioned to me how much she liked the way the Russians, in upper-level classes, had incorporated the complication of changes of direction, even turns, into almost every movement, something she says the French system had never done. Today, her classes strongly reflect the Russian influence in this area, both in the centre and at the barre, where she includes all types of pirouettes, as well as *fouettés à terre* and *en l'air, flic-flac en tournant, détournés,* and *soutenus en tournant.*

Her comparisons of the French and Russian Schools led Besobrasova to some interesting insights. She notes *flic-flac* as an example. "With Egorova, we did the initial *flic* the Italian way with a straight leg and the *flac* with a bent knee. The Russians do both movements bent. I realized the root was different. Theirs was closer to *petit battement* with its half-opened leg beats. Personally, I think of this movement as part of a progression: *petit battement* has the small leg openings and the accent is in, *flic-flac* uses both the half-openings and a *frappé*-like movement on the end, and *battement frappé* uses a full opening with the accent out."

Besobrasova credits Rudolf Nureyev[11] with teaching her a great deal about the Russian syllabus. She remembers fondly the times during which Nureyev and the great Danish *premier danseur,* Erik Bruhn, worked together in her studio in Monte Carlo. While Besobrasova watched, often entering into the energetic discussions, Bruhn and Nureyev taught each other the fine points of their two different methods (Danish and Russian).

Besobrasova held her first session of graded examinations open to students outside her own school in 1969. The candidates were pupils of teachers who for several years had been attending special pedagogical seminars offered in the summers by Besobrasova. In these first examinations, 120 students participated. By 1973, the number had risen to 500. Today, approximately 400 students annually take the exams, which are offered each Easter. Her program is used by teachers in Australia, Switzerland, Italy, Spain, Germany, Japan, Korea, and, of course, France.

What those who have attended her teaching seminars find most useful, she says, is the guidance she offers them in how to correct students. Drawing upon her in-depth knowledge of anatomy, she also gives teachers advice about helping students overcome any physical problems. She tells teachers that they must learn how to *see* their students. To help them analyze their pupils' physiques, she offers them the following checklist:

1. Check students' backs for scoliosis.
2. Observe how students' feet are placed when they are standing. Are they rolled (pronated)?
3. Check for a lack of symmetry in the stance. For example, does one arm hang out from the pupil's side while the other is next to his hip?
4. Observe students' bodies from down to up, not vice versa. Problems in the upper body are often the result of something down below.
5. Observe students each day with "new" eyes, because with time some things can get better, but others can get worse. Also, there is always the danger that a teacher's eye will become accustomed to a student's crookedness.

One day in class, Besobrasova watched a girl walking to place in the centre and exclaimed, "You walk like a Russian doll—rocking from side to side. Walking, if you're going forward, is transferring the weight from back to front, not side to side!" She told me that she carefully observes how people walk. "It shows me their inner organization and balance." In a dancer's run, she notes, you see the impulse, the vitality of that person.

Besobrasova, who can often be seen in class squatting next to a student in order to hold the student's feet firmly in proper alignment, is very emphatic about how teachers should use their hands when making corrections. "I always grumble when I see teachers poking, kicking, or pushing students," she says. "If you make a correction with a physical touch on a student's body, then you have to get a physical answer to what you are doing. So you must be patient with your hands. You must wait for the muscles underneath your hands to act. This is how you will know the body has registered the correction, and you must have the sensibility to feel not only when the muscle responds, but also how much it has responded. Teachers must be able to analyze how a pupil's muscle works. Does it, for instance, stretch, then relax right away? Some children have difficulty concentrating for more than half a second. They give an impulse, then they relax, and the muscle is again fluffy, without any vitality." With pupils such as this, she says, it makes no sense to teach them new movements. "First you must teach that child how to make a muscular effort and to keep that effort, because only a sustained effort will produce power in the muscles." Many children, she notes, don't understand that inner muscles exist. "It's an absolute mystery to them, " she says. "You tell a child to pull his tummy in, and he may pull on his skin. He sees his stomach sticking out, but he doesn't know at all what to do. He does not understand that he has inner muscles that must be activated." To illustrate to such students what she's talking about, she has them shake her hand in a greeting. If a student has what she calls a "fluffy hand—like an old piece of tissue—a hand without bones, muscles, nerves or energy," she squeezes his hand and asks him to squeeze hers. When he does so, she will say, "It's not enough. Press on me." Then, she says, often the student will press, then release, press, and again release. "I try to get them to hold the pressure on my hand. Many children are initially incapable of this, and, if they can't do it with their hand, believe me, they can't do it with their feet! It means they have no command to make their muscles obey."

Besobrasova has a series of exercises on the floor for each muscle group. "As soon as students get the idea on the floor, though," she says, "I make them get up and do it in a standing position. Then I will use it in a dance movement." As an example, she cites working on the action of the gluteus medius on the standing leg during *battement tendu*. First, she will have the child use the muscle while lying on the floor. Then she will show him a picture of the muscle and demonstrate where it attaches on the skeleton. Then she will place his hand on her own body so that he can feel the action of the muscle. Finally, she will place her hands on him as he does the movement. After she is certain that he feels the muscle, she will have him do the *tendu* first on one leg, then on the other. Sometimes, she notes, students have difficulty transferring the muscular action from one side of the body to the other. Again, she will help with her hands. She tells the child that, contrary to what he may be thinking, the movement does not go from side to side. "Try to think of maintaining the same center line in your body when you switch from *tendu* on one leg to *tendu* on the other. If you do this," she tells him, "you will be obliged to hold your muscles." The final step in the entire procedure, she says, is, of course, to get the action into the student's muscular memory—something that can be achieved only through much repetition.

Also important to teachers who study with Besobrasova is the way she teaches them to visualize the body. "It's really important to see the body as a whole," she explains. "You will see that if a dancer changes even the slightest aspect of placement, the whole body responds. If the placement is incorrect, the body compensates, but, if it is correct, movement and balance become easier." One day, as I watched class, Besobrasova turned to me and said something that I will never forget: "Dancers," she remarked, "think balance is something you just do on *demi-pointe,* but to be graceful, as well as technically successful, you must be on balance in *plié* and in the air, as well."

Besobrasova remembers that Violette Verdy[12] "always used to say that I had X-ray eyes because I never see the flesh, only the bones. That's how I have the faith to know that I can correct the body of a dancer, because if you have too much flesh, you can get rid of it. If the density of the muscles is wrong, you can change that. If there is underdevelopment in the muscles, you can develop them. What you have to place are the bones and the joints, and if the joints work correctly, the muscles will be perfectly set in and will grow according to the weight of that body and the possibility of that body. I cannot, for instance, correct the tibia. It's just one bone. But how the tibia relates to the ankle bones—that I can change."

She says one of the nicest compliments she has ever received was from a professor whose specialty was the physical rehabilitation of people injured in accidents. After watching her classes, he told her: "You've showed me through your teaching that there is no limit to the physical possibilities of humans. You use your students' bodies in the right way without negating their potential." Besobrasova elaborates on what he meant: "For instance," she says, "if you lift your leg turned out, there is practically no limit to the height you can achieve. If you don't turn out, your bones inside will touch one another. You will squeeze and squash and suffer and be unable to lift it." She continues, "When we lift our leg to the back, the natural possibility is only about 17 degrees, so we must turn out to get it higher. I think this is one of the reasons the Russians use counterbalance [i.e., tilt the body forward] so much in arabesque. They create the impression of great height with the back leg even though the angle of the leg really does not change. I don't think it's a loose back that gives a good arabesque as much as a loose hip joint and correct placement of the spinal column."

She is critical of the practice followed by many professional ballet academies of dismissing students for purely physical reasons. "They have absolutely no humanity sometimes," she exclaims. "How can you have a student—a girl with faith, dreams, and artistry—and just throw her out because she grew too tall or didn't grow tall enough? There are no centimeters that can measure talent!" Besobrasova adheres to a different policy, not only because of the realities of the situation in her school, but also because of her belief in the possibility of changing a student's body. "I am not in a position to be as choosy about the physiques of dancers admitted to my school as, for instance, they are at the Paris Opera. When you have a Sylvie Guillem [one of the brightest young stars of the Paris Opera Ballet], with a body so perfectly suited to ballet, all you have to do is to teach her to dance. But with a student of mine, I might have to build *every centimeter* of that body." She notes that this is never an easy task. "Each student," she says, "presents unexpected difficulties."

Besobrasova's extensive knowledge of anatomy grew out of her search to heal her own physical problems. Months of being bandaged after her childhood operation left her with a badly asymmetrical ribcage. In mid-life, she sought relief from her chronic back pain from masseurs and chiropractors. From all of them, she learned. Today, a human skeleton, to which she frequently refers while teaching, hangs on a stand in one corner of her studio. On another wall is a large anatomical drawing of the human back. It is composed of several overlays of clear plastic, on each of which is painted a different layer of muscles. Each plastic page can be lifted to reveal the set of muscles underneath. The bottom page illustrates the spine and adjacent bones of the torso. Besobrasova often uses this visual aid to explain to students which muscles they must use to hold their backs properly, showing them the difference between the surface and deep muscles of the back and how they relate to the skeleton.

Sabrina Lenzi, a principal dancer with the Stuttgart Ballet, is one of the many dancers who have come to Besobrasova for help with rehabilitation. "I had a bad back," she recalls, "a slipped vertebra, and the doctor's prognosis was not good. Marika and I searched together for a new way of working for me. She placed my back, gave me exercises, and made me aware of the feeling of how I had to hold back—actually, when I should do more and when I should hold back. She worked with me on visualization, and the anatomical pictures she showed me helped a lot in understanding which muscle was holding what."

While Besobrasova regularly employs such visual aids to get her point across, she says the choice of words used to communicate with students is also critical. "My husband," she recalls, "was a lawyer and a very intelligent man. He always told me: 'A few words should be enough to explain something. If you have to put together twenty phrases so that people will understand something, they will never listen to you for so long. You have to be short and concise." She cautions teachers to "make certain that absolutely every word you pronounce is a word the child understands, because you can put him on a completely wrong path if there is only one word in a phrase that he misunderstands. For instance, if you tell a student to stretch his knee, he may then push on the bones in his joint and later, if he is hyper-extended, have a very big problem. It would be far better to say 'Stretch your muscles.' The bones, after all, cannot stretch themselves." She also advises teachers to "make sure that a student knows and understands the name of every movement."

Besobrasova's advanced classes are often fast and difficult. Her barre is especially strenuous and complex. In tempo, her exercises are far more French (i.e., fast) than Russian—an irony, considering they are primarily based on the Vaganova syllabus. I was instantly struck, however, by how relaxed and assured her students looked in spite of the speed and complexities of the exercises. I asked Besobrasova to what she attributed this admirable lack of tension. She cited two things: her focus upon correcting asymmetry of the body (which she believes creates tension) and her emphasis on breathing.

Over and over again as I watched her teach, I heard her entreat her dancers, "*Respirez*! [Breathe!]" In the stretching exercise with which she begins every class, her students take a deep breath as they raise their arms and then exhale audibly as they drop over (*cambré* forward). Her focus on breathing arose from her work with yoga. "Because of my childhood bout with pneumonia and pleuritis," she says, "I always had trouble with breathing and stamina." Noticing her difficulties, her husband brought her books on yoga, one of which, she remembers, stated: "If you want to master your body, you must learn how to relax it." She says she practiced for hours lying "like a stone" on the floor trying to learn how to relax. "One day," she says, "a place in my back suddenly went crack-crack-crack and relaxed, and I remember that first wonderful feeling of less tension. I realized it was what I needed. I was twenty-nine and from then on it took me a year to start to understand. I learned about breathing—started listening to my breath. I wanted to apply what I was learning to dancing. I thought that perhaps when they had told me that I had a bad heart, it wasn't really that. Probably, it was that I did not breathe properly."

Today, Besobrasova regularly includes relaxation classes in her curriculum. She hopes that sessions such as these will become a lifelong habit for her dancers. "Relaxation on your own," she emphasizes, "is terribly important. You have to learn how to be completely alone in silence. It's how you learn to be in charge of yourself." One of the young ladies who had been studying at the academy for some months told me how much Besobrasova's relaxation exercises had helped her. "When I came here," she said, "I was always so nervous in my head that I couldn't feel anything. Now I'm much more aware of the inner workings of my body."

During the relaxation class, the dancers lie silently on the studio floor. The louvered shutters are drawn, closing out the sunlight for half an hour. Besobrasova, eyes closed and waistband loosened, sits comfortably in a rattan chair at one end of the room. In a slow, husky voice, she takes the students on a verbal tour of their bodies. "Undo the knot in the back of your throat," she coaxes softly. "Don't hold your cheeks. Relax around your nose and eyes. Relax your forehead and look into it. It is pink. You are happy, serene. Relax under your hair."

Coaching her students in correct breathing, Besobrasova tells them not to pull the air in (i.e., gasp). "You don't have to be a vacuum cleaner," she says. "If your body is not tense, you will let the air in naturally." She remembers the wise words of a yoga teacher in Paris: "The air will enter where you want if you open up and allow it to do so." In dance classes, Besobrasova advises students to let their breath out before doing something difficult. ("Throw your air to your feet.") She tells them to begin inhaling only at the moment the movement becomes difficult, such as mid-pirouette, rather than at the initial moment of the turn. "You will see," she says, "that this will help sustain you on *relevé*." She uses the analogy of adding air to a balloon to help it go up.

I was intrigued by another aspect of Besobrasova's teaching that also seems to have a direct relationship to yoga. At the end of class, she has the students stand absolutely still for about fifteen seconds. "Find the inner calm within yourself," she directs. "You must be able to stand quietly without agitation, even if the music is still very strong. You must not vibrate to that music. Instead, you must produce a silence that is just the opposite of what the music is suggesting. This is very important. To me, it means that you are flexible enough to agree to any way of hearing the music and using it in your body."

Musical training is so central to Besobrasova's classes that she has refused to compromise on the quality of her piano accompaniment. In order to satisfy her standards, she uses recorded music, custom-made for her

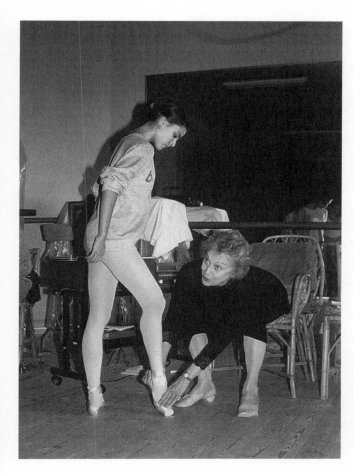

Marika Besobrasova explaining how to use the foot on *pointe* to a student after class.

classes by her favorite pianist, an accompanist for the Paris Opera Ballet. She has ready for use hundreds of classes she has prepared with him. So skillfully does she operate the tape recorder[13] that the flow of her class is never interrupted. And the inspiring music is so perfectly matched to her exercises that I understood exactly why she chooses to work in this rather untraditional manner. (Most professional teachers prefer to teach with live piano accompaniment. Not only does it free them from having to work recording equipment—usually an annoying distraction while teaching—but it also allows them flexibility with tempo changes, something that recorded music can never provide.)

Besobrasova's custom-designed accompaniment is especially vital for those classes that she structures differently from a traditional ballet class. "I often give special classes for the ladies that begin with a toe barre," she says. "Then there are separate classes for men, as well as *pas de deux*. My pianist has always understood the special needs of each." Together, they have also prepared many exercises to teach children musicality. Some of them were inspired by Russian books she received on the subject. Each of the beginner and intermediate classes in her program contains a section in the centre, just after the barre work, called *exercices rhythmiques*. In these exercises, students learn such things as the difference between strong and weak beats. They may, for instance, walk on the strong beat, then stand still or walk on tip-toes on the weak beats. She has designed exercises in which the children must listen for two different phrases, one on which they run and one during which they stand still. Often, in all her classes, the piano music on the tape deliberately stops for a few counts mid-exercise. The dancers keep moving. (Sometimes, at the barre, this happens in the four counts allotted in the accompaniment for changing sides.) She is deliberately challenging the students not to lose a beat and to be exactly on the music when it comes in again.

Besobrasova has strong thoughts about rhythm: "I think that music is the base, though movement is certainly possible without music. (Ballets, after all, can be done to words, which have their own rhythm.) In silence, though, there is a rhythm produced by the body of the dancer, by his heart-beat, by anything he can listen to—a beat without music. If there were no rhythmical support at all (in silence, words, or music), to me there could be no dance. Even if I dance without any music, my own breath is to me already rhythmic. I believe that without the shape created by rhythm, there is no art. To me, art is born through the association between the vibration to which you dance and the vibration of your own body. Art, after all, is a certain technique through which you create. If you create chaos, it will stay chaos. We have to understand that and then work on our ability to follow any kind of rhythm asked for by a choreographer. Fokine used Chopin, then came Stravinsky. I remember struggling with *Petrouchka*. Today, you can be asked anything—Phillip Glass, for instance, with all that repetition in which you will have to find a support. You will have to produce something, create some melody. If you don't have the sensibility of obeying a choreographer through musicality, how will you relate to his choreography?"

One day while I was sitting next to her in class, she turned to me and said, "It's strange to me that dancers rarely feel the musicality of the arms. They'll do the rhythm of the feet correctly, but with uncoordinated arms!"

She finds that she must constantly remind her students to listen while they are moving and to match their body movement with the dynamic quality of the music. She will point out, for instance, how inappropriate it is to jerk during a sustained chord. She tells them an anecdote about the great Japanese ballerina, Yoko Moroshita, whom she coached for years: When asked how she could dance so musically, Moroshita replied that "every part of my body listens to the music."

I asked Besobravsova how she deals with unmusical students. She admitted it is difficult. "I try to make them understand that they don't communicate at all with the music, that they are not using it as a support, that they neither breathe, nor vibrate with it. And I point to them every time they are early, or late, or just deaf!"

She remembers a conversation she once had strolling in Kew Gardens with Massine.[14] Massine insisted that when students were unmusical, he simply found it impossible to work with them. Besobrasova remembers saying to him, "Excuse me, but I do think one can teach them. First of all, I make them feel not only the beat, but the division between the beat and its subdivisions more and more until they become aware that they are neither on the beat nor between it. They are nowhere! When they realize that they are ignoring the music, and if they are willing to progress, they will think it over and start to feel what it means."

Besobrasova remembers that she once had a rather well known, but very unmusical, ballerina in her class. Her pianist, she recalls, was the first to have the courage to raise the issue. "You know," he told the dancer, "you're never with me." With great tact, Besobrasova seized the opportunity to address the problem. "When we do our preparation," she told the ballerina, "the pianist is corresponding with you. He is sending you a message at that moment that unveils what he's going to play, but you never listen to it. That is why you are beginning the exercise late." Besobrasova says that she had to present this comment delicately, given the status of the ballerina, but, she says, "We did it with love. You can't hate your students just because they try your patience to bits. If you do, there will be no possibility to change them."

Besobrasova's advanced morning classes cover an enormous amount of material, moving from exercise to exercise with little pause. Her manner of working is quite different from most teachers who compose a new class each morning. She composes all of her classes for the year in the summer, when she works with her pianist. During the following months, she progresses through one class at a time—all are written out in a large notebook—working on the same class for as long as she feels it is necessary for the students to master the material. It takes her about a week to teach one entire class to the dancers. Each day she adds new exercises until all the combinations have been learned. After initially teaching an exercise, she spends very little time on explanation in subsequent classes. Her corrections are brief and to the point. Because the students have already learned the exercises, perfecting them is primarily a matter of repetition.

Some of Besobrasova's prepared classes have as many as ten allegro *enchaînements.* Therefore, it is generally impossible to cover all the material in a single ninety-minute class. This does not concern her. Because she works with the same students every day, she enjoys the luxury of being able to spend more time on one part of a class one day and less on it the next. Her barre is always very complete, but, if time is short, she may omit, for instance, the *grand allegro* in the centre. Obviously, this method of working is possible only in her own school in Monte Carlo where she sees the same students once or twice a day all year long. She assured me that when she guest-teaches elsewhere, she follows the more common practice of composing a complete class on the spot.

One of the most unusual aspects of Besobrasova's classes is her willingness to combine aspects of the Russian School with those of the French. The first allegro exercise in her centre work, for instance, is very French (i.e., fast, small, full of complex footwork) and the second, heavier, more even, and very Russian. The first skims lightly across the floor; the second presses into the floor. Thus, her dancers, trained in both the French and Russian methods, are uniquely well rounded. They have both great speed and great strength. Her *pointe* classes, however, are decidedly French and provided me with one of the highlights of my visit. Rarely have I seen a teacher so thoroughly warm up the feet, nor demand that they be used in such a variety of articulate ways. Not only did the students get up and down, on and off *pointe,* in every conceivable manner (rolling, pressing, springing, and using *assemblés* and jumps) and with every imaginable tempo and dynamic, but they also focused on the presentation of the foot, the beauty of the shape of the foot in the *pointe* shoe.

Two or three times a week, Besobrasova holds a special afternoon class in which she answers any questions the students may have about material in the morning class. After discussing their questions, she will often compose on the spot a special exercise that deals specifically with the problem being discussed. She does not do a barre in these classes and limits herself to taking three questions in each of these ninety-minute sessions. She considers these classes terribly important. "I find when I discuss things with them," she says, "that they have sometimes totally misunderstood what I said in class in the morning. I remember every word I said, and sometimes they have understood exactly the reverse! It's a disaster!" she exclaims, "but if you sort it out in the afternoon, you are clear for the next day."

Although convinced that students must be intelligent and knowledgeable about their dance technique, Besobrasova is also quick to caution them about the danger of letting their thoughts interfere with their natural coordination. She was much influenced by the book *The Inner Game of Tennis.* "You have to be confident," she warns her advanced dancers, "that the body knows what you have taught it. You can think before and analyze after, but when you push, pull, balance, counterbalance, and move forward or backward while dancing, these are reflexes, not thoughts. If you think while you are dancing, first of all, you will be late musically and second, your coordination will be ruined. When you dance, you dance!"

At the end of each week, everyone—staff and students—meets together for an hour. Besobrasova, in her perpetually hoarse and high-pitched voice, presides over these sessions like a queen bee. Clearly, her vitality and commitment to detail energize the entire school. These meetings allow her the opportunity to reiterate with no-nonsense authority rules pertaining to the behavior of her residential students. During the session I observed, she covered such topics as diet, behavior in their dorm rooms (some of the young men were becoming a bit rowdy), and rules pertaining to leaving the premises. Because she has many international students, some of whom have only begun to study French, she often repeats what she has said in several languages just to make certain that everyone understands. It is not unusual in any of her ballet classes for her to switch back and forth among French, Italian, Russian, German, and English, depending upon whom she is addressing.

The full school meetings also allow time for discussion of dance concerns. Besobrasova sits at the front of the room, students clustered around her feet, with her faculty sitting on either side of her. (She has three excellent full-time ballet instructors who share the teaching load at the academy with her.) She asks each of the teachers what he or she has noticed in classes during the week. If, for instance, a teacher mentions that the students seemed to be having difficulty with hand-eye coordination, Besobrasova will spend time talking about the importance of this aspect of dancing, clarifying any questions students may have. She herself may question the students, testing their memories by asking them to repeat to her something she said to them in class earlier in the week. There is much repartee; the session seems less like a lecture and more like a family meeting. A strong sense of friendly community exists among all who work and learn at Casa Mia, and it comes from the top. Besobrasova—with her disciplined work ethic, kindness, and impeccable manners—sets a perfect example for all around her.

As her former student Elisabeth Carroll remembers: "Marika gave a lot of herself and expected as much back from her students. This meant that our work, like hers, had to continue outside of the classroom. We had special exercises—ones that did not require a fully warmed-up body—to perform at home or while traveling. These included foot and hand exercises, *port de bras,* the study of poses in front of the mirror, breathing exercises, yoga, relaxation, and drawn and written explanations of classroom exercises, to name a few. Other special exercises done before and after class, such as floor barre and flexibility exercises (using a stick) for the back, helped develop the necessary awareness of one's power deep inside the mind and body; eventually, I was able to make the connection and relate all these to movement. In short, Marika taught us all that was necessary to know and beyond. . . . She instilled in me the ability to perform any movement I was ever asked to execute."

I was curious about how Besobrasova cultivates taste and artistry in her students. She told me that she tells dancers from the beginning of their training: "We are not gymnasts. All our effort must be hidden, our faces pleasant, our eyes alive, if we wish to produce an artistic impression with our movement." She says that she parts company with those teachers who emphasize the development of virtuosity at a young age. "I go slowly, up to a certain point," she says, "in order to have time to deal with artistic details. They must learn these things at a young age; otherwise they become slam-bang dancers." She explains to her students that parts of their bodies, such as their feet, can be used differently, like the hands of a pianist. "How you bring your foot onto the floor is important," she tells them. "It can hit the floor, slap it, slide on it, or press on it. If you have none of this sensibility, what kind of an instrument will you be for a choreographer?"

She tries to implant in her students an awareness of what is beautiful and what is ugly. "Only when this awareness is awakened," she says, "will the child be conscious of what he has to do, what he's really done, what he wants to do, and how he does it. If we do not develop this awareness, we will never have an artist in front of us, only a little mechanic—maybe a good mechanic, but not an artist."

I asked Besobrasova what she finds most difficult about teaching. "When your pupil is visibly talented," she replied, "nothing is difficult. The problem comes when you have to find where a student's talent is hidden. If you have a physically talented child without character, you cry every day because you see that, my God, it's all there, but you can't pull it out!" Her biggest challenge, she says, is to produce artists. "If you give me a bad foot," she explains, "I will undertake many ways of working with that foot until, finally, I will get a decent foot. But when I start to work on musicality, it can be like pushing my head against the wall!" She says that the most difficult part of her job is not teaching dancers to do new movements, but getting them to do the new movements on a "pure, clean body" without any old, bad habits. "Sometimes," she says, "you have to destroy the image they project in order to make necessary changes. If you don't, you are just gluing something on top of the mistake."

I was amazed at Besobrasova's energy. Her long work days, during which she sometimes teaches three classes, would exhaust many half her age. During my stay in Monte Carlo, she would return to her apartment at about 7:00 P.M., and, after preparing dinner, as tired as she was, she willingly continued our interviews. She would lie on her couch, her dog curled at her feet, with my small tape recorder on her chest. One evening, she even insisted on giving me some of her special therapy ("heat and healing power from my hands") for a bad ankle with which I was suffering.

I was particularly delighted to watch her teaching a late afternoon class one day for "the babies"—a large group of tiny three- and four-year-old would-be ballerinas in tousled ponytails and pink leotards. I can imagine no other world-renowned teacher of her stature who would deign to undertake such a pre-beginner class (she calls it *Classe d'Initiation à la Danse*), yet Besobrasova clearly enjoyed skipping and clapping to the music with these round-tummied, pink-cheeked tots. Guiding them through a little simple barre work, some floor exercises, and a bit of *port de bras,* she was both regal and effervescent. At the end of the sometimes chaotic hour, holding the hands of two little girls, one on each side of her, she first walked, then danced exuberantly, in a big circle, like the Pied Piper, with the rest of the class following. She was well aware that from this class a future ballerina might emerge, and she was there to see that the right foundation was laid, that it was a joyful experience for all.

It seems as if almost all major dance stars arrive at Besobrasova's school at one time or another. Several past students who are now dancing professionally visited to attend class while I was there. Often, she is asked for advice on developing roles. Her effectiveness as a coach is well known. As Stuttgart Ballet soloist Elizabeth Hertel remembers: "When Marika helped me with my role of Olga in *Eugene Onegin,* she explained to me that every movement must be very big in order to project to the audience—not a little movement from the heart, but a big movement from the chest—and how everything moves together. For instance, if you fall or have to run backwards, it all comes from the middle of the chest. She will sometimes try to show you with her own body, but more often she uses manipulation as a tool—her hands pushing and pulling on your body all the time. She pulls the beauty of the movement from you."

I wondered if, at seventy-three, Besobrasova entertained any thoughts of retirement. "My academy is a very pleasant instrument," she replied, "because, due to my residential facility and scholarship fund, I am able to have many very good students. But, it is a lot of work. It's very hard to keep the whole machine—dance classes, general studies, international students, education of children, *and* education of parents—moving." However, she noted that her own beloved teacher, Egorova, was still teaching at the age of eighty-seven. "And Kschessinska[15] lasted to one hundred!" She confided that she missed celebrating her fiftieth year in the classroom. "I didn't tell anyone," she told me with a little smile. "I think I'll go for my sixtieth!"

Classroom Quotes from Besobrasova

"Even if you have a good instrument, you still have to learn to play on it, how to make it obey."

"The preparatory *port de bras* is to prepare your *inner* self to dance—to be exactly moving with the music, rather than having the music fly around your ears someplace."

"There are many lights and other distractions onstage. This is why one must build balance inside oneself—find one's center."

"Be really *with* the music, not next to it."

"Take care to keep the fluidity in your *plié*. One goes down to come up, not to go down."

"For *tombé*, Nureyev always used to say, you have to fall over the shadow of your foot, and for *piqué* you have to step onto the shadow."

"I am your teacher, but you are the teacher of your body."

"When you do *port de bras,* don't give all the importance to the arms. Give some of it to yourself, to what you feel—and show it."

Order of the Exercises in Besobrasova's Class (advanced class, 1½ hours)

1. Exercice Preparatoire, including cambrés, various foot and Achilles tendon stretches, tendus, demi-ronds de jambe, light swings of the leg (with the knee bent), and passés turning in and out
2. Demi-pliés and grands pliés with cambrés
3. Slow battements tendus
4. Faster battements tendus without plié
5. Battements dégagés lent
6. Battements tendus jetés (dégagés) rapide
7. Ronds de jambe à terre
8. Battements fondus
9. Battements frappés with flic-flacs
10. Ronds de jambe en l'air with adagio movements
11. Stretches
12. Grands battements
13. Petits battements
14. Cool-down exercise facing the barre, with grands pliés, cambrés, etc.

CENTRE

1. Adagio followed by tendus en tournant and pirouettes
2. Ronds de jambe en l'air with adagio movements
3. Exercice rapide (pas de bourrées)
4. Grands battements pointés
5. Temps levés and échappés
6. Fast petit allegro enchaînement (assemblés, temps de cuisse)
7. Medium allegro (sissonnes, pas de chat, entrechat six)
8. Coupés grands jetés en avant en diagonale
9. Grand allegro with grand jeté entrelacé, grands jetés, grands fouettés sautés
10. Changements
11. Port de bras à composé

The Roots of Tradition

THE PEDAGOGICAL LINEAGE OF MARIKA BESOBRASOVA

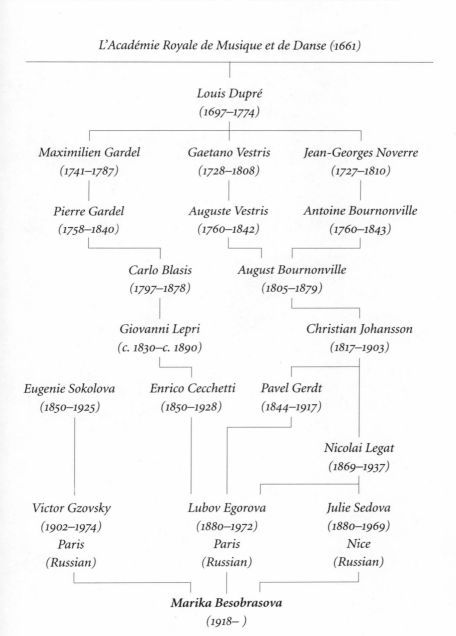

L'Académie Royale de Musique et de Danse (1661)

Louis Dupré
(1697–1774)

Maximilien Gardel
(1741–1787)

Gaetano Vestris
(1728–1808)

Jean-Georges Noverre
(1727–1810)

Pierre Gardel
(1758–1840)

Auguste Vestris
(1760–1842)

Antoine Bournonville
(1760–1843)

Carlo Blasis
(1797–1878)

August Bournonville
(1805–1879)

Giovanni Lepri
(c. 1830–c. 1890)

Christian Johansson
(1817–1903)

Eugenie Sokolova
(1850–1925)

Enrico Cecchetti
(1850–1928)

Pavel Gerdt
(1844–1917)

Nicolai Legat
(1869–1937)

Victor Gzovsky
(1902–1974)
Paris
(Russian)

Lubov Egorova
(1880–1972)
Paris
(Russian)

Julie Sedova
(1880–1969)
Nice
(Russian)

Marika Besobrasova
(1918–)

2 Willam Christensen

Willam Christensen making a point during class in Salt Lake City in 1990.

*W*illam Christensen's career as a ballet teacher has spanned nearly three-quarters of a century. Although he retired in 1975 as artistic director of Utah's famed Ballet West, which he founded, he continues to teach almost daily in Salt Lake City. He has been the recipient of numerous prestigious awards, including both the Dance Magazine and Capezio awards.

After a brilliant career in vaudeville in the 1920s, Christensen, a virtuoso dancer, settled in Portland, Oregon, where he established a large dance school and, in 1934, founded the Portland Ballet. In 1937, he moved to San Francisco, soon becoming the choreographer-director of the fledgling San Francisco Ballet. There, between 1939 and 1944, he created four major classical ballets, including *Coppélia* and the first full-length productions of *Swan Lake* and *The Nutcracker* to be produced in America. In addition, during his fifteen-year tenure with the company, he choreographed thirty one-act works and more than one hundred opera ballets.

In 1951, at the urging of Utah Symphony Orchestra conductor Maurice Abravanel, Christensen left the San Francisco Ballet in the hands of his famous dancing brothers, Lew and Harold, and moved to Salt Lake City. The intensive touring schedule of the San Francisco Ballet had made it increasingly difficult for him to care for his first wife, then gravely ill with multiple sclerosis. In Salt Lake, he created the reputable Department of Ballet at the University of Utah—the first ballet department in college dance in America. In 1963, he established the Utah Civic Ballet, which evolved, under his direction, into Ballet West in 1968.

"Criticize

with love."

I first met Christensen in 1989 when he was invited to teach a master class at the Ballet Aspen Summer Dance School. He had founded this school in the Colorado Rocky Mountains in 1969 as a summer home for Ballet West. So enchanted was I with his class that I arranged to visit him in Salt Lake City. He was eighty-seven years old when I interviewed him there in 1990.

"IF I SIT DOWN when I'm teaching, I get tired," Bill Christensen told me with a delightfully impish grin under his little white mustache. Although he has been training dancers for more than seventy years and now struggles with limited mobility because of a hip operation, he has no intention of retiring. As he told me with more pleasure in his voice than regret, "I've tried to quit a couple of times, but then I get a talented student or two, and I can't leave 'em."

Christensen conducts a highly energetic two-hour class almost every afternoon and often choreographs small dramatic ballets for his students. He believes that dance without drama is pointless. "Now, *expression* or give up!" he boomed one day as the class was about to begin a *grand allegro* combination. He confides that he has little patience with most plotless contemporary ballets. "I'm not anti-modern," he says, "I'm anti-amateurish junk. Somebody's got to understand that what we do has to be theater and not something people get bored with." Christensen told me that someone had recently taken him to see a performance of a contemporary ballet set to Beethoven. When asked afterward what he thought, he remembers replying, as diplomatically as possible: "I'm very grateful Beethoven is dead."

Christensen's strong opinions about what works in the theater (and what doesn't) stem not only from his extensive experience as a choreographer, but also from his early years as a popular vaudeville performer. "In 1927, at the beginning of my dancing career," he told me, "I organized a little troupe with my brother Lew and went to Los Angeles. We did a Russian finale that audiences loved. My uncle called us 'Le Crist Brothers' to make us sound more exotic and foreign. Later, we picked up a lot of Moiseyev-style Russian character stuff from this guy Burkoff with whom we joined forces in Chicago. He taught us all sorts of spectacular lifts—the kind of virtuoso stuff that was called 'adagio dancing' at the time."

Eventually, Willam, Lew, and the two ladies who danced with them became the famous act "The Christensen Brothers." Their parents moved east from Utah so that their father could conduct ("mostly Delibes and

Strauss") for the troupe. Christensen recalls: "We finally got to play the Palace. We were the only dancers who did straight ballet in vaudeville. We were virtuosos. Stopped the show almost every night!" He is a great believer in the theatrical value of virtuosity. Referring to the famous Italian ballet dancers of the nineteenth century, he told me: "The Italians deteriorated because their dancing was *only* about tricks. But, the fact is if there is *no* virtuosity, the audience gets bored. Without both drama and virtuosity, our dance is no longer exciting theater. People would rather go see an exceptional basketball player. They come to the ballet to see an unusual athlete. Perhaps we have a shortage of men in ballet because we haven't emphasized the heroics of male dancing enough."

To foster exciting dancing, Christensen not only encourages virtuosity in class, but also focuses on developing dancers' personalities. He is noted for his remarkable talent for knowing just what to draw out of each performer. As one former student explains: "He has that 'human electric.' He can get new students in his class with plain faces and, within an hour, they're dancing like they never did before!" Jocelyn Vollmar, a former ballerina with the San Francisco Ballet who began studying with Christensen when she was twelve years old, recalls: "He was always saying, 'Sell it!' when we danced. He'd urge us to 'make it interesting enough so that someone would want to look at it and buy it if it were for sale.'"

As a prime force in American dance in this century, Christensen has every reason to take pride in his many accomplishments. He is, however, a remarkably humble man. Blessed with a marvelous capacity for always seeing the humor in life, he kept me laughing both in class and out for the five days I spent with him. He arrived to teach each day neatly attired in a slightly worn wool sports coat, holding his stick like an elegant walking cane. Although always the perfect gentleman, he is not at all pretentious. In fact, he cultivates a kind of down-home-on-the-farm American earthiness in his conversation. "You betcha!" he'll often roar.

More than anything else, one is struck by his obvious delight in all things related to dance. He's full of stories from the past: "When I was a young fellow, I remember seeing Pavlova when she danced in Salt Lake City. It was like I was at a football game—I got so excited I wanted to stand up!" But he is also full of curiosity about the present. "When I was younger," he laments, "I used to go everywhere, see everything. Now [meaning since his retirement as artistic director of Ballet West in 1975], I feel a bit out of touch." There is sadness in his eyes. His face came alive, however, when I described an especially exhilarating performance by a current young Joffrey Ballet ballerina. "Oh," he said, shifting forward to the edge of his chair, "I would have liked to have seen *that!*"

His infectious enthusiasm for his art form fills any studio in which he is teaching, and one soon sees it reflected in his students. Tomm Ruud, a former leading dancer with Ballet West and the San Francisco Ballet who began his training with Christensen at the University of Utah, considers Christensen the most influential person in his life: "He was always full of things to color your imagination. He was a very hands-on teacher. He would push you around, mold you, explain to you, give you suggestions and ideas to make you think about things in another way, not just, 'Why don't you do it?' If one idea didn't work, he'd keep saying something else, keep giving you feedback. He was the sort of person you'd do anything for because it just seemed as if there were only one goal in mind: That we were all going to do a good job as dancers." Ruud also found Christensen's consistency inspiring. "He was just always there," Ruud remembers, "and I said to myself, 'If this sixty-year-old man can come to class every morning, I can certainly be there (I was twenty)!'"

Although Ruud and other former students obviously regard Christensen as a paternal figure, I found much that was delightfully childlike in him. His dignified personality mixes charming innocence with an inner calm wrought by years of life experience. He is given to speaking in parables, a form upon which he relies heavily in the classroom. "Keeps me from getting in trouble," he grins. He espouses the philosophy that "if you give it to them straight, they won't get it. I try to make sure the dancers really have to think about what I'm trying to say." One of his former students remembers Mr. C, as they call him, saying, "Now, when you finish those pirouettes, it's got to be like Maxwell House coffee." "But," the student remarked, "he'd never say 'good to the last drop.' You'd have to figure that out for yourself."

One cannot fail to notice similarities in personality between Christensen and the great entertainer and comedian George Burns, perhaps because both cut their theatrical teeth in vaudeville in the 1920s. Chain-smoking, diminutive, and unimposing in appearance, Mr. C uses his fertile imagination and well-honed abilities as a stand-up comic to command attention in the classroom. His perfectly timed humorous asides, delivered with a deadpan face, vary from subtle to slapstick. "There's so much repetition in ballet," he told me in his rasping, long-time smoker's voice. "If I can get a laugh out of 'em, it helps to get them to do something." One day, to a girl who

Willam Christensen demonstrating a grand allegro combination in class.

had momentarily lost her concentration in an adagio exercise, he commented: "You lifted your arm *this* way and the rest of the class did it *that* way—well, maybe you're just a Democrat in a Republican town."

Corrections, as Christensen well knows, are always much easier for students to swallow when given with a dash of humor. At this, he is a master. "You might be poor," he chided a student one day who did only two pirouettes, "but you can afford three pirouettes." And, to a young man who seemed to doubt himself, Christensen commented, "Ted, you did that exercise much better today. I remember the last time we tried it, you got so depressed you went home and bought a cat." The whole class grinned. Hardly straitlaced—he is a great admirer of women, evening cocktails, and slightly off-color jokes—Christensen is not above occasionally shocking his students. "It makes 'em pay attention." He elicited a blush and a giggle one day when he told a teenage girl who had her back shoulder raised in 1st arabesque, "Dear, you've already got two lumps. You don't need a third."

Christensen also does not hesitate to have a little irreverent fun with the French ballet terminology: "Now put undershirts on it," he directs students with a sly grin when he wants them to add *entrechats* to a *petit allegro* combination. He also elicits giggles when he sometimes jokingly refers to *grands battements* as "grand mothballs." The only things which are sacred in Christensen's class are those that truly matter: discipline, an intelligent approach, and a true love of dance.

His famous walking stick, by now almost a natural extension of his body, is used in the classroom, he says half-jokingly, "to keep the pianist in line," never as a weapon of intimidation. However, he has been known to throw it to the ground in frustration, once even splitting it in half. "We all went home early that day," relates a long-time student. "He couldn't continue if he couldn't tap time with his stick."

Christensen's exceptional musicality, apparent in every exercise he choreographs, extends far beyond stick-tapping. He is descended from a large, music-loving family—Mormons who immigrated to Utah from Denmark in the 1800s. Christensen recalls that "everybody in our family was a musician." His uncles founded a ballroom fancy-dancing school, Christensen's School of Music and Dancing, in Utah at the turn of the century. "We were poor kids, so to speak," he told me, "but we were rich 'cause we had the background in music. My Danish grandfather was a fiddler, and he also taught folk dancing, so we learned little court dances and pioneer dances as children. They'd have to gather us up because little guys don't like to dance with little girls, but we did it."

Most of Christensen's childhood was devoted to music, not dancing. He first concentrated on the piano, then later, in his early teens, formed a Dixieland jazz band in which he played the horn. Thus, it is hardly surprising that he is able to instill in his students an understanding of music that is both confident and impressive. If dancers in his class are not ready to begin when the music starts, Christensen comments wryly: "There you are with your violin and the bow hanging." Generally, though, his musically astute students charge into the preparation for an exercise without the slightest hesitation. To develop their musicality, Christensen often has students simply listen to the music without either counting or dancing. He also coaches them about manipulating their use of music to dramatic advantage. One former student recalled that Mr. C would often ask them to "feather the beat" in an onstage walk, meaning each step should be slightly behind the music. "Adds a little schmaltz," Christensen would say.

He insists on good classical music from his accompanists and varies the meter of his exercises constantly. One of his musician uncles, he says, used to assign human characteristics to the different instruments in the orchestra, explaining that "the violin is the lady; the cello, the male romanticist; the bassoon, the comic, the laughing boy; and the oboe, the oriental." Christensen thinks that's probably why he grew to enjoy the color of great orchestral music. It told stories. In class, he often uses musical terms to describe movement quality: "I want your legs staccato and your arms marcato." And to a student obviously dancing behind the beat, he remarks dryly, "If you're going to be unmusical, you're going to have to marry a private conductor."

Christensen remembers his leap from musician to dancer as being prompted by adolescent hormones as much as by the beauty of ballet. He was fifteen at the time. He recalls: "My Uncle Pete, the dance teacher, came up from Salt Lake to our little town of Brigham with these three girls, little ballerinas. 'Gee,' I thought, 'it might be nice to dance.' The girls looked good to me," he remembers with a twinkle in his eye, "and besides, they were graceful."

He immersed himself in ballet studies with his uncle, then the best dance teacher in the West. Soon, he was introduced to his uncle's mentor, the famous Stefano Mascagno,[1] who had a ballet school in New York City. Mascagno had retired from the stage, and Uncle Pete, who was devoted to the Italian, brought him to Utah to teach a six-week summer course. Christensen recalls: "I took the course. Uncle Pete warned me, 'Willi, you'd better practice your *assemblés.*' I found out why. Mascagno was very strict—old school. He'd put a line of chairs in the back of the room, and, if you didn't do it right, he'd make you go stand behind the chairs. I was fascinated by the perfection of his footwork. He'd been trained in Italy and danced at La Scala. As soon as I could, I went to New York to study with him. Every time I'd run out of money, I'd leave New York and return to study with my uncle in Utah. Then I'd borrow money again and go back to New York City. I was always running out of money."

Christensen and his uncle Pete actually owed their connection to Mascagno to another uncle, Moses. (Mo Christensen eventually left Utah to establish a music and dance school in Portland, Oregon, where he later founded the Portland Symphony.) Christensen recalls: "My Uncle Mose was president of the Dance Teachers' Association, which still exists today. He believed there had to be a science to teaching dance. He knew there was one in music and in literature, too. He thought there must be more than just going here and there and learning little dances—fancy dancing, it was called in those days."

Following his instincts, Mo Christensen had gone to New York City in the early 1900s in search of a serious dance teacher. He had heard of Mascagno, who was reputed to be "a little difficult to get along with." Undaunted, he went to see him and asked to study with him. "Mascagno,"

Christensen remembers, "had leading dancers from the Metropolitan Opera Ballet in his classes and didn't quite know what to do with this big amateurish guy from Utah. But Mo got himself the requisite satin pants and sash and showed up for class, and they became friends." Uncle Mo discovered that there was indeed a science to teaching dance.

Christensen recalls being "thrilled with Mascagno's classes because it all made sense, although I could never understand why it had to be so strict." Thus, the dancing Christensens, first Mo and Pete and then later their more famous nephews, Lew, Willam, and Harold, were most strongly influenced by the Italian School. Christensen recalls: "Mascagno was a contemporary of Cecchetti's [see p. 36, n. 9], only a little younger. I was told the two of them sometimes got into arguments about technique and background while walking in the street. Apparently, they'd get so riled up that they'd stop and create a scene. The police would have to tell them to move on."

He continued: "In Mascagno's little old 63rd Street studio, there was only one lavatory for girls, none for boys. We'd go into the studio and change our clothes and put them, folded up, on a bench with a pillow over them. Then we'd go out into the hall and hear the music start. The door would open, and the girls would go in and curtsy, 'Good morning, Maestro.' And then we'd have to bow. And he'd clap his sticks, and we'd go to the barre. He didn't vary his barre work until you got to the advanced level—not a dumb idea to start with, you know, though later on I don't recommend it—but he would correct it. We gained the technique rapidly because of the repetition every day. It was very much like Cecchetti's technique. We learned to brush *assemblés* and land with *ballon.* It was remarkable. You didn't put your heels down on the fast stuff, but, of course, you did on the slower jumps like *assemblés* and *sissonnes.* You see the method in the Kirov today. Mascagno's technique was not still; it was flexible. He had a pianist. I would say his was the first legitimate school in America. Later the Russians came and moved in."

Christensen was also greatly influenced by Mikhail Fokine (see p. 360, n. 6). Even after he had established his own large school in Portland in the early 1930s, Christensen returned to New York City often to study with Fokine. He remembers: "We took class in his beautiful house on Riverside Drive. You'd do an arabesque, and your foot or hand would be out the window because the room was so small. He used to say, 'I want your neck long like a swan, not short like a pig.' He didn't like the Italian method. He wanted everything freer. It affected me very much. It was just the opposite of what I'd learned, but I enjoyed it. I was so affected by *Les Sylphides* that I went back to Portland and staged a *Chopiniana* there. I think I appreciated Fokine's soft, plastic quality because I understood music well."

Although Christensen's classes are primarily derivative of the Italian School in which he received most of his early training, one sees bits of Fokine in his teaching, as well as the influence of Balanchine (see p. 359, n. 3). Throughout his life, Christensen maintained a close friendship with Balanchine and his School of American Ballet in New York. He made frequent trips there in the 1950s to watch Pierre Vladimirov teach. "I admired Vladimirov," Christensen told me. "I thought he was one of the great teachers in our country. Balanchine was a choreographer and very musical, but Vladimirov was a much better teacher. I remember he wanted us to go up and *then* do our *tours*. If you didn't apply yourself, he'd never pay any attention to you, but if you had your eyes open and listened, he'd stay right with you. I'm one of the few characters that saw him dance, and it was frightening. Not because of great emotion, but because *everything* was there. Perfect! He used to rebound. His *ballon* was elegant. I was told later by Russians that he was one of the greatest to come out of the Imperial School."

Christensen's favorite recollection of his friendship with Balanchine was the following: "You know, he never complimented anyone. Once, though, I went backstage (one of my dancers from Utah was in the New York City Ballet then) and he said, 'Hey, Christensen, who's going to teach the dancers when we die?' And I thought, 'That's a nice compliment.'" Christensen also noted that when he created the first American production of *The Nutcracker* for the San Francisco Ballet in 1944, Balanchine's memories of the Imperial Russian Ballet production were invaluable. (Christensen had never seen the ballet, only heard about it!)

Like most great pedagogues, Christensen does not believe in the exclusive use of any one teaching system. As one of his former ballerinas in the San Francisco Ballet, Jocelyn Vollmar, puts it, "He believes if it's good, it's right, and if it's not beautiful, he doesn't care who invented it. He won't use it." He feels there are valuable aspects in all the systems, none of which precludes the others. "You can make a wonderful technique out of using them all," he says. "That's the way I've always taught." Typical of this open-minded approach is his advice to his students whenever they have the opportunity to work with another teacher. "Give 'em what they want," he tells them. "Don't ever say, 'Well, that's not the way my teacher in Utah does it.' Even if the person up there is a complete idiot, show them respect. You can learn something from everyone." When quizzed about how strictly he adheres to certain elements of the Italian School, he replies that, of course, he finds himself frequently adapting his material and adding new elements to it. "You have to," he says. "It's like religion. If you don't go with the times, you die out. You've got to always keep learning." There is one aspect of classical training, however, from which he never deviates. "Students have to learn all the directional poses (*croisé, écarté,* et cetera). That's old school. It's like the Bible. A lot of schools," he says with obvious dismay, "don't teach them. They teach everything flat. But if you've learned these poses well, you're lucky, because they're beautiful. They were created for a reason."

The material in Christensen's ballet class covers the full range of ballet technique. Clearly, though, turning and jumping are his favorite portions of the lesson. His students maintain that he can teach anyone to turn well. Much of his success in this area may be due to sheer repetition—pirouettes in one form or another appear throughout the barre work, as well as in virtually every one of his centre exercises. "Pirouettes from 4th position are easier," he says, "but pirouettes from 5th are a better training. If you can turn from 5th, you can turn from any position." He favors difficult exercises from the Italian School in which pirouettes from 5th are done in a series. His brother Lew, he says, was an exceptional, virtuoso turner. "One of the best! He and Balanchine used to practice together, taking turns counting for each other. Lew taught Balanchine how to turn like the Italians." One immediately thinks of the many virtuoso solos Balanchine choreographed in which sequential pirouettes *sur la place* are featured.

Watching Christensen's classes with their emphasis on balances on half-toe at the barre, I saw how carefully he prepared his dancers to align their bodies properly for pirouettes in the centre. No wonder they turned so well! In fact, extensive *relevé* work is an integral part of their training. When one day he asked them to repeat an entire adagio exercise in the centre on *demi-pointe,* few even blinked. Christensen told me he relates balance to sculpture: "If a sculpted form is a little out of balance, it bothers the eye—like a picture that's crooked. For pirouettes and things to have balance, the body must be placed over the ball of the foot, and it's got to be as accurate as a sculpture."

In the allegro portion of his lessons, Christensen emphasizes fluidity, urging his students not to stop between the brush and the jump or between the landing of one jump and the beginning of the next. He recalls one of the unusual ways in which he, as a dancer, perfected his own allegro technique: "Something happened when we were touring in vaudeville with Mascagno and wanted to practice before the show. We waited our turn in back of the movie screen, and the manager would come backstage and say,

'Don't jump. You can't practice.' So we had to practice landing soundlessly. We learned to go down in full *plié* after *tours,* and we never made a sound. We developed a *ballon* that was unbelievable—landing easy. Mascagno made us do *entrechats sixes* in and out of *grand plié,* insisting that we never stop (at the base of the *plié*). It was awful. Your muscles hurt, but you never smashed your knees. I guess the way we developed as dancers was kind of accidental, but we had a love for it!" Christensen notes that he does not inflict Mascagno's "*sixes* from *grand plié*" exercise upon his own students!

To build his students' stamina, he has them perform many repetitions of each jump combination. Former Christensen dancer Tomm Ruud remembers Mr. C as saying: "If you can do it ten times in the studio, you'll be able to do it once onstage perfectly." Ruud continues: "He would tell us there was no such thing as marking and expecting that suddenly in performance we'd be fabulous. He never allowed us to mark. Marking was something I learned *after* I left Ballet West."

Christensen adores filling his jumping exercises with *batterie.* As a result, his students are experts at fast, precise footwork. He says with regret, "You hardly see beats in any school anymore. I think some teachers and choreographers feel that now that we have so many bigger stages, we need more of the big, expansive, Russian stuff and less of that small, fast footwork. But, as a pianist once told me, 'I can play all sorts of beautiful things, like Debussy, but my concert is no good unless someplace I have my fingers crossed.'" Christensen sees a clear analogy here with dancing. "The scope of the art for the body moving to music, if it's properly taught, is very broad. Choreography is most interesting if the entire range is explored."

When asked, all of the former Christensen students I interviewed identified one of the most important aspects of Mr. C's teaching as his emphasis on developing each dancer's dramatic abilities. As one student told me, "He always says, 'The easiest thing is to run onstage and look pretty.'" Nothing frustrates Christensen more than a dancer with a deadpan face. "Do you have no soul?" he'll ask. He is fond of pointing out that "every movement should express an emotion." His students say he teaches them how to change their faces, that for every emotion there is an appropriate expression. "He'll give examples," one told me, "of how you must color your movement. 'Pathos,' he'll say as you do an *arabesque penchée,* 'Show pathos on your face.'"

As do all teachers, Christensen adheres to certain practices that he has found to be especially effective over the years. The classes I observed were conducted without the traditional use of studio mirrors. He believes the

Willam Christensen commanding a student to "Stay!" in arabesque.

positions of classical ballet must be practiced without the mirror, by feeling them. He enjoys telling an old anecdote about Nijinsky: "A fan of Nijinsky's once said to him, 'You dance so beautifully, it's a pity you can't see yourself perform.' To which Nijinsky, calling attention to his mental mirror, replied, 'Madam, if I couldn't "see" myself dance, I couldn't dance well.'" Christensen constantly stresses the development of his students' visual perceptiveness. When a student does something well, he stops the class and has everyone watch. Then he asks, "What do you think? Why is the balance good? The shoulders nice? The arms, *plastique*?" He tells his students that their ability to be visually discerning will help them in all endeavors in life, whether or not they decide to become dancers. He says if they're "blind," they're in trouble because "it's like a musician who can't hear pitch. He'd better do something else." He feels students learn how to correct themselves better from watching others—more so than if they rely only on his corrections. "A teacher who gives a blueprint for everything," he pronounces, "is a rotten teacher."

During his classes, Christensen often works on a one-on-one basis with individual students. The manner with which he shows respect for each of them is one of the most beautiful aspects of his teaching. "He has an aura about him that suggests he could be an intimidating man," says one student, "but he never is. He's extremely kind." Former Ballet West dancer Tomm Ruud remembers learning a valuable lesson from Christensen about how to treat dancers: "I was choreographing once and screaming and yelling at the dancers, probably being really malicious because they weren't making my ballet look fabulous, and he turned to me and said, 'Be careful, Tomm, that you don't destroy their magic.' I've never forgotten those words."

When working with students, Christensen has definitely perfected the art of turning a negative into a positive. Like all caring teachers, he scolds and corrects, but always does so while simultaneously building up his students' egos. "If you'd fix that *port de bras*," he tells one young lady with a smile, "you'd be a very good dancer." His optimism is infectious, and students eagerly renew their efforts. When he booms across the room, "Why don't you bring your arm down like you're *somebody*?!" it seems a reinforcement of his belief in that individual's worth. To the gentlemen in the studio he occasionally issues a stern "Now, guys, *get* it!" but I heard him really yell only once: "You give up," he shouted to a student who stopped midway across the floor. "You must *never* give up!"

Christensen has no patience with lethargic dancing. As he commented wryly to the young men in class one day when he felt they were using about 50 percent effort: "You men retire early." Former student Jocelyn Vollmar remembers that Christensen "was always spurring us on. He would never let us relax or take it easy. He was always needling us to do more and more. I think that's what I liked about him because he made us pull it out of ourselves no matter how difficult conditions were. And that has always stood with me as a dancer and a teacher. . . . I try to tell my students that it has to come from within them. It can't come from a book or a teacher because sometime they're going to have to function by themselves. The teacher isn't going to be there."

Perhaps as a way to foster self-resilience in his students, Christensen took the time one day to allow each student in a large class to perform sixteen counts of leaps and turns across the floor *alone.* The dancers watched and applauded each other's efforts. As each student rose to the occasion, Mr. C had the rare opportunity to concentrate on, and correct, each individually. Obviously, both for him and the students, the benefits of allowing such solo exhibitions once in a while far outweighed the not-so-efficient use of classroom time.

Christensen makes a definite distinction between an "exercise" in class and a "combination." He will have the students repeat a single movement several times in sequence (an exercise) from the diagonal, for instance, and then later insert this movement into a dancey combination. It is typical of him to build an advanced class by repeatedly embellishing what was initially a simple exercise. He does not hesitate to deviate occasionally from traditional class structure because, he says, "I do one thing and it suggests another, or I see a problem and decide to emphasize solving it. For instance, I've had to redo the shoulders of every student here [he demonstrates a caved-in chest]. If you're serious as a teacher, you see these things and try to fix them; if you're not, you just teach steps."

As a teacher and person, he expresses concern about one of the greatest injustices of the contemporary ballet world—the extreme selectivity regarding dancers' physiques. He comments that the average woman has a long body and short legs. "To lengthen her line," he says, "she wears high heels. This is what Balanchine saw when he started preferring ladies whose knees were up around their waists. Now, everyone picks ladies with that look." He pointed to two short, stocky 18-year-olds practicing perfect *fouettés* at the end of his class. Neither had the prerequisite lean, long-legged look of today's ballerinas. Therefore, as Christensen knew, their chances of gaining employment in the professional ballet world were slim. "What am I going to do with these sharp ladies?" he asked in anguish. "They're virtuoso technicians. They deserve to dance! It's a tragedy!"

When asked what he feels are the most difficult aspects of classical ballet to master, he identifies elevation and *pointe* technique. Like all teachers, he has often had to deal with mothers eager to see their daughters on *pointe* before they're ready. Christensen, grinning, says he tells them: "Sure I can put your daughter up there. That's easy. But I'll have a hell of a time getting her down." As he told me, "To go up and down softly—God, that takes time!" He objects to the practice predominant in some American schools of female dancers executing the entire class, including barre work, in *pointe* shoes. He feels this precludes the full use and articulation of the foot, a skill that is always stressed in his classes. He is also a strong advocate of "soft arms, not stiff," and, in spite of the limited mobility he must now endure, one occasionally catches a lovely glimpse of the former dancer within him. Briefly laying his stick aside, he will demonstrate a flowing *port de bras* from, for instance, the Bluebird Variation in *Sleeping Beauty*. One sees instantly why Mikhail Fokine once declared that Willam Christensen had "the best style of any male dancer in America."

I enjoyed watching how informally Mr. C holds court after his class each day. He retires to a small waiting room to enjoy a cigarette. (In deference to his students, he has given up smoking during class.) One by one, his students stop in, some to chat a bit, some just to plop themselves down on the old couch next to his chair and listen as he talks. The young men especially seem to idolize him. When, one day, one sheepishly asked him for a loan "just till next week's paycheck," Christensen reached for his wallet without hesitation, no doubt remembering his own hungry days as a young student in New York. "I know you're good for it," he said, handing over a bill. "Is that enough?"

His advice to young teachers is short and to the point: Learn your art; be musical; and have a thorough knowledge of anatomy. About his students he says, "I want them to have expression, not be dull, and then to have a feeling for music because the body's an instrument. It's a visual, moving art."

Classroom Quotes from Christensen

"It's poetry to do a simple thing."

"If you do an exercise weakly, it's like mumbling when you're speaking."

"A *glissade* is two half *battements*."

"Make that movement very noble—as if you're too rich to even sweat."

To students dancing noisily on *pointe:* "Dancers should be seen and not heard."

His commentary about the performances of "over-the-hill" ballerinas: "It's like trying to boil an old chicken to make it tender. It doesn't work."

To ladies frantically waving their arms all over the place during an *enchaînement:* "You've got enough energy in your *port de bras* to run a laundromat."

During the early days of the San Francisco Ballet: "Ballet should not have to wear a European label to be accepted."

Order of the Exercises in Christensen's Class (advanced class, two hours)

BARRE

1. Demi-pliés and grands pliés with bends of the body
2. Tendus in 5th with tendu double (toes only) in 2nd
3. Tendus in 5th with demi-rond par terre
4. Tendus with temps lié (sliding chassés through the open positions)
5. Passés relevés and balances in attitude
6. Tendus jetés (dégagés) in 4 counts with flexed-foot petits battements
7. Exercise for entrechat six with flexed-foot petits battements
8. Ronds de jambe à terre with pas be basque traveling away and back to barre
9. Développés with demi and grand rond de jambe
10. Développés with bends of the body
11. Frappés with pirouettes
12. Petits battements with développés and preparation for fouetté rond de jambe en tournant
13. Quick ronds de jambe en l'air at 30 degrees with pas de chat away from and back to barre
14. Ronds de jambe en l'air at 90 degrees
15. Stretches with the leg held high à la seconde
16. Stretches with the leg in attitude back and penchée arabesque
17. Grands battements

CENTRE

1. Adagio/port de bras
2. Tendus with épaulement and pirouettes
3. Pirouettes
4. Turns from the diagonal in coda tempi
5. Changements and pirouettes
6. Assemblés (repeated with battus)
7. Enchaînement with jeté battu and pas couru
8. Coupé jeté manège with jeté élance in 1st arabesque
9. Coupé chassé-coupé jeté en diagonale finishing with chaînés
10. Cabriole and brisé enchaînement
11. Fouettés turns for the females, tour en l'air for the males
12. Révérence—bow that includes a single pirouette finished on the knee, a deep port de bras to the floor and recovery to the initial standing position

The Roots of Tradition

THE PEDAGOGICAL LINEAGE OF WILLAM CHRISTENSEN

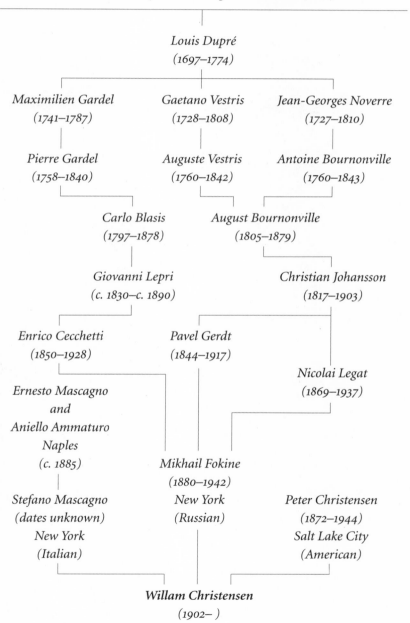

L'Académie Royale de Musique et de Danse (1661)

Louis Dupré
(1697–1774)

Maximilien Gardel
(1741–1787)

Gaetano Vestris
(1728–1808)

Jean-Georges Noverre
(1727–1810)

Pierre Gardel
(1758–1840)

Auguste Vestris
(1760–1842)

Antoine Bournonville
(1760–1843)

Carlo Blasis
(1797–1878)

August Bournonville
(1805–1879)

Giovanni Lepri
(c. 1830–c. 1890)

Christian Johansson
(1817–1903)

Enrico Cecchetti
(1850–1928)

Pavel Gerdt
(1844–1917)

Nicolai Legat
(1869–1937)

Ernesto Mascagno
and
Aniello Ammaturo
Naples
(c. 1885)

Mikhail Fokine
(1880–1942)

Stefano Mascagno
(dates unknown)
New York
(Italian)

New York
(Russian)

Peter Christensen
(1872–1944)
Salt Lake City
(American)

Willam Christensen
(1902–)

3 Janina Cunovas

Janina Cunovas demonstrating for a class at a Russian ballet
seminar in Tampa, Florida, in 1990.

*J*anina Cunovas has lived and taught in Australia for more than forty years. A native of Lithuania, she received her dance training at the school of the Lithuanian State Ballet, graduating in 1934. Upon joining the company, she went on tour to London and Monte Carlo, where they performed the classics to considerable acclaim. During World War II, she fled Lithuania and joined the Vienna State Opera Ballet. In 1949, Cunovas and her family emigrated to Australia where, in subsequent years, she taught for many ballet schools including the Borovansky Academy of Russian Ballet, the Australian Ballet School, and the Victorian College of the Arts. She has also worked with the Australian Ballet, with which she appeared in 1985 in the cameo role of the Ballet Mistress in *Gaîté Parisienne.*

Cunovas is unusual in that she may be the only Soviet-trained teacher in the world also certified to teach the Royal Academy of Dancing syllabus; she gives classes in both the Russian and the R.A.D. methods. She also speaks five languages (Russian, Lithuanian, German, Polish, and English) fluently. For several years, beginning in 1987, she traveled to the United States each summer to assist the late Jurgen Schneider in his Russian teaching seminars. It was during one such seminar that I first had the privilege of observing Cunovas teach. She was seventy-five years old when I interviewed her in Tampa, Florida, in 1990.

"Your body is

an instrument

with which you

must produce

music."

JANINA CUNOVAS is the embodiment of early-twentieth-century aristocrat-ic elegance. She defies her age by virtue of an inner glow and, with her beau-tiful carriage and energetic stride, puts most of us, far younger, to shame. To watch her teach is to understand the meaning of the word "ballerina."

In the classroom, the always chic Cunovas wears flowing silk dresses—street clothes, rather than dance attire. Often, when demonstrating, she delicately lifts her skirt to one side. The refinement of this gesture, used to reveal her legs slightly, is beautiful to see. Quite unconsciously, she presents a perfect example of how to manage a long-skirted costume gracefully—something every aspiring ballerina needs to learn.

Cunovas is typical of the "old school" Russian ballerinas. She demon-strates in class as if she were on the stage—with enormous charm. Aware of the effectiveness of flirting (in a way most modern young women are not), she does not hesitate to use her deep-set, dramatically made-up eyes in a provocative manner. Also captivating is the beauty with which she softly ar-ranges her fingers in the classical positions. As she often tells her students: "You must be expressive not only with your face, but also with your hands."

Among Cunovas's most likable traits is her humility. One of her former students, Terri Charlesworth, who now directs the Graduate College of Dance in Perth, remembers: "Once I said to Janina in a rehearsal, 'Oh, that's a lovely *port de bras* you've given them,' and she replied, without even think-ing really, 'Oh, we had such wonderful masters as teachers.' And I thought to myself that that statement sums her up. She won't take a compliment for herself; instead, she pays tribute to the people who taught her." In class, Cunovas delights in prefacing a comment or correction by saying, "My teachers used to tell me." Not only are these memories charming, they also serve to remind her students that what they are practicing is part of a very long tradition. "You have to believe in what your teachers taught you," Cunovas says, "and carry on that tradition. Everything I say is from the mouths of my teachers." She was trained in Vilna, Lithuania, and even though she has been living and teaching in Australia (a country with a strong allegiance to English ballet) for more than forty years, she has never altered her devotion to the Russian system in which she was schooled.

Cunovas was born in 1915 in Lithuania. For the first five years of her life, she lived in Moscow where her family had moved in an effort to escape the horrors of World War I. She remembers the time as being "very difficult be-cause of the Revolution." As a child, she always dreamed of being a dancer, although she has no idea how the thought entered her head. "I was always skipping and running," she recalls, "and everyone called me 'the little balle-rina.' But my parents dismissed my dreams. They were very old-fashioned and thought that naughty things happened in the theater. They wanted me to be a doctor, or perhaps a nun!"

The family returned to Lithuania in time for Cunovas to enroll in el-ementary school where, as luck would have it, one of the compulsory courses was "plastica," a class in free-form dance studies. The teachers en-couraged Cunovas's talent, and her desire to be a dancer grew. She remem-bers: "When I was nine, I saw the notice in the newspaper for the audition for the Lithuanian State Choreographic Academy. There was only one ballet school and one company in Lithuania then—no such thing as private stu-dios existed. My auntie who lived with us took me to the audition. We did not tell my parents. There were about one hundred kids. They examined our physiques. Eventually, I was called back for a second audition. There, we did little walks and danced—polka and waltz steps—familiar steps that everyone knew because Lithuanians sang and danced a lot, especially at so-cial functions. An interest in the arts was second nature to my people. Well, they took thirty-eight children, and I was chosen, so then I had to tell my parents. My mother, who was quite religious, was a bit upset."

Cunovas remembers her training at the Lithuanian school as being very strict. All of her teachers were Russian. "Everything was provided for you—tights, shoes, everything—so it was expected that you would work hard," she says. Half of her day was devoted to academic studies and the other half to dancing. She says she will never forget the elated feeling of total exhaus-tion at the end of each day: "When I went home at night, I remember my body feeling very light—as if I weighed nothing—as if I were not even touching the floor."

Cunovas recalls that her teachers could be "very nasty—when we did not work as hard as they wanted us to, they'd tell us to 'go home, bake cakes, and get fat!'" Younger students, she says, were always given lots of encouragement, "but when we got to be about fourteen, then they really became very demanding." She remembers one event in particular: "I made the mistake of going out with a friend, or something, instead of going to class. And it was like the end of the world when I came back. I was very scared." However, she says, she was never told by her teachers that dancing must be her entire life. Indeed, to this day she believes it is important to maintain a balance in one's life. "If dancing is the only thing in your life," she says, "you can get a bit funny in the head. Dancing is a *part* of my life."

Lest that statement be misinterpreted, Cunovas quickly adds that one must be totally serious in the pursuit of a dance career. She is fond of reminding students of something her own teachers would often say: "We will never ask you why you are here in ballet school, but we will let you know why you will have to go!"

In spite of the strict nature of her training, she remembers it with great nostalgia. "There were no more than eight students in each class," she says, "so we got lots of personal attention. And what I liked best was the interest the company members had in each of us. They'd come and say, 'No, no. Do it that way!' It was as if they were grooming us." Among those teachers whom she remembers with grateful fondness was Georgiy Kiaksht, who for many years was ballet master of the both the Lithuanian school and company.

Cunovas graduated in 1934 at the age of eighteen, after nine years at the school. She immediately joined the Lithuanian Ballet Company and feels fortunate to have been there at the time when Anatole Oboukhoff[1] and Vera Nemtchinova[2] had arrived from Russia to be principal artists. She studied under both and remembers them as wonderful dancers. "The Leningrad teacher, Lopokov, was also sent from Russia to give the company pedagogy classes," she recalls. "I was not very enthusiastic. I thought to myself, 'I don't need that. I only want to dance and maybe someday be a rehearsal assistant.' As a matter of fact, I hated teaching. But Lopokov, who was a year with our company, always said, 'You never know what's going to be.' He was right. I never planned on being a teacher, but now I'm glad I had those classes."

As soon as Cunovas joined the company, she left with them on a three-month tour to London and Monte Carlo under the auspices of René Blum.[3] In both places, the company enjoyed a huge success performing a wide range of standard ballet classics including *Raymonda, Giselle, Coppélia, Sleeping Beauty,* and *Prince Igor.* She soon married a fellow company member, Boris Cunov, a wonderful man ten years her senior, to whom she was proud to be wed for more than fifty years until his death in 1992. She remembers that the theater in Lithuania "was like our home." Not only ballet, but also opera and musicals were produced there. The company's ties to the Russian ballet were close. Many famous Russians performed with them. In particular, she remembers Asaf Messerer:[4] "He had fabulous elevation!"

Cunovas, who loved the repertoire she danced, attained the rank of soloist-*coryphée.* Asked for recollections about herself as a dancer, she giggles

Janina Cunovas looking into the mirror while helping a young student place his arms correctly in a pirouette preparation.

and admits, "I was a little bit frightened about turning, but, onstage, fear got me through my pirouettes!" She and her husband danced with the company until 1944, when the Germans invaded Lithuania and the bombing started.

As fighting continued, Cunovas escaped with her family to the safe haven of Allied displaced persons camps in Austria, hoping to find a way to emigrate to the United States. This proved impossible; they did not have the necessary American sponsor. They danced with the Vienna Opera Ballet until the city was heavily bombarded, then left for Innsbruck, joining a large group of dancers of other nationalities who performed for Allied troops in many theaters in Allied-occupied territory. After the war, Boris Cunov organized a company in Ausberg with Lithuanian dancers gathered from across Europe. The Red Cross helped the troupe obtain materials for costumes, and Janina's brother, a well-known artist, Vaclovas Ratas, designed the sets. With everyone helping to create the choreography, they produced *Coppélia* and traveled with it throughout Germany.

In 1949, Cunovas, her husband, her sister, and both their families decided to leave for Australia. "At that time," she recalls, "Australia would take you if you would sign a paper agreeing to work for two years after your arrival anywhere the government assigned you. We wanted," she explains, "to get as far away as possible from the terrible wartime experiences in Europe."

Once in Australia, they were faced with having to integrate themselves into a very different culture. She and her sister, who had also danced in the Lithuanian Company, discovered that no one wanted ballet teachers who taught Russian technique. (Forty years later, she notes, things have changed a great deal. Russian technique is now very popular in Australia.) She was lucky, she says, to land a job immediately in the Linley Wilson School, the best ballet school in Perth, where they had settled. However, she soon realized that to survive as a ballet teacher in Australia, she would have to learn the widely preferred Royal Academy of Dancing[5] method. She prepared herself and took the R.A.D. exams, which she says "cost a lot!" She was also battling an unanticipated language barrier: "I knew a little English from school, but when we got to Australia, everyone used slang and talked so fast that I couldn't understand a thing. I was very upset!"

For Cunovas's husband, the move from Europe marked the end of his dance career. He was assigned to work as a cook in a Greek coffee place. "He had a rough time," she admits. One of her longtime Australian colleagues thinks Cunovas survived this difficult transition period because of her natural gift for grace and diplomacy. "She was always very quiet. In class, she gave lots of lovely, delicate poses. She was never pushy. She was content to stay in the background. Also, she has always maintained a positive, spiritual outlook on life. As a person, she has always wanted to be happy and, with her wonderful sense of humor, can keep everyone around her laughing."

After completing all levels of the R.A.D. exams, Cunovas was certified to teach and, to this day, gives seminars in the R.A.D. method all over Australia and New Zealand. She has prepared many students for their R.A.D. examinations and says, "Honestly, they looked better because they benefited from my knowledge of the Russian School. And I was never penalized for that— for including a bit of head, just a little touch of the Russian style. I always got good results. After all, in R.A.D. the syllabus gives you steps, but each teacher has the responsibility to tell students *how* to do them. I teach *tendu,* for instance, as I was taught to do it in Russia—correctly!" She also admits that wherever she goes to do R.A.D. work, she often asks if she can give a few Russian classes as well. "The students enjoy it," she says, and obviously she, too, relishes any opportunity to work in the style she loves most.

Cunovas remained in Perth until 1958, when she moved to Melbourne and began teaching in the school of Edouard Borovansky,[6] the man considered the father of Australian ballet. "Both of us," she recalls, "taught the

R.A.D. syllabus, as well as the Russian method, because, of course, the students wanted to take the R.A.D. exams." Borovansky, who had come to Australia on tour with the De Basil Ballets Russes and had chosen to remain, was a Czech who had danced with Pavlova. When Borovansky died, Cunovas began to teach for the Victorian Ballet Guild. When it folded for lack of funds, she taught for the Australian Ballet, and then, later, at the Victorian College of the Arts. Now, she fills her time traveling to give seminars in Australia and New Zealand. In the late 1980s, she enjoyed going to the United States, where she assisted Jurgen Schneider, former ballet master of American Ballet Theatre (and an expert on the Soviet method), in his summer workshops on the Russian syllabus.

"A class must be beautifully balanced," says Cunovas, and hers always are. Aside from her magnetic presence, what struck me most as I watched her teach was the exquisite simplicity of her exercises. She is careful not to crowd too many steps into one combination. "If muscles get overcrowded, muscles can give you an unpleasant surprise," she remarks. She believes that to develop technique, one must keep exercises simple and gradually build stamina and virtuosity.

This approach also gives her plenty of opportunity to focus on the development of artistry. "We used to hear 'Be graceful' all the time," she says. "You don't hear that so much anymore. It's a pity. I'd like to help my ladies achieve more grace, delicacy, and femininity." Often she urges her students: "Don't just do mechanical exercises. Be a little artistic." Many students, she says, appear to have nothing inside. "That's why in the children's classes in the Russian School, we give what we call 'dancing steps,'" she explains. "We don't bother how they do it, or about turn-out or stretch, as long as they dance. We do it to see if they have feeling and the ability to show it. In each class, we give five to eight minutes of this dancing. In the beginning-level classes, this includes walking, running, small *balancés*, something to contrast with the dry exercises. It's the only way to develop expression, not just with the face, but with the hands, too." It is in this aspect of training that she feels the West could improve, and it is one of her signature areas as a teacher. Nowhere else have I witnessed such a creative variety of simple, dancey steps as Cunovas employs in her beginner and intermediate classes. Included are a wealth of slow and fast walks, runs, little gallops (*chassés*), and *balancés;* she choreographs them in all sorts of patterns: on the diagonal, in circles, facing all directions, and moving backward, as well as forward and sideways. Her students clearly love these opportunities to "just dance." She remembers that her teachers used to say that all students had a little flame inside them, that it was necessary to "blow so much that a big flame happens." "You can't let a child get lost," she says. "You have to bring out the artist inside of each one."

One of the keys to developing artistry in ballet dancers is the focus on *port de bras* (arm movements). Dancer Cosima Borrer, who studied as a child with Cunovas and then danced with the Vienna Opera Ballet, told me: "I was fortunate enough to have private lessons with Madame. They were very long, very tiring, and very meticulous sessions. Things were drilled into me that I do automatically to this day. Long periods of time were devoted to simply the 'preparation' of the arm before the legs had even moved. It is such a small movement, this *port de bras*, but how difficult to perfect! To hold the elbow still, to keep the upper body motionless, to follow the fingertips correctly with the eyes. She condensed and explained every movement and then wanted me to make it breathe and articulate. As a young girl, my patience was almost at an end. At that time, I did not see the importance of it. Now, as a professional dancer, I repeat that movement hundreds of times each week. Thank goodness, Janina taught me right!"

Cunovas remembers her own teachers in Lithuania telling her, "You must speak with your arms. We need to hear a song." (And she remembers, as a child, wondering how she could possibly sing with her arms!) Her students in Australia, she says, thought she was being funny when she first told them, "Don't talk with your arms. Sing!" After one learns the positions, she explains, one must study the passage, the movement between the positions, because "that is one's language, one's song."

In 1990, while I was observing Cunovas at the Russian Ballet Teaching Seminar in Tampa, the great Leningrad ballerina Irina Kolpakova was also giving classes. To illustrate her point about *port de bras*, Cunovas said to me, "Watch how Irina demonstrates. It's so alive. It's like she's talking—like a bird singing." She was right; Kolpakova's *port de bras* was exquisitely vital, and so, I observed, was Cunovas's. Both were an inspiration. As one teacher, a longtime fan of Cunovas, remarked while attending the seminar, "When I watch Janina teach, I watch her more than the students—the lovely coordination of the head, eyes, and fingers and her lovely sensitivity to music. For me, she's the artist in the room."

Cunovas told me that her greatest reward in teaching is to work with a student who responds well to corrections: "When I see a girl, not yet established as a dancer, and I correct her, and straightaway I see the result, it's the biggest pleasure." She smiles at the thought, then continues: "Not everyone can be a dancer, you know. You have to be born with a gift, but if you do not have the talent and determination to work, nothing happens. You must believe in your teacher and accept what she says."

Cunovas's devoted former student Cosima Borrer recalls that sometimes accepting Cunovas's recommendations had its problems. "Whenever I was injured," she told me, "Madame's suggestion was to put wine bottle corks in a cloth bag and place them over the pulled muscle or strained area. I'm still not sure if this was very effective—only that it was very difficult to get a good night's sleep with a bag of wine corks under my leg!"

Cunovas confesses that in spite of the joy she feels when, for instance, she watches her students perform in end-of-the-year recitals, she occasionally finds teaching very frustrating. "It really takes so much out of you," she says. "In Russia you might teach one or, at the most, two classes a day. Sometimes in Australia I have taught as many as five. And at the end of a day like that, you just hate it! It can also be hard if you have something you want to give students, and they are not receptive (probably because it is different from what they have learned in the past)."

She says sometimes she can get a bit angry or worked up while teaching. But she never completely loses her temper. One day I watched her patience dwindle at the timidity of her students. Disdainfully, she remarked that they were "wasting time," but as quickly as the cloud appeared over the classroom, it vanished. The next moment she was flashing her lovely smile and saying, "O.K., darlings, now try this." Teaching "business girls" in Australia who just came to class for pleasure, she says, taught her diplomacy and instilled in her the philosophy that "the best way to get something from a student is in a nice way." Although she tries to be very friendly with students, she is also careful to maintain her position as a respected authority figure. One day in class a student stood with her hands planted on her hips, watching Cunovas demonstrate. Cunovas turned and quietly asked her to put her arms down. She felt it was rude of the child to assume such a stance in front of her. "I stick to old tradition where manners are concerned," she says. "All classical ballet is based on tradition, and manners in the classroom are part of that tradition."

I enjoyed watching how carefully Cunovas chooses her words when making a correction. "I never get personal," she told me, "but I do try to show that I care for them. I would never say to a student, 'You have ugly feet.' Instead, I might say, 'Your feet are not quite good, but they can be nice if you use them well.'" This kind of positive encouragement was often visible when I watched her teach. I remember her asking a student, "Can you make a longer leg? I bet you can!" She is also a great advocate of using hu-

Janina Cunovas performing a port de bras exercise in front of her students.

mor to release tension. She elicited giggles from a class of young girls when, one day, in an effort to remind them to think about their hands, she held her fingers out in front of her like claws and chimed, "Monsters in town!" Former student Janet Tait, who is now a principal artist with the West Australian Ballet, told me: "Janina has a sense of mischief which is *most* effective at keeping her pupils light-hearted, while at the same time making them *want* to achieve."

When I asked Cunovas to remember the funniest thing that had ever happened in her classroom, she told me the following story: "I was correcting a boy in class in Australia. He had his legs in much too wide a 2nd position and was going too low in *pliés*. I told him he would have trouble with his knees if he continued to bend so low. 'Oh, Madame,' he replied, 'it doesn't matter—I already have problems with my knees.'" She shook her head, smiling.

A stickler about placement, Cunovas is a master at using her hands to make a correction. "You must touch students lightly, though," she warns, "in order to make sure they *feel* the correction." Sometimes, however, she breaks her own rule. One day she marched up to a student who was standing in 4th position preparing to do a pirouette *en dehors*. "Humph!" she said, putting one fist on her hip, sinking into one leg and looking him directly in the eye. Abruptly, she gave him a shove on the side. Flustered, the student lost his footing. "No!" she said, "Your feet must be *planted* on the ground in a preparation. Try again!" The next time, the student stood his ground when she shoved. "That's right," she said approvingly.

One of Cunovas's favorite methods for making students aware of the precise nature of the classical vocabulary is to ask, "What's two and two?" The class is usually a bit dumbfounded at the simplicity of her question. However, when they finally unanimously answer, "Four," she poses the real question: "So," she says, "one answer. So why do I see one hundred different arabesques when I ask for 1st arabesque? There's only one. It's the same as in mathematics!" She fondly reminds them that "style and expression can be different, but technique and musical counts—those we must make all together in precisely the same manner."

Cunovas identifies the two most difficult problems with which she must work as helping students achieve turn-out and getting their shoulders open (i.e., achieving the correct classical stance in the upper body with the shoulders pressed down and back while the chest is held lifted with a wide open feeling across the collarbones). She says she's very careful about forcing turn-out. "It must be done slowly," she says, "bit by bit, and only a few really have the capacity for it." She tells students: "Lightly lift from the hips. Then you can turn out better. If you sit—shrink—into your hips, you can't do it." She remarks that in the Russian School, one does not teach anything until the body is well placed "because on good placement, all technique grows. If you're not placed, you can't do anything." She feels that here lies one of the biggest differences between the Western and Russian Schools. "In Western training a girl without strong placement might be told to keep her leg low in a *développé* and to lift her body. In Russia, by the time she begins to learn *développés,* her body is already strongly lifted and placed, so I would ask her to raise her leg."

Cunovas does not count in class. If the students are being unmusical, she will stop the class and demonstrate what she wants, accompanying herself by singing, "Rhrrm-ta-tah. . . ." By demonstrating, rather than using a lot of words, she is striving to increase the perceptivity of her students. "In my training," she recalls, "we were taught that we must have a 'student's mind,' one that would enable us to absorb the lessons." Cunovas empowers students by setting up situations in which they must make aesthetic decisions. When they do a half *port de bras* arm preparation in a haphazard, distracted manner, she claps, "Stop!" "Now," she says, appealing to their intelligence as artists, "I will show it two ways, and you tell me which you like better." Unanimously, they pick the version in which she coordinates her head, eyes, and hands in a meaningful fashion. "Because it's *organized*," Cunovas says triumphantly.

She exhibits endless patience in explaining details such as the method used to lower the arm from 2nd position to 5th position *en bas:* "The hand and the elbow must be soft. No fancy movement. No flick of the fingers!" Invariably, in lower-level classes, she will have the accompanist add a musical phrase to the end of an exercise in order to accommodate this careful arm-lowering. She is a great believer in giving students time to establish poses and "feel like dancers." "Don't stand hunched and shrunken, girls," she says. "We have to show *all* of our figure." She also explains differences in dynamics, often using analogy. "*Fondu* must melt like ice cream," she says. Then she demonstrates a fast, jerky *plié:* "Now, that's not melting!" And she will point out changes in dynamics within a *port de bras.* "When you lift your arm to 1st position and open to 2nd," she instructs them, "it must complement the character of the exercise—either strong or soft." As a footnote she adds, "And your eyes must follow the arm as it opens and then look very far away."

Former student Cosima Borrer recalls: "Nothing we studied in Cunovas's classes was too small to be important. The eyes were one of her pet themes. She hated it when the pupils were positioned in the corners of the eyes. So we had exercises to train the eyes. My dedication to Madame went so far as to lead me to practice these exercises during school lessons. I'm sure my classmates doubted my sanity as my eyes suddenly went round and round, up and down, side to side! There were also exercises for the fingers. These I could practice more discreetly under the desk. Janina Cunovas still doesn't wear glasses—something she attributes to the strength of her eyes. I'm hoping I have as much success!"

During the jumping exercises in her classes, Cunovas encourages ebullience. "Jump higher," she urges students in a dancey *arabesque sautée* combination. "Enjoy yourselves and dance!" One day in class, when the young men got a bit carried away, losing their classical form, she cautioned: "That's not enough. Fleas can jump, too. You have to jump *and* dance!"

Cunovas insists that dancers push off for jumps using their whole foot: "I didn't hear any swishing there on those *assemblés. Brush* your foot—slide it along the floor like in *tendu jeté.*" Again, during this part of class, one hears her refer to her past. "As my teacher used to say," she reminds students while placing them in formation to begin a large *sissonne* exercise, "Jump from the mountain. Show me flight!"

One of the loveliest aspects of Cunovas's class comes at the end. After leading her students through a proper classical *port de bras,* she does a variety of nonacademic movements to increase their awareness of their arms and hands. These may include wrist rotations, rippling pushes through the hands, and a variety of circular movements of the arms. One day she finished with the arms in *demi-seconde,* palms to the floor, and fingers vibrating in the manner of the Songbird Fairy in Petipa's *Sleeping Beauty.*

Every day, after the final bow, after the applause has died down, Cunovas gathers her students around her for a little chat. "What did you learn today?" she asks. "What are we going to think about for next time?"

Classroom Quotes from Cunovas

"Technique you can get from a teacher, but expression must be your own."

To students at the barre: "*Tendu* out—you work. *Tendu* in—you work. At no point do you do nothing!"

On maintaining arm poses: "If I hold my arms, they will hold me."

On *port de bras:* "Do a drawing in space. Don't fling your arm open. You don't feel a thing that way."

To students waving their arms without control during an exercise: "My teacher would say that the mosquitoes were biting you!"

On jumping: "The floor is my trampoline."

Order of the Exercises in Cunovas's Class (intermediate class, 1½ hours)

BARRE

1. Pliés
2. Battements tendus
3. Battements tendus with flex and plié in the open positions
4. Battements dégagés with pointés and dégagés en cloche
5. Ronds de jambe à terre with relevés lents and cambrés
6. Battements fondus relevés and ronds de jambe en l'air
7. Battements frappés (singles and doubles) with balances in passé
8. Battements développés/enveloppés/relevés lents and cambrés
9. Grands battements and balances in passé

CENTRE

1. Port de bras and développés
2. Battements tendus and pas de bourrées
3. Sissonnes tombées pas de bourrée with grands battements and pirouettes en dehors and en dedans
4. Changements, temps levés in 1st and 2nd, and changements en tournant
5. Glissades, assemblés, petits jetés, and sautés arabesques
6. Medium allegro combination
7. Port de bras and révérence

The Roots of Tradition

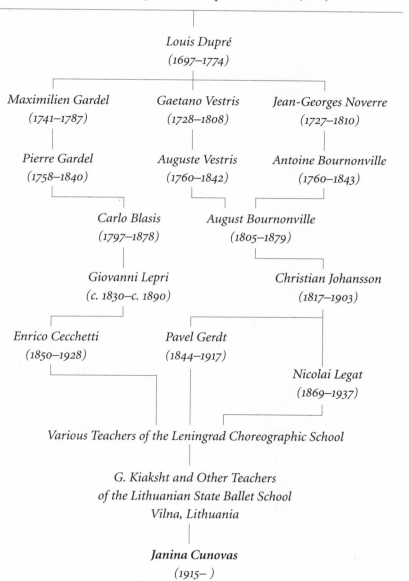

L'Académie Royale de Musique et de Danse (1661)

Louis Dupré
(1697–1774)

Maximilien Gardel   Gaetano Vestris   Jean-Georges Noverre
(1741–1787)   (1728–1808)   (1727–1810)

Pierre Gardel   Auguste Vestris   Antoine Bournonville
(1758–1840)   (1760–1842)   (1760–1843)

Carlo Blasis   August Bournonville
(1797–1878)   (1805–1879)

Giovanni Lepri   Christian Johansson
(c. 1830–c. 1890)   (1817–1903)

Enrico Cecchetti   Pavel Gerdt
(1850–1928)   (1844–1917)

Nicolai Legat
(1869–1937)

Various Teachers of the Leningrad Choreographic School

G. Kiaksht and Other Teachers
of the Lithuanian State Ballet School
Vilna, Lithuania

Janina Cunovas
(1915–)

4 *Gabriela Taub-Darvash*

Gabriela Darvash making a humorous remark during class in New York City in 1991.

*G*abriela Taub-Darvash, a native of Romania, has lived and taught in New York City since 1973. Her students appear in major ballet companies throughout the world. As a coach, she has worked with principal dancers from the Kirov Ballet, the New York City Ballet, American Ballet Theatre, and Dance Theater of Harlem. In 1980, she produced the first American female gold medalist in international competition, when her student, fifteen-year-old Nancy Raffa, won the Prix de Lausanne in Switzerland.

Darvash received her training in Romania and in Russia, at the Vaganova School in St. Petersburg and GITIS in Moscow. Before emigrating to the United States, she was artistic director and resident choreographer of the State Opera Ballet in Cluj, Romania. I began observing her classes in 1978 and have continued to do so whenever I am in New York. She has always been patient with my questions and generous about sharing her knowledge. I consider her one of my primary mentors, a major influence upon my own development as a teacher, and am immensely grateful to her.

"The closer we can stay to what is natural for the body in this artificial technique of ballet, the better we will dance."

GABRIELA DARVASH strides into her classroom in Broadway's theater district. Her lips are painted bright red, her elegant fingers adorned with large-stoned rings. Even though she wears huge earrings, there is something delightfully tomboyish about her. Perhaps it is her very short hair or her solid, no-nonsense stance. Here, one senses, is a woman who could command a ship or unsettle a Senate investigative committee. Madame Darvash is no wilting violet. "Good morning," she says briskly.

Her eyes quickly survey the room through large, owlish glasses. They alight briefly on a girl standing at the barre. After a quick vertical scan of the young lady's leg-warmer-encased body, she remarks dryly, "You're dressed for skiing, darling, not dancing." Several students try to suppress grins. One of the things they relish about Madame is this caustic mix of truth and humor. A brilliant, highly cultured woman with an acerbic wit, Darvash is a keen observer of the world. Her often memorable comments about the study of ballet and about life are often both very funny and deadly serious.

The pianist begins, and Darvash moves easily through the labyrinth of barres intersecting the studio floor. "Relax your elbows on the barre, and turn your heads so you don't get stiff necks," she advises. She weaves slowly among the students, addressing them individually by name, lightly touching one here, another there. Pausing momentarily, she lifts her eyes and calls to a young man on the opposite side of the room: "Now, you bend, Chris, salowwly." Her English, one of the six languages she speaks fluently, is heavily accented and embellished with voluptuously rolled r's. She pauses by a young dancer whose *port de bras* is overly expansive. "Now, what happens?" she chides. "It's a drama already and we're only doing *pliés.*"

Often, she uses humorous questions to get her point across. "What did you see between your legs down there?" she asks a student who has indulged himself by remaining too long in a *cambré* forward. Such pointed remarks elicit smiles of recognition throughout the studio. At one time or another, all her students have been the object of her fearfully truthful tongue. Her voice, what she calls her "dictation," can be loud, even piercing, but is more often urgent and coaxing. Sometimes, sensing the need for a more intimate correction, she will pause close to a student and speak in a gentle voice audible only to the student. She may be tough, but she is not insensitive. And, as she is fond of saying (although, perhaps, only half-seriously), "If you like, do what I say. This is a democracy here. Everything is optional. I just give advice."

More than anything, Darvash prides herself on cultivating thinking students, ones who use their bodies in an intelligent way. She is absolutely adamant about the need for dancers to understand some basic anatomy. "I ask kids to tell me which is the loosest joint in their bodies. They guess—'my knee? my hip?' They don't know! I ask them how, if they don't even know how their bodies are functioning, they can expect to be able to do pirouettes?! I want them to know that movement is the result of a command from the brain. I tell them: 'We are animals—read a zoology book—we are called homo sapiens, and we are distinguished by our ability to think. If you decide to think, then I am interested in you.'"

Darvash herself has spent her life thinking. Well-educated, she is a rarity in the ballet world, where most artists early on sacrifice their academic schooling in order to devote themselves single-mindedly to dance. Her mother, also highly educated, saw to it that Darvash had an extensive education, particularly in languages and music. Only after much pleading was she finally allowed to study ballet. Today, Darvash cites reading as her hobby and cooking and cleaning as her relaxation. A pacifist by nature, she objects to "violent movies and everything about violence. More and more, I wish I could work for anti-violent activities to try to humanize our society. Perhaps teaching beauty and elegance is part of that mission."

Darvash was born in 1930 in northern Romania, near what was, at that time, the Romanian border with Czechoslovakia. (With an evil twinkle in her eye, she is fond of warning students, "You better watch out. I'm from Transylvania, you know—where Dracula comes from.") After living in two villages, the family eventually moved to Timisoara when she was ten. There, for four years during World War II, Darvash remembers that each night at 2:00 A.M., the family was awakened by sirens. They ran to the bomb shelter in the basement, staying until 4:00 A.M. before returning to their beds. As the planes passed over en route to Yugoslavia, her family never knew, she says, whether they would be bombed or not. Food was rationed, particularly for Jewish families such as hers, who received a quarter of everyone else's allotment. Today, she wonders what effect four years without a single night of uninterrupted sleep must have had on her as a school child.

Difficult as those years were, Darvash also remembers her joy when, finally, she was allowed to take ballet classes. Twice a week, she went to a teacher who soon began using Darvash to demonstrate for students who had been studying much longer than she. "I must have had a lot of natural facility," she says, "because this teacher did not really explain to us how to do anything. I just picked it up. It was an amateur school, not very good, I'm afraid. Most of the students were society girls who came to the classes because that was something well-bred girls did." Darvash found herself bored with the curriculum, as well as the teacher, and did not enroll for a second session. Soon after, however, her mother took her to the opera as a birthday present. Darvash was fascinated by the professionalism of the spectacle. On her own initiative, she discovered that there was an opera school and that, if one were admitted, not only was tuition free, but there might be the opportunity to be a "super" in the opera productions.

Darvash was accepted by the school and remembers from then on practically living at the Timisoara opera house. She attended regular academic school in the morning, then dance classes at the opera in the afternoon, often staying to take part in performances in the evening. "I knew all the operas by heart," she says. She respected her ballet teacher very much, but is critical today of the old-style method in which she was trained. "He had a little stick," she remembers, "but he really didn't teach. He just gave the combinations, and if you could do them—good. If you fell out of your pirouettes, you got a bad mark. If you learned combinations fast, you were excellent. He'd say things like 'point your feet' or 'lift it higher,' and that was it."

During her last three years of high school, Darvash performed with a troupe comprised of musicians, singers, and dancers, many of whom also worked at the opera house. It had been formed by the Workers' Union. She remembers being sent into the countryside to learn Romanian folk dances because she picked up movement so quickly. This experience resulted in a lifelong love of character dance, which she also teaches. As a performer, it was her forte. "I never tell my students that I was a great classical dancer," she says. "I was a character dancer. I never had the physique for classical dance." Even had she wished to become a ballet dancer, she says, it would have been unheard of for someone with her education to have simply stopped her studies in order to join the opera ballet. Therefore, when she graduated from the Lyceum (high school), she accepted a scholarship from the Romanian government to pursue her university degree in the USSR.

She arrived in Moscow in September 1949 with the intent to enroll in the choreography program in the Lunarcharsky University of Performing Arts, also known as GITIS.[1] However, upon seeing a performance of *Romeo and Juliet* at the Bolshoi, she was overwhelmed by the technical level of the dancers and realized that there was much about classical ballet she still wished to learn. She left for Leningrad (St. Petersburg), where she enrolled in the Vaganova school (see p. 361, n. 10) in a special class for foreign students preparing to be teachers. She spent two-and-a-half years there absorbing everything "like a sponge." For six months she watched Vaganova privately coaching the great Hungarian ballerina Nora Kovach, an experience she terms "unforgettable." Darvash often speaks about Vaganova. In one class, she announced, "Today is Vaganova's birthday," and proceeded to pay tribute to the great Soviet pedagogue by teaching the students one of Vaganova's lovely *temps lié* exercises.

Darvash's mentor during her years in the USSR was her teacher at GITIS, the great Bolshoi dancer and choreographer Leonid Lavrovsky.[2] "To me," she says, "he was a hero. He had to bear the burden of working as artistic director at the Bolshoi during a period in Russia when censorship was drastic." Although her admiration for Lavrovsky and the artistic aspects of Soviet ballet never ceased, it was during Darvash's time in Russia that she first questioned certain aspects of Soviet dance pedagogy. "Vaganova," she says, "never asked for more than two pirouettes. She wanted them absolutely clean with a perfect finish. When I went to Moscow in 1952, I could count on one hand the number of dancers who could do thirty-two *fouettés*. When, later, I arrived at the Kirov school, I found that very few could turn there either. The minute I started doing what they said—forcing my turn-out to an extreme I didn't have, holding my chest open in the wrong way—I, too, was unable to turn, even though I had always had a natural facility for pirouettes. They taught preparations with the weight on both legs in *demi-plié,* and there were various other instructions given, such as 'hold your back,' 'hold your arms,' and 'don't tilt your head.' But they didn't teach students *how* to turn. Either you knew naturally or you didn't turn. I noticed that the ones who turned well did not take momentum from a *demi-plié* with weight on both legs. They kept their weight on the leg they were going to *relevé* on. The other leg helped them push up."

When she left the USSR, after seven years, with a magna cum laude diploma in choreography and direction from GITIS, Darvash was determined to return home and develop methods for rectifying many of the problems she had observed in Soviet ballet training. Upon arriving in Romania, she was appointed artistic director and resident choreographer of the State Opera Ballet in Cluj. She remained in that post for fourteen years, choreographing approximately forty ballets and receiving three high awards from the government for her outstanding contributions to the arts.

The ballets ranged from full-length classics such as *Cinderella* and *Swan Lake* to shorter contemporary works. At the same time, she also taught ballet and drama in the Cluj Ballet Academy. Her primary interest, however, was then (and still is) choreography, and it is a painful source of frustration for her that she has not been able to produce more of her own work in America. Nevertheless, she has enjoyed considerable success with productions of *Cinderella, Coppélia,* and *Giselle,* which she staged for her students in the mid-1980s in New York City.

Judith Fugate, a principal dancer with the New York City Ballet and a devoted, longtime Darvash student, danced leading roles in these productions. "She's been integral in shaping the dancer I am today," Fugate told me. "I have been very lucky to have Madame work with me, not only as a teacher, but also as a coach and choreographer. In all my years of dancing," she added, "I have yet to find a better coach. She has an incredible eye and will find nuances and details to bring out an individual's personality and technique. For me, she remains a constant inspiration."

Another Darvash student, Anthony Basile, who now dances in Europe, also commented on Darvash's abilities as a coach: "She has an eye for the stage—how something's going to transfer from the studio to stage. What something looks like in the studio is not necessarily what it's going to look like onstage. When you put something in a proscenium arch, it changes. For instance, something that looks straight up close, may not from the stage. The lines our bodies form must form a harmony with the space we dance in. Also, from a distance, you're more aware of the spaces in between the angle of the leg and torso—for example, the space inside the leg in *passé.* It's not something you're as conscious of up close. Darvash looks at these things in each student and coaches on an individual basis."

Without doubt, Darvash fine-tuned her abilities coaching dancers during her many years directing the ballet company in Cluj. In the 1970s, however, her life changed drastically. When the Romanian government suddenly began to permit Jews to emigrate, she and her husband, neither of whom bore any fondness for the Communist regime, made the courageous decision to leave for the United States. "They processed my exit papers very fast," she says. "As director of the ballet, I had been given a beautiful villa in which to live, presumably so that I could entertain foreign visitors in style. They wanted that villa! When I left, the First Secretary of the Communist Youth Organization moved in!"

Soon after her arrival in 1972, she was hired as the resident choreographer and teacher for New Jersey's Garden State Ballet. She stayed with the company four years, staging well-reviewed productions of the classics, as well as several of her own choreographic works. Then, in 1976, she opened her own studio on the upper West Side in Manhattan. At the time, it was one of the few places in the United States that provided Kirov-style training, although Darvash's methodology departed in some important ways from the Soviet system. The school flourished until 1988 when, like many other victims of the real estate boom in the city, she lost her lease. Today, she is a member of the faculty at the Broadway Dance Centre, where she teaches three classes each day. She will tell you proudly that even with this strenuous schedule, and even though she is in her early sixties, she never sits down while teaching class. She doesn't believe in it. She's proud of her energy, as well as of the fact that she has never become bored or burned out as a teacher. "I'm constantly refreshing my classes with novelties and talk about the future, for which I believe we need to study," she says. "We shouldn't be studying ballet just to preserve a few works from the past."

Darvash's advanced morning class is filled with professionals from ballet and Broadway, a few serious teenagers, and several adults, some of whom are teachers or retired dancers. I noticed one young lady who had rushed in late. She had a fabulous technique and was, Darvash told me, a successful modern-jazz dancer. The girl worked beautifully, but had a rather nonballetic body, lacking well-arched feet. Darvash is extremely proud of the fact that, with her method, which stresses careful, anatomically correct use of the body, she has helped many students with less than ideal physiques overcome their problems and become professional dancers.

"They must be talented, intelligent students and dedicated workers, of course," she says, "because talent is something I can't give. It's something you have to be born with and then develop." (Darvash is fond of a famous saying by Tchaikovsky: "The undeveloped talent is a lost talent for the professional arts.") I asked her how she recognizes talent. "The first thing you have to see in a child is the *desire* to dance," she answered, "that it's in his or her blood. Then the child must have the ability to hear music, to go with it—that you have to be born with!" If all this is evident, she says that with her method she can teach anybody to dance. "He may not look as pretty as someone with an excellent physique for ballet," she states, "but I can teach the coordination to anybody, if he or she is intelligent." She continues: "To be a good dancer, you must be an artist with perfect musicality and expression. Every movement you do has to make sense (and I don't necessarily mean in terms of a story). Some have this gift from nature, but others can be taught, although not to a perfect degree, of course. It's the same in music. Not everyone will be a superstar like Itzhak Perlman, but many will be able to play well in the orchestra."

Darvash has always thought of dance as a skill that demands a system of teaching just like any other profession. Such a system is especially necessary, she notes, if a teacher is dealing with students of varying degrees of physical ability. "Natural talents are great," she remarks, "but they don't appear in the world often enough to fill our theaters with good dancers. There has to be a method." She cites the great ballerina Galina Ulanova[3] as one who was definitely the product of a system. "Do you know," she asks, "that Ulanova did not have a good body at all—big knees, no neck, square shoulders? All through her schooling, she received only 3's (the Russian equivalent of a C). She succeeded because of the thorough and effective Soviet training program. Our profession must be dignified by strong theoretical basics that every teacher must know."

She fears that if the theoretical part of ballet training is not brought to the level of that in other professions (such as music), the future of the art form is threatened. "We are behind the times," she says simply. Darvash is talking about the development and maintenance of training methods that will command respect and admiration for the field of ballet. "I've cleaned up lots of messes," she says, "that were the result of lack of theoretical understanding. For this situation to change, every teacher must know how the body is built; how to develop its mobility, strength, and stability; how that body must move after it has been developed; and, finally, how all of this serves an artistic purpose."

Darvash breaks down her principles on training ballet dancers into a progressive series of chapters: "The first chapter in training dancers must be to teach them that bones don't move, that muscles move the bones. They must know that each of the joints in our body is not equally flexible and mobile. They must know what we can develop and what we can never develop no matter how much we train. (Our elbow, for instance, will never be able to bend in more than one direction; it does not rotate.) After that, we go to the barre to develop mobility in our joints and strength, not just in the leg muscles, but in *all* our muscles—back, stomach, everything that is used when we lift our leg up, or move, or jump. Students must be taught how to align the bones on the supporting side so that they support the weight of the body, so the muscles can relax, easily holding them. One doesn't want to

Gabriela Darvash coaching New York City Ballet principal dancer Judy Fugate.

work in such a way that one destroys the tendons, nor should one try to do things that are anatomically impossible anyway. Then we go to the centre and start moving. (And, incidentally, this is *not* the place to work on developing turn-out! You simply cannot work at the extreme degree of turn-out in the centre that you did holding onto the barre.)

"In the third chapter, we must explain that when we move, we use energy, which has strength and direction. Energy must be directed toward one's purpose. How much you use depends on what you want to do—more for *grand battement,* less for *dégagé,* for instance. When you move, you belong to the world of physics and mechanics just like any other machinery."

Placement is a continual area of concern for Darvash. "It is my fate," she says in mock exhaustion, "to push popos [backsides] up my entire life!" Over and over again, she reminds students that "when you align your bones properly, the muscles will be able to support them in a relaxed way, and your mind will be free to think about other important things like being expressive musically through movement." She explains to them that when their alignment is off, their muscles will grip in an effort to maintain the body on balance and that in such a tightened mode it is "impossible for anyone to be expressive in a natural way. All you will express is that you are struggling!"

Darvash's student Judith Fugate, a New York City Ballet dancer, remarks: "Learning to align the body the way Madame teaches is crucial if one wants to be confident to move at any speed, in any form, that choreography may require. In addition, I have found that since studying with Madame, I have had far fewer injuries—something that is very important to me—to any dancer—in this strenuous profession."

Darvash constantly warns students about the dangers of working incorrectly. She is adamant that her students not tuck their pelvises under. "When you tuck every day," she says, "you are systematically destroying the most sensitive joints in your body—your knees and lower back." When her students stand poised in 5th *relevé,* she tells them: "Just straighten your back knee. If it's bent, you're tucked under. Don't tuck! It's a misalignment of the bones." Students easily grasp Darvash's corrections because they are logical and clear. For instance, to a student straining in a *cambré* back, she warns: "If you put your head back straight in that backbend without turning your head to the side, you constrict your respiratory pipe." Such explanations make perfect sense, and rarely have I seen a student perplexed in her class. She is fond of saying, "1-900-COMMON SENSE.[4] That's me!" Then she'll grin and add: "I advise in other things, too, you know. Not just dancing. Let me suggest, for instance, how to find a husband," she says to a young lady who is looking at her feet while dancing. "Don't stay looking at the floor. Look up and around. See who's out there."

Nancy Raffa, a Darvash protégé who went on to dance with American Ballet Theatre, as well as with companies in South America and France, feels she's especially fortunate to have benefited from Darvash's wisdom outside, as well as inside, the studio. She remembers: "My mother, who was Madame's accompanist, took me to study with her when I was ten-and-a-half years old. Madame took a special interest in me and, because I came from a very poor and difficult family life—my father was ill—became almost like a surrogate mother. Sometimes she took me home after classes. There she'd teach me about dance history and tell me stories about the great Russian dancers in her time, and those from previous times—what special attributes each had brought to the dance world. And she'd tell me stories about what life was like in Europe. I'd be included in parties with all her Hungarian friends. She considered it part of my cultural education. She also took me to performances. She believed in the importance of exposure to all the art forms."

Raffa is grateful not only for the cultural education she received from Darvash, but also for "the huge memory bank of technical information" she has from Darvash's classes. "I can still hear her voice giving me corrections," Raffa says, "and if I really concentrate and think back to all she taught me, I can usually self-correct myself now when I'm having trouble with a movement—which is good because you don't always have a coach with you when you're out there in the professional dance world."

Darvash, by nature a scholar, is fond of categorizing things for her students. "Do you know," she asks them in class, "that we have five ways to shift our weight from one leg over to the other? Like someone patiently reciting a shopping list, she enumerates: "Walking (which is a gradual weight shift), *temps lié* (also a gradual shift), *tombé* (an instant shift that is a fall into *demi-plié,* but can also be done onto a straight leg), *piqué* (an instant shift usually, but not always, executed from *demi-plié* to a straight leg on *demi-pointe*), and, finally, *coupé* (an instant exchange of legs that happens in the same place)." However, at the basis of all such pedagogical dissections is Darvash's strong adherence to the principle that "as humans we have developed reflexes for natural movement—sitting, walking, bending forward—and the closer we can stay while dancing to these natural reflex patterns (which prevent us from falling off balance), the better off we will be. Ideally, we should master the movements of ballet to the extent that they appear as natural as movements we use in daily life. That will make it possible for us to use our bodies as instruments through which we express ourselves. We must always remember that our primary concern as dancers lies not with technique, but rather with what we want to express with our movement."

One day she asked the class, "Do we walk without changing our weight?" She stood penguin-like in 1st position and, with difficulty, attempted to shuffle forward. Everyone giggled. "Nobody does this," she said. "So how can we dance not shifting our weight?!" Darvash expresses frustration with the fact that there are ballet teachers who teach students *not* to shift the weight over the supporting leg when executing *battements tendus.* "Some say, 'Imagine you have a third leg,' or 'This is the way to strengthen your inner thighs'," she sighs, "but the fact is, if you do not shift your weight, you cannot lift your working leg. You can only *tendu* like that. And I believe that *tendus,* while they are certainly exercises for the feet, should also prepare you to dance later on, to move with pointed feet, not just stay in one place!"

She is also adamant about the issue of pushing one's heel forward in line with the toes in *relevé.* "It is absolutely anatomically incorrect," she says. "For that matter, even with perfect natural turn-out, it's physically impossible. Even Semyonova[5] doesn't teach it that way. When the heel lifts from the floor, it's natural for it to go a bit behind the toes. If you insist on trying to push it forward, you will pronate (roll onto your big toe) and your knee will bend." She tells her students that at the barre they may increase turn-out in the hip by pushing the working thigh back and holding the supporting side, but they should never force it from the feet. "You'll get tendonitis or knee problems," she warns them. "And, anyway, why push the heel so far forward if on *relevé* it cannot be?"

Another commonly taught practice with which Darvash strongly disagrees is rotating the lifted (working) leg in 2nd position so that the heel and sole of the foot are presented forward. "When we stand in a perfect 2nd position with our feet on the floor, they are in profile. Our soles face the floor. They are not visible." To continue making her point she asks a student to stand in profile and lift her leg to 90 degrees. "If you try to rotate the leg and push the heel forward in this position," she says, "you will have to tuck the pelvis under to do it, throwing your spine out of alignment. Also notice that the leg has moved in front of your hip, so you are no longer able to get a proper 2nd position with the leg directly to the side of you."

I was also interested in the technically effective method Darvash asks her students to use in order to maintain stability when getting up and down in *relevés*. "When you *relevé*," she tells them, "you lift your heel toward your toe, but in reverse, don't think about lowering and taking your weight back toward the heel, away from the toe. If you do, you'll fall. Instead, keep your weight over the toe as you lower the heel. It's an image," she says.

To make students even more conscious of correct placement, Darvash asks them to visualize themselves from above. "If you're going to be a dancer," she tells them, "you need to be able not only to judge your movement in the mirror, but also you need the imagination to perceive how this movement looks from behind yourself, as well as," she pauses, pointing skyward, "from above your head." The ability to do this is important, she feels, to achieve the correct positioning of the limbs in relationship to the torso. It is also essential for maintaining a vertical axis during turns.

Teaching students to turn well is one of Darvash's primary interests and major strengths. In class, she often compares turning to driving. "If you're going to drive," she says, "you prepare the best conditions to start your car. It's the same in pirouettes. You prepare for success first by not having any weight on the leg that must start the turn—the leg you will lift from the ground." She has found her analogy to driving very effective because she says "everybody knows how to drive a car." She tells her students: "Whether I'm going to go fast or slow, I still have to push the gas. For a slow speed, I push less—for faster, I push more, but I have to learn how to push it, as well as how and when to push the brake." She cautions them about using too much momentum before they are ready to control it. "You never learn to drive a car at 90 miles an hour," she reminds them. "Work on slow pirouettes first." When, in class one day, a student did seven pirouettes and fell off trying to finish, she looked at him incredulously and remarked, "When you take that much momentum and fall, it's as if you pushed the gas and drove into a wall because you did not know how to step on the brake." She constantly reminds students: "Like I always say, we function in dancing like any other machine. That's why we should use the body with knowledge, so that we don't destroy its parts. They're hard to replace."

In addition to dealing with the control of momentum, Darvash also addresses several other specific areas with regard to turns: the coordination of the arms and hips, the manner of *relevé,* and the impetus provided by the leading, or lifted, leg. All her axioms are broken down and practiced in a variety of combinations both at the barre and in centre. "I give exercises," she says, "that teach the coordination of all factors that make a turn successful." When analyzing how the arms work in pirouettes, she again returns to comparisons with a car. "I tell my students (although it may sound crazy) that in turns their arms have the same function as the ignition key. You know," she says, "if you push the gas, but the ignition key has not been turned on, the car won't move. The leading arm (that which is on the side to which I am turning) must go a split second before the *relevé* turn. I even compare it to going through a doorway. First you have to open the door."

For the purposes of turning, Darvash identifies one side of the body as the leading side and the other as the pushing side. "If you turn to the right," she explains, "your right side is the leading side." To illustrate this thesis in a beginner class, she asks the students to face her. "Now, walk to the right," she commands. All turn and step onto their right legs. "You see," she says, "it's natural. Turn to the right—lead with the right." Quickly, however, she reminds them: "It's the hips that do a turn, not only the legs." She continues: "Every turn is based on both sides of the body beginning to move simultaneously (i.e., the pushing hip must move at the same time the body begins to assume the pose for the turn)." To illustrate this fact, she says, "I sometimes give simple turns in my centre *tendu* combination from an unusual preparatory position from which it will be impossible to turn unless both sides of the body move together." She cites an example of a pirouette *en dehors* begun from *pointe tendue croisée devant* in *demi-plié*. "It will only be possible to execute a balanced half, or at the most single, turn from this position," she states, "and you will not be able to do it at all unless you ideally coordinate all the factors that later will make it possible to do multiple turns from a more comfortable position—4th, for instance. That's why I give such exercises." Repeatedly, she stresses that when a turn begins, the standing side of the body (hip and upper torso) must be held in one line and move in one piece without any twisting whatsoever.[6]

Darvash breaks turns into two categories. "Is this a 'prepared' or an 'unprepared' turn?" she asks a student. She explains that in a prepared turn (such as one from 2nd, 4th, or 5th position), the weight of the body in the preparation is entirely placed on top of the leg on which you will turn. In an unprepared turn (such as a *piqué* turn), the weight is transferred from the leg on which you are poised in *plié* onto the one on which you will turn. "This is much more difficult to do," she says, "but most important in unprepared turns is to realize that the knee of the leg you lift to *passé* [*retiré*] must lead the turn because it is the point farthest away from the axis of the body." This is why, she says, *piqué* turns *en dedans* in *attitude derrière* or *arabesque* are among the most difficult turns to master because the position of the leg in back of the body makes it impossible for the lifted leg to lead the turn. "It puts a drag on your turn," she says, "and it is very difficult to get on top of your supporting leg because the lifted leg really pulls against the directional force of the turn, especially in arabesque, where the foot is so far from the axis of the body." Mastering such turns, she admits, takes much patience. One day in class, acknowledging her students' frustration with an *en dedans piqué arabesque* turn in the adagio, she said in a positive and encouraging way, "We'll practice that turn another day. It deserves more attention." As one of her students told me: "She won't get mad at you if your pirouettes don't always work, only if you don't know *why* you fell!"

I asked Darvash about this. "Many factors go into making a turn work," she told me. "It's like cooking. You can prepare all the ingredients beautifully, make the appetizer, and then forget to turn the oven off and burn it. This can happen with turns, too!" However, she feels that with practice and conscientious application of the logical rules she teaches in class, anyone can learn to do good pirouettes. She has no patience with students who leave their pirouettes to fate. "This is the only profession I know," she says, "where dancers turn green in preparations as if they are praying that it will work. I don't want to teach dancers who don't know why they fall, then try again and *still* don't know!"

Timing, of course, is central to executing good pirouettes. Often in class she will hike up her skirt to make her legs clearly visible as she demonstrates. An excellent turner, she is living proof that her theories work. "Every turn produces centrifugal force, so you must squeeze the legs close to your axis *fast* to counteract the force which will push them away from each other." She gets a laugh when she demonstrates how badly one can be thrown off one's balance if one hesitates to do this, leaving the working leg momentarily floating out in space, as a turn begins.

Darvash often incorporates turns into the barre work. One day when several students fell into the barre at the end of a pirouette, she stopped the class and said: "Some of us turned very well, but some collided with the barre at the end. I'd like to remind you that this is *partnering* I'm teaching here. Your hand must *glide* onto the barre, not grab it."

In turns, as in every other aspect of classical technique, Darvash returns time and again to her central principle: the necessity, while dancing, to stay as close as possible "to what we do naturally." When she catches a student spotting the mirror instead of the corner in a series of *chaînés déboulés,* she stops the class and comments: "Why is *jeté* forward easier than *jeté* backward? Because everything we do in life is done going forward. Why should *chaînés* always be done spotting the direction to which you're going? Because it's easier to go forward if you look in the direction you're going. Try walking forward and looking backward. I can't understand why anyone teaches to spot in the mirror while turning diagonally downstage!"

Darvash applies the same commonsense principles to the way she teaches her students to jump. To illustrate the importance of weight placement in relationship to jumping, she holds a student's arm out at 90 degrees to the floor and then punches it up from below. "If you want to go up," she tells them, "you must *push* from underneath, so be sure your body is over top of the leg you're pushing from and not leaning back!" She also notes how essential it is to execute correctly the preparatory movement into a jump. When a student awkwardly performs a *glissade en avant* before a *grand jeté,* Darvash exclaims, "You walk like a tango there—all twisted up! You can't take off into a jump like that. Your hips must face the direction of the step." The use of the arms, she reminds them, is also crucial. Demonstrating a lift in her arm, chest, and eyes, she tells students that "my arms *act* to create an illusion of going up. You can't jump if you push your arms down!"

Although Darvash is a product of Soviet ballet training, which favors a slower jump than either the French or American schools, her allegro combinations are usually very brisk. She explains her preference: "Generally I feel the lighter the jump and the less I see the person on the floor, the more I see them in the air and the more exciting it is. I do not allow students to sit in *plié.* The longer they are on the floor, the more strenuous their jumping looks, and I don't want to see people struggling to get up. The ideal jump for me would be what a ball does when it bounces. Does it stay on the floor?!"

Double *tours en l'air* are a tricky, virtuoso jump required of all male dancers. Darvash reminds her young men that "double *tour* must be done in the hips—not just changing the legs." She is the only teacher I have ever heard address what must happen in the torso to absorb the shock of landing from a double *tour.* "When you finished that *tour,*" she told one student, "you did it like a car slamming on the brakes. Remember, in the air you have no contact with the ground. If, when you descend, you want to cushion the impact, you must continue to spiral the body into the direction of the *tour* just a little bit as you land."

Every Darvash class ends with a joyful leaping combination. She often introduces it as if she were serving dessert, announcing with a smile: "This is just a pleasant flying exercise." Getting students to move during jump combinations is a constant challenge for her. She elicits laughs in class when she resorts to one of her favorite sayings: "My dream is to invent a little engine to put in the popo to get dancers to move—then I could retire rich!" Her former student Anthony Basile remarks, however, that Darvash is concerned with much more than simply encouraging students to sweep across the floor. "She starts first of all," he says, "with the idea that what she's teaching and what we're doing is dance and that it's something human—rhythm and movement—that comes, perhaps, even before we speak. Others don't see dance or movement first. They see the feet or the legs. Dancers, of course, can really get into that. It's O.K. for our world, but it doesn't make a connection to society. The public doesn't want to know what it takes to make good feet or extension. They come to watch a performance, and they can get bored if what they're seeing is only a lot of legs and feet, but not the human part of it. Darvash works on developing that part, as well. I really must thank her for giving me this particular vision about dance."

Darvash constantly reminds students that while she wants them to be serious and concentrated in class, they must also remember that they are preparing to be performing artists. "You can't think," she lectures them, "that the quality you will need onstage will just happen. In fact, your face muscles will work the same there as they do in class. And you are mistaken if you think you can learn how to use your face in a few separate coaching sessions. This is not something you learn separately any more than we give separate classes for arms and head. Would you take a separate class with me just to learn how to walk onstage?" One day, as a group of students came across the floor with long faces doing a bouncy jump *enchaînement,* Darvash remarked: "It's sunny outside today, girls. Don't go to church. Go to the park." Their faces immediately lit up.

Of course, Darvash is concerned about developing expressivity in the entire body. "When we dance," she says, "our body is the instrument through which we express ourselves on the stage. A dancer is a performer. He trains for a lifetime to get onstage and perform because he wants to be seen, and wants to want to be seen again. He hopes to create that contact between himself and the viewer—that magic." One day, when her students awkwardly staggered, stiff-legged, through a simple *pas de bourrée* under,

Darvash stopped the class and said, "I must remind you that this is all to achieve an artistic goal. So what, if you manage not to fall doing a movement? What does it matter? If you do the movement badly, it means nothing. Everything you do must serve your art. You can do two pirouettes and be expressive—and you can do twenty and be boring as a day of fast." Then after chastising them, she turned, characteristically, to using humor to finish her point. "*Pas de bourrées* are so easy, children," she said. "Why do them with a face that is tortured? Look at your audience. In the old days we used to use *pas de bourrée* to ask to get married [i.e., to flirt with the audience]. If you're charming, you can even use a *pas de bourrée* to ask forgiveness from the audience after you fall off that arabesque!"

Darvash is noted, as a *New York Times* review of one of her productions stated, "for instilling in all her pupils an extraordinary stage presence."[7] She tells her students that they must be interesting when they dance, and she applies the same standard to her teaching: "I'm talking to you now, but if you do not listen to what I have to say, it's my fault because I have not been able to capture your attention. It's the same with dancing. Just because you do two beautiful pirouettes doesn't mean you have the quality to capture an audience."

I was interested to hear her discuss the need for dancers to differentiate between the way they use classical positions in dramatic ballets and the way they use them in technical *divertissements*. One day in class she used the pose 2nd arabesque to demonstrate her point. Normally in this position the head turns and looks downstage at the audience over the shoulder of the front arm. "If you were dancing Juliet, though," she said, "and you wanted to indicate where Romeo had just run offstage, it would be perfectly logical to turn your head to look over the hand stretched forward in that direction. This head placement, appropriate and desirable for such a dramatic moment, has nothing to do with the classical positions that we study in class." She continued: "In *divertissements*, though, we do use the proper classical poses. And although we are simply showing off our technique, we must still have an inner monologue which says, 'Look how skillful I am. I'm enjoying showing off my technique, and I hope you are enjoying watching.' So, darlings, you cannot do a variation with a terrified expression on your face because I will worry—the audience will worry!"

Darvash prides herself on cultivating individuality in performers. Former student Nancy Raffa remembers Darvash urging students "Never to forget the Transylvanian touch, which for her was the little things in her teaching method about technique, the movement of your arms, special qualities that make your dancing clean and sparkling. When I won the Prix de Lausanne," Raffa recalls, smiling, "she said, 'That's because of the Transylvanian touch!' She told us never to forget the fact that there was no one else like each one of us. She wanted us to have confidence in ourselves and to know that each of us had certain things to give to the dance world that no one else had. She'd always tell us we must always be ourselves onstage, that what was special inside each individual was what would make each of us sparkle. And if we had been born with special gifts as dancers, then we must always offer them to our audiences."

Another important aspect of artistry Darvash stresses is musicality. She, herself, is marvelously musical and uses a wide range of musical forms in class, including, among others, tangos, mazurkas, tarantellas, and Spanish waltzes. Sometimes, her musical construction is unusual and challenging. "I have to make this a little different," she explains to the students, "because we will not dance our whole life on symmetrical eight-bar melodies." She rarely counts and never claps in time to the music. Instead, she occasionally slaps her thigh. Often, she asks the class to identify a piece of music the pianist has played. When one day a student pipes up with the right answer, she is delightfully surprised. "Yes! Faust—it's ballet music!" In one class, exasperated at the unmusicality of the dancers, she threw up her hands, turned to the pianist, and said sarcastically, "I'll buy a drum, Olga, and you can go shopping." In a moment, though, she regained her patience and explained what she wanted. "An adagio is a musical concept," she stated, beginning to sing a bit of Saint-Saën's *The Dying Swan*. Then she sang the same melody *pizzicato* and asked, "Is this an adagio?" She asked the students to avoid clipped, jerky movements and urged them to mirror the sustained quality of the music, linking all the steps smoothly.

Darvash also uses music as a tool. When, during an adagio exercise, she asked the students to hold the end of their *développés*—a physically difficult thing for all dancers to do—she turned to the pianist and said, "Olga, play a bit longer there. It's always easier to struggle with a nice melody." However, when students are overindulgent and hold poses too long, she's quick to remind them that "there's a limit to fermatas—which we have all over the place in ballet—it can only go as long as the violin can draw the bow. Music is not a rubber band that you can stretch forever."

I enjoyed watching how Darvash—who often refers to herself as the class "policewoman"—made students aware of each other and of the space

Gabriela
Darvash dem-
onstrating a
grand allegro
combination
in class.

around them in class. (Professional dancers must constantly negotiate obstacles—scenery, props, other dancers—onstage. In addition, they frequently dance on different stages, each with different proportions. Thus,
spatial awareness and the ability to make split-second adjustments in their
movement trajectories are important parts of their training.) One day,
when two students crashed into each other moving across the floor during
a big jumping combination, Darvash got a laugh when she remarked wryly,
"If you don't understand in *grand allegro* how to stay in your own track,
then we'll have swans in *Swan Lake* that will end up in blood lake!" She is
probably the only teacher in the world who views having poles (columns
that support the ceiling and, in so doing, disrupt the floor space in many of
the big dance studios in New York City) in a positive light. "This pole is the
best invention," she says patting one in the centre of her studio. "It teaches
you to adapt to your surroundings. What if a dancer falls in front of you

onstage? Do you just step on her?" She finishes her dissertation on courtesy in the classroom with one of her favorite analogies: "I can't say enough that this is not a subway station here, where you just push no matter what!"

In fact, the carefully structured progression of a Darvash class is as unlike the chaos of a subway station as it could be. She begins each class with a slow, relaxed combination at the barre that lasts approximately twelve minutes. It consists of *tendus, pliés,* body bends, gentle stretches, and what she terms "unclassical moves" that she feels are necessary to warm up the body. These include various standing stretches for the feet and Achilles tendons that were recommended to her by a relative who coaches a basketball team. "It really doesn't matter what we initially do for warm-up," she says, "as long as we warm up the tendons, ligaments, and muscles." Occasionally, on cold mornings, she begins class by having the students jog lightly around the room. "Would it surprise you, " she asks them, "if I said that if we start with *tendus* our feet will get warm, but not the rest of our body?" She points out that the movements of classical ballet technique are not something that the human body was born for. "I'm in no rush in the morning," she says. "We better warm up well enough to be ready to do all those technical things with our bodies." The first three exercises of a Darvash barre are slow and even. They allow plenty of time for careful placement, stretching, and breathing.

Her long first combination includes *grands pliés,* but never in 4th position. These Darvash omits because she is convinced that it is impossible to do them safely. She feels doctors would agree with her "because if you have the weight placed equally on both feet in 4th, the back knee will turn in as you descend. It is impossible to keep it turned out in line with the foot, and, if you try to open the back knee to turn out the thigh, you will throw the weight onto the back foot." Omitting *grands pliés* in 4th position is one of several departures she has made over the years from the Soviet system. She justifies her decision not only for anatomical safety, but also because choreography very rarely calls for a *grand plié* in 4th position. "If a dancer has to do one," she notes wryly, "it's like having alcohol once in a while, which is very different from being an alcoholic."

After the *pliés,* Darvash gives a slow *tendu* combination, always in 3/4 time because, she says, the third beat gives students a bit more time to really point their working foot. She asks students to do these *tendus* easily, without too much force. She even goes so far as to tell them that the working foot need not be stretched at top energy in this exercise. She feels that the foot needs time to become fully active, that it must ease into the speed demanded in later exercises. "These are not dramatic *tendus*," she tells them.

This exercise is followed by another slow *tendu* that includes *demi-ronds* and slow *relevés* in 1st position—the position she always uses to begin work on *demi-pointe*. After that, she gives a fast *tendu* combination in 2/4 time, which is sometimes (to save time) an accelerated version of her previous *tendu*. She frequently alternates the way her *tendus* are accented; sometimes the accent is out, sometimes in.

At this point, twenty minutes into the barre work, Darvash makes a major deviation from the traditional order of the barre. Instead of *dégagés* (*tendus jetés*) following fast *tendus,* she gives *ronds de jambe par terre* because she feels that the students' bodies need the relief provided by a slower exercise. She comments: "It's like alternating running and walking. It's natural. It gives the body a chance to rest." The *rond de jambe* exercise includes various *cambrés* and slow lifts of the leg to 45 degrees. I was interested to see that in a deep lunge executed with a *cambré* front, Darvash instructed the students not to turn out their extended back legs (i.e., to keep them parallel) as they slid into the lunge until they reached the bottom of the position. She explained that doing the slide with the back leg turned out would put unhealthy pressure on the inside of the knee and the ankle. Even more important, she stated, is the fact that executing the lunge with the leg parallel stretches the area in the front of the hip—the place, she points out, where a human being needs to stretch most. "This is where you are tightest," she says. "Try a backbend and you'll feel the pull in front of your hip. Then, for contrast, bend forward. You can go more than 90 degrees forward before you have to curve your spine. This is where we are loosest—in the back of the pelvic joint."

Never does Darvash's *rond de jambe par terre* combination include the thrown *grand battement jeté en rond* that is almost always a part of this exercise in the Russian system. Darvash is absolutely convinced that including such a strenuous, violent movement so early in the barre work is potentially harmful for the body. When she does use this movement at the barre, she includes it in the final *grand battement* exercise.

After the *rond de jambe,* she does a fast *tendu jeté (dégagé)* combination that often includes *passés (retirés)* to warm up the dancers' hip joints. "I never have students lift their legs to 90 degrees before I've had them lift them bent," she says. "It's easier bent than straight—not so hard on the pelvic joint."

I was interested to hear Darvash instruct students to use 3rd, instead of 5th, position when doing a fast series of *tendus jetés (dégagés)*. "You have no time to put the foot in 5th each time it comes in," she said. "If you try to do so, you will compromise the speed and precision of the working leg, including the ability to form a perfectly pointed toe. Also, if you close 5th, you're already sitting in your supporting hip (this is the only way anyone, even someone with perfect turn-out, can get into 5th; it's how the bones are). You don't want to do this. You want to be able to move fast and never lose your placement on the supporting leg." She also notes that most dancers must bend their front knee slightly in 5th position and "we don't want that in fast *dégagés à la seconde* because here we are practicing the sideways leg action for beats. And we don't bend our knees in beats, do we?"

Darvash admits that her use of 3rd position is unusual, and I have never seen it used in any other advanced ballet class. Most teachers use it only in character class, or with children in the very beginning of their training as preparation for 5th position. "But," as Darvash says, finding further justification for her action, "we have five positions in classical ballet. What for, if not to use all of them?"

The fast *tendus jetés (dégagés)* are followed by *fondus*, usually in combination with *ronds de jambe en l'air* and balances in *retiré*, and in advanced classes, *fouettés* at 45 degrees. This exercise is followed by brisk *frappés*, usually to a fast gallop, which may include pirouettes. "Don't jam your knees," Darvash instructs the class. "*Frappé* is completed at the end of the toes. And, please, direct your energy up with each leg opening, not down into the floor." Throughout Darvash's barre, which becomes progressively complex (both musically and choreographically), there is much use of *relevé* work and various turns. Frequent opportunities to transfer the weight away from and back to the barre are provided. One cannot sleep through such a barre. Every exercise is designed to prepare students for moving, for centre work. As she tells them: "You are not developing your bodies so that you can stand in one place!"

In recent years, Darvash has begun to include stretches in her barre after the *frappé* exercise and before the adagio. She often begins them with the inside leg placed on the barre in *écarté derrière*, in which position the students bend in all directions—side, back, and forward. She says in a "closed" academy situation she would never include stretches at the barre, but that in "open" classes in New York City everyone wants to do them, and, of course, she is able to supervise that they are done correctly. She feels it would be preferable for students to stretch after class, noting that class time is valuable and best spent on other areas of technique in which one needs the eye of the teacher more.

Darvash finishes her barre with an adagio, followed by a *grand battement* exercise. She begins her centre work with an elaborate *tendu* combination. "I put pirouettes, difficult rotating movements (such as *fouettés en tournant à terre*), and other complicated transitions into my advanced *tendu* combination. After all, *tendu* is basically a warm-up exercise. Why do just that? I use this first centre exercise to accomplish various other things. I can even prepare them for double *tours*. However, all these complex coordinations are done in this exercise without momentum, but just making sure that the hips and upper body move simultaneously, as they must in all turns."

It was these elaborate *tendu* exercises with their complex turning coordinations that most fascinated Russian teachers when Darvash returned to Moscow in 1989 and was invited to give a seminar at her old university, GITIS. "With this exercise," she says a bit smugly, "I proved to them what I had felt for years—namely, that they did not know how (nor were they teaching their students how) to stay on top of their supporting legs." They were receptive to her ideas, she said, because "I was one of them. I had graduated from that place with a diploma of excellence." She feels there is a big contradiction between what the Russians say to do at the barre regarding placement and the reality of how one's body works when it is in the centre. "I gave them a class," she says, "and they were so surprised when they fell over in one of my centre *tendu* combinations. They were amazed at how easily I did it!"

After this initial *tendu* combination, Darvash does a *fondu* exercise with pirouettes. Sometimes, she adds elements of adagio in this exercise and then skips doing a full centre adagio. Normally, before jumping, she gives a *grand battement* exercise, although time constraints sometimes limit her ability to do so. She says it's the only exercise she feels guilty about leaving out. One solution she occasionally uses is to incorporate *grands battements* into the first centre exercise. "Of course," she explains, "if I'm not able to do a separate *grand battement* exercise, big jumps always use them."

If Darvash is concerned about what she has to leave out in order to complete her class in an hour and a half, she should not be. She covers an enormous range of material in every class, primarily because of her expertise at combining several elements into a single combination. For instance, every exercise in the centre, including the jumps, has some form of turn in it. It may be as simple as a half *soutenu* turn or a *changement en tournant,* or as complex as a *grande pirouette* finished with a *fouetté.* And she never skimps on the allegro portion of her class. The students usually jump for a half-hour. One day, when they finished a *petit allegro* gasping, Darvash remarked, defending the stamina demands made by the exercise, "I give classes so that if you should get a job, you won't choke at the first rehearsal!"

I was intrigued to see that after her first small jumping combination Darvash did not progress, as many teachers do, into a bigger jump exercise. Instead, once again in a major departure from the pattern in Soviet methodology, she places the main turning exercise of her class here. She feels that "if I give this pirouette exercise after the adagio, it's monstrous [i.e., strenuous]." She continues: "After the adagio, I give an upbeat allegro exercise to get the students' attention again. It's like when you hear a slow song and then, all of a sudden, there's a change in tempo. It attracts your attention and you become differently involved. So, with this first jump here, I wake them up and make sure they feel a bit of electricity—a new current in their bodies."

By the same token, having the pirouette exercise follow the small jumping gives her students the opportunity to regain their stamina. Once again Darvash is thinking—as she did at the barre—about the fact that alternating a strenuous activity with a less strenuous one is healthy and natural for the body. (It is interesting to note that this is exactly the conclusion that trainers for marathon runners have embraced in the last few years with their support of cross training.) Her pirouette combinations are lovely and difficult. She notes how much more important turning has become to the technique of classical ballet in recent years and feels that such an exercise is an essential part of her class. She says that she tries within any given week of classes to cover almost all forms of turns in the classical vocabulary. "Everything they might need," she says cheerfully. "And if they remember my recipes, they'll be prepared for any choreography." She uses a variety of preparations for getting into the turns and insists that the dancers move into them well so that they do not become accustomed simply to planting themselves in a still pose before a pirouette. She tells students: "The preparation must be just another step in the flow of the combination."

Darvash admits that in order to teach, she must be as much a psychologist as a theoretician. Fortunately, she is a gifted stand-up comedian and, as a result, there is frequent laughter in her classes. Her vibrant commentary alternates between gentle scolding, comic imagery, and a variety of commonsense bons mots. "May I remind you of that old Hungarian motto 'God doesn't punish with a cane'," she says slyly, shaking her finger at a student who has fallen off a pirouette because he did not listen to what she had told him. One day when the class failed to absorb her correction, she reminded them that "in the old days, before blenders, mothers had to chew the food before giving it to their babies. Well, I have chewed for you. Now, all you have to do is swallow!"

As quick as she may be to criticize, Darvash will also compliment students when they do something well. "That was excellent, by the way," she said to the class one day after a turn combination. And she is not without sensitivity to a student's need for a bit of encouragement. After one young man, a former gymnast now struggling with learning ballet, had tried repeatedly without much success to master a *grand allegro* combination, Darvash commanded him: "Please do three of your back flips for me, so I know that through the study of classical ballet you have not forgotten how to do them." Eagerly, the student propelled his body across the studio floor in this virtuoso gymnastic feat and received enthusiastic applause from the other students. His tension was relieved, his ego momentarily stroked, and Darvash remarked, "Great—at least I didn't spoil that which you were trained for!"

When Darvash demonstrates an exercise, she often prefers that students watch her by looking at her reflection in the mirror. This is particularly true when she is making a correction. If, for instance, she is explaining something about the position of the back, she will stand with her back to the mirror and ask students to view her in the mirror. "If students are standing around me and watching from different angles, they may miss my point," she says. "The position of my body in relation to theirs when I give a correction is very important."

Also important to Darvash is the location in the studio from which *she* views the students. During centre work in class, she often stands against the barre in the back of the studio, a vantage point that permits her, using the mirror, to observe the dancers from the front as well as from behind. In addition, she explains, from the back of the studio "it's easier for me to see all the students, not just the one opposite me." As she stands there peering intently at them from over the rims of her large eyeglasses, her body remains still in a relaxed pose with one hand on the barre, the other on her hip. "Hallelujah!" she yells when they do a combination correctly. "Now, turn your head to the audience. They pay for the ticket!"

Generally, the complexity of her classes keeps the dancers mentally alert. However, like all students, they occasionally daydream. Darvash has fun with the situation, embarrassing them into paying attention again. She asks a boy whom she has caught staring out the window, "Tell me. What's new down there on Broadway?" And when several dancers, waiting for their turn to dance, settle blank-faced in a line leaning against the barre at the back of the room, Darvash remarks: "There you stay, like birds on the wire, and if one of you moves, you'll all move!" Former student Anthony Basile told me, "It's one of the cardinal sins in her book to let your mind wander in class. She insists that you're in it, awake, living every moment. I was never good in school because I was hyperactive and scatterbrained. No one taught me how to study—until Darvash. She taught me how to concentrate and direct my energies. For that, I'm very grateful."

Although Darvash occasionally becomes frustrated and angry in class, her students seem to enjoy the fact that she is "constantly on our case." Her ironic remarks can sting a little, but they usually elicit smiles as well. When the dancers sucked their lips in concentration during a tricky allegro one day, she remarked: "Mm-mm—what a tasty combination. You all dance like Campbell's Soup ads!"[8] As Anthony Basile says: "You can trust her. She's not afraid to say, 'No good.' If she says it's good, it is. If not, it isn't."

Only occasionally does Darvash completely lose her temper, and students learn to weather the storms. One dancer obviously felt very bad one day after Darvash in a fury threatened to quit teaching. The young lady arrived for class the next day bearing a bouquet of daisies. "We love you," she said, presenting the flowers to Darvash. "You can't quit now. I'm just starting to get things."

In an effort to check their retention from class to class, Darvash constantly interrogates her students: "What do we call this pose?" or "What do I always say about this step?" At the end of each lesson, she gathers them around her for a mini-lecture, a five-minute discussion of, perhaps, a particular technical point, during which she asks questions and repeats her rules. She hopes she is cultivating thinking dancers. She is patient with students who come to her studio with a different way of doing something (a pirouette preparation, for instance). "Yes," she says, "you could do it that way if it's the choreography. It's another possibility, but today we'll do it this way." In fact, she wants her students to learn as many ways to do movements as are possible. That way, she knows they'll be even better prepared for professional careers. As she says: "My whole teaching method has one main purpose: to help students master technique easily and securely in order to become great performers."

Darvash remembers students by their eyes and says dancers are always surprised when they return after a long absence and she remembers them. Of course, many students with whom she has had long associations, especially those who are now professional dancers, always return with great anticipation whenever they are in New York. Almost every day at least one such former student arrives bearing flowers for Madame. The mutual affection is clearly evident, and Darvash cannot resist having a little fun with these students. "How is it that you two got so fat?" she one day teased a pair of dancers just returned from a stint with a regional company. "You get a job with a salary, go to the suburbs, and start cooking. Well, at least this week I know that you will starve in New York."

In spite of her propensity for humor in the classroom, Darvash is profoundly serious about her responsibilities as a teacher. "Teaching should not be a dogma," she says. "It should adjust to necessities. We live in a society that constantly changes. I still learn every day myself! I try to find out what the companies that function today need." Indeed, she can often be seen, fashionably dressed, in the audience at New York dance events—not only at ballet performances, but at other types of dance programs, as well. Justifying her taste for all styles of dance, she remarks: "There are only two kinds of dance—good and bad." She tries to challenge her students in class with movements that may be required of them when they are someday seeking roles in contemporary companies. "I am not interested," she states emphatically, "in a profession that's being practiced only to reproduce our five or ten inherited classical ballets—those works in which the corps de ballet actually doesn't need to do one pirouette." She continues: "I am interested only in a form of art that develops just like human society develops. I don't want to teach an art form that is obsolete. I'm interested in teaching dancers to be better than they were 150 years ago."

Classroom Quotes from Darvash

"Anyone studying classical ballet must know that this is the most sophisticated way of movement. Why? Because it is the least natural, yet is good only when it looks natural."

"Classical means pure. Everyone knows what a classic suit is, for instance—simple—no frills."

"The art of coordinated dancing is to move only the parts of your body you need to and isolate the others—keep them still."

"When a student does not look at himself in the mirror, he deprives himself of the possibility to go forward by 80 percent. If you can't see, you can't dance. Because it's a *visual* art."

"If I show it once more, I'll warm up and you won't."

An old Romanian peasant saying Darvash often uses: "The slower you go, the farther you get."

"If you don't remember your lines, you won't become an actor—If you don't remember combinations, you won't become a dancer."

"The eyes are the windows of the soul."

Order of the Exercises in Darvash's Class (advanced class, 1½ hours)

BARRE

1. Warm-up tendus, cambrés, demi-pliés, and grands pliés
2. Slow battements tendus
3. Battements tendus with rises on two legs
4. Fast battements tendus
5. Ronds de jambe à terre
6. Battements tendus jetés (dégagés)
7. Battements fondus and ronds de jambe en l'air
8. Battements frappés
9. Stretches, adagio
10. Grands battements

CENTRE

1. Battements tendus with various turning movements
2. Adagio
3. Simple small jumps
4. Petit allegro with batterie
5. Medium jumps
6. Pirouette combination with elements of fondus
7. Grand allegro
8. Stationary jump (usually containing entrechat quatres or sixes)
9. Port de bras and révérence

The Roots of Tradition

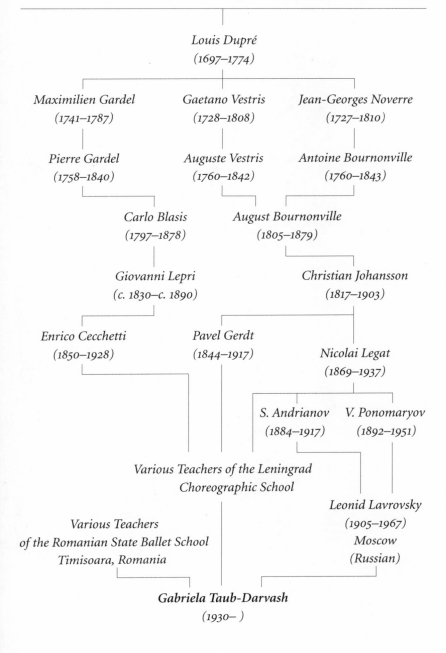

L'Académie Royale de Musique et de Danse (1661)

Louis Dupré
(1697–1774)

Maximilien Gardel
(1741–1787)

Gaetano Vestris
(1728–1808)

Jean-Georges Noverre
(1727–1810)

Pierre Gardel
(1758–1840)

Auguste Vestris
(1760–1842)

Antoine Bournonville
(1760–1843)

Carlo Blasis
(1797–1878)

August Bournonville
(1805–1879)

Giovanni Lepri
(c. 1830–c. 1890)

Christian Johansson
(1817–1903)

Enrico Cecchetti
(1850–1928)

Pavel Gerdt
(1844–1917)

Nicolai Legat
(1869–1937)

S. Andrianov
(1884–1917)

V. Ponomaryov
(1892–1951)

Various Teachers of the Leningrad
Choreographic School

Leonid Lavrovsky
(1905–1967)
Moscow
(Russian)

Various Teachers
of the Romanian State Ballet School
Timisoara, Romania

Gabriela Taub-Darvash
(1930–)

5 David Howard

David Howard working with American Ballet Theatre principal dancer Cynthia Harvey at his school in New York City in 1991.

*D*avid Howard, whose school is based in New York City, is one of America's most renowned teachers. Howard, a native of England, received his dance training at the Arts Educational School in London, where, in 1954, at the age of sixteen, he won the coveted Adeline Genée Silver Medal. From 1955 to 1957, he appeared at the famous London Palladium in a number of variety shows. Later, he joined the Royal Ballet's second company, where he was a soloist for seven years. In 1963, he spent a season dancing with the National Ballet of Canada, then returned to Europe to perform in a number of productions, including cabaret with the famous Bluebell Girls in Paris and Monte Carlo and, in London, two musicals: Bob Fosse's *Little Me* and Lionel Bart's *Twang*. He also appeared on television and radio and in films.

Howard began teaching in the Arts Educational School in London in 1965, but moved to New York in 1966, taking advantage of an offer by Rebekah Harkness to work as an apprentice teacher with the newly formed Harkness Ballet School. He stayed with Harkness eleven years, teaching for both the school and the company, and eventually becoming the school's co-director (1970–74) and then director (1974–77). During this time Howard established his reputation as one of the most sought after coaches in New York. Among those dancers with whom he has maintained long-term working relationships are Gelsey Kirkland, Mikhail Baryshnikov, Natalia Makarova, Darci Kistler, Patrick Swayze, Wes Chapman, and Cynthia Harvey.

In 1977 he opened his own school in Manhattan, followed in 1986 by a move to the much larger David Howard Dance Center near Lincoln Center, where he was still teach-

"The end of one movement must become the beginning of the next."

ing in 1995 when he was interviewed for this book. Always in demand internationally, Howard has guest-taught for the Royal Ballet, the San Francisco Ballet, the National Ballet of Canada, the Béjart company, the Joffrey Ballet, the Metropolitan Opera, the Juilliard School, and American Ballet Theatre, among others. He has coached several dancers for international ballet competitions, most notably Katherine Healy for her victories at Jackson and Varna and Jennifer Gelfand and Edward Stierle for their Gold Medal performances at Jackson in 1986. Howard is the honorary president of the Schweizersche Ballettberufsshule, Zurich, where he has guest-taught since 1984. In the United States, he has filmed several videocassettes on ballet technique and one on exercise titled "Shape Up," co-produced with his assistant, Peter Schabel. He has notably elevated the level of musical recordings for ballet classes with tapes produced in collaboration with two fine pianists, Lynn Stanford and Douglas Corbin. Howard, whose teacher training seminars are well known, served as president of the National Regional Ballet Association for three years, and, in 1983, was honored by the Dance Masters of America Award "for his outstanding contribution to American dance."

DAVID HOWARD's wizardry in the classroom is something dancers feel in their bones. For years they've flocked to him in large numbers, and today he is perhaps the best known, most popular ballet teacher working in America. Both great professionals and dedicated amateurs attend his classes; they work together, side by side, in the invigorating atmosphere Howard creates from the moment he steps into the studio.

Watching Howard's classes, I immediately understood the appeal of his fine, dry, British wit and his dynamic, well-constructed exercises. But it took longer to comprehend the philosophy behind his unique kinesthetic approach to teaching dance. His theories are gleaned from years of hard examination of his own teaching, as well as much experimentation. He has never been afraid to try new ways to help dancers improve. Some of his ideas have withstood the test of time; others have been cast aside. Although he himself was trained very academically in the best of British ballet tradition, he is, perhaps, the least traditional of all the teachers I interviewed for this book.

Coordination is Howard's major focus. An overall look at his classes reveals him to be far less concerned about analyzing individual steps and far more concerned with teaching dancers to move in a dynamic, natural-

looking way. To do so, he concentrates on linking steps together kinestheti-
cally and rhythmically, using effort in the body as economically as possible.
One of his longtime students, New York City choreographer Diane
Coburn-Bruning, comments: "It really took a few years before I came to
understand his entire concept, though 'concept' is, perhaps, too concrete of
a word. He's not dogmatic about it. It's built into his classes—the musicality, the circularity of motion, of energy. And even if you can't get everything he's after right away, there's something so satisfying about the attempt because his movement makes perfect physical and intellectual sense.
His classicism is very contemporary. To me, it seems as if it should have
been like this for all ages."

From a kinesthetic point of view, Howard defines all movement in terms
of circular shapes and opposing forces. He embraces that law of physics
which says that for every action there exists an equal and opposite reaction.
"The correction I make most often," he says, "is that dancers must counter
the upward lift in their bodies by directing their energy down into the floor.
This provides them with a wealth of power. You must push against the floor
to anchor your work. You can't just work against space. If the energy is not
initially directed down, nothing will happen on the way up. A jump, or a
turn, is the result of a thrust—like on a trampoline. The work is done on
the way down with the reaction happening on the way up."

Howard asks students to envision their arms and legs inscribing arcs in
space as they extend outward from the axis of the torso. "Line is an illusion,"
he says. "It's something we see and feel only at a certain point. So when we
do something like a *tendu* or a *piqué* arabesque, the impetus should begin
from high up in the torso, travel down through the body, underneath the
working leg and out. I ask students to feel the movement as a circular thrust
which, at the last minute, turns into a line, then glides out of it."

He elaborated on this concept: "A *tendu* does not go out and in, the way
most people are taught. It goes down through the leg, underneath it, and
out. In a sense, we go 'under' the floor, not along it. It's the same in *chassé
arabesque*. To overcome inertia, the body must lift first, then the energy is
thrust down, 'under' the floor, and out to display the straight line arabesque pose at the end." Howard compares this way of moving to the circular action of a piston driving a wheel. "A lot of dancers," he says, "get a mis-
understanding academically of straight up and down, out and in."

Much of Howard's kinesthetic theory has been derived from his work
with movement specialists, principally Joanna Kneeland, with whom he

worked in his early days as a teacher at the Harkness School, and later Eric Linder, a Swiss expert in biomechanics with whom Howard has co-taught several European workshops. "I think what a lot of dancers try to do," he told me, "is to make every muscle in the body feel the same, but the muscles in the leg don't all have the same function. They're not all 'pulling' muscles. The calves are the depressors, and the feet use a feeling of pushing down, not a feeling of pulling up. One does want that upward look in the body— the lift—but one does not necessarily achieve it by lifting everything up. The energy pattern that produces it is the result of several different types of muscular feelings."

Howard was not always so focused on kinesthetic theory. A fledgling teacher when he arrived in America in 1966, he remembers giving a basic class similar to the ones he'd had himself as a student—"mostly R.A.D. (see p. 364, n. 5) and Russian training from George Goncharov,"[1] he says, "plus I added some of my own ideas." His classes, he says, were totally different then from now. But, regardless of how much his teaching has evolved over the past thirty years, he repeatedly stresses how fortunate he was to have had the benefit of a rather traditional British ballet education. "I did all the grades in R.A.D.," he recalls, "and I think a syllabus is a very good thing for training children. In America, certain things like naming steps or doing things in reverse are a problem for a lot of dancers. Much of their training has been acquired in bits and pieces—a little here, a little there—and a lot of it has been based on simply copying what their teacher did. I call it 'follow the bouncing ball.' It stops and they stop! But in England, I had teachers (principally Eve Pettinger and Marian Knight) who would mostly sit in a chair and say, 'Now, dear, put your feet in 5th and do a *temps de cuisse* over and a *pas de bourrée* over with the back foot and a *sissonne en avant*,' and you did it. It was an education. I was also fortunate to study mime with Karsavina[2] (that dates me a bit!). So when I started to teach, I had that material to fall back on, but I also started to look back over all the syllabi and consider what might be lacking in them. Were there gaps that I could fill in?"

This kind of precocious curiosity was evident in Howard from a very young age. He was born David Edwards in England in 1937. During the war, with his father away, he and his mother (he is an only child) were evacuated from London to Holyport, a small town near Windsor Castle. Also evacuated there was the Cone-Ripman School of Dance, which enjoyed an excellent reputation, having produced famous dancers such as Gillian Lynne and John Gilpin. The school was run by the three Cone sisters. "Miss

Gracie taught," Howard recalls, "Miss Lillie played the piano, and Miss Valerie collected the money." Howard remembers that Grace Cone went to the local education committee and convinced them that Maypole dancing should be taught in the schools. One day, a woman named Elizabeth Davies arrived at Howard's school to do just that. He recalls that he went up to her and said, "But I want to be a ballet dancer." He was eight years old. "She patted me on the head, told me to be quiet and get to the back of the room, that we were going to do Maypole dancing." Howard is not sure why at such a young age he had decided so definitively on ballet. "My mother," he says, "had taken me to the Chelsea Palace when I was about three to see a vaudeville show. Somehow, I guess, I had just decided I wanted to be on the stage and be a ballet dancer."

After two years of Maypole dancing, the persistently ambitious Howard was driving his teacher crazy. "She came to see my mother, whom I apparently was also driving mental," Howard recalls, "and they decided that I should attend the Cone-Ripman School in London which was, at that time, changing its name to the Arts Educational School. It was the first school in the West to combine vocational and academic training in the same institution." Howard was given a scholarship and remembers having the best time of his life there. "I was the naughtiest boy in the world," he recalls. "I was impossible and precocious and was often put out of the classroom. Once some of us were taken on tour in an educational program called 'Ballet for Beginners.' We students performed in the first part of the program. In the second part, professional dancers did excerpts from the classical repertoire. One of the ballerinas fell one night, so the next night I went up to her before she went on and said, 'Miss Gordon, I hope you don't fall again tonight.' With that, she went to the stage manager and I was sternly reprimanded. I was fifteen at the time and didn't know very much."

While at the Arts Educational School, Howard completed all levels (Grades through Solo Seal) of the Royal Academy of Dancing ballet exams, as well as exams in tap and ballroom. At sixteen, in 1954, he won the Adeline Genée Silver Medal.[3] Soon after, Howard left school and went to work as one of the dancers in a show at the London Palladium. He stayed for two years, working alongside many well-known variety artists of the time, including Danny Kaye, Judy Garland, Rosemary Clooney, and Eddie Fisher.

It was during this time that Howard changed his name. "When I went to join British Equity," he recalls, "there were already three David Edwardses listed as members. To avoid confusion, they suggested that I change my name. Well, I thought up all these fancy-sounding Russian names and then one day, looking through the phone book in Holyport, I saw 'David Howard.' I thought it sounded good, so I took it. Many years later when I went to dance with the National Ballet of Canada and had to join the union over there, I discovered much to my dismay that they had both a David Howard *and* a David Edwards listed as members. I signed my contract as David Heward!"

"After I had been dancing at the Palladium for some time," recalls Howard, "my father asked me if that was how I intended to spend my life. He thought I should join a ballet company. I'd had an offer from Festival Ballet in London when I was fifteen, but hadn't been able to take it because I was too young to go on tour." As luck would have it, a friend of Howard's father knew the great Royal Ballet ballerina Margot Fonteyn. He arranged for Howard to speak with her. Howard went to ask for her advice and was surprised by what she told him: "She said I should join a company with an opera house because the most important thing was that I should be paid for what I did."

At about the same time, Grace Cone, Howard's former teacher, received a letter from Dame Ninette De Valois, the director of the Royal Ballet, inquiring about Howard's whereabouts. De Valois had remembered him from his winning the Adeline Genée Medal. "So I went and auditioned for the Royal Ballet and ended up staying seven years," Howard says. "I was a soloist in the second company, but also worked a little with the first company." Then, in 1963, he left for a season with the National Ballet of Canada in Toronto. It was not a happy experience. "I don't think there was anything wrong with the job," he says. "I just think my drive to dance in a ballet company was over."

He cured his depression in Paris and Monte Carlo, joining the famous Bluebell Girls revue. "I loved every minute of it," he remembers. "While I was there, I took classes with Franchetti,[4] who tried to discourage me from giving up my ballet career. I loved his classes. He was very supportive and I really think I improved a lot technically with him. He brought back the joy I'd had before in London in Maria Fay's[5] classes." Fay had helped Howard through some of his dark days at the Royal Ballet. "I worked with her for a long time, found her fascinating, and loved her adagios," Howard says. "I remember quite a few things she said and the way she'd link things together. She was a most inspiring teacher."

However, after much soul-searching, Howard, then twenty-four, finally decided to give up his ballet career. He returned from Monte Carlo to London to dance in a variety of television and stage productions, including Bob

Fosse's *Little Me,* in which he performed for a year and a half. He remembers it as a grueling situation: "Fosse was a hard taskmaster." During the run of the show, Howard started to develop a back problem. Perhaps worried about his future as a dancer, he began teaching a few classes at the Arts Educational School. One day when he was in the office of his agent, Sylvia Fisher, the phone rang. It was Rebekah Harkness.[6] She was starting a new program in New York and was looking for three apprentice teachers. "I said, 'That's me!'" Howard remembers. He met with the Harkness Foundation spokesman and arrived in America on 6 October 1966—a date he's never forgotten.

"I don't think I ever would have become what I am now," he says, "if I hadn't come here. I've seen so much more. I was a bit conservative when I arrived. I suppose I had a bit of a 'plain Jane' approach. Living in America seemed very different to me from Europe. There was an energy and physicality here that didn't exist there. People in America are more aggressive, more 'what-you-see-is-what-you-get.' No one beats around the bush. The way I was trained, students never said two words to their teachers. Here, there's much more openness. I think it's very healthy."

Howard was lucky to arrive in the midst of one of the most prolific periods in American ballet history. All three major companies—the Joffrey, American Ballet Theatre, and New York City Ballet—were thriving. In an effort to encourage the spread of excellence in dance outside New York City, the Ford Foundation had decided to generously fund several regional ballet companies. And Rebekah Harkness, an American heiress who loved ballet, had decided to spend a considerable fortune creating the finest ballet company and school she could envision. She refurbished a mansion on Manhattan's upper East Side and recruited reputable teachers, choreographers, and dancers to help make her dream come true.

Howard arrived as an apprentice teacher, but soon became a favorite of Mrs. Harkness. He began to assume greater and greater responsibility. He remembers his heavy teaching schedule: "I taught the scholarship students, as well as the company, as well as an open class every day. But, it was really ideal because I had much more flexibility in the classroom than I have now. With the scholarship students, I could spend twenty minutes on a single step, and if we ended class with that step, it was fine, because I knew I'd get the same students later in the day for a second session. These kids had a two-hour morning class, a break, then a second class that dealt with a kinesthetic breakdown of different aspects of technique—barre, allegro, turns, etc. We'd take an hour and just work on one single area. Also, there were never more than fifteen students in the room, and, with the fifteen-year-olds, I had only six! I taught the girls separately from the boys. It was very good individualized training. I also worked with eight-year-olds in the children's program. Later, we even had an adult beginner program, so I was teaching the whole spectrum of levels."

Mrs. Harkness soon asked Howard to go on tour with the company. He remembers the experience with mixed feelings: "I was put on tour teaching people basically the same age as I was—dancers like Helgi Tomasson, Finis Jhung, and Larry Rhodes—who were ten times better than I ever was. It was a challenge! I had lots of problems when I began working with the company. Half the dancers didn't want to take class with me and half did. So I had to conduct myself in the most professional way, trying to forget that I had been brought over to experiment with ideas of kinesiologist Joanna Kneeland. Instead, I just taught a good basic class. After a couple of years in the company atmosphere, I nearly had a nervous breakdown. Mrs. Harkness came to the rescue one time and sent me down to Nassau for a month to recuperate! The fact is, I wasn't prepared for that responsibility. I was just beginning to teach and a bit out of my depth. It was a little bit unfair."

During his eleven years at Harkness, Howard recalls that he was very much "the new, ambitious, bright kid on the scene." He remembers being very eager, wanting to learn everything he could, but also that he was head-strong and probably rubbed others on the faculty, as well as some dancers, the wrong way. "I'd fight with people and disagree. I wanted to prove my point." However, he is proud of the training program at the school that he and the well-known California teacher Maria Vegh developed together. "It was a fine school," he says. "We picked a good faculty. There are things I think we'd do differently now if we did it again, but we turned out some very good dancers. Mrs. Harkness took care of all the finances, which was wonderful. She was sometimes difficult to deal with, but I had great love and respect for her. And as time goes on, I believe she'll be even more respected for what she did. I mean, she put her money where her mouth was. Most people do the opposite."

Howard left Harkness in 1977. He was offered the position of ballet master by both Robert Joffrey and American Ballet Theatre, as well as the directorship of the Metropolitan Opera Ballet. Instead, he decided to strike out on his own, opening a studio near Lincoln Center. By then, he had developed a loyal following among some of New York's most illustrious professional dancers. During his last years at Harkness, Mrs. Harkness had given him a studio and pianist for three hours each afternoon. Leading dancers such as Gelsey Kirkland, Mikhail Baryshnikov, Helgi Tomasson, Robert Weiss, and Peter Martins came to study with him. Word spread and Howard's classes at Harkness House soon became the "in" place for dancers in New York.

"We used to experiment," Howard remembers. "We used to spend three hours on one thing. Maybe turns, maybe placement. Whatever we wanted to do that day. And that's how I developed my rapport with a lot of these dancers who, when I opened my own school, continued to support me." Cynthia Harvey, a ballerina with American Ballet Theatre who began studying with Howard during that time, recalls her first class with him at Harkness: "I started with David in 1975, just eighteen months after I'd joined ABT. I went because I saw a sudden major improvement in a young soloist in the company, Richard Shaefer. I asked him what he'd been doing. He told me he was going to David Howard. I asked if I were allowed to do that. (Being in the corps de ballet, you know, I wasn't sure I was allowed to study anywhere else.) He said, 'Of course,' so I took off to Harkness. At that time David was working with several people from NYCB, as well as Gelsey and Helgi. My first class with him I remember he did those balances at the barre he does, and I couldn't let go of the barre. He actually came up to me and said: 'By the time you let go of the barre, the music will have stopped playing, the audience will have gone home, and you may as well be working at Woolworth's.' I thought to myself, 'How dare he talk to me like this, em-barrass me in front of the whole class,' but after class I went up to him and asked him to please explain how I could find my balance. He did; so I wanted to go back and learn some more. I had a pretty decent technical foundation from the place in California where I'd been trained, but there were certain things about musicality and phrasing and taking risks that I've learned since I've been with David. First of all, I loved the atmosphere, the fact that there were so many professionals in the studio through whose dancing I could see what he was trying to get at. I felt like a real student. I still do. I never stop learning from what he has to say."

Interestingly, if you ask Howard who he feels has most significantly influ-enced his teaching, he'll tell you that it is all the dancers he's ever worked with. "I have great respect for the wonderful teachers I had in England," he says. "People like George Goncharov, Anna Northcote, Eve Pettinger, Marian Knight, Vera Volkova, Maria Fay, and Raymond Franchetti (in Paris) all were important forces in my life. But as a young teacher, I was very fortunate to work with wonderful, wonderful professional dancers right from the beginning. Not many have that opportunity. I started literally at

David Howard counting for the dancers during a grand allegro combination.

the top, and, although I think I helped dancers like Gelsey Kirkland, Peter Fonseca, and Natalia Markarova a lot, I think I learned more from them than they from me."

Seeing how these great dancers moved, how their bodies reacted, considerably influenced the way Howard's classes began to evolve. "I watched their body language," he recalls. "I tend to watch what people do rather than listen to what they say. I started to build many harmonious things into the exercises in order to make their bodies (and minds!) feel as good as they could, while at the same time demanding some of the academic things that you have to do." Howard feels his ideas are still evolving. "I don't think I've finished exploring yet," he says. "I'm still trying to put it together in a better way, make it feel better on the body, or sometimes even antagonistic. Both of those feelings can produce a good result, though, obviously, with the latter, you have to be careful. After all, you want people to return to your class the next day. Otherwise, there'll be no continuity."

"In the past, sometimes I heard people say about my class that it felt like a massage," Howard remarks ruefully. "Well, actually, I don't think class should feel like that. I understood what they said, but it bothered me, too. I believe students should very rarely put themselves with a teacher with whom they feel totally comfortable. It's much better to put yourself with someone with whom you feel slightly uncomfortable because in this situation sometimes you do your best work and are able to push to a new level."

Howard says he always gives serious consideration to comments made by his students: "Makarova used to criticize everything I did. She helped me a great deal." But he also has a strong mind of his own. What he does in class today is the result of years of teaching. "Every type of class I give," he says, "is different, whether it be a company situation, or children (whom I love to teach), or an open class in my school. I try not to have a set class, but I do have a set pattern of things I do, a set structure, although I may change it a bit from time to time. I often videotape my classes to have a look at what's happening. I'm not so set in my ideas about schooling that I'm inflexible. I try to do whatever it takes to get people to be better."

Today, Howard's barre lasts thirty-five to forty minutes. Because the combinations tend to be short, they can be taught and learned in minimal time. His exercises, which often include a generous amount of repetition, are usually executed on both sides without pausing in between. Throughout the barre, there is a major emphasis on fluidity and *plié*. Approximately thirty minutes into class, Howard provides the opportunity for students to release muscular tension, giving them time (with music) to stretch on their own.

Howard does not adhere to the common practice among many teachers of starting the barre with foot exercises. "Unless it's very cold," he says. "Otherwise, I don't like doing it because it takes the thought down to the foot instead of keeping it on the total body. I think of everything as the total body, with the energy starting from the inside and going out through the muscular system to the extremities." He prefers to start with *pliés* in 2nd position, which he feels is the least stressful position for *grands pliés*. "I believe that *plié* is a body movement and not a leg movement," he states. "It's the body that motivates the lowering rather than just the knees bending."

Howard's regular student Diane Coburn-Bruning uses the words "ebb and flow" to describe how he paces his class. "The exercises, including those at the barre," she says, "are as fast as anyone's, but he carefully builds to this speed. For instance, he'll have you do a slow *tendu* exercise on both sides, then the second time through he'll either double the amount of *battements* in the same time, or increase the musical tempo."

It was shortly after his early and not entirely happy experience teaching the Harkness company, Howard told me, that he began to question the way his *tendu* exercises were constructed. "I decided that they were not slow enough in the beginning," he says. "Also, I joined certain barre exercises together and started to use my own ideas about blending one area into the next. Lately, for the past three years, I've been building *pas de chevals* at various speeds into my barre work. I realized that all the *battements* I was doing—*tendus, dégagés, grands battements*—were what I call 'under and out' steps in their circular movement thrust. *Pas de cheval* is the opposite feeling—over and out. For me, it's like riding a bike; it pushes you higher. I felt it was important to work on this type of circular action too."

Howard is very specific about what students should feel when executing *battements.* He describes the feeling of the working leg in *tendu* as two opposing forces: "over" (the top of the arch) and "under" (the inside of the leg). In spite of the fact that he has worked with many New York City Ballet dancers over the years, he departs from the Balanchinean practice of overcrossing the leg in *tendu devant.* "The inside of the thigh should lengthen in that position," he says. "If you overcross it, it gets too contracted. It's hard to keep the length."

Body bends (*cambrés*) with *port de bras* are incorporated into almost every barre exercise in Howard's classes. He says he added these because he noticed dancers always doing them on their own between exercises. "And I started to think," he says, "about how I could get everyone to coordinate their breathing with these bends—with every movement they did, for that matter, in and out of classical ballet shapes." Not only do Howard's *cambrés* at the barre provide a welcome release of tension for dancers' bodies, they also develop the kind of flexibility in the torso demanded by contemporary choreography. Following Howard's example, more and more ballet teachers these days are incorporating such bends into their barre—a major departure from the traditional manner of devoting barre exercises almost exclusively to legwork. Many of Howard's bends begin with the body going sideways, then forward or back. He favors these over the more commonly used straight forward and back bends. Again, he is using a circular approach to movement. However, it is important to note that Howard follows every *cambré,* most of which happen at the end of an exercise, with a rise and balance in order to re-center the body.

In the past, Howard has been known for incorporating short periods of nonballetic strengthening and flexibility exercises into his classes. "I used to do a pre-barre therapeutic warm-up," he says. Reluctantly, he's dropped this practice. "It's the reality of teaching open classes," he says. "At Harkness, with the same students every day, all of them knew my warm-up. But, now, with different people coming in and out every day, I'd have to continually take time to explain these exercises because otherwise, not knowing what they were doing, the students would do themselves more harm than good."

Howard also used to include ten minutes of floor exercises after the barre. He eliminated them for roughly the same reason he no longer gives a pre-barre warm-up, although time was also an element. In recent years, he's been forced for economic reasons to cut his classes from two hours to one and a half. "If I could," he says, "I'd put the floor work back in. It was very beneficial. I placed it after the barre work because it was a way of pulling the class together. Sometimes a class can fall apart at that point. Doing these exercises was a way of centering the energy in the classroom. Vibrations in a class are important to me. I'm very sensitive to them."

Howard feels that most of the movements at the barre should relate to those in the centre. "So, for instance," he says, "rising up and down with the knees straight is something I rarely do. Of course, if a dancer was very hyperextended, I might concoct an exercise with rises on straight legs to get her to focus on not pulling back in the knees, but, generally, I ask students when rolling down from *relevé* to release their knees as soon as the heel begins to contact the floor—just as if they were coming down from a jump. No one locks their knees when they land and then bends them afterward!" He works on this coordination with a particular *piqué-relevé* exercise (see p. 308) that he is fond of inserting near the end of the barre work.

His desire to relate barre work to the centre also influences the structure of each of his classes. "I use the first centre adagio to bridge the space between barre and centre. I'll incorporate in it elements of things I've used at the barre—either patterns (for instance, changing the weight sideways) or things I've noticed we need to concentrate on," he states. "I try to tie things together in a logical way, rather than just pulling steps out of the air. I'm not nervous about repeating myself movement-wise. I don't try to become original. I want to make a sort of journey. We're going in this direction today."

After this first adagio exercise in the centre, Howard usually gives a fast-moving combination with *tendus,* sometimes in combination with *ronds de jambe* and *relevés.* "I see these *tendus*," he says, "as a change-of-weight exercise in which the legs move *through* 5th position. I have never thought of 5th as static; to me, it's a position of transition. It is also the position in which dancers most easily feel ballet's natural sense of opposition, the result of the fact that we work turned-out."

Following this *tendu* exercise, Howard starts working on direction changes, expanding on circular patterns of movement even more than he has done at the barre. This third exercise is inevitably a waltz with pirouettes and *balancés.* "To me," says Howard, "a *balancé* is a step that moves down, under, and out; it is not simply a *balancé* forward or back. In the same way, I feel a *pas de basque* is an over and out step. It's always been the energy pattern of a step that has interested me more than the step itself." This third centre exercise often includes tempo changes that require students to go from one step to another with little or no time between the two movements. "You've got to store energy and immediately do the next step," Howard tells them. He explained that this kind of challenge was closely related to what they would have to do onstage. Thus, in constructing these exercises, Howard says he's constantly updating what he does, keeping his eye on what's happening choreographically in the dance scene.

American Ballet Theatre principal dancer Cynthia Harvey, who gives Howard most of the credit for her development as a leading dancer, reflects that "he has tried to get me to dance through the combinations, rather than concentrate on accuracy. I have a flow of movement now that I did not get from my original training—my dancing no longer looks like classroom work. It's about connecting movements. There's always a life going on inside the body. Potential energy, I call it. You're always ready to go. He's instilled that in me, and that the steps between are as important as all others." Indeed, Howard often seems little concerned with academic correctness, perhaps because many of his students today are well-trained professionals, but also because he has a definite aversion to position-oriented dancing. His longtime assistant, Peter Schabel, remembers that "a group of teachers from R.A.D. came to watch his class once and commented that it was very nice, but didn't he think the arms looked a bit sloppy. And he said, 'God, I hope so. There's nothing worse than those rigid arms that you see everywhere.' It's his basic philosophy, I think, that if you get people moving, you can get the body to work in a more coordinated fashion, and once that happens then all of the details become easier to fix. But if your body is regimented in a way that becomes rigid, then it becomes very difficult because you must break down before you can start to fix. He was almost delighted about those sloppy arms."

While he may not insist on academic correctness in certain arm positions, Howard still has plenty to say about *how* students use their arms. "Don't flitter and flutter your arms around aimlessly in space," he'll tell his dancers. "Your movement has to have weight!" He believes there must be resistance in *port de bras* in order to give movement power and believability. "Girls," he warns, "especially need to be careful because, being fine in bone structure, their arms tend to look lightweight." And he can be caustic about mannerisms: "When you start using the wrist like that," he told students one day, "you'll want to do it more and more. Pretty soon you'll be doing wrist dancing instead of ballet."

Interestingly, in a major departure from tradition, Howard seldom asks students to reverse exercises. He explains: "When I was a student, we reversed everything, and it was such a waste of time. As a dancer, you don't ever use it. Not that I think one only has to practice things that will be useful in terms of future choreography you'll dance, but there's so much more time you can spend, if you don't reverse steps, working on the things you *do* have to do. I remember watching one well-known New York teacher once. His class spent at least a half-hour reversing an exercise, and, in the end, he was still the only one who could do it!" However, Howard is quick to say that his feelings about reversing things are probably related to the type of open class he's now teaching in New York. "If I were working with a group of youngsters," he said, "I'd do much more of that. With children, I'd be following a much stricter pattern of syllabus. Explaining everything. All the positions and steps from academic methods like Cecchetti's (see p. 361, n. 9). It's very important. They have to have that first. My open classes here are not the right environment for children, who need to be schooled, disciplined, and have everything explained."

I asked Howard if there were other aspects of traditional ballet training from which he distanced himself. "Yes," he replied, "I don't use *flic-flac*. I just find it an hysterical step. I can see its value. It's got that whipping around motion, but when dancers attempt it in class, it becomes 'groping-the-barre time.' For the same reason I tend to stay away from turns at the barre. Unless the barre is set far enough away from the wall, you find yourself stabbing your hand. So I stay away from things like that and do other things to build a sense of rotation—turning slowly, feeling one side of the body against the other."

He also admits to reservations about the wrapped *cou-de-pied* position. "I find it more cosmetic than anything else," he says. "The wrapping feeling is something you can't use other than at that time. You can't use it when you jump because you shouldn't wing your foot. You can't use it when you go on *pointe*. It's a shape that is obsolete after it leaves that position. So I generally tend to stay away from it. Obviously, if I had a group of kids to whom I had to give schooling over a number of years, I'd feel an obligation to make them aware of this position, but I'd get them out of it as fast as I could."

Howard teaches *frappés* both with the flex-point action of the foot and with a fully pointed foot. "With boys," he states, "I generally make them work with flex-point, because most of them need more activity in the feet anyway. Whereas, if I'm working with girls whose feet are already well developed, I don't mind them doing the *frappés* pointed." Interestingly, Howard refers to the pointed foot position as unnatural. "It's what I call a pre-set feeling in the leg," he says. "It's like standing on *pointe*. You're assuming an unnatural form right away."

He also has strong convictions about how to teach *rond de jambe en l'air*. "To me," he says, "it's a double *ballonné*. The first thing you have to get going is the in-out action of the leg, then develop the shape. If you start with the circles first, often the right leg action never comes. So I start students just moving the leg in and out, not even telling them what it is. And if someone asks, 'Isn't this *rond de jambe en l'air*?'" he says, only half-jokingly, "I tell them that I really don't know. Later, I put the circle in."

Several times as I watched Howard teach, he employed special nonballetic exercises designed to help his students feel a particular coordination. Once, he had them just bounce with tiny jumps in 6th position. "Feel the ankles release and relax," he told them. "No steel wool there. The more you exercise the joints, the better; the more you tense, the more the arthritic condition continues." Another time, when he thought the dancers, who were jumping in 1st position, were neither holding their shoulders down nor pressing their feet through the floor enough in *plié*, he had them clasp their hands, stretch their elbows, and hold their arms straight down, pressed against the front of their bodies. They repeated the *temps levés* holding their arms in this position. Strangely enough, jumping in this unclassical pose produced the desired result in both feet and shoulders.

Howard feels turns are one of the most complex areas to teach. "When we learn to jump," he says, "we all stand there and there's only one way to go—up. But with turns there are a lot of variables in the way different dancers approach them. Everyone finds—or doesn't, if they don't search for it—a natural counterbalance unique to their own body. Some people turn well à la seconde, some on their knees, some with their arms out, some with them in, some en dehors, some en dedans, some not at all. It's finding that counterbalance in the body that's crucial."

Leading American Ballet Theatre dancer Wes Chapman, whom Howard coaches privately, recalls: "David told me that pirouettes are not a position that's held and then you turn. Instead, he teaches that it's an adjusting balance that rotates. He'd have me just stand and take the body around to feel how to bring the left side around, the right back, the left around, right back, etc. That's the feeling you have to have to turn, especially in chaînés. You're constantly adjusting. People are fond of saying, 'Just get up there and turn,' but you can't do that. You have to get up and move around the spine, put the left side around the right. There are so many things that you can do."

Another aspect of dancing that Howard has discovered is critical to a student's success is eye coordination. "Eric Linder, the Swiss biomechanics expert with whom I've co-taught several seminars," Howard says, "taught me that a lot of people who don't progress in terms of motor problems (co-ordination) have problems in using their eyes. Eric did a lot of good exercises for that, pointing out that the eyes are the first things that affect our movement because they are what warn us of approaching danger. And I've noticed that when people 'tune out' in the eyes, suddenly they become very uncoordinated in the body." In one class I observed, Howard chided his students about where they were looking during an allegro combination. "The level of your eyes must change in relationship to the level of thrust of your body in jumps," he told them. "You can't just glue your eyes on your feet in the mirror. It looks a bit sinister. Lifting the eyes helps get the body up."

In structuring his exercises, Howard prefers to create short combinations that the dancers can repeat several times. "If you do an exercise only once," he says, "the body never has the chance to develop habits." He guards against long combinations that contain too many elements. "You can lose the point of the exercise that way," Howard states. "I always try to feel that the idea behind the combination is to get the body to do something. I never think in terms of trying to put together a pretty step. It either serves its purpose or it doesn't. If it turns out pretty, fine. But class is not choreography. I think of a choreographer in terms of someone who invents movement. What we do in class is dance arrangement. I do it as musically and interestingly as I can." Regardless of what he calls it, Howard's method of designing combinations is hardly dry or academic. He uses a large variety of linking steps that change daily. "I like to change the character, the feeling of movements, within a combination," he explains, "because that's what happens in choreography. It's never all jumps, never all *relevés* or *piqués*." For instance, he will often put a *relevé*, such as an *échappé à la seconde*, or a *piqué attitude* into the middle of a jump combination. This requires his dancers to make a deliberate change in movement quality from the bouncy jumps into the controlled, driven action of the *relevé* or *piqué*, then back to the jumps again.

Howard is a great believer in the hypothesis that it is the exercise, rather than anything he might say in class, that teaches students how to do a movement. If anything, he prefers to err on the side of undercorrecting. "I try to keep the interest up in terms of being helpful, making suggestions (try this or try that)," he says, "but I'm not necessarily particular on 'this is the arm I gave, therefore you have to do that arm.' Of course, if it gets too out of hand, one has to stop. But I prefer not to waste time stopping. Instead, most often I let the dancers do a combination a couple of times and, then, see what it looks like. Most of the time, problems I've spotted initially get solved through repetition."

Howard says he tries to construct his exercises in a way that deliberately challenges the body to make intelligent choices. "The dancers discover very fast," he says, "that if the weight isn't going in the right direction on one step, then the step to follow won't work quite as well." In short, unlike many teachers who bombard students with a lot of intellectual, verbal instruction, Howard prefers to trust the natural intelligence of the body to activate itself in the face of difficulty.

I observed this modus operandi in a company class that Howard taught at American Ballet Theatre. He deliberately put a very tricky weight change into a men's exercise by inserting a *renversé* just before a double *tour*. After class, he commented: "If they didn't complete the *renversé* all the way around to the right place before the *tombé-assemblé* preparation for the *tour*, they could not manage to do the *tour* and land in 2nd position as they were supposed to. They might have been able to do a *tour*," he added, "but not one into 2nd."

In class, Howard's presence is pure energy. Indeed, at the end of the ninety minutes, he is as profusely soaked in perspiration as are his students. His slender, slightly stooped physique and long blond hair give him a gentle, English-poet look that is in direct contrast to the highly charged manner with which he leads the class. "Ready? Off we go now!" he'll chirp merrily before a quick *petit allegro*. His assistant Peter Schabel comments: "One of

David Howard leading his students through an adagio.

the things I've noticed about the few great teachers I've had the privilege to observe over the years is their ability to energize a room. It's their voice, their presence; it changes the whole room when they start to work. David's one of those people. I haven't seen too many others who could do this. It's not just that his exercises are well conceived and that they work in a kinesthetic way, it's that there's something about his presence that gets you to zero in and work at a more concentrated, energized level. That's a quality of a great teacher. I asked Baryshnikov about his teacher, Pushkin, once—what his class was like. He told me: 'Just an ordinary class, like everybody else's, but what he did was make you work better, at a higher level.' That's what David does. You learn to enjoy the working process."

Howard claps briskly throughout his classes. "I wish it were not such a habit," he says. "I started to clap when I had great problems with my throat. Sometimes I try to hold my hands and not do it, which is better, I think, because one is able to stand back and observe without getting so involved." He has watched videos of himself teaching and felt that perhaps, with his clapping, he was driving the students too hard. (Dancer Cynthia Harvey comments: "David's is the most aerobic class I know of.") Howard says it's hard to judge "because there on the spot you feel you can drive them some-times, and other times it just seems really necessary to clap to keep their energy level up."

Howard also traces his clapping to his famous working relationship with the fine ballet accompanist Lynn Stanford, who died of AIDS in 1991. "Lynn brought about a great change in my life because he was such an inspiring improvisatory pianist. We came from very similar backgrounds, knowing all the old show tunes and that sort of thing, and he was a great support to me. He gave me a lot of confidence in rhythmic response with accents and syncopation. I frequently used to do exercises with a two-against-three rhythm, or three-against-two, when Lynn was here. I enjoyed that. I worked with him twelve years. He got me going. And that's when I started to clap. Now, I wish I didn't. Some pianists don't like it."

Howard says he had trouble adjusting when, after Stanford passed away, he began working with other accompanists. "Music is very important," he says. "To me it's one of the driving things in the class, and I'd just like to say how much people like Lynn Stanford and Douglas Corbin and several other pianists here have contributed to my work." Without Stanford, however, Howard has had to search for another way of working. "I think I'm doing that right now. I had a unique situation with Lynn, but things change, and that's why I feel I must be constantly looking and re-evaluating my class and what it is that works about it." Interestingly, Howard notes that recently some of his dancers observed that he now seems less focused on what's hap-pening musically in the classroom, and more focused on the students.

Perhaps. But the fact remains that Howard is an extremely musical teacher. "Rhythm is one of the key ingredients to learning," he remarks. One day, as his students prepared to repeat a waltz pirouette combination, Howard asked them to change what they were doing on the last two counts. The first time, they had finished with two *soutenu* turns (*glissades en tournant*) on counts seven and eight. Now, he asked them to fit three *soutenus* into those two counts—not only a technical challenge, but a musi-cal one, as well. (He told me later that he also occasionally even asks for four turns in these last two counts.)

Much of what he wants musically Howard conveys via his voice. His usually clipped British accent can become soft, low, and full of breath as he coaxes students through exercises: "I often try to talk in circular patterns rhythmically," he says, "like onnnnne and two." He stretches his words to match the music. In a *fondu* exercise, he will sing along with the music, drawing his voice out equally on the *fondu* and *développé*. When the students repeat the combination, he makes his voice sound heavier, more drawn out on the *fondu* than on the *développé*. He wants them to change the quality with which they're doing the combination the second time around. After a *développé* exercise, he says, "It's not in and owwwwut; it's in and out!" Then, in a slightly mocking tone that elicited smiles around the studio, he added, "You do things slow, slower, slowest and soon you'll find you're not moving at all!"

There is nothing passive about Howard's presence in the studio. He clearly demonstrates every exercise; then, as the students dance, he circulates among them gesturing with his hands how a leg should turn out or a foot press into the floor. He touches students often, lifting an arm here, correcting a sway-back there, or leaning over to hold a foot firmly in his grip so that it cannot sickle. Usually, however, his hands are quite gentle. To straighten a swayed back, he places the fingers of one hand on the student's upper back, then reaches around to the front with his other arm and, with his palm twisted to face out, places the backs of his fingers against the student's rib cage. Somehow, this seems a more delicate, less aggressive way of making a manual correction than, for instance, pressing the student's ribs between both palms. If a dancer seems to have too much tension in *grand plié* in 2nd position, Howard will stick his fingers into the student's hip joint at the base of the *plié* and wiggle them.

Howard has thought much about how best to correct students. He chooses his words carefully: "When I tell dancers to get higher, they'll often say, 'You mean, pull up?' and I never mention the word. Never ever. I say 'lengthen,' 'elongate,' 'stretch'—all of the words with potential. To my mind, 'pull' doesn't have a potential sound. I think sound plays a great role on the body, and if the word has the right sound, then there's potential for the muscular system to be able to get the same feeling. But words like 'hold' I very rarely use."

"It's also important how you say things," he remarks, "how you deliver the material. Instead of saying 'Don't,' I try to say, 'Have you ever thought of' or 'Why don't you try.' Instead of 'Can't you hear what I'm saying?' I prefer 'Have I made myself clear?'" He does not like negative vibrations in the classroom. No doubt one of the reasons he is so popular is that he maintains a healthy, respectful atmosphere in his studio. Often, he relies on his understated British sense of humor to take the sting out of corrections. In one class, after spotting a student whose 4th position preparatory lunge for a pirouette was too wide, he commented dryly: "It may look pretty, but remember that a preparation is a preparation to do a step. The way you're doing it, it could be a preparation for a disaster!" As dancer Cynthia Harvey reflects: "Although his remarks can be a little cynical, he always gets people laughing about themselves—and at the same time he gets right down to exactly what it's about."

In spite of years in the classroom, Howard says he still gets very nervous when he teaches. "People don't realize it," he says, "but to combat this, I have a whole regimen that I go through in the morning. I get up and meditate for about twenty minutes, trying to tune myself in to the energy of the universe. In class, I try to tune myself in to the energy of the people in the room. As a teacher I have tremendous respect for people's bodies. So I feel very fortunate that they place their bodies in my hands for that amount of time. I always try to do the best for them that I can."

One of the things he enjoys most about teaching in his own studio in New York, Howard says, is the variety of people who show up for his open classes. "Years ago," he told me, "I was obsessed with youngsters. Now, I'm not. I like working with people with much more mature minds and bodies. I enjoy struggling away with the fat ladies that come in, or the school professors, the nurses, doctors, dentists—I enjoy that! I find if one has people in class who are perhaps taking dance for fun, along with the serious professionals, it puts things in perspective. When you see an adult struggling in class, you suddenly realize as a teacher that some of the things you're asking for are almost impossible! Ballet technique has been refined to such a high level nowadays."

Howard says he is not concerned about inspiring people in class—though, in truth, that is exactly what he does. "I don't try to inspire," he says, "I try to encourage dancers to be faster, or slower, or stronger, or to turn more, or to develop artistically, rather than just concentrating on technique (although, certainly, it is through technique that one expresses oneself). I try to develop a love of movement. I can be witty or pointedly critical at certain points. I've gotten a lot lighter over the years. But during my time at Harkness, I was very intent on making dancers do what I wanted them to do rather than seeing things from their perspective too."

Early on, working with the Harkness company, Howard says he was very sensitive to criticism from dancers. ("I went through a time when everyone said my classes were too easy. Now," he laughs, "I'm going through a time when they say they're too difficult!") He remembers that Finis Jhung, with whom he worked closely, gave him a very interesting bit of advice: "He asked me why I was always so worried about the people in the back of the room." Howard remembers Jhung telling him "to forget about those people and just worry about the people who are really interested in what you have to say." He told Howard not to try for 100 percent approval. "If you get 50 percent or 75 percent, he told me, you're doing well, and it was from that point on," Howard says emphatically, "that I made a major improvement as a teacher."

Howard also remembers another important piece of advice. "I used to write everything down. If I taught four classes a day, I wrote four before I taught them. I was totally prepared." One day, while the company was on tour in Monte Carlo, Rosella Hightower, the well-known ballerina and teacher from Cannes, watched class. Afterwards she said to Howard: "You know, you're obviously a very earnest young man, and I think you have the makings of a good teacher, but you're not teaching at all." He remembers being a bit hurt. "She told me," he recalls, "that you have to look and see what's in front of you and deal with that. And if you can think of something that can help at that point and it's something you've prepared, fine. If not, then you have to search within yourself." One day, Howard remembers, he left his notebook at home. At the studio, trying to think what he would give in class, he momentarily panicked. "But," he says, "it was from that small crisis that I really started to develop, to be able to think of things on the spot, as well as, perhaps, use material I'd thought of before class. (He still carries a notebook in which he jots new ideas for class.) I'd do my home-work. I was prepared, but not in the same way with every single moment of every class completely planned ahead of time. Today, I generally think through the whole class four or five times in my head, thinking what I'd like to do, beforehand. And then, depending on what's in front of me, some-times I don't do one thing I thought about!"

Another valuable piece of advice Howard remembers came from the great *danseur noble* Erik Bruhn. He warned Howard to be careful about demonstrating: "You don't want people to look like you," Bruhn said, quickly adding that he did not mean this in a bad way. "But students gener-ally tend to pick up on all your bad points, and if you have any good points, they usually miss them completely!"

I asked Howard what he felt was the most difficult aspect of being a teacher. "To be consistent day after day with the level of your work," he answered. "And not get too moody—to always try to give a good class." He mentioned that one of the most disconcerting realities of teaching is the fact that occasionally one has students for many years who never seem to improve. "Your work has had absolutely no effect on them whatsoever," Howard says, shaking his head in disbelief, "no matter what you've done—in some ways they've gotten worse! That's really depressing."

I asked him if there were any particular areas in ballet technique with which he struggled. I was surprised by his answer, because the construction of all his exercises seemed to me so effortless. "I have trouble sometimes with adagios in the centre," he said. "I think it's because I don't understand the rationale behind holding one's leg up for a long time, unless one is doing it with a sense of making the body work, too. Anyway, I often don't like the way my adagios come out construction-wise. That's the part of the class I get nervous about."

He also confesses to feeling "bogged down" sometimes by the big allegro combinations. "After years and years of teaching," he remarks, "one eventually feels that one has done every step in every possible pattern, and the challenge comes in keeping yourself interested as a teacher—that's the key—because if I'm not interested in what I'm doing, the students never will be. So I've got to try constantly to find different ways of creating these combinations without necessarily copying what others do. Those are the two areas, adagio and *grand allegro,* I spend the most time thinking about."

One of the nicest traits in Howard's personality is how supportive and encouraging he is, both in and out of the classroom. He will always follow a biting comment with positive reinforcement. One day, when his students' arms lacked correct classical form in an adagio, Howard snapped: "Most of you just stick your arms up as if you haven't a problem in the world. Well, you've got lots of problems. That's the problem. They're multiplying by the minute!" Then, when the chastened students held their shoulders down as they lifted their arms, he changed his tone of voice. "Now, that's it!" he praised them enthusiastically. "That's the best you've looked in years!"

I asked how he managed to balance being both friend and teacher to his students. "Well," he admitted, "I've had problems with kids standing outside my doorstep with two suitcases in each hand, ready to move in. I've had people write ten letters a day to me, people fall in love with me—one girl even left her husband, she told me, to be with me, but generally it hasn't happened that often." Howard tries not to get too involved with his students. He's always willing to help, but says, "I don't think you can be a pal—

come into the room and gossip with students. It's your duty as a teacher to lead, propel, encourage, and give as much information as you can—bring everything to a higher level. You've got to drive students, and I don't think you can do that if you're chatting with everybody in the room."

When he leaves the studio, Howard does not take work-related concerns with him: "I'm not fanatic at all about it. I care a lot about what I do, but I can get away from it very, very easily." Among Howard's non-dance interests are collecting old movie and theater posters, as well as any Betty Grable memorabilia he can lay his hands on. He's also a great fan of the Peruvian popular singer Yma Sumac, who has an extraordinary five-octave range. "I've known her for nearly thirty years," says Howard. "She's a great friend. Most people are surprised I'd be involved with people like that." Howard's assistant, Peter Schabel, says of Howard: "Basically, he's a fan. Especially for odd people in show business, the fun side of it. Perhaps it goes back to his years at the Palladium. He loves that aspect, things like old terrible dance routines in the movies—like Barbara Stanwyck in *Lady of Burlesque.* He's a tough audience though. His eye is too trained. This is probably one of the reasons he tries to avoid going to the ballet at all costs!"

Howard has another unusual hobby: "I'm also quite talented as a hairdresser," he told me. "I was actually interested in being one when I was younger. A friend of mine who was a famous hairdresser told me you either have a talent for cutting hair or you don't. I said, 'It's a bit like dance really, isn't it?' And he said, 'Yes, it's exactly the same. You can't really teach anyone to do it. You can bring out the qualities, but they have to be there.' So I went one day to his shop, and he said to me, 'There's a girl over there. There's a pair of scissors. Cut her hair.' I got hold of the comb, combed it down and looked at her and just cut it. And he said to me, 'You're doing exactly the same thing as you do in dance—following what your eye sees—the way everything falls.' He told me I'd do it quite well, and I nearly went into it. It's instinctive. I always used to do my mother's hair. And a lot of people's in the Royal Ballet, too. In my early days in New York, I used to cut the hair of many dancers whom I coached. For me, it's like getting into another area, and I can just cut off the ballet world."

Over the years, Howard has done much more for dancers than cut their hair. His generosity is well known. When American Ballet Theatre was locked out on strike one year, he told the dancers they were welcome to take classes with him free of charge. He's been known to pay needy dancers' doctor's bills and rent, as well as to buy costumes for young choreographers' work, which he regularly showcases at his studio. He gives scholarships to many of the young people who study with him, and has never taken payment from dancers with whom he has developed close coaching relationships. "We help many, many people here," Howard says earnestly. "And that's part of being in this business. I was helped when I was younger, and I believe very much in passing that on. I think you have to give back to your profession."

Howard is also extraordinarily generous in his attitude toward other teachers. He believes that there are many good things in all the various methods of teaching ballet. "I have always believed that no one teacher has the only answer," he states. "All we do as teachers is pass our students between us, and I'm happy if, when they're not working with me, they're working with someone else, as long as they're working. No one teacher can claim to have trained a dancer. The person who has really put it all together is the dancer who has made decisions about what to take in and how to assimilate and use the information."

Howard encourages students to be willing "to invest the time and curiosity to explore something—with anyone." He feels many dancers want instant results. "If you can give them those," he says, "they'll listen to what you say, but instant results technically don't always produce changes in the quality of one's dancing. They may give you the turn or the thrust or whatever, but not the quality. That takes time." He is fond of telling students that "to be a good dancer, you must be curious about the profession. You can't just dance. So much else is important—like the drama of it. You must be in love with the theater."

And what advice does Howard offer an aspiring teacher? "Leave as many problems of your own outside the door as possible. Keep an open mind and be prepared to change your ideas. Don't say: 'It was better in my time!' Remember, if you're having trouble with students, it's not that they don't want to get better. They all want to get better. It's just that we as teachers haven't found a way to help them do it. Be prepared to see people improve in front of your eyes so that maybe you have to dig a bit deeper to come up with more new challenges for them. You must keep learning from your dancers, good and bad. And don't worry if the class hasn't worked perfectly that day. You'll always have another chance!"

Classroom Quotes from Howard

"You must work with a minimum of effort for a maximum of result—not the other way around."

To a student sitting in an incorrectly placed preparatory pose for pirouettes: "You have nothing to help you get up from that 4th position except perhaps a miracle—and they're not giving those out this year!"

"Don't think of the 5th position *plié* in a series of jumps as the beginning or the end of anything. Think of it as the middle, the thing that links your jumps. This will give it the right quality of rebound. You mustn't stay in it."

On placing the arms correctly during an *enchaînement:* "You may think about it before and discuss it afterward, but you must *correct* it as you're doing it."

"The days are long gone—and they're never coming back—when ladies wore long gowns and all you saw was this gorgeous foot extending out from under the hemline. You must turn out the *whole* leg when you point front and rotate all the toes. Don't just wing the foot."

"Effort that is not worked the right way will not be rewarded."

"Link steps together with a pause, not a stop. There's a difference!"

"You have to resist hopping during a pirouette like you resist coughing during the opera. Otherwise, it becomes a habit very quickly."

On holding the arms *à la seconde:* "You must have energy coming from the inside of the arm, as well as from the outside; otherwise the body looks caved in, too rounded."

"Lift up your body from the teeth, not just from the hips!"

Order of the Exercises in Howard's Class (advanced class, 1½ hours)

BARRE

1. Demi-pliés, grands pliés, cambrés, and rises
2. Slow tendus in 1st position
3. Tendus in 5th position with temps liés
4. Dégagés (tendus jetés) in 1st position
5. Dégagés (tendus jetés) in 5th position
6. Pas de chevals
7. Ronds de jambe à terre
8. Frappés
9. Adagio
10. Ronds de jambe en l'air with petits battements
11. Stretches
12. Grands battements

CENTRE

1. Adagio
2. Tendu enchaînement
3. Waltz enchaînement with pirouettes en dehors
4. Pirouettes en dehors with relevés in arabesque and piqués en tournant en dedans
5. Changements and temps levés with pirouettes en dehors and en dedans
6. Petit allegro enchaînement with échappés, ballonnés, and grands jetés
7. Batterie: enchaînement with petits jetés, ronds de jambe en l'air sautés, and pas de chat
8. Grand allegro with assemblés portés and grands jetés développés
9. Coda turns en diagonale (piqués, fouettés, chaînés, etc.)
10. Changements and rise and balance

The Roots of Tradition

THE PEDAGOGICAL LINEAGE OF DAVID HOWARD

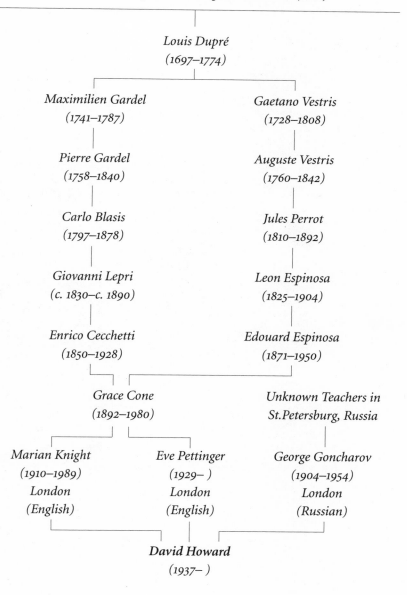

L'Académie Royale de Musique et de Danse (1661)

Louis Dupré
(1697–1774)

Maximilien Gardel
(1741–1787)

Gaetano Vestris
(1728–1808)

Pierre Gardel
(1758–1840)

Auguste Vestris
(1760–1842)

Carlo Blasis
(1797–1878)

Jules Perrot
(1810–1892)

Giovanni Lepri
(c. 1830–c. 1890)

Leon Espinosa
(1825–1904)

Enrico Cecchetti
(1850–1928)

Edouard Espinosa
(1871–1950)

Grace Cone
(1892–1980)

Unknown Teachers in
St.Petersburg, Russia

Marian Knight
(1910–1989)
London
(English)

Eve Pettinger
(1929–)
London
(English)

George Goncharov
(1904–1954)
London
(Russian)

David Howard
(1937–)

6 Larry Long

Larry Long conducting an advanced class at the Ruth Page
Foundation School in Chicago in 1991.

*L*arry Long is recognized as one of the preeminent teachers in the American Midwest. Since 1971, he has directed the Ruth Page Foundation School of Dance in Chicago, which, with more than forty former students in some twenty-five professional companies, enjoys a reputation as one of America's finest ballet schools.

"Dance with color!"

Long began to study ballet at the age of seventeen in southern California. Five years later, in 1958, he joined the Chicago Opera Ballet under the direction of Ruth Page. His talent for teaching and staging ballets was soon apparent, and Page appointed him ballet master in 1962. During his first years with the company, he was much impressed by the style and technique of visiting dancers from the Royal Danish Ballet. In particular, he was greatly influenced by the Danish company's renowned Russian teacher, Vera Volkova.

Long continued as both dancer and ballet master with Ruth Page's International Ballet until the company disbanded in 1969. From 1963 to 1968, he was also the artistic director of the Midwestern Music and Art Camp, a summer program run by the University of Kansas in Lawrence. After the demise of Page's company, Long joined the National Ballet of Washington (D.C.), where he served as ballet master from 1969 to 1970 under the direction of Frederic Franklin. The following year, he was invited to become ballet master of New York's Harkness Youth Ballet, with whom he toured Europe. Soon after, at the request of Ruth Page, he returned to Chicago to assume the direction of the newly established Ruth Page Foundation School of Dance. He has been there ever since, except for a year and a half in the mid-1970s, when he undertook the artistic direction of a successful, but short-lived, English-based company, Ballet International. Today, in addition to teaching and overseeing the school, Long continues, as he has for many years, to direct the lavish annual production of *The Nutcracker* at Chicago's Arie Crown Theatre. In addition to accepting many engagements as a guest teacher, Long has also been responsible for restaging, both in Chicago and major cities elsewhere, several ballets choreographed by Ruth Page.

"BEE, BEE, chicky, bom-bah, bee, pah-wom!" Larry Long doesn't count when he teaches. He scats! His voice, rhythmically commenting on the music, guides his students through the combinations. "Rrrra, pah, diggy, diggy, dee, HA, HA, HO!" he sings, emphatically pounding the head of his teaching stick on the floor. Music to him is much more than a mathematical collection of counts. It is phrasing and nuance, pauses and spurts, allegro and adagio. "Don't count it out like a pedometer," he tells students. "Sing it!" Long is adamant about good musical accompaniment when he teaches. "Without it," he remarks, "my brain shrinks to the size of a chick pea." This is hard to imagine. With a fine memory, polished over many years as ballet master with several companies, he is an enormously inventive teacher, musically and choreographically.

Now almost sixty, the trim, gray-haired Long still moves across the studio floor with great ease. He reflects on how accidental it was that he ever became a dancer. "No one in my family was in the theater," he recalls. But his mother, who had once been a singer with her own radio program, saw to it that her son took music lessons. He started at seven, becoming accomplished on both the trumpet and the French horn. When he was two years old, his family moved from his birthplace, Des Moines, Iowa, to Sunland, California, a little town on the fringes of the big Tujunga Canyon near Los Angeles. Long remembers a childhood centered on outdoor activities: "I rode horses and hiked, never wore shoes in the summer, and practically lived in a bathing suit."

In high school, he worked with the gymnastics team. "I was involved with them from the tenth grade on, competing in tumbling and the free exercise. I guess I had natural ability—I was very loose and pliable, with a certain amount of strength." During his senior year, the coach decided that the team could benefit from ballet lessons. "So, once a week," recalls Long, "all very hush-hush, of course, he hired a local ballet teacher to come give us a class." Much to his surprise, Long soon found himself enjoying these lessons very much.

"In our little town," Long remembers, "there lived a rather peculiar lady whom everyone called 'the Baroness.' No one knew if the rumors about her aristocratic background were true, but, as it turned out, they were." The Baroness DeBarkov was a White Russian[1] whose husband taught political science at the University of California. Long did yard work for them for extra income. One day, he told the Baroness about his new-found interest in ballet. "Well," she told him, "if you're really serious about studying ballet, you should study it right."

She introduced him to a friend of hers, Alexandra Baldina,[2] who had been a member of the Diaghilev Ballets Russes in Paris. As one of the three leading ballerinas in Fokine's *Les Sylphides*, Baldina had danced alongside Pavlova, Karsavina, and Nijinsky. In June 1954, when Long graduated from high school, he decided to continue studying ballet with Madame Baldina.

"She lived in a very big place on a hill, and I worked around her house and yard in exchange for three lessons a week," he says. "She taught me in a little outdoor, screened-in summerhouse with a wooden floor. The space was very small, but it didn't matter since, in the beginning, she concentrated totally on barre work. The first lesson literally was *pliés*. For the entire hour, we did nothing else! The second lesson she added *tendus* to *pliés*, and it went on like that until I'd learned the entire barre."

Because the space was small and they were working without music, Baldina did very little centre work. "We began pirouettes," Long recalls, "and did just a few beats." He remembers enjoying Baldina's stories about the old days in Czarist Russia. Although he cannot recall much specifically about her lessons, he readily acknowledges the impact she had on him. "Whether or not it manifests itself today in my teaching," he says, "I don't know. But she made me aware of working on something to the point of—I won't say 'perfection' because nobody reaches perfection—but certainly not being satisfied with simply getting by, just getting through it. She introduced me to ballet in such a way that it was an absolutely serious thing. It wasn't something one just did as a pastime."

Today he sometimes says things in class he remembers Baldina saying to him: "For example, the way she taught pirouettes, which I think is a very, very old, particularly Russian way of doing them. You would always spring off the pirouette into a finish, either in 4th or 5th. She also told me not to worry about hopping during a turn—that I'd find where my balance was that way. That someday I wouldn't hop. And I like that idea." Long feels this approach encourages students to take a chance with staying up in a pirouette. "I always tell my students," he says, "that a pirouette finishes on the leg you are turning on, not the leg you put down."

After Long had been studying with Baldina for about eleven months, she decided he needed to be in regular ballet classes with space to move and musical accompaniment, neither of which she could provide. Two former students of hers, Paul Petroff and Nana Gollner,[3] had a school in Van Nuys, California, and she recommended that Long study with them. By that time he had become quite serious about dancing; the longer he studied, the more he had begun to consider it a possible career. "My father was very, very upset," Long recalls. "He was anxious for me to become a musician. After all, he'd paid for my lessons all through the years, and he knew nothing about dancing except the usual misconceptions. He had let me get by while I was with Baldina because I had a job and was earning a little money, but when I decided to stop music lessons and go study with Paul and Nana, he laid down an ultimatum. Either I gave up dancing, or I moved out of the house."

Gollner and Petroff offered Long a scholarship. When, by accepting it, he found himself without a place to live, they generously agreed to let him move in with them. "I left home," Long recalls, "and I didn't see my father again until I got my first job with Ruth Page's company and came home to California on tour. We reconciled then. My mother, however, was more amenable to the whole thing. Dancing wasn't what she would have chosen for me, but she was unwilling to object to the point of causing a rupture between us. So all the time I was living with the Petroffs, she and I kept in contact by phone."

Long studied for four years with the Petroffs. "They were really surrogate parents for me," he recalls. "For instance, on my twenty-first birthday, they bought me the first suit I ever owned. They took me places. They introduced me to a kind of cultural experience I'd never been aware of. I ate things with them I never would have otherwise. After all, my family was very middle class. My father was a carpenter. So I learned everything from the Petroffs, more than just how to dance."

He took a morning class with them every day, then usually two classes in the evening—an advanced one and a slower one. In addition, he danced in many of the performances that Petroff staged. Long remembers one occasion very well: "Paul and Nana were dancing in a production of *Vagabond King* and had choreographed a little *pas de trois* for two girls and me. Madame Baldina came to a performance and came backstage afterwards. I was very nervous because I had always held her in such high esteem. I asked her to tell me what she thought. She answered in her heavily accented, halting voice, 'Oh, boy,'—she always called me 'boy'—'you just like smoke. You see it, but nothing there.' Well, this made a great impression on me. It certainly was not a compliment, but it was undoubtedly something I needed to hear because I was very full of myself for having danced so soon. I believe she meant that my stage presence was considerably lacking, for the dancing was very simple. I was a real neophyte at that time."

What wasn't lacking, Long remembers with a laugh, was the amount of makeup he had on! "Paul had given me all the Royal Ballet books to look at," he recalls. "I'd never done a makeup before. He came into the dressing room at one point and practically shrieked in terror because I had copied at least one of everybody's lines in the Royal Ballet—and there were, at that time, considerable lines to copy! I must have looked like the rear end of a baboon."

Gollner and Petroff, who were married, were major sources of inspiration for Long. They were, however, very different from each other as teachers. "Nana was a very technical, unemotional kind of teacher," he says. "She was an extremely beautiful woman—one of the leading ballerinas of Ballet Theatre at that time. She was a very strong technician, a marvelous turner and jumper who could dance on *pointe* in her bare feet." Petroff, on the other hand, was never a strong technician, although Long notes that he never actually saw him dance at the height of his career. "He was a Dane," Long says, "who joined De Basil's Ballets Russes when it first regrouped after Diaghilev's death. His real name was Paul Peterson, but he changed it when he joined the company.[4] He had beautiful *port de bras* and was a well-known leading dancer in De Basil's company. As a teacher, he was much more romantic than Nana. His combinations were more choreographed, more dancey, with lots of *port de bras*. Hers were not. She did exercises, if you can appreciate the distinction."

Long notes that, as teachers, the two of them complemented each other very well. "But, if anything," he remarks, "I was probably more influenced by him than her because his classes seemed more dance-oriented." He feels that today he teaches quite differently from both of them, with the exception, perhaps, of questions of taste and structure in the centre work. "For example," he says, "it was the general rule in both their classes to do everything in sets of four eights: eight *grands battements* to the front, eight side, eight back, and eight side again. Then we repeated the same around on *relevé,* then again with *battement développé,* and finally around with *battement-passé* in. That's thirty-two in each direction. It was grueling work, but I must have had the kind of constitution that could withstand such heavy classes."

Today Long does not believe that such a system is necessarily the best way to train. He first questioned it when he began to teach professional dancers in Ruth Page's[5] company. "As my wife, Dolores [Lipinski],[6] can testify," he remarks, "my early classes were probably quite horrible because at that time I really wasn't thinking about teaching. I was just giving a rehash of what I'd done as a young man. But I began to think about it when the girls in the company started complaining that their thighs felt like thunder. After all, dancers by that time [the early 1960s] had started to adopt a very different style. They were more lean and drawn out. They didn't need to build up a tremendous store of muscles. So I was forced to rethink what I was teaching and why, to ask myself what it would produce."

Long had joined the Page company, then called the Chicago Opera Ballet, as a dancer in the fall of 1958. He had left the Petroffs a few months earlier to go to New York. He laughs at the memory: "I was sure that after four whole years of training I would take New York by storm!" After all, he had already performed not only at the Hollywood Bowl, but also in a production of *Coppélia* staged by Alicia Alonso[7] at the Greek Theater in Los Angeles. "So," remembers Long, "I got on a bus and went to New York, auditioned for a summer stock job, was pretty lucky and got it." The job was in Kansas City, where he met Patricia Klekovic, a ballerina in Ruth Page's company. She suggested he audition for Page. "So on the way back to New York at the end of the summer, I stopped off in Chicago," says Long.

Page, however, was noncommittal, and Long continued on to New York. There he took classes with Valentina Pereyaslavec[8] and William Dollar,[9] then auditioned for American Ballet Theatre. "I didn't make it," he remembers, "but Ms. Page was at the audition and spoke to me afterward. Then I auditioned for the Ballets Russes de Monte Carlo. Again, I didn't make it, but Ruth was there, too, and spoke to me again. The same thing happened at my next audition, for Margaret Craske at the Met, but this time Ruth invited me to come audition for her once more. She was having a few dancers over to Steinway Hall. Again, I wasn't selected, but just as I was leaving, she called out asking if anybody did tumbling or acrobatics of any kind. So I did a tumbling run, or something, and she offered me a contract. I got the job not because I could dance, but because I could do a back handspring! I was twenty-one and probably far from ready for a ballet company. I'd like to think that my technique continued to improve once I joined Page."

Long did his first tour with the Chicago Opera Ballet in 1959. "Ruth Page," he recalls, "was an independently wealthy woman, but in those days she actually made money on her company—about $100,000 at the end of each tour, which she then used for the following year's new productions." The company toured under the auspices of Columbia Artists Management—5½ months on a bus traveling four hundred miles a day to one-night stands, most of which were community concerts where the income was assured. "We were thirty-two dancers, fourteen musicians (augmented in each city), and a crew of seven," Long remembers. "Our scenery and equipment traveled in a semi-tractor trailer and one smaller truck—an eighteen-footer. So we were quite a large undertaking for that time. The only other companies that toured in the States then were American Ballet Theatre and the Ballets Russes de Monte Carlo."

In 1961, Page found herself without a ballet master and approached Long. "In those days with Ruth," he recalls, "being ballet master didn't really mean too much. All I did was give warm-up classes before rehearsal. I don't know why she asked me to do it, except that she had taken an interest in me early on. I was one of those people who, when she choreographed, she'd ask to step forward and try things. Also, I have always had a very good memory." Long's wife, Dolores, recalls: "Larry was always the one in rehearsals to say, 'Two days ago we did this on count five. Why are we doing it on two today?'"

In his typically self-effacing way, Long says he thinks Page offered him the position of ballet master "mainly because she couldn't get anyone else to agree to do it!" His decision to accept the responsibility turned out to have been a very wise move. "By that time," he remarks, "I had realized what kind of dancer I had the potential to become. Unfortunately, it wasn't at all the kind of dancer I wanted to become. In the Petroff school I had been practically the only boy, and they had encouraged me a great deal. When I went to New York, I carried their hopes with me and saw myself ultimately as a prince. However, I soon realized I was more of a *demi-caractère* type. In those days, dancers were more pigeonholed than they are now. If you looked a certain way, you became a certain kind of dancer. I was on the small side. I wasn't handsome and didn't have a princely bearing, so I became a *demi-caractère* dancer, which actually is a wonderful category to be in. I did a lot of absolutely super roles, but I knew I wasn't going to do the Prince in *Swan Lake* or any other heroic sort of parts. So, perhaps, when Miss Page offered me the position, I accepted because I had already subconsciously realized that I needed to prepare myself for another path in dancing."

He soon discovered that he loved teaching. "It was very, very interesting to me," he recalls. "And I started to really make a place for myself in the company, rehearsing ballets to a much greater extent than any previous ballet master had done." He admits that he was very nervous about teaching, but says he never prepared classes. "Maybe I'm fortunate in that I can usually teach cold," he says. "I like to be free to take a class where it needs to go on that particular day, depending on the people that are there, what their strengths and weaknesses are, and what I see during barre that needs to be addressed. I'm fortunate in that I don't get stuck very often. So I don't prepare now and I didn't then, though probably there were many in those days who wished that I had!" His wife, Dolores, who has been taking his classes ever since Long began teaching, begged to differ: "I think Larry's a better teacher now than then, because he's done it for thirty years, but the real talent for his teaching was always there."

Watching Long teach, one notices that shortly after the beginning of the barre, a theme for the day starts to develop. Something catches his attention, perhaps a lack of weight in students' *pliés,* or a lack of articulation in the way they execute a *petit développé.* Cleverly, he manages to insert movements that address that particular problem in almost every exercise. "I try to attack the same problem in as many ways as I can," he states. "For example, if we're working on how to hold the leg correctly in 2nd, I'll do more than just *développé* to 2nd. I'll also give *demi-ronds* in which the leg must be carried side, and jumps with the leg in 2nd, and *grandes pirouettes* in 2nd, both *en dehors* and *en dedans*—from 2nd position! I'll emphasize how the shape of the thigh in 2nd must be maintained in *plié,* as well as *en l'air.* And how the issue is not just sticking the leg up there to the side and holding it, but also getting the leg into 2nd in as many ways as possible."

Janet Shibata, a former soloist with American Ballet Theatre who is now one of Long's devoted students, comments: "Larry's classes are not given to satiate your ego. They're classes to work, providing you with constant challenges mentally, physically, emotionally, and musically. From the first note, there's some sort of challenge confronting you. And once you start to attain one level, he presents another for you to work on. So you're constantly growing."

Larry Long commanding young male dancers to stay in the air during a grand allegro combination.

Long recalls that he did not always have such a deliberate approach to teaching. "The first time I really felt as if I was teaching and not just giving a class was in 1963," he says, "when I was appointed artistic director of a summer arts camp run by the University of Kansas." There, at the Midwestern Music and Art Camp in Lawrence, Kansas, Long had his first experience teaching young people. "It was very, very different from teaching company dancers," he recalls. "I truly had to take into consideration the varied backgrounds and knowledge of the people I was teaching. They came from many different teachers all over the States. It was very challenging. Much more so than teaching Page's company."

None of the thoughts that came to him, he supposes, were unique revelations. "But they were new to me," he says. "For example, I started to question how deep one should go in *pliés*. In 2nd, a lot of dancers went down below the level of their knees, as far as they could go. I decided that if you *plié*d that deeply, the chances of things happening to your body that you really did not want to have happen were greater. I didn't think it was either wise or necessary." He also thought about the standard half *port de* *bras* that accompanies *grands pliés*. He decided the hand should elongate in 2nd, then lower to a point just outside, rather than inside, the knee. "It shouldn't come across the line of the body," he felt, "until it begins to lift to 1st. That way you avoid that position of looking like you're trying to lift a heavy rock between your feet."

It was at this time that Long began doing the first three *tendus* at the barre in a very specific pattern. He still adheres to it today. He gives the first slow *tendu* in a 4/4 or 2/4 time, the second one in a 3/4, and the third in a quicker 2/4. "I began doing this because these young people needed the time in the first *tendu* to pay very close attention to balance and carriage. I put the second one to a waltz—more flowing—so that the *tendus* would not become bogged down or pedantic, so that the body would begin to move, to dance. I have never felt that barre work should be separate from dancing. From the time you walk into the studio, you should be thinking about dancing; barre work leads you to dancing. A lot of people disagree with me, I know. They think the barre is to prepare the body for dance, but I believe there's another kind of preparation that needs to be done, and that it can be done at the barre. This is what my second *tendu* is designed for. The third one is a culmination of the two that precede it. You're moving with more force, more energy. It's quicker, more sharp and precise, more delineated."

Long remained director of the Kansas summer camp program until 1969. He also began to give master classes at various schools. His main job, however, was teaching the dancers of the Chicago Opera Ballet. Many famous guest dancers performed with the troupe, including Rudolf Nureyev (see p. 36, n. 11), who made his American debut with the company in March 1962. "He was brilliantly exciting, as good as Baryshnikov," Long recalls, "but in a very different way because they are two very different animals." Long told me how grateful he feels to have seen so many unforgettable performances in his lifetime: "First and foremost, in my memory, are Alicia Alonso and Igor Youskevitch in *Black Swan Pas de Deux* and *Giselle* with American Ballet Theatre. Then, Eddie Villella in *Prodigal Son*. And I remember the first time I saw Jacques D'Amboise. It was in *Filling Station*, a silly little ballet really, but he was really impressive, and just nineteen years old! Then, all those marvelous performances by Nora Kaye. And it was extraordinary to actually be in performances with Nils Bjorn Larsen as Dr. Coppelius. He was incredible—very unique. It's wonderful to have lived long enough to have seen all these people who are just names in books now!"

We talked about some contemporary dancers. He spoke in his quiet, earnest voice, slightly raspy as a result of years of smoking. (He's tried repeatedly, he told me, to break the habit, but without much success.) "I've always been a great admirer of Baryshnikov and Gelsey Kirkland. But I'm so mad at her!" he exclaimed. "I almost took it personally when her book[10] revealed all that business about her because she was too good to have had all those things happen to her!" Such a comment reveals Long's rather sensitive nature. "I think about failure a lot," he told me. "I think it's part of my lexicon!" He recalled an incident early in his teaching career that left him really shaken.

"Galina and Valery Panov, who had left the Kirov ballet, were dancing with us in *Die Fledermaus*. They were in class every day and, naturally, I was very nervous, especially as Valery can be rather outspoken. One day he came to me and said: 'You know, you have a lot of potential to be a good teacher, a lot of talent, but do you mind if I tell you something?' I said, 'Of course not! I'd be delighted.' And he said: 'You don't teach dancing. You just teach preparations. Too many preparations in your class. All this dancing around in the centre. You should just teach *assemblé*. Just *jeté*. If you did that, you'd be a wonderful teacher.' Well, my mind was absolutely blown. I thought 'Oh my God, I'm a terrible teacher. I can't do it. I should stop.' It really blew me off, until I thought, if I did that, I'd be like any other teacher who does that. How many ways can you just teach *jeté, jeté, jeté*? Not a lot. And if there is anything unique about the way I teach it is the fact that I don't just do *jeté, jeté, jeté, jeté*. And, finally, I came to the realization that it may not be the way he would think a good teacher should teach, but that's the way I teach—good or bad. It's just the way I do it."

Catherine Yoshimura, a former leading dancer with Ballet Met and Les Grands Ballets Canadiens, who was completely trained by Long and Lipinski, recalls that Long "always seemed to think he had so much to learn in teaching, so he would invite guest teachers for his summer courses and he would sit in and listen so attentively. I think he'd learn more in those classes than we would! But in his endeavor to find the right teaching method, he never lost his own style or strayed from his own convictions about principles of technique. He never believed in overstressing the joints in one's body. He firmly believed that one must work with what one was born with. But he did stress that one really had to work within that framework; dancing didn't come through an act of God! It came from hard work and intelligence. He urged us to read—and not just books on dance. (His own library was impressive.) He always said there should be punctuation and phrasing visible in one's dancing, like a well-written paragraph."

Long says his wife used to keep notes on all his classes. "Even when I look back ten years ago," he remarks, "I realize I'm teaching differently now. I taught in a more dry, less choreographed fashion before." He continues: "The longer I teach at the level I teach now—advanced and professional— the more important it is to me that class, especially at that level, has to contain a lot more elements than just the physical education, the steps, etc. Particularly nowadays when young people tend to listen to a certain kind of music less often. They need to learn phrasing or become aware of phrasing in movement—how movement can change, how the same movement can be done differently in terms of accent and emphasis on where the movement is coming from and where it's going, etc. This is especially important for dancers who are close to getting a professional job, where they're going to be asked to express something through dancing. I think it's essential that they're aware of these things in class."

He also believes in exposing his dancers to a wide range of choreographic styles. As his student Janet Shibata notes: "You'll find yourself doing a Russian *grand adage* at the barre, then, in the centre, doing some *petit* complex footwork of Bournonville[11] with a lot of *ballon*. Then, all of a sudden, he'll ask for a pirouette prepared with a straight back leg like in New York City Ballet. All within one class. So you're never tied down to a particular way of doing things because the next day you're going to do a step in a totally different way. This keeps you alert all the time, and, if you have a strong base, you'll find it's easy to go from one style to another. This is rather unusual because most teachers stick to one system. But the result of what you get here with Larry is that later, when some choreography is thrown at you, you'll have a flash of recognition and understanding."

As I watched Long's classes, it was clear that his teaching has been strongly influenced by the Bournonville technique. He had his first exposure to it when the Royal Danish Ballet toured America, accompanied by their great teacher, Vera Volkova,[12] in 1959. "They were performing at the Chicago Opera House," he recalls, "and we were rehearsing there. Ms. Page invited Volkova to teach our company. Also, I saw every single performance the Danes gave. I was absolutely shattered by the Bournonville technique. I loved it! I also thought Volkova's class was extraordinary. She was such an inspiring teacher, very simple, but very encouraging, with a warm and giving kind of personality. What about her classes was so absolutely wonderful I can't really remember, though I do remember certain exercises—like the *frappés* with that "Japanese" *fondu* I sometimes give (see p. 316). Her classes had a kind of extraordinary flow to them. She stressed soft, juicy *pliés*. I often say now that *plié* isn't a place you go, it's a movement. That's very typical of what I remember of Volkova."

He also remembers her classes as being "very opening in the hip," and one sees this trend in his own classes. "It's a very conscious effort on my part," he says, "because I like the feeling I get in my own body doing it, and I like the effect it produces in the dancers. It's the reason I often put *ronds de jambe* into other exercises, such as *tendus*. I also often combine exercises—*frappés* with *fondus,* for instance. Probably much of what I do stems from her, but I can't say exactly. I wasn't teaching when she came, or even thinking about teaching yet. I was only a young dancer in my second year with the company. Also, a lot of her concepts came to me secondhand when Henning Kronstam and Kirsten Simone (principal dancers with the Royal Danish Ballet) came to work with us later. They were great promulgators of Volkova's methods. They taught us a lot, and we were constantly getting little bits and pieces of them saying that Volkova would do this or that."

Long was so taken with Volkova and the Danish company that he actually went to the director, Nils Bjorn Larsen, and asked if he could join. "I told him I'd give up my citizenship and become a Dane if I could only dance with the Royal Danish," remembers Long. "Of course, he told me it was totally impossible. Only years later, did the Danes begin to admit foreigners into their ranks. But, at that time, I was just completely enthralled by the technique, by the way they moved, and I think, to a large extent, by the inventiveness of the Bournonville *enchaînements,* which were very challenging to me. I've always liked the style and the way the steps are put together. I enjoy it when I can do something like that in class."

Long notes that the only *pas de deux* he ever felt truly successful dancing was Bournonville's *Flower Festival of Genzano.* "I had done both *Don Quixote* and *Nutcracker pas de deux,* but just between us, they were not my cup of tea. However, I really pride myself on the way Dolores and I did *Flower Festival.* I could jump that way. I appreciated that kind of movement and I had great success with it." He remembers thinking when he first saw the Bournonville ballets: "I could do *that;* I could never be Solor or Albrecht, but that's something I could really do." And, he told me, had the Danes taken him in, "I think I'd be speaking to you today in Danish."

Fortunately for several generations of American dancers, Long stayed in Chicago. He is, however, extremely modest about his accomplishments. As former student Catherine Yoshimura told me: "Larry was never the pushy type of teacher who needed to pat himself on the back and announce to the world, 'I am so-and-so's teacher.' I think he was just happy to be part of so many dancers' lives—and not just the ones who made it into companies like ABT, or NYCB, or San Francisco Ballet. He was proud of the folks that got into Louisville, or Des Moines, too, or who became doctors and housewives. He was interested in teaching people to be good at whatever they did. 'If you're going to do this *tendu*,' he'd always say, 'do it the best you can. Why waste it?'"

Comments such as this are typical of Long's down-to-earth approach to teaching ballet. He is fond of reminding students that "dancing is really just organized falling about. When you do something," he advises them, "you have to know where you're going to fall next. It must be premeditated; otherwise one thing doesn't prepare you for the next. You must know where you're going to fall, what you're going to fall into, and how it's going to take you to the next thing you fall into." His students are fortunate, because Long, like all great teachers, makes such movement transitions easy; his combinations, with their beautifully rhythmic and logical choreography, are exceptionally danceable.

His talent for constructing wonderful combinations is, no doubt, due largely to his innate musicality. "Music is the single most important thing to me in my class," he says. "It's what I agonize most about." Therefore, fostering musicality in his students is a major focus. "Don't go ahead of the music," he tells them. "You have to start the exercise on time and finish it on time. What you do between those two points—well, we can discuss it." He often sings to them in the pauses between repeats of an exercise in order to give them an idea of how to phrase or accent a combination. This, instead of words, makes what he wants very clear. "Don't forget the 'and-ah,'" he cautions them. "It's a very important part of the music." After a pirouette combination, he asked his students, "How many beats are there in a measure of 3/4? Three, right? So, you have to dance to all three beats, not to two. After all, waltzes are great because they give you that extra beat on the end. Use it!"

Catherine Yoshimura remembers that "he'd encourage us to study an instrument, but mostly he would 'sermonize' on the importance of our hearing the music when we danced or when we watched dance. He was so intuitively musical himself that when he saw someone who couldn't dance on the music, I think it puzzled him. But, instead of just screaming at these people, he would demand that his pianists play strong, clear rhythms so that unmusical students could try to train their ears. If that failed, after years, he would throw up his hands and make up a joke about how maybe these people 'should look into hearing aids'."

To help emphasize the rhythm and dynamics of certain exercises, Long teaches with a stick—a three-foot wooden cane with a round metal head on it. "I think of it as a percussive instrument," he says. "I use it more often than not to communicate with the pianist. And to make comments about musicality or accents to the dancers. I never poke anybody." However, he is not above smacking it loudly against the floor to snap students out of lethargy. "Mostly," he told me, "I use it upside down with the heavy end, the round brass ball, close to the floor. Like this you can get a marvelous sewing-machine kind of rhythm going. I never used a stick when I was teaching with Page's company. I think I started it when our school moved here to Dearborn Street because I found the room so big." He told me that the cane he uses today is the second one he's had. "I broke the first one. I used to throw my cane in class every once in a while. I think I thought it was romantic," he says smiling sheepishly, "like when Cecchetti threw his chair or something. It was an affectation, so I hardly ever throw it anymore. The students bought this replacement for me."

Long uses his voice in class as emphatically as his cane. He is fond of saying things in threes. "Think, think, think," he claps, halting an exercise. He also has a little ritual with threes in which he repeatedly questions students. They have learned to repeatedly answer. "That step's a what?" "*Brisé*" (softly). "A what?" "*Brisé*" (louder). "A what?" "*Brisé*!"

I asked Long what he looked for in a student. "A desire to learn," he answered. "The most talented are not always those with the most physical facility. They're the ones who want to know how and why something is done, rather than just dancing blindly, aimlessly." I asked him what he thought the requirements were for someone aiming to be a dancer. "Insanity," he joked, but quickly became serious. "Today," he stated, "there is an expectation of a certain level of physical facility without which you are unlikely to have a career in ballet." He noted that this was not always the case, particularly for young men. "The renowned Danish *premier danseur* Erik Bruhn was probably responsible for changing people's expectations of male dancers," Long added. "And believe me, he was considered suspect in many quarters because he danced at a certain technical level that was greater than the norm at the time."

To elaborate on how much the technique of ballet has changed, Long related his own experiences when he first went to New York in 1958: "I had been taught to do pirouettes with my foot up at my knee, but when I got to New York, I was told very pointedly, very directly, that men didn't turn with their foot at their knee, that that was feminine. Women turned that way. Men, they told me, turned with their foot in the middle of their calf. I was also told that it was unmasculine to dance on three-quarter *relevé*, which is where I had always danced. In New York, my teachers said men should be on a one-quarter or half-point at most. And I was told to lower my extension. I was naturally loose so my leg went up in arabesque, and I had a high *développé* to the front and the side, but I was told then that men didn't dance like that. Well, that's all changed now. Nowadays, all dancers, even men, have to possess a certain physical facility that is greater than when I started to dance—more turn-out, extension, that sort of thing. Line wasn't important for a man when I started. Nobody cared if a man could do an adagio or not. If you could do an *entrechat six,* a double *tour,* two or three pirouettes, and you could pick up the girls, you were pretty much safe. But that's not enough today."

Long regrets that now there is so much focus on the necessity of having the perfect physical instrument. Another important aspect of good dancing, he says, is often overlooked: "A certain individuality is necessary, a certain personality—so that you see more about a dancer than their physical attributes. Often, nowadays, you see dancers who are quite acclaimed and they are simply very, very good technicians, but not very interesting personalities. I think there were more personalities in the old days, primarily because you had the kind of repertoire that demanded it. Today, because of the greater physical possibilities that dancers present to choreographers, the technique has grown so fast that it has now been the focus for some considerable time. And to be a superb technician, to be able to do all these incredible things, does not necessarily require personality. So the emphasis lately in the ballet world—I'd say in the last ten years—has been on technical prowess."

Obviously, Long, who in class frequently urges his students to "add some spice" to their movement, is concerned about nurturing dancers' personalities. His student Janet Shibata recalls that Long once "asked a girl in class if she ate oatmeal. She said no. He told her to go to the corner store after class, buy a box of oatmeal, and eat the whole thing just out of the box. We all thought that sounded terrible. But he said, 'That's what you dance like, like raw oatmeal. If you want it to taste good, you have to add butter, sugar. Your dancing has to have fat, cholesterol!' And everyone started to dance more."

Long told me that he doesn't think a teacher can "develop a personality that isn't there, any more than I think you can suppress one that is. But if it's there and repressed," he believes, "you can get it out. It's like squeezing a dry orange. You can squeeze, squeeze. If there's no juice, you won't get any, but if there is some, and you squeeze hard enough, you'll eventually get some out." Long paused for a minute. "Actually," he said, "I don't think a teacher can bring personality out. The person has to be the one that realizes there's more, is aware of it, and brings it out of himself. A teacher can only make a student aware that something's lacking."

Long qualifies what he means by personality: "I'm not talking about a dancer having any great sort of personal charisma; I'm talking about personality in terms of movement, about a dancer who makes no secret about how he or she feels about movement when dancing. Baryshnikov, to me, is a dancer of great personality because, for instance, when he does *Other Dances*, he does that movement in such a unique and distinctive way that you know he understands what he feels about the music and choreography. His interpretation is unique. It's not abstracted. The way he does it is, in fact, a comment upon the music. Conversely, he does something like *Push Comes to Shove*—which would be very easy movement to kind of lose oneself in and not, in fact, say anything at all, just stick to the counts, get through it, and it's over—but Mischa always comments on what he does. It's never totally and completely abstracted, devoid of thought. Dancing is in fact *how* you get from point A to point B. It's much more than just making it through."

Never, when Long teaches, does he forget that he is teaching people to be performing artists. "You know," he chides them, "there has to be something going on above your neckline, too." He begs students not to glue their eyes to the mirror. "Please do me a favor," he pleads, "and do that whole *grand allegro* combination without looking in the mirror once—and don't look down! I guarantee you won't disappear from the face of the earth. Also, look where you're going every once in a while. That's always a good idea." He told me that he tells his dancers to look anywhere except in the mirror "because with some of them I get the feeling that they think if they took their eyes off the mirror, it would be like the Twilight Zone, they'd cease to exist or something. Their only reality is when they can see themselves in the mirror." He sounds exasperated.

Larry Long helping a young girl place her arabesque correctly at the barre during pointe class.

If students move in a matter-of-fact, unphrased way, Long tells them their dancing is "downright upright"—one of his favorite phrases, culled from something he once read. "I try to get them to make their dancing more interesting," he says, "not so square and boring. They can do whatever they want as long as they make it interesting, *à la* Bolshoi, *à la* whatever. But don't do it without accents, head, dynamics." Many of his exercises seem designed to challenge students' awareness of the variety of interpretive possibilities within a single combination. For example, in one class he gave a first allegro exercise that consisted of four *changements* followed by a *tombé, pas de bourrée, chassé* into an arabesque pose *à terre*. He pointed out that while the *changements* could be rather "square," the *pas de bourrée* to the pose needed to contrast them by being "more romantic."

Without doubt, one of Long's greatest talents as a teacher is his gift for making perfect analogies. The entire class smiled in recognition one day when he turned to a dancer who had just landed quite out of control, with a great thud, from a *grand jeté* and said: "Please don't collapse in on yourself like an old Halloween pumpkin—you know how they begin to fall in on themselves? Don't let your fangs droop!" His student Janet Shibata comments: "What his analogies do first is make you think. Then, you apply them to your own body. Then, in the end, they make you laugh at yourself. You laugh if you try something, it doesn't work, and you realize he's 'right on.' Or you laugh at the fact that, yeah, it could look the way he's described it and it shouldn't! So, no matter how you look at it, his analogies make your approach positive, not negative."

Long's wife, Dolores, says her husband often compares dancing and steps to food. "Dancers in class used to come up to me and ask whether or not I'd fed him," she laughs. I was amused one day to see him poke the rather unpulled-up thigh of a young lady and remark, "There should be some semblance of firmness there, dear. I shouldn't be able to stick my finger in like brie." But Long's knack for witty, perceptive analogies probably has less to do with food fantasies and more with the fact that he's an avid reader. "I used to read a lot of biography," he told me, "although novels hardly at all. I like politics and history—mainly nonfiction, though on vacation I read mysteries. I don't read for inspiration. I just do it because I'm an inveterate reader. I love it." He says certain books have made a great impression on him. "As a young man," he recalls, "I read *Atlas Shrugged* and *The Fountainhead*. I remember thinking a lot about the concept of selfishness not being negative. I liked *The Dance of Life*. I don't read self-help books. I'm not really an introspective person at all. I'm pretty much what-you-see-is-what-you-get. No hidden depths to my personality. For better or for worse. If I think, I do so intuitively. My analogies in class probably do come from my reading. If I hadn't been a dancer, I probably would have liked to have been a writer. Mostly because I like books. I would have liked to have been someone who made a book. I think that's tremendously impressive."

I admired the very clean and logical construction of Long's classes. Nothing ever seemed rushed, although the class was chock-full of challenging material. "Something I learned when I first started to teach is that you can't get it all in, in one class," he told me. "Nobody can make a dancer in one class. So I think about teaching someone about dancing over a number of years. It used to bother me if I didn't get to this exercise or that, or a student didn't seem to learn in a class—that is, she wasn't better at the end of the hour-and-a-half than she was at the beginning. It bothered me a lot! I felt so inadequate. I used to worry if I didn't do every beat there was to give, or *grandes pirouettes* in every class. There are wonderful teachers who actually do that. It's very intimidating, but I've stopped worrying about that.

And, if I find I've neglected to do something in class, I'll make a conscious effort to correct that."

The other thing he's learned, Long told me, concerns his relationship with students in class. "I've had to accept that I'm one person with forty students in a class," he says, "and that I can't change myself for each one of those people. I have to understand, and they have to understand, that they have to adjust to me, because then it's one on one. If I adjust, it's one on forty, and I can't be forty different people in a class." I asked Long if he ever encountered problems with students. "If I have problems with a student, I don't anguish about it," he told me in his typically matter-of-fact way. "If it becomes really protracted, I will have a talk with that student and try to discover what the problem is. I may suggest that maybe I'm not the right teacher for him or her. Which brings me to the third thing I've learned: You can't be the proper teacher for everyone. It's not possible. No matter how much you'd like to. I'm sure there are people who come to me and leave saying, 'Gee whiz, I think he's terrible and I'm going to go someplace where I can get good training,' or, 'I can't work with him.' And when you're a young teacher that does make you feel bad."

It is hard to imagine that Long would ever have a problem with any student. His honest, committed, humorous style creates an open, comfortable atmosphere in the classroom—one in which students are never afraid to converse with him. One day, he stopped to work with a young man on the preparatory position in 5th before a double *tour*. "Don't *plié* and twist your rump around so I can read the label on the back of your tights," Long joked. The boy, grinning, offered to tuck the label under. "Either that," Long replied dryly, "or change it so that I can read something more interesting than 'Danskin, Size C.'"

Some of his studio commentary is directed toward the entire class, some toward individual students. It can be encouraging: "Well, it was better, Jordan. At least I saw the effort. You get 'A' for effort." Or, if called for, much more pointed: "You're like an editor, George. You do one step 'cause you like it and then kind of *change*, not quite *do*, the next one." Sometimes, he is downright enthusiastic. "Sheila, beautiful! Bouncy!—that's what *ballon* is all about," he called out one day during a *grand allegro*. As Long obviously knows, most corrections are much easier to swallow when seasoned with humor. At this, he is an artist: "Oh, galoshes, galoshes," he moans, looking at the students' flopping feet in *pointe* class. "It looks like your *pointe* shoes were made by L. L. Bean!"

Given the breadth of ballet vocabulary at the advanced level, Long must make daily choices about what to include and what to omit in each lesson. "But," he told me, "I never leave out inside and outside pirouettes. I never leave out a good introduction to jumping, something easy, not too fast. And I try never to leave out *grand allegro*. It's very important for both boys and girls to really jump around. It's often slid over in girls' training. Emphasis for them today seems to be on adagio, which I will skip sometimes, though my barre always has adagio elements." He makes sure that he includes, on a regular basis, certain *grandes pirouettes* like those in *attitude* or arabesque.

There's a free, easy, open quality to Long's combinations in class. His movement never seems like drill, although—cleverly disguised—it often is. He is fond of inserting hidden challenges into what initially might seem like a simple exercise: four *changements,* for instance, followed by a fast *développé relevé* that must be momentarily sustained at full height, before moving on to the next step. All his movement seems to flow very naturally. Never are his exercises dry or awkward. Rhythmic and dynamic contrasts abound. "What you're doing is fine," he tells a student. "It's the *way* you're doing it that needs fixing. Make those *tendus* sharper than the *glissade* and *chassé.*" There are constant cautions from him about making a step too big, or too small, and, therefore, out of size within the design of an *enchaînement.* "Movement, as opposed to just a bunch of steps, sometimes means that some steps need to be understated rather than overstated," he wisely tells the dancers.

Long often demonstrates to make his point. He is an inspiring sight— beautifully light on his feet and the epitome of masculine grace. He can move big and fast. His feet, clad in well-worn jazz shoes, are always impeccably pointed and turned out. His *port de bras* is free and relaxed-looking. Not one mannerism surfaces in anything he does, and he is extremely articulate when showing exercises. The way he pulls his whole body up off his hips is a perfect example of lifted placement. Showing *dégagés* at the barre, his leg action is effortless—the in and out are both light as air. "Small, juicy," he tells students. *This,* I thought, watching, is preparation for *petit allegro!*

Long wears comfortable jazz pants and a polo shirt in which to teach— nothing fancy. Knowing a picture is worth a thousand words, he does not hesitate to distort his body, silently chiding students by demonstrating an awful, sway-backed stance to get his point across. During the centre work, he most often perches, straight-backed, on a high stool in front of the mirror. His legs hang turned-out over the sides, feet dangling, while his arms do the *port de bras* along with his students.

He is adamant about motivating the movement of the arms from the center of the body out, rather than from the fingertips in. The use of his arms as he demonstrates, moving through several positions, is very specific. "Round," he will correct a student with awkward-looking arms, "not big, but shapely." To another, whose elbow has dropped in 2nd position, he says: "Don't catch water in your elbow." When they begin allegro work, he reminds the dancers of his rule about *port de bras* in jumps: "The arms lead on the ascent, follow on the descent." When the students' *port de bras* is not exactly what he has set, he remarks with a smile: "Well, a lot of what you're doing with your arms is nice. I like it almost as much as what you're *supposed* to be doing with them."

Long's barre has a rolling, organic quality to it, especially in the beginning as he eases students toward the sharper, faster movements that will follow. He starts with *pliés* in 2nd position, after which he often includes a *cambré* forward and back with the feet parallel rather than turned-out. (This is an excellent warm-up stretch for the back of the legs.) Following are *pliés* in 1st and 5th positions. He is fond of reminding students that "*Plié* is not a place—it's a movement. Don't make it geographic." He told me that when he was young, he had always felt frustrated when his teachers told him to resist going down in *plié*, as well as coming up. "None of that stuff about dynamic tension makes sense to me," he says. "I don't understand where that's all coming from. When you go into a *plié*, you want to control it enough so that you can control the speed, fast or slow. But I don't see any point in resisting going down when the whole point is to go down and stretch. Then when you come up, just come up. Don't be so analytical about it!"

He cautions students about this same kind of overly analytical approach to *tendus*. "Don't get religious about it," he tells them. "It's an exercise, just do it." In no way, though, is he advocating a lack of precision. "Messy, messy, messy," he'll say if he isn't satisfied. "We'll call that practice." He wants *tendus* to be cleanly articulated both physically and rhythmically. "Place that foot like it's precious," he says. It is characteristic of him to give *battements* with many changes in tempo—in four counts, two counts, and one count—within the same exercise. For instance, he might give four *dégagés* in one count each, followed by one that is drawn out over four counts. He is uncompromising about how the leg closes: "5th position is 5th position," he states. "It's not on or about 5th position!" And for Long, dance is not only technical precision, it's also conversation. "Don't just shake your legs in *petit battement*," he directs students. "Be articulate. You have to talk with them. Don't mumble. Your feet have to be like a percussive instrument!"

At the barre, Long commonly alternates bending and straightening the supporting leg within each exercise. For instance, an exercise might include a *passé* on a straight supporting leg, followed by a *développé plié*, followed by a *demi-rond* straightening. This alternation, of course, is not only good for warming up, but also forces students constantly to readjust their placement, just as they must do dancing in the centre, moving up and down, and changing from one foot to the other. Long finds himself continually reminding students "to *plié* on your bones." He explains, "What I mean by that is: Don't let your muscles carry your weight. Let your skeleton carry your weight so that one bone is placed on top of another." He often reminds students that their necks are part of their spines. When a student tilts to the side in a *relevé arabesque*, he stops the class: "No, no," he chides. "Don't ever do that. You've got to go up in that *relevé* square. If you're all tilted over to the supporting side like that, your body is confused. It's like living on a hillside all your life. You never feel level."

Long is particularly careful about placement in extension. "My young dancers all the time come into class, go down on the floor, and pull their foot behind their ear," he told me ruefully. "They do all these sorts of contortions, none of which are directly applicable to what they're going to be doing at the barre—because in none of those things do they make any effort to maintain a parallel line through the hips, from one hip to the other." He admits that he likes high extension, but not if it means sacrificing placement. As he told a young lady overindulging herself one day in the height of her extension: "Be careful when you're feeling good. You might just be doing the worst thing for yourself." Reflecting both his good taste and his common sense, Long is fond of telling students to hold their legs "not high, but perfect!" And, lest they forget what is holding them up, he reminds them: "Shape your supporting leg well, too!"

"Most of the time," Long told me, "I let dancers take their legs high in *fondus*, almost like an adagio." In essence, Long's *fondu* exercise, which comes after *frappés*, is his adagio at the barre. Only occasionally does he give a separate adagio exercise, and usually it's as much a *port de bras* as an adagio. "Extension is a very personal thing with me," he remarks. "When I was young, I had the ability to do high extension, and I liked it because I could do it. So I understand when a lot of dancers, particularly nowadays, like to do it because they can." He continues: "Sometimes today, it's a bit of a battle to get dancers to keep their legs down. It's as big a battle as it was in the old days to get 'em up." Placement, as well as height, during extension is obviously foremost in Long's mind. I watched him correcting a student in *développé à la seconde.* He restrained the young man from pushing his thigh back. "It's not *where* the leg is in space, the geography, that makes 2nd," he told him. "It's the rotation of the leg in the hip!"

Long urges students to be equally careful about placement in turns. "Not in segments like a grapefruit—all in one piece," he tells a student whose body parts seem to go in many directions during a pirouette. He wants students to concentrate on getting to a pose and holding it when turning and cautions them about the use of excessive force. "You're taking the whole world around with you in that turn," he told one young man who did an exaggerated *rond de jambe* into a pirouette *en dedans.* "I just want two turns in *passé.* Not a half-turn in *attitude* front, a half swiveling into *passé,* and a turn falling out of it!" When a more timid student, at the other extreme, barely managed to turn at all, Long urged her, "Go for it. If you don't make it, you don't make it. It's a class. But give it a shot at what it's supposed to be." One day, Long offered the men in class one of his personal solutions to a common problem with double *tours en l'air:* "I never thought about taking just one foot—the front one—to the back," he told them. "I thought of both legs changing simultaneously—the back one coming front, as well."

One of the best aspects of Long's class is the allegro work. He encourages his students to be fearless, to eat up space. "Feel extroverted in that jump," he tells them during a *grand allegro.* Stylistically, his *enchaînements* are closest to Bournonville's, with a loping quality and as much emphasis on the *plié* as on the ascent. He wants the feet beautifully presented. If the girls are wearing *pointe* shoes during jumping exercises, he reminds them that "you've got your satin boots on, so you have to use your feet the way you do in *pointe* dancing." He differentiates between various types of jumping. After a fast *terre à terre* combination with a series of tiny *petits jetés* in it, during which he wanted the focus to be on the feet, he corrected the dancers: "Still too much action in the hips!" Usually, however, he wants the body to be very much involved in jumping. "Some jumps are done just with the feet," he says, "but on most you have to jump with more than your feet—meaning the big muscles of the legs and buttocks—you have to really thrust yourself up there. Otherwise, it's just ghastly, both to do and to watch." In one class,

Long approached a girl after a *sissonne* exercise: "Well, Heidi," he remarked, "you're going up without jumping. That's amazing! We'll have to get *The National Enquirer* of ballet in here." She giggled. He put his hands on the back of her head, under her ears, and lifted her as she repeated a *sissonne*. They did it three times. "Well," he told her, "isn't it a rarefied atmosphere up there? You could get heady. You could learn to love it!"

Long often asks students to reverse combinations in class. Knowing how they dread this process, he is not above teasing them a bit. One day he gave an exercise that consisted of three jumps in 1st position, followed by two *échappés sautés* to 2nd and two *changements*. After the students did it once, he commanded, "Reverse it!" He paused devilishly, enjoying the momentary panic on their faces. "Anyone figured anything out yet?" he asked. Then, as relief spread across their faces with the realization that it is impossible to reverse this exercise, he smiled at them paternally, saying, "You never want to panic when someone says, 'Reverse it.'"

With an eye toward flow and coordination, Long carefully coaches students about transitions. He stopped a *sissonne simple, assemblé* exercise one day in order to emphasize the coordination and timing of the foot action between the two steps. "You must lower the foot from *cou-de-pied devant* down to brush out *as* the jump is descending," he told the dancers. "If you do it after you're down, it makes the transition to the *assemblé* jerky."

He made his point about students' lack of elevation in *grands jetés* in a less academic manner. Climbing off his stool, he did two great, floppy *grands battements devant*, the first with the right leg, the second with the left. Each hit the floor with a large splat. "A *grand jeté* without two legs off the floor," he told the class, "is just a big walk."

In addition to his popular open professional-level class every morning, Long also teaches another advanced or *pointe* class in the afternoon. Amazingly, he is an excellent *pointe* teacher, a talent rare in a man. (Traditionally, men in ballet do not dance on *pointe;* therefore, male teachers seldom have a good understanding of the intricacies of this particular area of ballet technique.) His combinations stress perfect articulation of the foot as it steps onto *pointe*. "Now, a significant movement!" he directs as the ladies do a sharp, low *petit développé* before a *piqué*. His *pointe* barre consists of fifteen exercises, each one dealing with a different aspect of *pointe* dancing, whether it be fast *relevé*, soft, controlled lowering through the foot, or balance on *pointe*. Most of these exercises are quite short and, therefore, easily repeated four or eight times. As usual, he has fun with the students. "Don't give me that monster-married-the-ballerina look in those walks," he exclaims, demonstrating a series of stiff-legged *emboîté* walks coming forward on *relevé* with his body lurching rigidly from side to side. "And remember," he adds, "you have to do these in a straight line, one foot replacing another, just like a drunk test!"

Clearly, Long—with his fine sense of humor, exceptional musicality, and sharp eye for detail—is a teacher of the highest caliber, so I was curious to know what he felt were the most essential ingredients for a good ballet teacher. He thought a while, then answered: "I don't think exercises or the structure of the barre make a good teacher. Naturally, a good teacher combines all these things, but the most important thing, I think, is that he is willing to learn as he's teaching, that he's willing to give and is committed. I've known so many good teachers who can't count 8's, or who don't put their exercises in phrases, or who don't do the same thing on both sides. But the best teachers are inspirers. All the rest is like frosting. It's the most important quality. A good teacher inspires people to believe that they're capable of doing more, as well as giving them the confidence to try doing something a different way, to go that extra step further, try harder. And part of inspiration is making people think in a way that they might not on their own—consider things like music, phraseology, and timing. The truth is that dance *is* an art form. And as hackneyed and perhaps embarrassing as it is to say, part of being an inspiring teacher is being an artist and helping other people to appreciate something like dancing in terms of art rather than in terms of just plain physicality, aptitude, talent, and facility." His former student Amy Rose, who went on to become a soloist with American Ballet Theatre and, later, Pacific Northwest Ballet, gratefully remembers Long doing just that: "His booming, singing voice and the rhythmic tapping of his ever-present cane scared and inspired me to great heights. He was always showing you that you could do more, move more, jump higher. And I never had to learn to perform because his classes were so wonderful that you enjoyed them, you *felt* the dance and so, in fact, you were already performing in your soul, not just plastering a smile on your face. Even now, as a seasoned professional who has studied with many great and famous teachers, I still find his classes the most difficult and always the most inspiring."

Classroom Quotes from Long

"Dancing should feel alive—at least aerobic. Don't dance like a ghost of yourself."

To a young man after a *grand jeté* exercise: "Ballet is not ladylike. You've got to get your legs open. And if you've got scruples about that sort of thing, then you're in the wrong business."

"*Petit allegro* is like petit point, not like macramé."

"*Pointe* dancing is not just what you do up there. It's how you get up and how you get down. You can get the right pair of shoes and the right ten toes and go across the country, but that's not *pointe* dancing. The hallmark of *pointe* is lightness. You don't want to haul yourself up there like you have a rock on your foot. It should be like gossamer."

"Don't think you'll get more out of your body by bashing yourself about. It's so mean, and it hurts. It hurts to watch! Be gentle but insistent. Be kind to your body."

"When you do *échappés sautés,* the most beautiful thing is to see you way up there in the air in 2nd position. It's like God sitting on a cloud. The legs like two arrows pointing straight down."

"*Plié* is a whole body exercise—not just the legs."

"You have to express three times as much when you have your back to the audience. When you're facing downstage, you can express something with just the arch of an eyebrow, but upstage you have to use your whole body to show me something."

"Bloody determination. It's good to have, but bad to show."

"Dance without *épaulement* is like food without any seasoning—no salt, no garlic, no sage. It's like plain boiled rice. It's got to have some curry!"

Order of the Exercises in Long's Class
(advanced class, 1½ hours)

BARRE

1. Demi-pliés, grands pliés, cambrés, and rises
2. Slow tendus with demi-pliés in 4th and 2nd positions and temps liés
3. Tendus in 3/4 time with demi-ronds
4. Faster tendus
5. Dégagés (tendus jetés)
6. Dégagés en cloche with fondus
7. Ronds de jambe à terre
8. Frappés
9. Développés with fondus and cambrés holding the leg at 90 degrees
10. Quick fondus relevés at 120 degrees
11. Ronds de jambe en l'air
12. Grands battements
13. Petits battements

CENTRE

1. Ports de bras
2. Tendus and pirouettes en dehors
3. Dégagés (tendus jetés) with small jumps and pirouettes en dedans
4. Petit allegro with changements, cabrioles, assemblés, petits jetés, chaînés, and piqué turns en dehors
5. Petit allegro with ronds de jambe en l'air sautés and petits jetés battus
6. Grand allegro with entrechats sixes, grands jetés développés, grands jetés à la seconde, six de volé, and pirouettes (tour en l'air for the men)

The Roots of Tradition

THE PEDAGOGICAL LINEAGE OF LARRY LONG

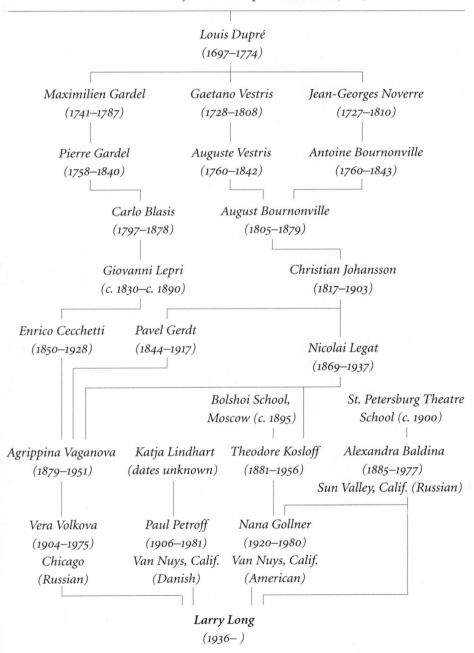

L'Académie Royale de Musique et de Danse (1661)

Louis Dupré
(1697–1774)

Maximilien Gardel
(1741–1787)

Gaetano Vestris
(1728–1808)

Jean-Georges Noverre
(1727–1810)

Pierre Gardel
(1758–1840)

Auguste Vestris
(1760–1842)

Antoine Bournonville
(1760–1843)

Carlo Blasis
(1797–1878)

August Bournonville
(1805–1879)

Giovanni Lepri
(c. 1830–c. 1890)

Christian Johansson
(1817–1903)

Enrico Cecchetti
(1850–1928)

Pavel Gerdt
(1844–1917)

Nicolai Legat
(1869–1937)

Bolshoi School,
Moscow (c. 1895)

St. Petersburg Theatre
School (c. 1900)

Agrippina Vaganova
(1879–1951)

Katja Lindhart
(dates unknown)

Theodore Kosloff
(1881–1956)

Alexandra Baldina
(1885–1977)
Sun Valley, Calif. (Russian)

Vera Volkova
(1904–1975)
Chicago
(Russian)

Paul Petroff
(1906–1981)
Van Nuys, Calif.
(Danish)

Nana Gollner
(1920–1980)
Van Nuys, Calif.
(American)

Larry Long
(1936–)

7 *Larisa Sklyanskaya*

Larisa Sklyanskaya looking into the mirror as she shows young students how to hold their legs at a Russian ballet seminar in Tampa, Florida, in 1990.

$\mathcal{L}$arisa Sklyanskaya was born and trained in Tallinn, Estonia, on the Baltic Sea. She danced as soloist with the Estonian Ballet from 1962 to 1967, then departed to join Moscow's Bolshoi Ballet, with whom she danced for fifteen years. In 1982, she left the Soviet Union to emigrate to America, settling in San Francisco. In 1986, Helgi Tomasson invited her to join the faculty of the San Francisco Ballet School, where she taught upper-division men's and women's classes until 1995. Currently, she guest-teaches across North America and is well known for her expertise in staging the classics.

I first observed Sklyanskaya at work when she staged *Giselle* for the Tampa Ballet in Florida in 1989. Watching her coach the dancers, I was immediately impressed by her exquisite attention to artistic detail. In 1990, I went to San Francisco and spent three weeks observing her classes and talking to her about teaching. I discovered, much to my delight, that Sklyanskaya had been a student of the great Bolshoi Ballet teacher Marina Semyonova, whom I had hoped to interview for this book. Unfortunately, I was unable to do so, because Semyonova, now in her eighties, was not well. However, I was pleased to be able to incorporate into this chapter much about Semyonova as remembered by Sklyanskaya.

"Good technique must be very solid and absolutely nonchalant."

"As a child," Sklyanskaya told me, "I was listening to music from my cradle." Her mother was a second violinist in the Tallinn Symphony, and Sklyanskaya remembers her "practicing all the time—music poured into my ears!" Today, the development of musicality is an area she constantly stresses with her students. She tells them that, for her, watching a dancer who is off (i.e., not listening to) the music is "as painful as having a tooth pulled without anesthesia!" She is sorry that many of them did not have childhoods filled with good music, as hers was. "When music comes with your first sounds, with speech, you develop a love and understanding of it—just to the melody—without knowing who wrote what. That comes later," she says.

In such an atmosphere, she might have become a musician had she not been taken to a ballet performance at the age of four. Her mother recalled that her young daughter came home, stretched her hands up to grip the edge of a table, pulled herself onto the tips of her toes and announced, "I am going to be a dancer." Her mother immediately had an attack of déjà vu. She recalled that as a baby Sklyanskaya had repeatedly kicked the blankets off her legs, and that a neighbor, who was a "settled gypsy," had, after observing this trait, prophetically remarked: "Hah! A ballet dancer!"

During her childhood, Sklyanskaya's parents continued to take her to the ballet. Inspired, she began to move instinctively whenever she heard music. Soon, her balletic improvisations at family musicales had so impressed her parents' neighbors that they decided the budding ballerina must be seen by a teacher from the local ballet school. An impromptu audition was arranged in their living room. "No one had taught me any ballet," Sklyanskaya recalls, "but I probably memorized something I'd seen onstage. Our neighbors played some music that I loved, and I just moved without being afraid or ashamed. When I finished, I remember I used the Dying Swan movement, with the hand finishing on the last note. Afterward the ballet teacher called me over and whispered in my ear, 'Listen, girl, I promise not to tell anybody, but can you tell me who taught you this dance?' Well, of course, I couldn't because no one had taught me. Probably, it was not even a dance, just a number of movements."

As the neighbors had predicted, the teacher was sufficiently impressed to arrange a formal audition for the seven-year-old at the Tallinn ballet school. Officially, Sklyanskaya was too young to be enrolled. However, upon seeing the child dance, the faculty decided to make an exception. Thus began what Sklyanskaya describes as "difficult, but golden years."

She recalls: "I was living at home. The first part of the day, I studied in the public school, where they didn't want to know of the ballet school's existence! Later in the day, I went to the ballet school, where I studied a completely different set of subjects. (In Estonia, the curriculum in the state ballet schools included many theoretical courses concerning art and music, but did not provide classes in regular academic subjects.) Sklyanskaya recalls that from her fourth year on, she was onstage almost every night: "It was tough, believe me!" However, she admits that she and her fellow ballet students were fanatics about their chosen art form. "We collected money and instead of buying even ice cream (can you imagine?), we saved kopeks to buy photos of dancers. We had all possible books about ballet. My father frequently went to other cities like Moscow and brought me everything on dance he could find. We read. We studied poses in old photos and copied them. Every single free moment, we devoted to that. Like crazy!"

Emmanuel Lurye, a former pianist at the Tallinn Ballet School now living in Los Angeles, remembers the young Sklyanskaya well: "There is an old Latin saying: 'Ubi bene, ibi Patria,'" he told me. "For Larisa, I would change it to: 'Ubi danza, ibi bene.' (There, where there is dance, is the best.) I remember that whenever she and I were both free and a studio was available, Larisa, blushing and apologizing, would ask me to come play for her. I always agreed because it gave me pleasure to watch how she improvised to my music. She was especially good in jumps. (She had the best jump in the school.) I remember one of the big school parties when everybody came—students, teachers, parents. The Big Hall was beautifully decorated and gifts had been prepared for the students. The young ones simply received them, but the more advanced students had to 'earn' them. The gifts were hung on ribbons and attached lightly at different levels on two walls. Students had to try to reach the prizes by jumping—the higher the gift, the better the prize. Well, when it came to Larisa, she made such a *jeté* that she got the best gift. Everybody applauded."

Sklyanskaya remembers much more than the joy of jumping from her student days. "We had a wide range of wonderful subjects at the Tallinn school," she recalls. "In Level 1, for a whole year we had eurythmics. I believe this was invaluable to me and that it is a terrible missing link in the development of musicality in dancers today. We did it a whole year and loved it—no positions, no exercises. We were given ropes and tennis balls and, while the music played, we had to throw balls to each other exactly on the music. The same with jumping rope. Everything had to be right on the music, though you could create your own rhythmic variations. And when you finished the whole year, even if you were deaf, something had been wakened in you."

In the years that followed, she studied historical dance, character, *pas de deux*, variations, stage makeup, painting, sculpture, piano, and music history and appreciation. She remembers that in the end-of-year examinations in front of a jury, their music teacher would play a few chords, and they would have to identify the piece of music and the composer. "It really developed our ears," she says.

Her curriculum also included theater and dance history—"both of which we learned beginning from the times of the Greeks!" she remembers. However, of utmost importance to her artistic development, she feels, was the course titled Acting in Dance. "It was difficult," she remembers, "because as teenagers we were like clam shells. It was necessary to open us. Fortunately, the teacher was wonderful." The class had nothing to do with old-fashioned mime, which, Sklyanskaya recalls, had by that time been abandoned in Soviet ballet in favor of a freer, more naturalistic mode of expression. "I remember one class," she says, "in which this teacher chose a Rachmaninoff 'Romance' to accompany us. She gave us a theme from *Eugene Onegin*, but she developed the plot further than is done in the original poem. She asked us to imagine Tatiana already married and with kids, but her love for Onegin has never died. Upon hearing of his recent death, she rushes to his home in the countryside, where she has never been, and storms into his study. We were asked to show by our appearance that we had been running, that our breathing had been stopped by both exertion and emotion. Then, we were directed to calm down and move around in this place where the man we had loved had lived. She gave us a few connecting dance movements so that we would not choreograph, but everything else, all our acting, we had to create ourselves." Sklyanskaya remembers that it was a big challenge, but "after you go through that subject, you learn so much about how to make your feelings visible in your movement—not in the empty, dance-like, decorative manner of pantomime—but in such a way that your dance becomes speech."

Today, in this country, Sklyanskaya worries about her students' lack of ability to act with their bodies. She is frustrated because they do not have the advantage of outside acting classes, and laments that she must try to find time within her technique classes to explore this subject. "Of course," she says, "there is *never* enough time!" But she constantly reminds her students of this integral aspect of dancing. "I don't like dancers who just stick their legs way up in the air," she will say to her class. "Personally, it doesn't impress me. You must be expressive with your body and make me see what your ears hear and your heart feels." One day she chided a student who had neglected to use her eyes appropriately: "Do you understand? Your body is your tongue. You're going onstage to talk. You can say a lot with a tiny gesture, so you must be aware of every little movement you make."

Sklyanskaya's training in Estonia also included many opportunities to perform. For this, she is grateful. "When you are onstage from such an early age," she says, "the stage becomes your home. It's a very important thing to go through. I believe the reason I never had stage fright was because while I was still a student, the stage became such a familiar place for me. I was occasionally very nervous backstage, but once I put a foot onstage, it was always as if I stepped into my own room and no one was around."

She also stresses how fortunate she was as a young performer to have worked alongside experienced senior artists. "In those times in Estonia, the dancers of two generations before us still performed on our stage. They may not have been very strong as technicians—we kids, fresh from the ballet school, were stronger—but their artistic ability, their belief in what they were doing onstage, was both great and contagious. So we grew among artists who taught us that the stage is life, not puppetry. Today it sounds outdated and sentimental that, for instance, in *Esmeralda*, when Esmeralda is taken to the guillotine, all the dancers onstage cried, really cried—but we learned about real feelings from these older artists. They were our inspiration. They taught us a lot. We never made jokes onstage. It was unheard of! It was a sacred place." Sklyanskaya is saddened when she sees how many companies today (even her beloved Bolshoi, she says) seem to have lost a commitment to this kind of dramatic intensity. "Technique," she says, "can come and go—a little bit stronger or weaker (stronger is better, of course!)—but if dancers don't have artistic goals, why do they go onstage? And I'm not necessarily talking about dramatic ballets. One can dance without a special theme, but one never dances nothing. You always dance something, some mood, some feeling, and not just empty, simple movements strung together."

Sklyanskaya was taken into the Estonian Ballet company early, while she was still in her seventh or eighth year in the school. (At that time, the school had a nine-year program. Later, it was cut to eight years. "It's too bad," she believes, "because the ninth year was really vital. It provided you with the opportunity to refine everything you'd learned in the eight previous years.") Once she graduated, she rose quickly through the ranks, dancing both soloist and principal roles. Myrta in *Giselle* was one of her favorites, no doubt because of her extraordinary abilities as a jumper. She remembers: "I had a wonderful coach, Nina Ulanova,[1] from Leningrad (our school and company maintained close ties to the Kirov). She was a very knowledgeable, intellectual lady who taught very good classes. Without her highly professional eye, I would never have been able to accomplish what I did in the Estonian Ballet. Ulanova explained to me what a critical role Myrta was in *Giselle*, Act II. And, when I heard I was going to learn it, I did one of those silly things you do only when you're young. I went at midnight to the cemetery—a village cemetery by the seashore, with the wind in the pine trees and the squeaking old gate. There was a little church with a shape full of shadows, and I went in and there was a sculpture in black marble. Well, you know, it was not very comfortable, and I started to dance Myrta's steps among the graves, mostly to calm my fears because I'm very afraid of darkness. Well, the more I was jumping, the more I started to feel that a strange wave was coming from my heels up. It was a cold, terrible fear, and the more I felt it, the wilder I danced. When the sensation reached my hair, I could no longer stand it, and I jumped over the fence and ran home. But it helped!" She smiles at the recollection.

As a footnote to our discussion of *Giselle*, Sklyanskaya remarked to me that it was only logical that the ballet was conceived during that period in history (1840s), when many people strongly believed that the spiritual world was just a continuation or extension of life. Performers today, she feels, need to understand such things about this ballet in order to know how to dance it. When she coaches a new Giselle, she compares the hopping spins in arabesque in the beginning of Act II to the spiraling journey towards a bright light described by people who have near-death experiences. "You see," she says, "Giselle's spins are a spiral swirling her into the next life."

During 1968, after five years with the Estonian company, Sklyanskaya suffered a problem with a pinched nerve in her foot. She was sent for treatment to the doctors at the Bolshoi Theater in Moscow. Because she was a soloist from another company, she was permitted to take classes at the Bolshoi while she was undergoing rehabilitation. As it happened, she was not completely unknown to the Bolshoi's artistic director, Yuri Grigorovich; she had worked with him when he had staged his ballet *Stone Flower* in Estonia. She had also captured his attention the year before when she had performed well in a choreography competition in Moscow.

One day, one of the teachers at the Bolshoi asked her why she didn't go to Grigorovich and ask for a position in the company. Sklyanskaya was shocked. It had never occurred to her that this was even a possibility. "In Estonia, we thought of the Bolshoi as a Mount Olympus, a place untouchable for us. Everyone there was on the level of gods in our minds," she recalls with amusement. Initially, she brushed aside the suggestion, but the teacher was persistent. She had heard there was going to be an opening in the company soon. She kept pushing Sklyanskaya to approach Grigorovich. Finally, Sklyanskaya found the courage to do so—after all, she decided, no one would know of her shame if he refused to consider her. Much to her surprise, he agreed to audition her, even setting the following Monday, the company's day off, as the date. Unfortunately, on that exact day, news of Leonid Lavrovsky's (see p. 364, n. 2) death reached Moscow, and Sklyanskaya went to the audition feeling that the timing was hardly opportune. But Grigorovich arrived as scheduled, gave her a short barre, a little centre work, and then, she remembers, "I began to jump like crazy from fear and a strange mixture of feelings." She had always been blessed with very high, natural elevation. (Even today, Sklyanskaya occasionally demonstrates a double *tour en l'air* in a men's class—a feat that always guarantees her instant attention from her young male students!) Grigorovich was obviously impressed with her jumps, as well as with her *fouettés,* which she says she always did better to the left and without arms! "It looks tricky," she shrugs, "but, for me, it was always easier." Then she showed him the difficult bird's solo from *The Little Humpbacked Horse.* She says she found herself speechless when "just like that he said, 'Well, I'd like you in my company.'" He explained that there was only one contract available, a corps de ballet position, but he promised her that if she took it, "she would not regret it." She remembers that the next day he showed up and watched the entire class she was taking. "They were shocked in Estonia when I told them I was leaving," she recalls, "because I had such a good position in the Tallinn company, but I was ambitious and anxious to grab this opportunity to perform with the great Bolshoi Ballet."

In the beginning at the Bolshoi, things looked promising. She was given a soloist coach and did a few outside concerts with other Bolshoi dancers. However, she was not cast in any of the company's main repertoire. "In a company of three hundred dancers, if you did not go bang on the door and request roles, you were easily overlooked," she says. "I did not know how to do that. I could never speak for myself, though I was always outspoken about others and about certain ideas. So, in effect, I got lost." She hardly danced for months, became depressed, and gained weight. Life was especially hard because she was trying to save money for an apartment, a difficult and expensive thing to acquire in Moscow. Short of funds, she remembers subsisting for months on nothing but black bread, sugar, and boiled tap water. "It was hardly," she says, "a diet for someone with a weight problem." Finally, she was assigned to corps de ballet roles. It was like a death sentence as far as her artistic hopes were concerned. "Once you're in the corps of the Bolshoi," she says sardonically, "just *try* to get out!" She remembers how difficult it was, after "tasting the joy of creativity" earlier in her career, to have to "put chains on my capabilities and the opportunity to develop as an individual artist." However, she got herself back into shape ("slender like a herring—just bones!"), and little by little began to be given more visible roles. She performed internationally with the company from 1969 to 1982, including tours to London in 1974 and New York in 1975.

During her years with the Bolshoi, Sklyanskaya had the opportunity to work with many different teachers, one of whom, Marina Semyonova (see p. 365, n. 5), eventually became her guiding light. She began, however, with Yelisaveta Gerdt,[2] a reserved personality whose class she describes as "painfully slow and academic." Sklyanskaya recalls: "Gerdt had been a beautiful dancer in her time and became a marvelous, renowned teacher. Although she was quite elderly when I stepped into her class, I remember her as queen-like, very elegant, dignified, and graceful. She was a very accurate teacher who spent a lot of time on details and nuances—showing them all beautifully—but I left her class because I started to lose my ability to jump, which was, by nature, always my strong point. She made you sit on your legs. It was timing and also the tempo of the music."

Sklyanskaya notes that Vaganova (see p. 361, n. 10) also used rather slow tempi for teaching jumps, even though Vaganova herself reputedly had a very quick jump (something her famous student, Semyonova, apparently inherited from her). Sklyanskaya says she has given a great deal of thought to the issue of jumping tempi. "I was trained in Estonia by Nina Kurvitz, who was in the last class of Vaganova and later became a pedagogical student of Kostrovitskaya (senior teacher at the Leningrad ballet school). Following the method of both these great teachers, Kurvitz used rather slow tempi for jump combinations. Later, in Semyonova's class at the Bolshoi, we jumped faster. This is the pattern in Russian training—slower for children, increasingly fast as dancers become more advanced. I completely agree with Vaganova's belief that a well-developed *plié* is invaluable, and, to develop it, one must allow time for the students to form their *pliés* well within each jump. In addition, a slower tempo is especially important for students who have weak muscles, as it forces them to really use their legs to lift their bodies off the floor. They cannot cheat. After a few months of work on these uncomfortable, medium tempo jumps, young dancers become much stronger. However, I believe that if you teach jumps at too slow a tempo for too long a time, the body does not respond. The students sit so long in *plié* that they can't get off the floor—they crawl up. Jumps have to be taught with the right timing in order to create the impression of flight— otherwise you'll get a turkey hop!"

After her experience in Gerdt's class, Sklyanskaya went to Asaf Messerer's (see p. 363, n. 4) class. "It was excellent—a great warm-up class," she remembers, "and popular with all the big stars in the company. It was an inspiration—almost an academy in itself—for me to take class alongside famous dancers like Plisetskaya, Maximova, Vasiliev, Fadeyechev, and Lavrovsky. This was the time when the Bolshoi was at the peak of its greatness, when dancers instilled their performances with grandiose meaning, and going onstage was one's reason for being." But Sklyanskaya found one aspect of Messerer's classes disappointing: "He never gave any corrections. Of course, there was the expectation that as a professional you were supposed to know everything yourself, but it bothered me. I believe that no matter how accomplished a professional you are, you still need another pair of professional eyes to guide you. We all need to continue to grow and we need reminders," she says. "I missed this in Messerer's class."

The following year she went to the men's class of Alexi Varlamov, an excellent teacher whose reputation, she regrets, was never known in the West. He died in 1978. "He had an endless sense of humor that kept the atmosphere in the classroom uplifted, high energy. He gave lots of corrections, and I learned a lot about male technique from him. It was interesting for me because I was always curious; like a cat, I always wanted to look behind the mirror." (Sklyanskaya's longtime nickname is "Koschka," the Russian word for cat.) She had good reason to be intrigued by the material presented in this primarily male class. For five years, while dancing with the Estonian Ballet, Sklyanskaya had also maintained a position on the faculty of the company's school, where she had taught intermediate-level boys.

Varlamov's men's class was not difficult for Sklyanskaya because of her easy, high jump, but she discovered eventually that it was not the best thing for her: "If you do a male class with a female body," she warns, "you develop the wrong muscles." It was by a stroke of good fortune that in 1971, while still searching for the right class, Sklyanskaya began to study with the most revered of the Bolshoi's teachers, Marina Semyonova. One of the greatest ballerinas in the history of the Bolshoi, Semyonova was, in the 1920s, the pupil upon whom Agrippina Vaganova developed her teaching theories. (In her memoirs, Vaganova writes of gasping at the beauty of Semyonova's natural *développé*.) "Unfortunately," Sklyanskaya notes, "Semyonova never became well known in the West. She stopped dancing far earlier than she should have."

Sklyanskaya remembers that one didn't just go to Semyonova's class—not in a company where other classes were available. Other Bolshoi teachers would permit dancers to come and go as they pleased, but not Semyonova. "She did not permit what she called 'foreigners' into her classes," Sklyanskaya recalls. "You had to be invited. This was because what she did in class was like an independent statement from everyone else. Inside the Bolshoi walls, all eight teachers were supposed to be doing the same things. Well, seven did, but not eight. Hers was the most sophisticated, the fastest class, and it was considered a privilege to be in it. She never just gave class. She *taught* it every day. Her corrections and explanations made the most complicated movement simple, logical, and beautiful."

"I was very fortunate to get in," she says. "One of the girls in the company wanted to learn the roles danced by Kitri's two friends in *Don Quixote* and asked if I'd be interested too. She was going to be coached by Semyonova. We went to her and she said to me, 'I don't rehearse anyone who is not in my class, so you come to class tomorrow, and I'll look at you.'" Semyonova did not say a single word to Sklyanskaya during that first class. However, at the end, she told her, "All right, you can come to my class and let's work."

Sklyanskaya remembers being very, very happy. "The next day, though," she recalls ruefully, "that happiness ended, because from day one with Semyonova it starts. You feel like a complete fool, like you have no education, nothing behind you. It was like an earthquake! She would look at you like a dart, an arrow, and declare in a loud voice, 'You look like an iceberg—an icy mass.' Well, first of all, you didn't know what she was talking about because not many teachers used analogies like she did." Sklyanskaya says she learned the power of verbal pictures from Semyonova and uses them frequently with her own students. One of her favorite Semyonova sayings—"Don't cut the branch on which you are sitting"—refers to maintaining one's placement over one's supporting leg. Unfortunately, many of Semyonova's best sayings do not translate well into English. "For instance," says Sklyanskaya, "she would say our feet looked just like dustpans. If you are familiar with the shape of Russian dustpans, this is very funny. On American ears such a comparison is completely lost. So I rely mostly on my own creativity where analogies are concerned. Anyway, I don't believe in copying other teachers. Even if you make the first copy, it's still a copy!"

She admits, though, that she cannot resist using Semyonova's words with regard to hands and arms. "Don't hold your hand like a gun or a shovel," she admonishes students, "and, please, go home to the kitchen, lay the chicken on its back, unfold its wings, and take a look. That's what your arms with their droopy elbows look like!" This always produces a laugh from the class, and the errant elbows immediately lift.

"Well," says Sklyanskaya, "it took me four months with Semyonova to relearn everything I thought I knew after my presumably top-notch, Leningrad-supervised schooling in Estonia. It was complete shock, complete frustration; so when new students come to me at San Francisco Ballet School, I know exactly how they feel, because I went through that. Semyonova requested complete understanding of your body. You had to be master over every inch of it, to have total control. And she wanted it to look easy. No show-off stuff, no rough seams. Even if you were doing something incredible technically, she wanted the onlooker to be able to think, 'I can do that; anybody can do that.'" Sklyanskaya elaborates on why she insists that her students strive for such total control: "What makes dance beautiful is the opportunity for endless nuance, and you can get this only if you can feel and master every inch of your body."

Sklyanskaya also describes Semyonova as demanding a "painful musicality." She taught her students that being musical meant more than just hearing the beat, even more than just expressing the music. "What she wanted to impress upon us," says Sklyanskaya, "was that a dancer must become a vision of the music, that the whole body is the music. This meant that the music went through you in arabesque, for instance, from the tips of your fingertips through the line of the arm, the cheek, nose, eyelash, eyes, all the way to the big toe. If we stood motionless in a pose, she reminded us that our bodies must continue to be 'a singing song.' That's how she taught; nobody else taught like that. Her classes were very, very unusual." Sklyanskaya does not mince words in her criticism of the other Bolshoi teachers of that time: "In a country of teachers who either said nothing, suggesting that as a professional you knew everything (which is ridiculous), or teachers who said things that were rather meaningless (often they did not even understand themselves what they were saying) or said things that were so insignificant that they hardly stayed in your mind for a long time, Semyonova was for me like a beacon of light."

Furthermore, Sklyanskaya remembers, Semyonova, who was also a leading teacher at GITIS (see p. 364, n. 1), had an astounding knowledge of anatomy. "She'd often make me aware of a muscle I didn't even know existed. Gradually, I came to understand how my body worked. I think it is a very bad thing that so many ballet dancers go through their educations today without anatomical knowledge. They dance without thinking, and the better body one has, the less one has to think because the body just acquires dance technique like a sponge. Such dancers leave school without any real understanding of what makes dancing happen. The tragedy starts when they begin to teach. They want to pass it on, but they don't know how. They have no idea why they did something so well."

Sklyanskaya spent thirteen years in Semyonova's class at the Bolshoi, all the time making new discoveries about herself as a dancer. In her last year in Moscow, knowing that she might soon leave Russia (effectively ending her dance career) and begin teaching full-time, Sklyanskaya accompanied Semyonova every day to her class for teachers at GITIS. "She dissected every movement, distilled it like a slow-motion movie. We learned how every movement developed from the beginning to the very end—how it worked, what made it work, which muscles were responsible for which movement. Semyonova went through the entire ballet vocabulary this way. Then she elaborated on which movements should go together, which shouldn't. (Some movements when put together in a combination are clumsy, artificial. In the worst case, you obtain a negative rather than a positive result from such combinations.) She prepared me completely for teaching. She taught about 'inner lines'—the inside of the leg, the bottom of the arm— and how they support the poses. She constantly emphasized the feeling

Larisa
Sklyanskaya
helping a
student jump
in men's class
at the San
Francisco
Ballet School.

of the air. 'Your arm,' she would say, 'in *arabesque penchée* must lie on a pillow of air.'"

Sklyanskaya corroborated what I had heard about Semyonova's fero-
ciousness in the classroom. "Yes, she had a short tongue, though, fortunately, she used it more often on others than on me. In spite of her talent as
a dancer and teacher, she could be incredibly mean. When she humiliated
me in front of the whole class, I burned like a fire. It was not pleasant, but
her students' discomfort did not concern her in the least." Sklyanskaya does
not agree with such tactics in the classroom. "It's one thing if it happens
accidentally without any intention to humiliate the student. Sometimes all

of us who teach say what we see and don't understand how painful it is for that person. That's unintentional, a different story. But, if it is done purposefully to hurt someone, I don't condone it. You cannot teach people through humiliating them." She remembers that the regulars in Semyonova's class were accustomed to their teacher's razor tongue and tended to forgive her. "For the newcomers, though," she says, "it was always very, very tough."

In the dance world, of course, it is not unusual for dancers to forgive cruelty or eccentricity in teachers or choreographers if they sense they are in the presence of greatness. (Stories abound of emotional pain caused to dancers by such luminaries as Antony Tudor[3] and Martha Graham.[4]) In Semyonova's classes, the students not only sensed they were learning from an extraordinary teacher, but were also occasionally treated to glimpses of her greatness as a dancer. Sklyanskaya recalls: "She came to class in her street clothes, never tights or leotards—it was unheard of in the Soviet Union for older teachers to put on dance clothes to teach. But, once in a while, if she was in a great mood, she would do something from one of her past variations. It was like a great piece of art. You wanted to see it again, but if you didn't, you still remembered it. One day she showed us Nikiya's first entrance in the second act of *La Bayadère*, when she sees Solor (who the day before has sworn love to her) sitting with the Princess to whom he has just become engaged. She did the *ronds de jambe* small, not high as some do it, and her *port de bras en rond* in the backbend was like a scream from the soul, like the trunk of a birch tree in the wind going from side to side, squeaking with pain. She gave dramatic motivation to every movement. Vaganova coached her throughout her career. Even when she was dancing in Moscow, she returned to Leningrad to have Vaganova rehearse her. I think the result was the combination of two great talents. After seeing that, it is very hard for me to accept anything else."

Sklyanskaya's career at the Bolshoi did not flourish as she had hoped, or as Grigorovich had hinted. She remained floating back and forth somewhere between corps de ballet and soloist rank. She had no talent or stomach for company politics, steadfastly refused to join the Communist Party, and developed a strong dislike for the many people who used their Party memberships to further their careers. "The less talented they were," she remembers, "the more they waved their little red passbooks and the more they won." She also admits to having been, perhaps, too outspoken, a trait that she acknowledges continues to cause her problems to this day. "I can't help it," she says. "I speak the truth. Maybe today in Russia they like that, but the 1970s was the wrong time to be so forthright with one's opinions." Although she found the situation difficult, Sklyanskaya is quick to add that she also considers herself extremely lucky to have been where she was: "It was a privilege to be a member of the Bolshoi for fifteen years. The Bolshoi stage was always for me a sacred place. Perhaps I'm too sentimental, but when I think of the whole history of the place, of all the dancers who went through it, just of the sheer beauty of the place, I can't help myself."

In 1982, she decided to come to the United States on a Jewish immigration visa. Although she arrived with her mother and sister, she chose to live apart from them and settled with her young son in San Francisco—"because of its beauty," she says. She had been to New York City on tour with the Bolshoi in 1975 and remembers thinking that it was not a city in which she would ever be able to live. Her leap to the West was an act of courage for she knew no one, had no money, and spoke no English. (She describes her command of the language back then by using an old Russian saying: "Two claps and three stamps!") Cruelly, as she left the USSR, all her books and mementos of her dancing career were taken from her by Soviet customs officials. She owns only one photograph of herself dancing; it slipped through by mistake. More than anything, she grieves at the loss of her library of art and dance books. Slowly, in the West, she has begun to build it again.

She came prepared to teach, knowing it unlikely that she would be able to find a position as a dancer. She was in her mid-thirties and well aware of the preference in the West for eighteen-year-old ballerinas. She was looking forward to seeing more contemporary ballet. She considered herself very open-minded. "My early years in Estonia—a very progressive place—had prepared me for Western choreography." However, she was shocked by the mostly expressionless dancing she encountered. "What I saw," she recalls sadly, "were bodies that were like string instruments from which the strings had been taken." As soon as she could, she began to try to remedy this situation in the classroom.

It took some time, however, for her to secure teaching jobs. She taught part-time wherever she could, including occasional stints as a substitute teacher at the San Francisco Ballet. At that time, the school's director, much to Sklyanskaya's surprise, was extremely wary of Vaganova training. Not until Helgi Tomasson was appointed artistic director of the company was Sklyanskaya offered a full faculty position in the school. She recounts with pain her early years in San Francisco: "It was complete disillusionment. I had to go on welfare, which I hated. The few classes I managed to obtain here and there simply did not provide enough money on which to survive with a child. I made $7.00 a class, and half of it went towards public transportation to and from the studios. I had no friends here to help me. I didn't go to Natasha Makarova [the famed ex-Leningrad ballerina, who was also living in San Francisco] because I didn't know her. In desperation, I began to work as a maid in households in the wealthy White Russian community (see p. 364, n. 1). It was ironic. These people had been taught to hate Soviets and we to hate them, and here I was scrubbing their bathtubs. Although some did embrace me with understanding and warmth, especially a family named Shouliakovsky, I experienced terrible depression, often wondering why I had left Russia. At one point, I even considered going back, but by then my nine-year-old son had become quite enamored of life in the United States. He told me I could go, but he was staying," she recalls, throwing her hands up with a smile, "so what could I do?"

It was during this time that Sklyanskaya met her American husband, Karl. He was a dancer in a local Slavic folk dance troupe that had hired her to coach them. He says he fell in love with her when he saw her jump and remembers it as "poetry in motion." Today they live in a beautiful redwood home Karl has painstakingly designed and built by himself high in the hills of Oakland. A great lover of nature (as well as cats and books), Sklyanskaya travels to nearby orchards to pick fruit, which she preserves in her kitchen. From her stove, she looks out her windows at the magnificent, undisturbed vista of a wilderness that borders their property.

Sklyanskaya says it took her a long time to adapt her teaching to Western dancers: "It was not the different style I couldn't accept. It was the complete ignorance. It made me very unhappy and often unwisely aggravated. I was not against contemporary dance. I love it! But if you speak of the professional ballet world, you expect there must be a fundamental knowledge, trained bodies that can do any style. Teaching, after all, is not about style. Teaching is about pulling out from the students' bodies everything that it is possible to pull out. And here I found a whole lot of bodies that could do nothing—incapable—even though many of them had wonderful natural ability." She recalls how impatient she was mainly because she had no idea how ineffective and incomplete had been these dancers' prior training. She remembers with regret that in one well-known studio where she was hired to take over while the director was out of town, the students stopped coming after just a few of her classes: "I was as much of a shock to them as they were to me!" Gradually, she says she learned to understand the psychology and roots of American dance training, how things developed here, where they came from, and she began to adjust her methods, though never her standards. "In the beginning, though," she says, "I felt as if I had been dropped here from the moon!"

Today Sklyanskaya's students at the San Francisco Ballet School are devoted to her. Katita Waldo, now a principal dancer with the San Francisco Ballet, says that although Sklyanskaya is demanding, "she never asks for what cannot be given. Nor does she ever withhold praise when it has been earned." Several students, however, told me that studying with Sklyanskaya can be difficult because she rarely acknowledges that something they do "is good." I asked her about this. She replied: "I disagree that kids have to be constantly complimented, that they grow on compliments, on a self-image that they are great, that any correction to them is painful, and sometimes unacceptable. Many of them have been trained this way when they get here. Many were the best in their hometown school. When they first are exposed to my demands, they become very fussy, very moody. If they fail at something, they may blame it on my 'crazy combination.' Some are just like ostriches with their heads in the sand in their denial of their own basic weaknesses. They already have so many faults in their muscle memory and are so close-minded, wearing blinders, that it is a big job to break through the walls they erect. As they progress, often in tears, they begin to understand. Sometimes it's practically atomic warfare! In the beginning, they think I hate them. Gradually they learn that all this screaming and pulling hair out from my skull comes from my love for them and true concern for their future, that just patting them on the hand and trying to hide their faults would be a very false process."

In spite of her demanding nature, Sklyanskaya is remembered fondly by former student Robert Henry Johnson, now a San Francisco area dancer and choreographer. "She's the most motherly teacher I've ever known," he told me, as he poetically recalled his early days at the San Francisco Ballet School: "I became more curious each day in her class—happy to see her rush in late, skipping the attendance book because she could not read or pronounce our names correctly. 'Let's just dance,' she'd say. She jumped higher than any of the men in class, her wild mane flying, it seemed, to the four corners of the world. I noticed the way she talked to us, the care. Strange pebbles would fall from her mouth: 'Do not do *pas de bourrée* like a cat with a wet paw,' or 'You look like an ostrich or giraffe in quicksand. Pull up. You have to feel your back.' We thought she was an alien from another planet. Maybe Russia is another planet—I don't know—but she brought light, mischievous light, from wherever it was she had been. It was contagious, making you want to jump higher, want to listen for what falls from the sky, want to see the dark and take it apart, bring it back to somebody like magic. Discovery. She longed for us to discover ourselves as human beings, which is very difficult to do in a ballet institution."

Johnson remembers wanting very much to please her, and then one day giving up because he felt his body was too different and could not assimilate the texture she had to offer. After class, he says, she followed him down the hall and said in very broken English: "You think because you are just beginning ballet at such a late age that you cannot accomplish this? You have good legs. They are strong. Nobody has legs like you. You have to hear the music and keep coming to class. That is all." Her words inspired him to stick to his studies. "I don't know," Johnson reflects, "how it is possible for a man to feel like a gardenia, unless he's outfitted totally in frills, and I'm not, but somehow she made you feel very precious and special. Perhaps more like a rare stone than a flower. If you are a prince or a princess, Larisa will tell you, demand that you recognize it, and, most of all, demand that you dance like one."

Sklyanskaya acknowledges that winning students over is her greatest challenge: "They arrive at the San Francisco Ballet School at all levels of ability and from all different approaches. I have to learn who they are, where they came from, and not offend them. I have to open them like flowers, but without a knife. Eventually, I hope they will embrace my ideas, because I believe in the system I am giving. But, in the beginning, they can be stubborn and attached to what they have learned before. Sometimes I am almost ready to give up because the result I want to achieve with these kids—and with the senior students I often have only a year with them in class—seems very far from what I can in reality actually do."

On the bright side, though, she notes that these American students have been responsible for making her a much better teacher. "I have learned from them—not because I made any kind of specific investigation—but just by watching them and observing how to take obstacles out of their bodies. Each individual body is a new challenge. You cannot put one rule to a hundred people. It doesn't work."

Sklyanskaya says that one of the most important things she wants to convey to her students is that they approach movement logically. "For instance," she will say, "if you want to scratch your right ear, you don't reach over your head with your left arm. So if you're going to turn to the right, you have to push your body in that direction, not do something illogical that works against what you really want to do." She continues: "If you stiffen your wrist and finger joints, you cannot write, so don't stiffen your arm if you want to make a good *port de bras*. If you make your knees 'rusty' so that they squeak and barely move, you cannot run. So when you take class, how do you expect to dance unless you relax these joints? It's just logic!" Former student Katita Waldo remembers this aspect of Sklyanskaya's teaching well: "Larisa is a master at making dance technique, and the use of it, easy. She makes even the most difficult steps accessible. She is able to take the mystery out of dance without diminishing the magic."

In addition to teaching dancers logic as it relates to technique, Sklyanskaya is also concerned about educating her students in artistic and intellectual areas outside of dance. She refers to these as "missing subjects" in the curriculum of most American dancers. A lack of familiarity with music and other forms of art, she feels, is seriously detrimental to the development of a dancer. "I try to push my students in these directions," she told me, "by endless talking, by giving images in class, comparisons with sculpture and painting. I encourage them to read, to go to museums, to learn the names of composers and their music. I bring them books. I try to explain that ballet is the quintessence of all arts, especially if you dance a role that requires you to convey an image. It is art and history. They have to absorb everything, and develop a photographic memory, so that when the teacher makes an analogy to something in class, they know what he or she is talking about. Unfortunately, often when I give an image to these students (such as referring to a famous work of art), I have to take a lot of precious class time to explain what I'm talking about. But it's important for them to know. What can you show through dance if you know nothing, if inside, you are completely empty? You're just lifting legs and making a number of turns, that's all."

She also laments her students' lack of exposure to many of the great classical ballets. "One day," she says, "I showed a videotape of Plisetskaya dancing *Swan Lake* to my senior girls' class. One girl had never before seen this great ballerina. The performance made her cry. Don't you think it is a shame that she had to wait until she was eighteen years old to see this?" Sklyanskaya says she rejoiced in the fall of 1992 when the Willam Christensen (see chapter

2) Dance Library was established on site at the San Francisco Ballet School, with many donated books and videos available for student use.

One day, as I watched her teach a men's class, Sklyanskaya asked a young man to name the dancer he most admired as a role model. Leaping to what he thought would certainly be a safe answer, the student replied, "Nijinsky." Sklyanskaya was momentarily caught off guard. In the era of Baryshnikov and Vasiliev,[5] this was not the answer she had expected. "What do you know about Nijinsky?" she asked, amazed. "Have you seen him?" "No," said the student defensively, "but I've read about him." "Well," scoffed Sklyanskaya, "don't believe everything you read. Be selective. If *your* mother wrote a book about you, *you'd* be the greatest dancer that ever lived![6] Nijinsky was great, for sure, but he's not the only great male dancer in this century!"

Most of the time in class, Sklyanskaya speaks in a soft, but insistent, whispery voice. When she makes an important point in class—one she wishes her students not to forget—she is fond of pressing her fist against the center of her forehead like a branding iron and commanding: "Burn forever!" She is still dancer-slim with long arms and legs and lovely feet. To teach, she dresses with little concern for fashion, in jogging pants or blue jeans, wearing sneakers or dance shoes on her feet. Her bushy black hair hangs in a long, thick braid down her back. With a radiantly pretty face, and big, soft, blue eyes framed, catlike, by thick black eyelashes, she looks fifteen years younger than she is. Her ability to sustain herself without shakiness on one foot on *relevé* for long periods of time, even while giving an explanation, elicits gasps of admiration from her students. "This is no secret," she tells them. "To stay on *relevé* the spine must simply be over the supporting leg." She credits her excellent sense of balance to her years with Semyonova who, she says, stressed stability because "without it, nuance is impossible."

She moves constantly about the classroom, often getting down on her hands and knees to correct a student's legs. Her prominently veined hands move from one dancer's body to the next, knowledgeably molding muscles like a sculptor. Her fingers are long, strong, and free of nail polish. These are the hands of a masseuse—confident, articulate, beautiful to watch, but in no way dainty. Former student Robert Henry Johnson remembers her hands well: "One time she showed me the ancient classical arabesque, as opposed to the 'à la se-besque' (as we students playfully called the contemporary Balanchine line, somewhere between *à la seconde* and arabesque). After she touched my back and leg and showed me where my body should be for the classical line, my entire attitude toward movement changed. I felt humble. Very proud that my body had facilities no one else imagined I had. I felt very quiet, but triumphant. I wanted to roar, though only a smile came over my face. This is Larisa's magic, her gift of knowledge of how and when. That is why she is constantly touching children. With her hands. No sticks or tools. Tactile. Nowadays," Johnson added with obvious disapproval, "many teachers sit in high chairs and never touch their students."

Over and over again, Sklyanskaya stresses correct placement of the hips. "The supporting leg is for support," she reminds her dancers. "If you cannot stand on your own leg, you are a cripple. Do not use the barre as a crutch!" With her hands, she opens students' upper backs and presses their shoulders down. "Stretch yourselves," she says, "don't shrink." When they face the barre to do an exercise, she reminds them, "Make your neck long. Don't choke yourselves with your shoulders. I want to see an interesting back." When students momentarily lose their aplomb, she asks, "Do you know we have a spine inside? What would happen if we took it out? Do you know that that's your technique?"

One of her most interesting concepts comes from Semyonova and concerns the manner of teaching students to *cambré* forward and backward. "Most teachers," she says, "will tell you to bend back from the center of your back. It's not always right. While flexibility from the shoulder blades must be developed, and used frequently, when you make a bend standing on both legs or in arabesque, the whole spine should be in use. Therefore, you must begin a backbend from your tailbone. When you start by lengthening these first four lumbar vertebrae, it puts your hips on your legs; then you make a long curve. It's very light and free." She continues: "It's more difficult to teach a bend forward than a bend back. You must start to roll over from the top of the forehead, not from the hips, which must stay over the legs. This makes it possible to *cambré* front on *demi-pointe* without losing one's balance."

She talks often about the forehead. "You must *feel* it in *attitude derrière* and in practically every other pose, as well. You must also feel a light sensation at the back of your neck, like an electric current, a tingling running up your whole spine through your neck. This keeps [i.e., stabilizes] you and gives your movement life as opposed to just staying like a shape from nature, like a beautiful stone. There is a great difference."

Sklyanskaya also stresses coordination of all parts of the body in building toward a final line. She demonstrates how, when executing a *demi-rond de*

Larisa Sklyanskaya demonstrating a port de bras exercise in front of a class in Tampa, Florida.

jambe en dehors at 90 degrees from 2nd position into the pose 2nd arabesque, both the arm and the leg must simultaneously dip slightly as the movement begins. Then she shows how, at the completion of the *demi-rond*, both the fingers of the front arm and the toe of the arabesque leg lift together slightly to finish the movement. It is attention to artistic details such as these that distinguishes Sklyanskaya's classes, and it is with these tiny finishing touches that her students struggle daily. She is relentless with her requests. I loved her explanation of how the students should finish an exercise standing in 5th position: "Even at the end of the combination, when the legs have finished doing all they can, the arms must still be lowering and the eyes dropping as the sound of the music dies. Then, at the very end, the eyes and chest lift as the sound is finally gone." Watching such teaching, I was reminded of one of my favorite sayings: "Details make the difference between the amateur and the professional, and between the professional and the artist." Clearly, Sklyanskaya is concerned with making artists.

Repeatedly, she reminds students to release unnecessary tension from their bodies. "Your necks are like steel today," she chides. "Try to walk around for five minutes after class like that and see if you can do it. You can't dance like that!" To a girl holding her breath, she says, "Relax, please. Go outside in the sun and look at the flowers and butterflies, the things in nature that you will dance about. How can you do this [she places both her hands around her own throat as if to strangle herself] if you are dead?!"

To students who have forgotten to think about turn-out when landing from jumps, she says: "Please remember when you do *plié*, no kissing knees!" Or, more matter of factly, she points to a student's foot that is rolling in and says, "Keep your little toe on the floor, or the entire line of the leg will turn in."

Her comments are often humorous and laced with irony. "Your legs are absolutely snoring!" she says to a class of lethargic young men one morning. "*Tendu* is an active movement!" When a class falls apart attempting a new exercise, she gets them all to laugh when she cups her hands around her mouth and spells out "B-A-D." Then she rushes into their midst to help. Her imagery can be very funny and absolutely to the point. To a student whose head was dropped too far forward, chin almost to her chest, she remarked, "Don't imitate a bull!" In one class I watched, she had been particularly hard on her young men. The lesson had progressed painstakingly with constant stops for Sklyanskaya's persistent (and, to the boys, maddening) corrections. Toward the end of the time period, sensing that she had pushed them about as far as she could that day, she decided to let them enjoy themselves. She gave them a big, dancey *grand allegro* combination. The boys threw themselves into it with the joy of animals released from their cages. They bounded across the floor with little thought to correctly forming the classical poses they had just been practicing for an hour and a half. Sklyanskaya could not keep the smile from her face. "Guys," she said, "I love you. I respect you. I know you are trying your hardest. But, my God, you look like flying closets! No shape! Like a piece of furniture flying through the air."

She can also be pointedly blunt, and, although her tongue may not be as razor-sharp as Semyonova's, it can bite. To a student obsessed with watching his feet in the mirror, she remarked, "You look in the mirror and don't see the whole truth. You look as if you are looking through a keyhole. You must open up and see *all* of yourself." She constantly admonishes them about how they use the mirror: "In a hundred years from now, killing yourself doing it over and over again, you will still be stumbling in place unless you use your eyes and your brain when you watch yourself in the mirror and, whenever possible, match corrections with physical actions." (Sklyanskaya is against closing the curtains across the mirror, especially for young students or those with lots of bad habits.) She is aggravated by the sight of a sleepy student. "Dear girl," she says with exasperation, "I am not your dentist. If you *must* yawn, turn your face away. This is very rude. I am sorry to give this lecture, but it is for your own benefit."

Calling the students out on the floor after the barre, she directs them to "set yourselves up like checkers." When modestly they leave an empty spot in the center of the front row, she gestures to the space with a smile and an invitation: "Who wants to be a star today?" She encourages them to present themselves in class as they will someday on the stage. When a student does a leap accompanied by an arm gesture to the corner, but looks down, she asks, "Do you say 'Hello' like that, with your eyes closed? Open your eyes!" To another, she says, "Keep that smile. It's very becoming to you." Sometimes, she is very direct. To a girl who is visibly struggling during an exercise, she remarks, "You don't make these funny faces [Sklyanskaya imitates—grimacing, furrowing her brow, and pressing her lips together] when you talk to your friends, so don't do it when you dance. Give me a nice beautiful smile."

I particularly enjoyed watching her correct students in turning exercises. To young ladies doing *piqué* turns *en diagonale,* she asked, "Do you walk down the street looking sideways? How many do? Raise your hands . . . No hands? So why do you do diagonal turns looking in the mirror? Spot the diagonal. That's where you are going!" As always, she is teaching her students to be logical. One day in *pointe* class, the girls were doing *passés relevés.* Sklyanskaya reminded them that when they lift their working leg to the knee it "should not make a swimming lesson [i.e., lift and circle away from the shin of the supporting leg]. "Remember," she told them, "correctly done, *sissonne simple relevé* is your key to pirouettes." She frequently tells students that their hips are like a steering wheel. "Do you drive?" she asks. "Turn them when you do a pirouette." When students, turning, pull their arms too close to their chests in 1st position, she says: "Keep your elbows rounded. With them bent like that, you look like you're holding a baby." She is fond of walking up behind a student whom she feels is not lifted high enough in *passé relevé* and saying, "Let me destroy your hairstyle for a minute." She puts one hand on top of the student's head, pulling a few hairs straight up, and the other on the back of the student's neck, lengthening it by placing her middle finger up under the skull and her thumb against the seventh vertebra. "Now, stretch yourself up," she commands, pushing her two fingers up and down, away from each other in a vertical line against the student's neck. She will also call two students to help her place another correctly in *passé relevé*. She has the helpers stabilize the balance of her demonstrator by holding the student's hands while Sklyanskaya gets down on the floor and guides the action of the student's knees. When a student's *passé* leg slides up and down the shin during multiple pirouettes, Sklyanskaya jokes, "Don't play the cello!" And when students somehow manage to save the finish of pirouettes gone awry, she remarks wryly, "Well, you survived, but it was an accident."

To develop students' *ballon*, Sklyanskaya emphasizes rhythm. "You must be like a bouncing ball and go evenly up and down," she tells them. She reminds them that keeping tension in their bodies "pushes the body down in jumps." She is also adamant about pressing the heels into the floor in allegro work. "If you desperately want to have shin splints," she says, "just keep jumping on *demi-pointe*." She reminds them that their arms can often be helpful when they're jumping, "like two wings." However, she demands that they be beautifully positioned. When one girl did a split *jeté* thrusting one arm straight up and the other out too far in back of her body, Sklyanskaya exclaimed (referring to the sharp angle formed by the arms), "You're crucified! No wonder you can't do anything!"

Sklyanskaya says she deviates somewhat from Semyonova in how she develops the allegro portion of her class. "Semyonova gave jumps practically without any preparation," she says. "The first jump in class could come out of nowhere, very fast, and the second one could be large *sissonnes ouvertes*. For people like me with a natural jump, it was O.K.; for others, it wasn't. But, even for those with a jump, I believe they started to build undesirable muscles. I regret terribly that I never had the opportunity to discuss this issue with her, but I have followed my own instincts. Semyonova's classes were so fast. I doubt Balanchine dancers could move that fast—I mean, correctly, with positions and *port de bras*. After *grand plié* she gave only one or two fast *tendu* combinations. I give a slower *tendu* exercise first because I believe one must never force the body to do what the body is not prepared for. That's how injuries come. I realized when I came to America that Semyonova's tempos would never work here, not unless people could be gradually brought up to that level. I build the allegro part of my class much more carefully: small jumps, medium jumps, big jumps, and then fast *batterie.*"

I asked Sklyanskaya what ingredients she felt were essential for a student to achieve success as a dancer. "There are lots of girls and boys born with nice feet and flexibility," she remarked, "but few are dancers in their souls and, unfortunately, few have the talent to learn. Both of these qualities are absolutely necessary. I especially believe in the power of intelligence!" One thing that distresses her is what she refers to as the "disease of narcissism" she sees in some dancers. What produces it, she wonders. Personality? Upbringing? Both? "It's impossible to fight this affliction," she says sadly, "and the worst is when narcissistic dancers become famous and are idolized."

Asked what advice she would offer young teachers, Sklyanskaya replied: "Never stop learning. Never think you know enough. Continue to learn and improve your teaching, because in the continual process of expanding your own vision, you will find yourself capable of giving more to those to whom you wish to pass it on."

Classroom Quotes from Sklyanskaya

On *petit battement* at the barre: "Your foot must move in and out like a silver bell, not like an ax against a tree trunk."

On rubber pants that students like to wear over their tights: "Take these home, put them over your head, tie them around your neck, and in one second you will feel what you do to your legs. You suffocate them!"

Again regarding the detested rubber pants: "I suggest you fold these up neatly, wrap them in silver paper, put a gold ribbon on top, and at Christmastime give them to your worst enemy."

"A pose in which you have not placed the head well is like an unfinished sculpture."

To the ladies in *pointe* class: "You must not look like your mother's electric mixer when you do those *bourrées*. Try instead to glide as if you have a cup of tea on your head and not a drop spills out."

"Make your fingers soft—like feathers."

"Look at yourself in the mirror with sober [as opposed to drunken] eyes. Don't admire and don't hate yourself either."

"You have to have a metronome inside of you even if there is no music."

To a student who has forgotten to point her foot: "Your foot is just like a rag in the wind."

"Your arm in 2nd will be much stronger if you feel [hold] it from underneath instead of from the top."

To a boy doing a backbend by pushing his hips forward: "You resemble an upside-down turtle in that position."

"Good classical dance is freedom in a cage of positions."

Order of the Exercises in Sklyanskaya's Class (advanced class, 1½ hours)

BARRE

1. Warm-up tendus
2. Pliés
3. Battements tendus with demi-plié
4. Battements tendus with soutenu and faster footwork
5. Battements tendus jetés (dégagés)
6. Ronds de jambe à terre
7. Battements fondus
8. Battements frappés
9. Ronds de jambe en l'air
10. Petits battements
11. Développés
12. Grands battements

CENTRE

1. Small adagio
2. Tendus and pirouettes
3. Fondus relevés with ronds de jambe en l'air
4. Grands battements
5. Small jumps such as temps levés
6. Small jumps such as assemblés
7. Petit allegro (petits jetés, ballonnés, etc.)
8. Medium allegro (sissonnes ouvertes, etc.)
9. Grand allegro 1
10. Grand allegro 2
11. Batterie
12. Changements
13. Port de bras
14. Révérence

The Roots of Tradition

THE PEDAGOGICAL LINEAGE OF LARISA SKLYANSKAYA

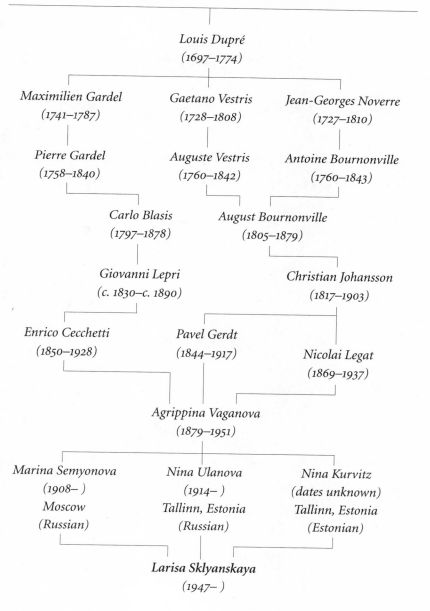

L'Académie Royale de Musique et de Danse (1661)

Louis Dupré
(1697–1774)

Maximilien Gardel
(1741–1787)

Gaetano Vestris
(1728–1808)

Jean-Georges Noverre
(1727–1810)

Pierre Gardel
(1758–1840)

Auguste Vestris
(1760–1842)

Antoine Bournonville
(1760–1843)

Carlo Blasis
(1797–1878)

August Bournonville
(1805–1879)

Giovanni Lepri
(c. 1830–c. 1890)

Christian Johansson
(1817–1903)

Enrico Cecchetti
(1850–1928)

Pavel Gerdt
(1844–1917)

Nicolai Legat
(1869–1937)

Agrippina Vaganova
(1879–1951)

Marina Semyonova
(1908–)
Moscow
(Russian)

Nina Ulanova
(1914–)
Tallinn, Estonia
(Russian)

Nina Kurvitz
(dates unknown)
Tallinn, Estonia
(Estonian)

Larisa Sklyanskaya
(1947–)

8 Alexander Ursuliak

Alexander Ursuliak demonstrating the pose *écarté devant* for his senior students at the John Cranko Ballet School in Stuttgart in 1991.

Alexander Ursuliak is director of the John Cranko Ballet School, the official school of the Stuttgart Ballet in Germany. He was born and raised in a Ukrainian community in Canada. At nineteen, he traveled to the Ukraine to complete his ballet studies at Kiev's Schevchenko Opera Ballet School, from which he received his diploma as Ballet Master-Pedagogue after three years. In 1960, he returned to Toronto to work with the National Ballet of Canada, where he both taught and performed. In addition, he also taught for Betty Oliphant in her newly established National Ballet School of Canada. Later, he moved to London, where he was hired as ballet master and assistant to the director of London's Festival Ballet. While in England, he was also invited by Beryl Grey to teach at the Arts Educational Trust.

In 1965, Ursuliak joined the Vienna Opera Ballet as assistant to the director, Waclav Orlikowsky, and was simultaneously appointed director of the Vienna Opera Ballet School. He remained there seven years, until 1973, when John Cranko offered him a position as ballet master with the Stuttgart Ballet. He has been associated with that company ever since. In addition to his regular duties as Stuttgart's ballet master and coach, Ursuliak has also frequently appeared in company productions in character roles. In 1990, he became director of the Stuttgart Ballet's professional academy, the John Cranko-Schule, to which he continues to devote himself full-time. He has been a guest teacher in America, Australia, France, Italy, Spain, Sweden, China, Hong Kong, and Japan, and has conducted summer teachers' courses with his friend Marika Besobrasova at her school in Monte Carlo. In 1983, he was awarded the Order of Merit by the German government for his contribution to the arts both in Germany and internationally.

"Who wants to work these days as dancers do? We are the last of the dinosaurs. We should be proud of that and carry ourselves accordingly when we enter or leave a stage."

THERE'S A LOT of philosopher in Alex Ursuliak—and a lot of stand-up comic too. Throughout his lively, thought-provoking classes, he bombards his students with information—anatomical, theoretical, artistic—as well as quite a few rules that apply to life. "Perspiration is good, but results are better," he warns with a wink, encouraging them to work carefully. As one of his former students, now a member of the Stuttgart Ballet, told me: "I always wanted to write everything he said down after class—not to forget it. He said so many things you never hear from other teachers, introduced us to so many new aspects of ballet."

Ursuliak is simply carrying on a family tradition. "My mother," he remembers, "coming from peasant stock, fed us a lot of proverbs—wisdom about daily living. Often, I believe, it was used tongue-in-cheek. We were never quite sure whether she was serious or not." And his father? "He was a philosopher," says Ursuliak, "and a great story-teller. He did a lot to develop curiosity in us." There were six children in the family, five boys and a girl. All became teachers, although he is the only one who embarked upon a career in the arts.

Ursuliak's admirable way with words is not the only aspect of his classes that can be traced to his childhood. The wonderful, rhythmic musicality of his exercises is certainly the result of the fact that he grew up folk dancing in one of Canada's tightly knit Ukrainian communities. "My first dance steps were those of the Kolomeyka, a Ukrainian round dance," he recalls. "We Slavs danced every Saturday night, and especially at weddings! The arts were integral to our family life. Being Ukrainian meant a lot of mandolin playing, singing, folk dancing, and poetry reciting at an early age. There were also a lot of concerts, choirs, and theater in our culture, so I became addicted to these sorts of things early on." He remembers playing the big bass drum at dances. "Then I'd get up and go out in the centre and throw a few dance solos. Naturally, I got to like being in the limelight," he says with a smile.

Ursuliak started ballet lessons at age ten, studying in Toronto with Freddy Seychuk, who had once been a soloist with the ballet in Kiev. "It was he who planted the seed in my mind," Ursuliak says, "that I might be able to make a profession out of dancing." During his teens, Ursuliak danced in nightclubs and in musicals such as *Carousel* and *Oklahoma.* His appetite for theatrical dancing grew, although at the same time, he was seriously studying to become a biologist. (One sees the influence of this former interest in the emphasis Ursuliak places on anatomical theory in his ballet classes today.)

In 1957, the Canadian and Ukrainian governments signed a cultural exchange accord. Ursuliak was nineteen and had been studying ballet for nine years. He decided to take advantage of the opportunity to go to Kiev to study. After all, Ukrainian had been his first language. He hadn't started to learn English until he was six. Also, he'd already learned a bit of Russian.

When he arrived at the school of the Schevchenko Opera Ballet, he was given a test. "I had no idea at the time why or what it was about," he recalls. "It contained all sorts of weird questions." As a result of the test, Ursuliak and four other students were placed in a special class in which the dance regimen was the same as everyone else's in the student body, but with an added emphasis on pedagogy. "The test," he says, "was to see if I had pedagogical abilities. Apparently, I did. Therefore, I was required to study a lot more than the regular students—intense classes in psychology, ballet and theatrical history, and literature. In addition, I did classes and performed with the company. As there were only five of us in this special class, we received a lot of attention."

He remembers these as pleasant years. "I was very intent on developing myself," he says. "My teachers never had to yell or scream to motivate me. Most of the time was spent absorbing—them giving, me absorbing. I was never abused. I try to do the same with my students—stern guidance when necessary, but that's it."

Ursuliak names Robert Klavin, a Soviet-trained teacher with whom he studied technique and *pas de deux* in Kiev, as the person who had the greatest influence on him. "I admired him a great deal," he remembers, "probably because, though not a super talent as a dancer, he was a very effectual human being on stage—extremely theatrical. He had learned to have a good career with only mediocre physical attributes. He showed me that it's not always the super-talented bodies that make theater. He made me aware that it's always an illusion. A dancer must work like a magician. Each moment on stage, or in class, must be well thought out. You're manipulating the whole time. He'd talk about how a jump could look big simply by the way one timed the takeoff. He reminded us never to come crashing down, but to go *into* the floor. Even if we did just a few pirouettes, he'd emphasize how important it was to hold them well and to make our finish look gracious—never forced. 'You must look as if you still have a lot of potential in yourself,' he'd say. And he was right."

Much later, Ursuliak remembers, he overheard Nureyev (see p. 361, n. 11) express the same sentiment when, speaking of multiple pirouettes, the great dancer commented: "It's never how many. It's *how*."

With the diploma he received after almost four years at the pedagogical institute in Kiev, Ursuliak could have taken a job as ballet master in any theater in the USSR. Instead, he married a Soviet ballerina, Galina Samsova, and returned to Canada, where they both joined the National Ballet of Canada. Almost immediately, he was asked to teach. "Celia Franca, the company's founder-director, and I worked a lot together," he says. "I tried to help her out in choreographing, mainly with character bits and *pas de deux,* where my experience gave me a bit of an advantage." During this period, he also became one of the first male teachers at the newly formed National Ballet School of Canada. "Betty Oliphant, the school's director, was very Cecchetti oriented," Ursuliak recalls, "but even with my Kiev [Soviet method] background, we never had a conflict. She let me do my thing. I've been lucky to have always worked in situations where there was a lot of mutual tolerance, where what mattered was the results. How you got them was left up to the individual."

Samsova and Ursuliak remained in Canada two years. In 1963, they joined London's Festival Ballet—she as a principal dancer, he as teacher. "I also co-choreographed a few things with Jack Carter there," he remembers. "I was very, very happy. We worked well together." Then, his marriage began to disintegrate, and Ursuliak decided to accept an invitation to go to Vienna. In 1964, he left London to assume the dual posts of assistant to the director, Waclav Orlikowsky, of the Vienna Opera Ballet, as well as director of the company's ballet school. There, juggling both jobs simultaneously, he worked from nine in the morning until ten at night. "I had only an hour's lunch break," he remembers, "and the schedule nearly did me in, but I certainly learned a lot working daily with both students, as well as professionals."

I asked Ursuliak to elaborate on the differences between teaching students and fully trained dancers. "Professionals," he told me, "are working on a performance, something very close at hand. So you must make sure that the buildup of the lesson and the choice of movements are conducive to that. It's much like preparing a racehorse for a specific race. One knows the turf, weather conditions, and how much speed and endurance are necessary. You also have to think about such things as injuries, tiredness, boredom, as well as about helping dancers who may not have performed in a long time. With the schoolkids, on the other hand, you're working long-term, and there isn't the pressure of immediate performance. One has months, even years, to get things done. However, what you *are* doing at the moment is leaving impressions that can make or break, that can divert or confuse, because these young people are looking at you every second. You're much more of a role model than you realize."

Ursuliak stayed at the Vienna Opera seven years. "It was a difficult theater to work in," he recalls, "but it was very educational because there are a lot of traditions there that sometimes get in the way—union problems, etc., so I had to learn to give and take, which is important in life because one doesn't always get one's way." He found living in the cosmopolitan Austrian capital exhilarating, and enjoyed working in the beautiful, historic opera house, assisting such luminaries as Nureyev, who came to stage his productions of *Swan Lake* and *Don Quixote*, Antony Tudor (see p. 369, n. 3), who staged *Pillar of Fire*, and Harald Lander,[1] who set *Etudes*. In addition, in Vienna Ursuliak met his present wife, Christl Himmelbauer, a dancer in the company. They have now been happily married more than twenty years and have a teenage daughter, Natasha, who, while not aspiring to be a dancer, studies piano, sings, and is (as was her father in his youth) passionately fond of musicals.

"The story of how I came to work with the Stuttgart Ballet is strange," Ursuliak told me. "During my last year in Vienna, my colleague, Orlikowsky, the director, had left. I took the company by myself on a successful seven-week tour of the United States. Then, a new director from Rome was hired, and it soon became clear to me that we could not find a common language. So I started looking for something else. One evening the Stuttgart Ballet was performing in Vienna. I was a bit late getting to the performance and, when I arrived, John Cranko, the company's founder and director, was pacing back and forth in the lobby of the Theater an der Wien like a caged animal. (Everyone else was inside watching the show!) We knew each other from Canada, where he'd staged his *Romeo and Juliet* in 1961. (Galina, my wife, had danced Juliet and I had played Lord Capulet.) He saw me coming and immediately said, 'Are you looking for a job?' I said, 'I am!' He asked how quickly I could come to Stuttgart. I said, 'How about tomorrow?' It literally happened that way. When the company returned to Stuttgart, I went with them. I gave class and was hired. I did the next tour with them to the USA, and then there was that terrible, tragic flight back . . ."

Recalling Cranko's accidental death from asphyxiation on the plane, Ursuliak explained: "John had taken some sedatives to try to get some sleep during the flight. I was the first to notice something was wrong with him. I tried mouth-to-mouth resuscitation, but to no avail . . . I still get nightmares."

From 1973 to 1990, Ursuliak remained with the Stuttgart company as ballet master and coach, working closely with many acclaimed contemporary choreographers including Kylian, Tetley, MacMillan, Béjart, Neumeier, Forsythe, Ek, and van Manen. Then, in 1990, he agreed to assume the responsibility of directing the John Cranko Ballet School. He continues to enjoy performing character roles in such Cranko ballets as *Taming of the Shrew* and *Romeo and Juliet,* and recently appeared in the role of the ballet master, Sergei Alexandrovitch, in the Stuttgart Ballet's popular production of the American musical *On Your Toes.* In 1989, he played the role of the already sick and aged Nijinsky in a short French film directed by Irene Jouannet. Over the years, he has coached many great dancers including Nureyev, Bruhn, Cragun, Haydée, Evdokimova, Donn, and Pontois.

Ursuliak concedes that when Marcia Haydée, then director of the Stuttgart Ballet, first asked him to take over the school, he hesitated. "I felt a bit old to be a father again," he laughs. Pressed for specifics about his dreams for the John Cranko-Schule, Ursuliak, surprisingly, denies having any. "I have no particular plans or changes I wish to make," he says. "I learned that from my father. With him it was never 'We're going to do this or that tomorrow.' It was always 'Well, we'll see what happens.' Of course, we have certain dates for exams and performances, but, really, I believe we shouldn't make a big deal about them. Every day here is simply part of a learning process." This is how Ursuliak sees life—as an evolutionary process. "I just want to remain a part of it," he says. "That's why I stay away from dogmas." He says one of the nicest compliments that he has received from his students in Stuttgart came after they'd just finished a performance. "They told me how sad they were when the performance ended because the process was over. They said they'd learned so much and had had such a good time preparing for it."

In relationship to what he can accomplish with the school, Ursuliak considers himself a realist rather than a dreamer. "I work with what I have," he says. "These kids have to go to regular German academic school in the morning, then they come to ballet school in the afternoon. So my time with them is limited. Also, there are budget restraints." However, Ursuliak does keep one important objective in mind. "My overriding interest," he says, "is seeing that my students develop as human beings and artists. If we can't achieve that," he remarks wryly, "then I'm the wrong person here."

He remembers once watching a videotape of a girl performing in a ballet competition. On the tape he could hear comments being made by people watching the performance. "They were saying things like 'Oh, look at those feet," he recalls. "I never heard anyone mentioning the *name* of the dancer. It's sad, but there's a lot of fetishism in ballet. If the audience comes only to see my students' feet, then I'm missing the boat. I want them to see what my students have to offer as far as what they have to say about this world they're living in. I want to produce dancers who use ballet as a means, not an end! And isn't our first priority as teachers," he asks, "to create a new generation of dancers who will inspire a new generation of choreographers, who will, in turn, create fantastic ballets?"

Ursuliak has very definite ideas about how to produce interesting artists. "Never rob a student of his self-esteem," he says. "If you do, you will kill creativity in students. Then you will have made dancers who are only mechanical, and what kind of an influence are they going to be on a choreographer? Completely mechanical! So the ballets will come out mechanical. But," he continues, "if you have a dancer who has not only technique, but also a flow—the Russians call it 'dousha,' meaning the soul is behind it— these dancers will influence a choreographer, even if he's a stone! He's going to have to melt somewhere along the line, and some of this will wear off and the choreography will develop some depth. So it's up to us pedagogues. If we'd stop pushing their legs up to their ears, pushing these extremes, and remember about aesthetics, we'd do better. After all, if you can't look at a dancer without first looking him or her in the eyes, then what are you looking at?"

Indeed, Ursuliak's philosophy seems readily reflected in his students, who dance with individuality and confidence, as well as a lovely innocence and naturalness. Even he was pleased, when I visited him a year after he had begun directing the school. "In spite of my madness," he says with a mischievous grin, "they've remained quite natural this year—a normal bunch of young people developing their abilities, but also developing as human beings at the same time. As soon as they start moving, you feel this humanness about them," he says proudly. "It's not just feet and arms, which, of course, we talk about in class, but the priority is first the person. The other things are simply there to get us from point A to point B."

The school adheres to the Russian system of training, a change in method that was made three years before Ursuliak took over. "It was done under my predecessor," says Ursuliak, "because the system in use simply was not turning out the kind of dancer that we in the Stuttgart Ballet, or other companies, were looking for."

"Many years ago," Ursuliak recalls, "I had the opportunity to translate for Ulanova (see p. 365, n. 3) when she first came to Canada. She was asked why there is a certain difference between Russian-trained and Western-trained dancers. Her answer was that dancers in the West had become slaves to the barre, never seeing where those exercises were leading. 'You see barre work only as itself and nothing more,' she said." Ursuliak elaborated on what she had meant, using an example from a class he had just finished teaching: "Today in class we did a *fondu* and a *coupé*. Now, where are they leading? Well, the *coupé* is the pushing off to jump and the *fondu* is the soft landing. Already, even at the barre, the child should have a picture of that in his mind."

Ursuliak commented that the German word for education, "Ausbildung," is constructed with the word "bild," or picture. (The word for imagination, "Einbildung," also uses this root.) "In other words," he says, "education is about pictures. Therefore, before I can educate a child, I must have a picture in my own mind. Then, I transmit it to him." Along the same line, he points out that the word for teaching, "lehren," comes from an old German word, "lehre," meaning "show the way." "If a child doesn't understand, it's nobody's fault," Ursuliak says gently, "maybe you're just not using enough ways to make your point clear. That's where our work comes in. It's much easier to just give a class than *teach* a class."

Ursuliak is fond of pointing out that the word "pedagogy" comes from the Greek roots "paid" (child) and "ago" (literally, to lead). "Don't forget that," he warns prospective teachers. "Don't forget what it's all about. Unfortunately, nowadays, 'pedagogue' is used mostly as a sort of title. It's no longer about a service being given."

All of the teachers in the Cranko School are from Eastern Europe. "They've all had dance careers and pedagogical training in the Russian method," says Ursuliak, "but each, not being Russian-born, has somewhat adapted their approach, cultivated a certain amount of flexibility. That's the undogmatic kind of teacher I want here—one that adapts the program, the method, to the child and not vice versa. I am not interested in fitting the child into the cookie cutter."

Ursuliak never tells his teachers that they must teach something one way or another. He trusts them. "There's always more than one way to skin a cat," he remarks. He was not always this way. "Twenty years ago," he confesses, shaking his head, "I was obnoxious—an absolutist. Things had to be done a certain way. Finally, I realized that usually as soon as you get knowledge, it's already changing! Truth, you know, is of the moment." He says he used to teach a very standard Soviet class, but has become much more flexible now. "I remember my teachers in Kiev," he says, "telling me, when I finished the pedagogy course there, to burn all my books. And they were right. You need books to get the basic information, then there must come a time of adaptation. Otherwise you risk staying at the same level. You'll become a very dogmatic teacher, your students will be very dogmatic, and they won't develop."

Ursuliak, who believes that he and his students are on a voyage of discovery together, would prefer that his students view him as a colleague, rather than an absolute authority. "I'm not smarter than they are," he says, "just older. All I have is experience, and experience is only subjective. I find it pretentious when people think their own experience is *the* thing." He remembers that his respect for his own parents grew in proportion to their ability to admit that they did not know everything, couldn't do everything, that they, too, had problems. "If, as a teacher, you put yourself on a pedestal," he warns, "then when you do not live up to students' expectations, the disillusionment of the students is much greater than if you'd simply admit you're just another sometimes fallible human being." He says he never feels pressure to prove anything to his students. "I think sometimes teachers start screaming and yelling when they fear students are catching up with them," he observes. "They get nervous. The good teacher keeps on educating himself, is himself constantly a student, in order to stay ahead of his students." Ursuliak advises teachers never to give a wrong answer because they don't want to admit they don't know the right answer, or because they don't want to take the trouble to search for it. "I've seen teachers give phony answers, and then when the students are still confused, they start yelling at *them*! When that happens," he remarks pointedly, "it's the teacher who has the problem, not the students."

If his students do something to which he takes exception, Ursuliak will discuss it with them and encourage them to talk about it. "I never say," he comments, "that there is only one way and that they have to do it that way." He believes strongly that students need to find things their own way. "Because if they don't live it out, discover it, with their own bodies, it's just fiction to believe that you've taught them something." Also, he warns that teachers must "be very, very careful not to become complacent, or to mentally put children in categories," with the assumption that what works with one child will work with another. "They're all different," Ursuliak says. "Nature, fortunately, has played its game with us. Each child is unique—although we humans look very similar—because nature is always evolving. It keeps on experimenting."

Ursuliak holds regular discussions with his faculty about methodology and about their students. He tries to visit each class, if only briefly, at least once a day. "There are 110 students in the school," he says, "and I feel I must know them all." As he strolls energetically from classroom to classroom, a bald-headed, slightly rotund figure with twinkling eyes and bushy white sideburns, he seems both elfin and paternal. In the halls, he often sings along with music that drifts from the studios. Clearly, he has favorite tunes. And in each class he visits, he does not hesitate to become involved in whatever is being studied, often offering comments or corrections.

I talked with Ute Mitreuter, a beautiful Soviet-trained East German teacher on the Cranko School faculty. She feels very fortunate to be working with Ursuliak, who has influenced a substantial change in her thoughts about teaching—for the better, she thinks. "Alex is a professional," she says, "with all necessary skills in his pocket. Dance, for him, is a philosophy of life. He's very open-minded. The way he talks and works with students—even problem students—is very special. He always knows how to approach, which tack to take. He draws pupils out of themselves. The most important thing he gives them is the knowledge of how to motivate and empower themselves. It's not discipline imposed from the outside, but from the inside. He believes they must work for themselves, not for the teacher, and that this will make them more successful in their careers. He lets them discover for themselves, for instance, that missing classes means bad performances."

Ursuliak credits his liberal philosophy about discipline to his upbringing. "My parents never laid a hand on me. One look or drop of the eye was enough to let me know I'd done something wrong. We lived with very simple rules. We were given responsibility and expected to live up to it." He tells students: "This is your class. If the concentration, awareness, isn't there, you won't profit." He does not feel it is his job to punish students. "I just tell them they're wasting their time. 'Life's too short,' I say. 'Whatever you do, whether it's sitting in a park or riding a bus, try to benefit from it.'"

Again, there's logic behind his philosophy. "As a dancer, you have to work with continuity, in a methodical way," he states, "and, if you work hard enough, long enough, you'll get results. It's like boiling water. Kept at the right temperature long enough, it turns to steam." He points out that

Alexander Ursuliak looking in the mirror as he corrects a student's hip placement.

tenacity and perseverance are what make a person successful in dance: "It's a risky business, and it takes an awful lot of work to make something even half-way consistent."

One aspect of classroom discipline about which Ursuliak is adamant is *not* allowing students to change the combinations in class. He tells them: "As a professional, you rehearse, and when you get to a certain point, you decide 'that's what I'm going to do in the performance' and you don't play with it anymore. You go onstage and do it as rehearsed. You don't start experimenting mid-performance! Afterwards, if you want to change something, you do it. Well, it's the same with class. Once it starts, it's the teacher, you, and the music. The teacher substitutes for the choreographer, and you do what he sets. It's not just warming up. You're training your body to respond to different needs and wishes. If you want to improvise (for instance, you think an exercise is too fast or you'd rather stretch longer in an adagio) do it *after* class, because when you do that you're interpreting what the teacher has given."

In class, Ursuliak may sound exasperated, but he uses commonsense explanations and humor to appeal to students. "Don't look at the floor," he warns them. "It will still be here when this building is demolished. If you look for it, you'll find it. It will take you right down to it." In line with his dislike of punishment, he rarely raises his voice except, perhaps, to emphasize the dynamics of a *plié* or *battement*. However, he is aware that even the most carefully worded correction can bruise a student's ego. "Dancers must learn early on," he says, "that sensitivity doesn't mean hypersensitivity so that they are not easily hurt or insulted. They must forget the subjective 'me' that's saying, 'I get too many corrections' or, conversely, 'I didn't get enough.' There's too much of this garbage going on too often in class," he says. "The quicker one gets rid of it, the better. You're not going to a psychiatrist when you go to class. You must be able to learn without having your name mentioned. Great dancers understand this, because it doesn't matter who's teaching class—they create the atmosphere for themselves that is necessary to learn. They take what they need out of class and leave the rest."

Ursuliak tells his students: "If you go out of class and you're screaming and yelling or you're so depressed, ask yourself why. What did you take in there? What did you do in that class that permitted things to go that far?" He reminds them that the great Soviet ballerina Ulanova once said, "When I go through the studio door, I leave behind the kitchen, the husband, the dogs, and my friends." He tells his students they must cultivate this ability to leave things where they belong and see things in perspective. "Then you'll make progress," he promises, "because there's no one stopping you but yourself. If you don't get anything out of class, you have to ask yourself, 'Well, where in the hell was I? What was in my way?'"

Having said this, however, he admits that he, too, is occasionally capable of an emotional outburst. "Sometimes I blow my stack," he says regretfully. "But I'm human, too, so why should I pretend I'm not? I believe that there is no such thing as the completely good human being or the completely bad human being. Most of us are in the middle. We're constantly learning to deal with aspects of our characters—what we received from our parents, what's genetic, what's the result of our environment. We're constantly evaluating and re-evaluating. But I always apologize when I blow it," he says. "At that moment something irritated me. And why shouldn't a child know that at that moment they were irritating? Why shouldn't there be a reaction? The one positive thing is that I know my kids will tell me if they disagree with me!"

Leading Stuttgart dancer Roland Vogel, who still studies with Ursuliak, remembers well the day his behavior as a young student invoked Ursuliak's wrath: "One day, unknown to us, he overheard my colleagues and me discussing a famous dancer we'd seen on television the night before. As senior students, we felt quite capable of critiquing other dancers, and I'm afraid we were speaking rather badly about this dancer. Alex was not pleased: 'You should have more respect for this dancer,' he told us. 'He made a big career, and you don't even know what it means to make a *plié*!' This was my first meeting with Alex. It gave me a big shock!"

Ursuliak holds regular weekly rap sessions with his senior students in which such behavioral or attitudinal problems are discussed, along with any other issues pertinent to their development, whether it be as people or dancers. The subjects may range from anatomy to therapeutic exercises, from dance history to diet, from drugs to family problems. The sixteen-year-old students giggled as they told me that he advises them to have a beer after a performance. "And he's adamant about sugar," they said. "He tells us that sugar in any form is unhealthy for us because it makes one's moods go up and down!"

On the day I observed a rap session, the students were to view a videotape of one of their recent performances. "Watch from a neutral point of view," Ursuliak instructed them. "Don't be too critical of yourself. Just see what's good and what needs to be fixed." Later, in a class, I noticed that he gently referred to the video as he offered a correction to one young lady. "Did you notice your head in the tape?" he asked her. One student told me that after she'd danced what she felt was a bad performance one night, Ursuliak encouraged her to stop crying. "You must live always for each moment," he advised. "Forget the past. You're young. Don't waste your time thinking about that which is already finished."

As with any state-subsidized school, admission to the John Cranko School is highly selective. I watched one morning as Ursuliak conducted a physical evaluation of a child after auditioning her in class. He has developed a six-part method of screening a student's physical suitability for a career in professional ballet:

1. To check turn-out (degree of external rotation in the hip joint), he had her lie on her back with her legs drawn up, soles of the feet together, knees dropped out sideways to the floor. He pressed on her knees to see how far they would go toward the floor.

2. To check back flexibility, he had her lie on her stomach and, while keeping her legs and hips on the floor, push up, arching her back.
3. To check her foot flexibility, he had her lie face up on the floor. Then, he lifted one leg straight up at approximately a 60-degree angle to the front. He held the lower leg in one hand and, with the other, bent the foot both ways—flexed and pointed—while simultaneously feeling the calf muscle. He tries to ascertain what type of muscle the child has—soft, pliable, quick to regenerate, or hard, with a tendency toward stiffness, which will probably result in problems with Achilles tendonitis. He also flexed the metatarsal arch by itself, bending the toes back as far as he could, pushing hard on the foot. He repeated the entire process with the other leg, since the flexibility of each foot can vary.
4. To check for flexibility in the hamstrings (i.e., potential for high extensions), he had the student stand and, with legs straight, bend over all the way forward from the hips. Also, in this position, he ran his hand up her spine, checking each vertebra, looking for any sign of fusion that would indicate lordosis.
5. Then, to check flexibility of the Achilles tendon, he had the child do *demi-plié* in 1st position.
6. Finally, he placed the child standing with her back against a wall, her legs parallel, feet together. Then he moved about eight feet away in order to view her from a distance. He was looking for evidence of foot deformation, knock-knees, or one hip or shoulder higher than the other.

Ursuliak's overall evaluation of the child, however, went far beyond the physical. "When you look at prospective students," he says, "you must look with two sets of eyes simultaneously. You want to know if they have the necessary physical attributes—enough turn-out and flexibility to ensure that they won't be miserable—but, also, you're looking for a kind of uniqueness, to see if this is a theatrical human being. It's something you notice immediately."

Even with selective auditioning, Ursuliak says he has very few perfect ballet bodies in the school. And often, older students (particularly males) are accepted even though they have received very little previous training. The always pragmatic Ursuliak rises to the challenge. A knowledgeable food and wine enthusiast, he compares the situation to cooking: "It's like having to prepare meals with only what you grow in your own garden because there's no grocery store you can go to." He enjoys telling an anecdote about a time when he was visiting Marika Besobrasova in Monte Carlo. "She had sixteen dancers over for dinner and I was cooking. All of a sudden she told me we had only one chicken. 'Do something!' she said. So I dissected it, pounded it up to make it look like a lot, and made a lot of sauce to smother it with. We had plenty of bread, and everybody just dunked and dunked in the sauce, and, do you know, at the end of the evening, we had half a chicken left!"

Of course, he says, it would be nice to have his senior classes filled with dancers with perfect physiques and years and years of solid basic training. "But, we don't have it," he states realistically. "When my teachers complain to me about this or that class being difficult, I say, 'What do you want me to do—shoot them?' They're there. We must just get on with it and do the best we can!"

Ursuliak arrives in his classroom each morning about fifteen minutes before the lesson is due to begin. Clad unassumingly in loose sweatpants, a pullover shirt, and well-worn black jazz shoes, he uses the time to warm up his back and feet and, often, to think about the class he is about to give. Kathy Bennetts, who danced with the Stuttgart company before becoming ballet mistress with the Frankfurt Ballet, remembers this pre-class period with Ursuliak: "You'd come into the room in the morning, and there would be Alex working out his combinations with such intensity that you didn't dare be lazy. You had to rise to his level. Even if he was no longer in shape, you'd still be inspired watching him because he did everything with such conviction."

The studio stays very quiet as Ursuliak readies himself to teach. Rarely does he speak to anyone during this period. He seems totally self-absorbed. Most of the students are also there early, sitting on the floor stretching or warming up their feet with Therabands. The atmosphere is one of concentration, a time of stillness during which all prepare their minds and bodies for the intensive ninety minutes of effort that lie ahead.

When the pianist arrives, Ursuliak begins to conduct the warm-up. It starts with slow *tendus* from 1st position facing the barre and continues, while he dictates, for almost ten minutes, during which time the dancers never stop moving. Beginning slowly, and gradually increasing in tempo, it is one of the best, most thorough pre-barre warm-ups I have ever observed. In the process of executing many different types of *tendus, tendus jetés (dégagés), pliés, relevés,* foot stretches, and *cambrés,* the students have ample opportunity to establish placement on top of their legs. Ursuliak even includes movements during which they must *temps lié* away from the barre in order to test their balance as they transfer weight from one leg to the other.

It is obvious from the way he structures his exercises that Ursuliak treats dancers' bodies with great care. And he expects them to work with the same kind of prudence. "Treat your body like a valuable antique car," he tells students, "like it cost $50,000. Take care of it. It's the most important investment you have, because its health determines your happiness." He was very specific one day when, after the warm-up, he chided one young lady who had allowed her ankles to roll in as she lowered from *relevé* into *plié*. "*Relevé*—the moment before you are in the air and through which you pass as you're coming down—is a very important moment," he told her. "You must be very aware at this moment of your turn-out, of the balance on one or two legs, of the way your heel leaves or returns to the floor. It's a vital moment in our technique, especially on the way down, as we control how the weight is absorbed into the floor."

Although his warm-up routine might seem to concentrate primarily on the feet, Ursuliak is a stickler about awareness of the total body. "It has always bothered me," he says, "that one visualized the five positions as something from the knees down. All you saw was the feet. For me, it's a question of are you standing in the position or *are* you the position? I believe 1st position is 1st from head to toe, fingertip to fingertip. Because when you compare how the body looks in 1st and, say, in 4th, it's not the same. It's not just the feet. So you don't just stand, you *are* the position. And when a child understands that, their basic posture improves, and they move differently—much lighter on their feet."

Correct anatomical placement is one of the major focuses in an Ursuliak class. Stuttgart dancer Roland Vogel remarks: "It's great the way he takes care of the body. I think that's the most important thing for him—that a dancer works in such a way that his body will last the entire duration of his career. He's great for this because he has X-ray eyes. He sees *into* the body!" Ursuliak says he spent a lot of time studying anatomy. "My challenge is to transmit this knowledge to dancers—to laymen—without it being boring. I try to simplify it," he told me. "Also, this information is particularly important to help certain less-skilled dancers develop an awareness of their bodies so they can catch up on certain things that they might have acquired unconsciously had they had the benefit of eight years of solid, traditional training."

Ursuliak uses his wealth of anatomical knowledge not only to help him with older students, but also with young ones, as well. One day he talked to me about one of the most common problems teachers face with beginning students, pronation or rolling over of the feet: "You must develop the calf muscle with special exercises outside of class *at the same time* that you begin to turn their legs out. If you don't, you will begin to have protrusions on the inside of the foot below the ankle, and the halor flexis of the big toe will become immobile. Turn-out without lower leg strength will increase pronation." He demonstrated the method he uses to show a child how to feel these muscles. He had one of the young students lie on the floor on her back. He picked up one of her legs straight, positioning it parallel, rather than turned out, and held her flexed foot firmly between his hands. He asked her to try to turn her leg out against the pressure of his hands. After doing this with both her legs, he had her stand up in 1st position and, by herself, try to feel these same muscles on the outside of her lower legs.

During class, Ursuliak's anatomical emphasis is on lifted, but relaxed placement. Former student Kathy Bennetts recalls: "He has this thing about staying calm on your supporting side—'Quiet on your supporting ankle,' he'd always say. He told us that any little extra movement in the supporting ankle is a sign that something's not right. He worked from the ground up on alignment. Your supporting foot had to be quiet and calm on the floor."

Ursuliak also stresses correct placement of the head on top of the spine. This, he tells students, is particularly essential for the execution of any type of *tour en l'air*. He is fond of pointing to his head and saying, "Four kilos," then, jutting his head forward, saying, "Eight kilos!" indicating how weighty the head can be if not properly positioned on top of the spine. One often finds him in class with one hand placed on the back of a student's neck and the other on the side of the face, under the jaw. In this position, he gently lifts the student's head up away from the neck. He notes that only the top two vertebrae really support the weight of the head. "If it isn't placed efficiently on top of these," he says, "you're going to have problems with stability and balance. If students can feel the placement—almost a suspension of the head—all of a sudden there's an awareness in the eyes. Even one's hearing improves when one is placed up there. In fact, the dancer almost looks arrogant, but that's not it. We talk about *port de bras,* but there's also *port de la tête.* In a deer, any wild animal, you can see the awareness in the head as they listen, and their agility is tied to that, to how the head is poised."

During the barre work in his classes, Ursuliak moves constantly, walking

Alexander Ursuliak using Spanish arm poses as he leads students through the *révérence* at the end of a class.

among the students, touching them when necessary, and frequently giving little hints of advice in a soft voice. "Keep your weight over your ankle, not back," he reminds a girl doing *relevés* on one foot. Sometimes he needs to say only one word. "Woof!" he barked humorously to a girl whose leg was not behind her in *attitude*. Sometimes he'll step in front of the student and, in an exaggerated manner, silently imitate the mistake being made. The student immediately gets the message. Throughout the class, he chooses his words carefully, and the brief speeches he offers after exercises give students much to think about. After a stern lecture, he will invariably make a funny remark, eliciting a laugh from the class and breaking the tension of the moment.

To observe his students in the centre, Ursuliak most often places himself at the side or the rear of the room, where he stands, leaning back against the barre, chin down, lips pursed, peering out intently from under his eyebrows. When a student does something incorrectly, he reacts, shaking his head with a slight frown. If he likes what he sees, the corners of his mouth move up slightly with delight.

Sometimes he counts in Russian, sometimes in German, sometimes in English. The students at the Stuttgart school come from all over, and, although all are required to study German, Ursuliak is often faced with a language barrier. He speaks Russian, German, Ukrainian, French, and English fluently, but does not hesitate to try bits of Japanese, Italian, Portuguese, and Spanish with students from other countries. Often, he needs no language at all. One day, he walked in front of a boy whose face was screwed in concentration. The student's body was overwhelmed with tension. Ursuliak took a wide stance, striking a taut, threatening samurai warrior's pose, clenching his jaw, face reddening. "Hah!" he grunted. The student laughed and relaxed.

Ursuliak's regular daily classes in his school differ somewhat from his company or master classes, which are always impeccably structured in the typical Russian tradition. He never pushes to cram a lot of material into any one class, but, rather, remains flexible to students' changing daily needs. "I'm not wedded to any single method," he told me. "There are days when I may not give *grands pliés* until *ronds de jambe à terre*, but then they'll get a lot of *grands pliés*." Along this line, I observed one senior class in Stuttgart that included not one pirouette and another without any large jumps! I asked him about this. "Most of the kids I work with at the upper level," he told me, "do not come to the school adequately prepared. There's a lot of work to be done with them and it's very intense, both in the classroom and out. I often give them exercises to do outside of class to develop more strength and flexibility. Physically, if absolutely necessary, I may allow them a bit of leeway where turn-out is concerned, but not with anything else. I constantly give them information, and I make them do a lot of repetition to catch up. We may do an exercise three or four times in the centre. There's no secret to it. You're trying to make up for lost time, so it means you don't just use class in the normal way, to warm up. It's all intensive learning. Sometimes, I'll eliminate some standard part of class because I'm working on something particular that day. I'm trying to cram it into their bodies, and, up until now, I've had a certain amount of success working this way."

His classes always have a theme—one that emphasizes a certain coordination or dynamic quality or even an individual step. On a day during which he planned to focus on the *développé* leg action in *ballottés* and *sissonnes développés,* he began by inserting an *enveloppé* movement into the third barre exercise—a *tendu* combination. He talked to the students about the difference between the muscles in the thigh (long) and the groin (short) and how strongly the short muscles must be used during the *enveloppé* to pull everything into the groin area. He noted the importance of pelvic and stomach control during the leg action. The fifth barre exercise was devoted exclusively to *enveloppés,* and the sixth—*rond de jambe à terre*—included a *grand battement en cloche* immediately followed by a *ballotté* (a jump that begins with the leg action of an *enveloppé*). The first centre exercise with *tendus* and pirouettes included an *enveloppé* movement at 90 degrees. Finally, in the jumping combinations, the students did *ballottés.*

The combinations in Ursuliak's classes are usually rather short—simple, though certainly not easy. In the barre work, there is a great deal of flexing and pointing of the feet, as well as many *pliés* on one leg with the other extended at all heights. There are also many *cambrés* of the body, and tempi are relaxed, allowing for plenty of time to hold balances in *passé* or *attitude.* I felt there was a deliberate effort on his part never to overtax or strain the dancers' muscles. When they are working, he requires maximum effort and concentration from them, but he obviously understands that one cannot work at this maximum level constructively more than a certain amount of time.

Former Stuttgart dancer Jan Stripling told me what he remembers most about the construction of Ursuliak's classes was that "they carried you like a stream. You hopped in and you floated into the various areas—the deep ones, the shallow ones where the speed is greater. And it was your own choice whether or not you wanted to go the faster or the quieter speed. You know how a river goes around curves? It really swirls you around, and he had the ability to do that to people. Even though there was a mass of people in class, all with their own individual needs and different demands—within the range of exercises you could go at your own speed of learning. I enjoyed it immensely."

As an observer, I, too, enjoyed the flow of Ursuliak's classes. Particularly impressive was the seemingly infinite number of ways he varied the daily regimen. Former student Kathy Bennetts recalls: "His way of lightening up the class would be to throw in a bit of character movement—it was his Slavic side coming out—a couple of mazurka steps in a turn exercise or a Spanish *port de bras* at the end. One was always swept along by his intensity."

I noticed that each day, Ursuliak seemed to sneak new challenges into the usual barre exercises. In *rond de jambe à terre,* for instance, one day he put *fouettés* at 90 degrees in the combination, the next *attitude* turns from 2nd position *plié,* and the following day *ronds de jambe* with one-quarter and one-half turns. In short, the routine was never routine.

There are, however, certain characteristics of an Ursuliak class that never change. He rarely, if ever, gives a separate adagio exercise at the barre. Bits of adagio movements are instead inserted into several of the other combinations. "What's the purpose," he asks, "of these long adagios when people's legs are up so long they're shaking? In what choreography do you see that? I avoid this kind of exercise, especially with dancers who are tired." His rationale also has something to do with psychology. "Most dancers see adagio exercises as something to be feared. You give the counts and already you see the hair standing up on their necks. I try to get rid of that fear element by putting adagio movements in here and there. And, at the end of the class, they may actually have done even more than the equivalent of one long adagio."

Another characteristic of Ursuliak's classes is his inclusion of many changes of direction at the barre, something in which he strongly believes. "If you wait until the centre work to do these, it's too late," he says. For instance, there are always *fouettés à terre* in his *tendu* exercises (used mainly to change sides).

I also noticed Ursuliak's repeated emphasis on *port de bras*. The arms and head, always used in a soft, natural manner, are very specifically choreographed into every exercise. His teaching about arms begins with how the students must hold the barre. Tongue-in-cheek, he often accuses students of holding onto the barre as if they believe someone is going to steal it! To a student who was suffering from repeated problems with a sore foot, he commented: "You cannot improve your condition if you stand incorrectly at the barre [shoulder up, hand placed on the barre in back of the torso] because you are never standing *on your feet*. You're standing on your arm!" And I loved the comment he made to a tense student who was gripping the barre with his elbow incorrectly rotated up in the air. "In Russian," Ursuliak told him dryly, "we have a word for that—*kazhydnniy*—which refers to putting a person in prison."

He can be very funny as he demonstrates how *not* to execute *port de bras*. During an allegro combination one day, he demonstrated an *échappé sauté* with a huge half *port de bras*. He was mimicking, ape-like, students who had lifted their arms too high and wide as they opened them to 2nd position. "Wilhelma!" he exclaimed, naming Stuttgart's famous zoo. He got a big laugh from the class. "This half *port de bras*," he told them, "is typical of the Bournonville school [see p. 368, n. 11], and Bournonville always used low arms. If you do it too big, you're cultivating the gorilla look. I'll send you to the zoo." Repeatedly, he will admonish students to keep their arms simple. "Too complicated, too complicated," he will declare. "Just look at your hand in that small pose and don't embellish by twisting your torso, looking over your elbow, or anything." To emphasize his point about simplicity, he asks the students to define the name of what they're doing. "*Port de bras*," he says, "means simply movement of the arms from one pose to another. Give me what's in the name of a step, nothing more."

He does not cling to any particular tradition in his approach to arm positions. "There are thousands of ways to hold your arms," he says, "but the *way* you do it must be attractive and organic. It irritates me, for instance, that today we see low arms so infrequently. Arms are so big and wide. When I was taught, we were told to keep our little finger level with our navel. Of course," he jokes, "on today's long-legged dancers most of their navels are in the middle of their breastbones!" His advice about arm placement is not simply aesthetic. "You could kill yourself with these karate arms," he tells a student one day, imitating the young man's violent arm slice to the side preceding a pirouette. "Keep it simple," he says. "The *passé* is enough to make you turn."

He has little patience for students who forget, or change, the *port de bras* he has set during an exercise. "Just working on one part of your body in an exercise is ludicrous," he tells them. "You're just defeating your own purpose. Coordination must never be taken for granted. It's something you have to fight for every day because there's a battle constantly going on in our bodies between the old cells that are being replaced and the new ones." Ursuliak believes this is what causes a lack of memory in the muscles. "The old is still partially there," he says, "and the new still hasn't acquired all the information."

Drawing attention to the way the hands must be used, Ursuliak tells students to remember "that our ballet history goes back to the time of Louis XIV. In order to keep the hand looking aesthetical," he says, "seventeenth- and eighteenth-century court dancers used a lot of those little mannerisms—though I wouldn't call them that. They're just logical changes of direction for the purposes of beauty and communication. During historical dances, one needed little re-finesses of the hand because there was always a dialogue going on. People used to make arrangements for their next meeting in someone's boudoir with such hand gestures!" He notes how ballet dancers are often criticized for having fixed positions of the hands—hands that never say anything! "Well," he says, "that's because we don't use them enough. The little transitions are important."

At the end of every class, Ursuliak leads his students through a long, improvised series of *port de bras,* often incorporating character (particularly Spanish) poses into his movements. "Rings on your fingers!" he tells them to remind them to keep their fingers separated.

His classes at the school frequently include former students, now Stuttgart company members, returning to the fold. Certainly they come because Ursuliak's wonderfully dancey moving combinations feel good to them, but I believe they are also mentally storing his wise words for the time when they, too, will become teachers. Indeed, Ursuliak has prepared many dancers for that mid-career change. At one point in his tenure with the Stuttgart Ballet, he decided to offer a teachers' course. Twenty-two company dancers signed up. "I was astounded," he says. "We met two or three times weekly for two years. We started from point zero. What is a *plié*? What muscles are being used? What is an axis? What is physiologically efficient posture? What is the psoas muscle?" He continues: "During this course, the level of these dancers' performances naturally increased. They improved because they were learning so much about their own bodies. So I felt like I was winning for the present day, as well as for the future of ballet in general. I knew these people would eventually go out and influence the world. And they have," he says proudly. "Reid Anderson is now running the National Ballet of Canada. Kathy Bennetts, Urs Frey, and Glen Tuggle are ballet masters in Frankfurt. Otto Neubert danced with the New York City Ballet and is now out west somewhere. And Richard Cragun, Egon Madsen, and Kurt Speker are working with our own company. It was beneficial for me, too. Conducting company classes and rehearsals with the people who were taking the teaching course became much easier because they had so much more information with which to work."

I asked Ursuliak whom he himself looked to for inspiration and learning. He told me that the writings of the Indian guru Krishnamurti continue to have a strong impact on him. He also named several others he has always admired, among them Gandhi and Martin Luther King. "I suppose," he says, "it's because of their commitment to nonviolence—to achievement without blood loss." He also mentioned John F. Kennedy, whose statement "Ask not what your country can do for you, but rather what you can do for your country" he has always revered. "And," he adds, "I love Mother Teresa's pure generosity. I find it inspiring that there are people all over the world who find strength in giving rather than receiving."

When one begins teaching, Ursuliak told me, one has to become selfless. "You must let go of egotistical ambitions for your students. It's their life, not yours. So why should you be ambitious for them? If you are, you will have problems and you're going to have disappointments. Remember: you're not there for yourself. You're there for them. It's difficult—sure—to leave the spotlights and go into the shadows, but it's a choice. If you're not willing to make it, don't become a teacher." However, he does not deny that his students' success gives him great pleasure. "I want you to be the best you can be," he tells them, "because if you're happy, then I'm happy."

I asked him what he thought his strength was as a teacher. "I believe it is that I know I am still capable of growing," he replied. "A good teacher is one who can remain a good student himself—always adapting and being flexible. A good student is a disciple who wants to learn. One who creates the atmosphere of discipline in which learning is possible by opening himself up and allowing things to come in. Actually," he said, eyes twinkling, "there's not a big difference between the two of them."

Classroom Quotes from Ursuliak

"Timidity is not a virtue—modesty is—timid is weak. So don't look down. That's where the worms and the ants are. Hold yourself up. Give people something to admire. Look up. Be confident. That's admirable."

"A lot of people, doctors, will tell you that in pursuing a dance career, you're ruining your toes or your knees. So what! Ordinary people have meniscus operations for bad knees and backs—and they've never done *anything* exciting with their bodies."

To a student standing too close to the barre: "The barre is your friend, but a distant friend. Don't get too chummy."

To a student struggling to stay on balance in *sous-sus:* "5th position on *relevé* shouldn't cost a hundred marks."

To a student holding his arms incorrectly *à la seconde:*
"The tightrope walker in the circus holds his hands in 2nd in *front* of his body. That's where the balance is—not in back of the shoulders!"

"On the way down into *plié,* the only thing you have to do is to control your turn-out and the speed of descent. Gravity—Mother Earth—does the rest. It's only as you come up that you must work."

"Never believe in the mirror. Just believe in yourself."

"When you have the opportunity to be ethereal, snatch it. Because it's so rare. When you look at the way most people slouch around going from point A to point B, you realize how beautiful it is when you get this rare exotic bird that's a dancer who goes through so much for something that lasts such a short time. So be ethereal. Keep your head up. It'll make things so much easier both mentally and physically."

Order of the Exercises in Ursuliak's Class (advanced master class, 1½ hours)

BARRE

1. Warm-up (approximately ten minutes)—includes tendus, tendus jetés (dégagés), various stretching exercises for the feet, demi-pliés, relevés, cambrés
2. Pliés
3. Slow tendus
4. Fast tendus
5. Tendus jetés (dégagés)and battements dégagés pointés
6. Ronds de jambe à terre
7. Fondus
8. Frappés
9. Ronds de jambe en l'air
10. Grands battements

CENTRE

1. Tendus, grands pliés, pirouettes en dedans
2. Traveling adagio
3. Tendus jetés (dégagés), pirouettes en dehors, chaînés
4. Grands battements with grandes pirouettes in arabesque and piqués en tournant en dehors
5. Small jumps: temps levés, emboîtés, assemblés
6. Medium jumps: Sissonnes, temps liés sautés en tournant
7. Grand allegro with grands jetés entrelacés
8. Port de bras

The Roots of Tradition

THE PEDAGOGICAL LINEAGE OF ALEXANDER URSULIAK

L'Académie Royale de Musique et de Danse (1661)

Louis Dupré
(1697–1774)

Maximilien Gardel
(1741–1787)

Gaetano Vestris
(1728–1808)

Jean-Georges Noverre
(1727–1810)

Pierre Gardel
(1758–1840)

Auguste Vestris
(1760–1842)

Antoine Bournonville
(1760–1843)

Carlo Blasis
(1797–1878)

August Bournonville
(1805–1879)

Giovanni Lepri
(c. 1830–c. 1890)

Christian Johansson
(1817–1903)

Enrico Cecchetti
(1850–1928)

Pavel Gerdt
(1844–1917)

Nicolai Legat
(1869–1937)

Moscow State School
(c. 1918)

V. Ponomaryov and
Other Teachers
of the Leningrad
Choreographic School

Various Teachers
of the Winnipeg Ballet
(c. 1940)

Boris Volkoff
(1900–1974)

Robert Klavin
(1929–)
Kiev, Ukraine
(Ukrainian)

Freddy Seychuk
(1929–)
Edmonton, B.C.
(Ukrainian-Canadian)

Alexander Ursuliak
(1937–)

9 Christiane Vaussard

Christiane Vaussard conducting class at the Paris Opera Ballet School in Nanterre in 1991.

*C*hristiane Vaussard is the senior women's teacher at l'Ecole du Ballet de l'Opéra de Paris. She has been associated with the Paris Opera Ballet her entire life. Vaussard entered the Opera school in 1933, at the age of ten, became a member of the company at fourteen, rose through the ranks, and was appointed *étoile,* or star, in 1947. During Vaussard's nearly thirty years as a Paris Opera dancer, she worked closely with many renowned choreographers, including Serge Lifar, Léonide Massine, and George Balanchine. On tour with the Paris Opera Ballet in the 1940s and 1950s, she danced in America, in London at Covent Garden, and in Moscow at the Bolshoi. She also appeared on several occasions on French television.

Vaussard was appointed professor at the Paris Opera Ballet School in 1964, a position she has held continuously since then. In 1969, she was also appointed to the faculty of the Conservatoire National Supérieur de Musique de Paris. Among her former students are some of today's brightest stars at the Paris Opera. Vaussard is the recipient of several decorations by the French government, including Chevalier de l'Ordre des Arts et Lettres, Chevalier de la Legion d'Honneur, and Chevalier de l'Ordre National du Mérite.

"Chantez votre danse" (Sing your dance).

CHRISTIANE VAUSSARD'S animated manner—she has an adorable swagger—always elicits small smiles from the teenagers in her classes. Try as they will to control themselves in the austere atmosphere of the Paris Opera Ballet School, they cannot keep the corners of their mouths from rising at the sight of the sparkling Vaussard exuberantly jetting across the studio floor. With her cheerfully energetic presentation, she makes dancing fun—even when it is technically difficult.

Only occasionally does Vaussard sit in class; more often, she paces—relentlessly prodding, pressing, and molding students' bodies with her expressive hands. Coaxing her students, her voice can be seductively guttural one moment, ardent and piercing the next. "You can't just tell a student something once," she told me. "You have to keep telling them!" She has a delightful, graceful way of lightly and quickly brushing the back of her fingers upward over students' *derrières*. "*Montez!*" she commands, urging them to lift their weight up out of their hips.

It is not hard to imagine the slim, delicately boned Vaussard as the Opera star she once was. To say she has charisma would be an understatement. She is charming, electric, and still possesses, in spite of her age, a glowing, vivacious beauty. For teaching, she wears flowing white culottes and always breezes into the classroom in a flurry of activity, untangling the leash of her tiny Yorkie (and constant companion), Romy, while quickly changing into her heeled pink ballet slippers. As each class begins, her chest lifts proudly, her back becomes elegantly straight. When she demonstrates an allegro step, her long, slim legs move with the staccato brilliance of two needles on a sewing machine. She was still performing—"Better than ever!" she says brightly—when, at the age of forty, she was appointed to teach at the Opera school. Today, in her seventies, to maintain herself physically, she adheres to a sugarless health-food diet, walks a great deal, and practices yoga, which, she says, "allows me to continue to do things I was able to do before. . . . Without it, I couldn't get up and dance!"

Vaussard is one of the few seventy-year-old teachers I have ever seen demonstrate a movement full-out in class. The first time I saw her do this, I blinked in disbelief! For a period of about three seconds, her entire body was transformed in front of my eyes. The years disappeared as she jumped into the air, impeccably executing a high *assemblé porté*. Her back was straight, her feet perfectly pointed, and her legs crossed tightly in 5th position *en l'air*! "Once in a while, I do these things," she says slyly. "It makes the students pay attention." One day, after finishing a lesson, Vaussard even hoisted her leg onto the barre in 2nd position to do a bit of stretching. "Just to see if I still can," she told me. She is still able to move faster than most of her students, and to see her demonstrate a fast *pointe* exercise (albeit off *pointe*) is a thing of wonder. Her feet fly! The speed at which she can execute a series of small *emboîté* walks forward boggles even the minds of her students. Sometimes her demonstrations become comic, such as when, showing the velocity with which she wished them to flick their foot to *cou-de-pied*, she inadvertently kicked her shoe across the room. She can also be deliberately funny. "*Pas comme ça* [not like this]," she said one day, striking an awful pose, tummy hanging, shoulders drooped, and mouth turned down.

Generally, though, she is somewhat more careful about how she appears to her students. "I do not want them imitating me. As a matter of fact, I always consider it a great compliment when people tell me my girls don't dance like me, but rather like themselves. That's my aim as a teacher. I especially wouldn't want them copying me now, at this age!" She says she still feels very young (and with her dark, naturally styled hair, she looks it), "but," she admits, "I don't like to see myself in the mirror anymore." The portrait she has chosen to use in the school's souvenir booklet is from her younger ballerina days. "I must show a positive, respectable image to my students," she explains, but then laughs, remembering that her maid, upon seeing the photo, exclaimed, "Is that you? But you were so pretty!"

Vaussard started dance lessons as a very young child. She came from an artistic family. Her great-grandfather, Gilbert Duprez, had been a tenor in Italy, and her grandfather, Leon Duprez, was a piano teacher at the Conservatoire. Her mother, who felt the petite Vaussard was in need of physical development, took the child to the great Parisian ballet professor Carlotta Zambelli.[1] "Because I was so young," Vaussard recalls, "Zambelli placed me at the back of the studio where I could learn by copying the older dancers. She thought I was cute and talented, so I studied with her twice a week until I was ten and old enough to be enrolled at the Opera School."

"Zambelli," Vaussard remembers, "because of her spirituality, was an extraordinary person. She was artistic, musical, and very exacting." Vaussard remembers Zambelli telling students: "If your feet aren't exactly *en dehors* [turned out]—*Tant pis!* [Too bad!] But if you're unmusical—*Dehors!* [Get out!]" As director of the Paris Opera Ballet school, Zambelli often watched the children's classes, providing guidance to young professors such as Vaussard's first teacher at the school, Mauricette Cesbron. During the

1930s, when Vaussard was a student there, the training of the young people was sandwiched between the classes and rehearsals of the ballet company. With difficulty, both groups, children and professionals, shared the backstage studios at the opera house. The arrangement was hardly ideal.[2] Vaussard remembers her daily schedule: "In the morning at eight I attended regular French academic school. At 1:30 P.M., I went to the Opera for my ballet class, followed by a French class there until 4:30. After that, we were done, and I went for classes with either Egorova [see p. 360, n.7], Zambelli, or Preobrajenska[3] in their private studios."

I asked Vaussard how Zambelli had felt about her studying with other teachers. (Nowadays, it is strictly forbidden for Paris Opera Ballet students to take classes outside the school.) "She didn't like it," Vaussard admitted, "but she was a lady of great intelligence and finesse. She knew that as a young girl I preferred, for instance, the more expressive Russian-style movements of Preobrajenska, who, incidentally, loved me very much. So, Zambelli growled a bit and complained (she preferred that children study more contained movement), but she did not try to prevent me from going. However, she warned my mother: 'Be careful where you take your daughter because she sees and remembers everything—the good and the bad! It all registers.'"

I was curious about Vaussard's recollections of the great Parisian teachers Egorova and Preobrajenska, both of whom are legendary figures in the history of ballet pedagogy. They were special, she told me, primarily because of the beautiful manner in which they showed their exercises. "They had charisma, great personality," she recalls. "Egorova was very Slavic, very Russian. She used big arm movements and was fond of small, rapid steps. During World War II it was very cold, so she wore gloves and boots and something on her head in the classroom. She was well known for her beautiful adagios. I don't remember them exactly, but I will never forget the expression in her body as she demonstrated."

As a young student, Vaussard remembers that after class she and her classmates were often required to return in the evening to the opera house, where they performed as extras. "I can sing all the operas—Wagner, Mozart, all! But we were always exhausted. I'd sleep through my school classes in the morning!" However, she recalls her childhood at the Opera as a very rich experience: "It was like being in a fairy tale. The Wagnerian operas impressed me the most." Unfortunately, there were very few parts for children in the ballet performances at the Opera. However, occasionally, special children's ballets were presented. She began to appear in these at age eleven. She remembers two: *Images* by Leo Staats[4] and *Jeanne's Fan*. "We also danced in a Chopin suite," she recalls, "in which we were little cupids. I loved that!"

As was customary at the time, Vaussard officially entered the Paris Opera Ballet Company at age fourteen. "Starting my career that young," she says, "I probably missed something in the way of life experience, but people didn't question such things then. Anyway," she says brightly, "*Je me sentais bien* [I was feeling good]. My life was *la danse, la danse, la danse.*" Coming up through the strictly regulated ranks of the Ballet de l'Opéra was hard. She says certain aspects of ballet technique, such as turn-out, did not come easily to her body: "I had to work on everything," she recalls.

As was required of all dancers at the Opera, Vaussard participated each year in the annual *Concours*. This tradition is unique to the Paris Opera Ballet. Once a year, the members of the company compete with each other for promotion within the Opera's hierarchy. For an entire day, one after another, the dancers perform solos from the repertoire in front of an illustrious jury.[5] There are six ranks in the company, from entry-level corps de ballet to star (*étoile*). As individual dancers move upward, they are rewarded with better roles, as well as increased salary and prestige. In Vaussard's day, the *Concours* was obligatory for all dancers. Now, it is optional. Dancers who wish promotion participate; others satisfied with their current rank do not.

Vaussard remembers doing the *Concours* every year, except for two years during the war when it was suspended. To move up to the rank of *première danseuse*, she was required to perform an entire act from a ballet. (Things are different now. Dancers compete with only two variations.) Vaussard danced Act I from *Coppélia*. The next day, officially her first in her new rank, she was presented with an unexpected opportunity. Yvette Chauviré, the Opera's leading ballerina at that time, became ill. On last-minute notice, Vaussard stepped in for her, dancing not only Act I of *Coppélia*, which, because of the *Concours*, she was well prepared to do, but also Act II, which she had never rehearsed at all. "I'd only seen it!" she recalls. "Fortunately," she adds, "I've always been blessed with an excellent memory."

Her initiation into the role of Odette in *Swan Lake*, Act II, was just as sudden. She was almost twenty-three and had been a *première danseuse* for a year. One night, a fellow dancer who was the understudy for the roles of the two big swans was called upon to dance. Disinclined to perform, she convinced Vaussard, who always knew everyone's part, to go on in her place. Vaussard remembers: "Half-way through the act, I was standing backstage in my swan tutu by the radiator. I was cold and tired and my *pointe* shoes were nearly worn out. Someone grabbed me and said: 'Get onstage!' The great Opera ballerina Lycette Darsonval, who had been dancing Odette, was incapacitated. Her leg had given out. Darsonval's partner, Peretti, dancing the role of the Prince, assumed the curtain would fall. He was very surprised when I, who had never danced Odette, appeared from the wings to finish the act with him!" Vaussard's phenomenal memory had once again served her well. "Of course, I knew the role," she says, "I'd watched it so many times. I loved it! Probably, I'd been dreaming of dancing it." The next day, as a result of her performance, she was appointed *étoile*, the top rank at the Opera. It was the beginning of January 1947.

I asked her about the war years in Paris in the 1940s. She recalled the Occupation as being very difficult: "The atmosphere was icy and anxiety ridden. People were being arrested and sent to Germany. I lost a lot of friends—young men. Our parents had to line up for food. My father had something to do with the French Resistance. My mother brought a Jewish friend home and hid her. There were nerve-wracking bomb alerts in the subway. Suddenly, you'd be stuck down there for two hours. This was a big problem where rehearsals were concerned, so my godmother bought me a bike to go to and from the opera house. (Unfortunately, it was a man's bike and I had trouble reaching the pedals!) One night, while I was at the Opera, our house was destroyed by bombs. My parents were in the cellar. It was six months before we found another house. We just moved around from one friend's place to another. But I had the Opera and it sustained me . . . when you're young you get used to anything."

It was during the war years that Vaussard met her husband, an American intelligence officer who spoke fluent French. He remained in France with her after the war. They had one son who is now a doctor. "It was very unusual for a ballerina to have a child in those days," she says. "I was the first one at the Paris Opera since Taglioni to do so!" She was twenty-six years old and danced leading roles in both *Les Sylphides* and *Swan Lake* when she was five months pregnant. "And I came back a month after my baby was born," she adds. "Probably too soon."

Vaussard's motto, she told me, has always been: "Life is hard work, and one must do a good job. Do everything you do well." Does she believe that she owes something of her success as a teacher to the fact that, without a

Christiane Vaussard guiding a student through an adagio at the barre in a senior
ladies' class at the Paris Opera School.

physique well-suited for ballet, she had to struggle so hard to become a dancer? "Perhaps," she answers modestly. "But if I am not a bad professor, it is surely because I had such good professors." She names Zambelli, Egorova, Preobrajenska, and Balashova[6] as the major influences on her when she was a young student. Later, as a dancer in the company, she studied with the great ballerinas Tamara Toumanova and Maria Tallchief, as well as Serge Lifar,[7] George Balanchine (see p. 359, n. 3), and Albert Aveline. "Aveline," Vaussard recalls, "was Zambelli's associate for many years. I remember him coming to watch her classes. Then, when she retired, he took over the direction of the school by himself (1935–58). He was ballet master at the Opera for fifty-five years, and he was a great pedagogue, very different from Zambelli. He was more influenced by the Italian teacher Guerra. He put a lot of research into his teaching, which was extremely structured. It was real work, and it was wonderful! He always corrected through a thought process. He was perhaps the greatest ballet master the Opera ever had. Like Zambelli, his musicality was fantastic. He staged all the classics. Balanchine liked him so much that he always requested that Aveline be the person to rehearse his ballets."[8]

I was curious about what Vaussard recalled from the classes of Lifar and Balanchine. "When I teach," she told me, "I mostly have three people in my head—Lifar, Aveline, and Balanchine. These were the greatest influences on me. Lifar's movement was always long. He wanted everything really pulled out, and he used lots of spirals in the body. Balanchine was much more square, straight in the body, clipped." The influence of all three is easily visible in Vaussard's classes. One sees Aveline, the most academic of them, in the exacting way she focuses on placement, Lifar in the sweeping *port de bras* she uses in adagios, and Balanchine in her sparkling, jazzy *pointe* and *petit allegro* combinations. "I worked with so many marvelous teachers that what I do today," she says, "is really a synthesis. For the arms, it's from one. For the feet, another. Nothing comes just from myself, from a vacuum. Nothing is just mine. One evolves with age and experience, and I also evolve with contemporary ballet. For instance, there's a Forsythe [the Frankfurt Ballet's director and choreographer, William Forsythe] ballet in the Opera's repertoire now, so it's necessary for me to give my girls exercises that will make dancing this ballet possible."

Vaussard's classes are filled with such exercises. Many of her combinations demand great speed; in others, the torso bends freely and fully, accompanied by *port de bras* that is large and sweeping. High extension in her classes is *de rigeur*. Her allegro combinations move across the floor at full throttle—*enchaînements* that reflect the athleticism and excitement of today's choreography. But this is only one side of Vaussard's teaching. Equal emphasis is placed on perfect articulation of all tiny movements— the presentation and turn-out of the foot in a *petit développé*, or the light, staccato precision of the toes in a series of fast *battements dégagés pointés*. Throughout all the exercises, students hear Vaussard's constant reminders about placement and balance.

"When you finish being an *étoile*," Vaussard told me, "you know nothing. It is when you begin to teach that you begin to learn. As a dancer, you know it in your body, but as a teacher, you must know it in your head." I asked her how she had prepared herself to teach. "I read a lot," she told me. "The Vaganova book and the Cecchetti book, which Zambelli gave me. It was her personal copy and contains her annotations. As I read these books, many things from my own training came back to me."

I asked her if her classes have changed over the years. She replied: "Certainly I hope so! Modern choreography demands it, but also as you grow older, your thinking expands and you move toward a synthesis of all you know—memories of your youth and of all the people with whom you have worked shape your classes. Using the ideas of one's teachers, incidentally, is not stealing. It's a necessity to pass along such good information! And I love new ideas. For instance, one of the ballerinas at the Opera showed me a *petit rond de jambe* exercise that Nureyev (see p. 361, n. 11) had taught her. I thought it was excellent, so I incorporated it into my classes. But I don't think the structure of my classes has changed much. Perhaps, however, as I've worked with so many people's faults and problems and know what is possible, I am now more demanding." Devoted former student Elizabeth Platel, now one of the Opera's reigning stars, remembers that Vaussard "never let us cheat—no tricks—you had to do it right without any compensating!"

Because Vaussard's choreographed combinations are unusually detailed and creative, I was curious about how much preparation she does for her classes. "I've been teaching since 1964," she told me. "In the early days, I wrote down all my classes, every year. Now, however, it's automatic. I know what must come after what."

Echoing a complaint made by many teachers, Vaussard laments that her classes at the Opera School are limited to an hour and a half: "There's never enough time!" she exclaims. In order to cover everything that she feels her

Christiane Vaussard 237 ～

senior girls must practice, she adheres to a rather unusual method: one day they do their class in soft ballet slippers; the next, they repeat the same class on *pointe*. Watching them do this was impressive. Many exercises, especially slow ones, are extremely challenging to perform in *pointe* shoes. Also, Vaussard has her students reverse every exercise, regardless of the difficulty. "It's for the brain *and* the body," she says. "When I was young, we always reversed everything! So did Aveline and Balanchine when they taught. After all, you have to be able to move backward as well as forward onstage. After you descend downstage in a variation, how do you get yourself back upstage? With your back to the audience? No!" And I watched with amazement as her students easily executed a fast series of *chassés* backward, upstage.

As a teacher, Vaussard is very specific. No detail escapes her eagle eyes. "I try to make every movement I give in class exact, precise, and beautiful," she says. "Afterwards, I want expression put into it. Students have to feel that they have something special to reveal—and not necessarily what the teacher wants them to give, but what they themselves feel individually through the music. Also, as movement, after all, is a reflection of the music, you have to be in the correct style of the music, whether it's ragtime or a Negro spiritual. Aveline always wanted us to sing the music. One can either do that or just feel the rhythm inside one's body." I observed her in class showing how to perform a step in several different ways to the same piece of music, and still be musical. "This is the richness of choreography," she said with the matter-of-factness of one stating a universal truth.

Vaussard is fortunate to work with highly skilled accompanists at the Opera School. "*Joli adage, Maestro, s'il vous plaît!* [A pretty adagio, please!]" she will call cheerfully across the room. The pianist, Michel Mitrovitch, plays a trial phrase. "No, let's save that one for another class," she may say, pausing to give him time to come up with another idea. Sometimes, she'll bring music she wants to class. Once, after the pianist had played an adagio she particularly liked, I saw her ask him for a copy of the music. Why? "To make sure he'll play it again sometime," she told me, winking. For allegro work, she has a preference for sassy ragtime music that is fun to dance to. *Grands battements* at the barre one day were done to the tune of "Hello, Dolly!" Regardless of the choice of music, however, all details of musicality in Vaussard's classes are impeccably coached. Every beat is clearly defined in movement. Nothing is ever unclear. "*Non, non, non,*" she cries in distress if the dancers stray rhythmically. "*Dansez avec la musique!*"

Much of her communication about musicality is done through the sound of her voice. Like a mockingbird, she ranges through a wide variety of high and low exclamations, whistles, coos, grunts, and whispers. Even in ordinary conversation, her animated voice moves from one dramatic sound to another with the versatility of an opera singer. This, coupled with her enchanting French accent, makes listening to her very entertaining. I suspect that even if one did not understand the language in which she spoke, one could understand a great deal simply from her delightfully varied intonation. In class, she shows how she wants the dynamics of one movement contrasted with those of another simply by changing her voice.

Emphasis on the contrast between a slow, "pulled" movement one moment and a quick, sharp one the next is one of the major focuses of Vaussard's teaching and, for that matter, of the entire French School. To achieve this contrast, which adds dramatic shading to their dancing, students are coached, for instance, in *pointe* work, to make their *relevés* (or *piqués*) sharp, then to use resistance lowering through the foot into the *plié* that follows ("Sharp, soffft!"). I first saw this approach used in *pointe* classes taught by Violette Verdy (see p. 362, n. 12), although, at the time, I did not realize how derivative it was of her French background. Now, having watched the classes of Vaussard and others in Paris, I believe the repeated use of this contrast to be one of the most beautiful aspects of French dancing, not only in the *pointe* work, but also in allegro combinations, where pulled-out moments of suspension between fast steps add significantly to the choreographic interest of the *enchaînements*. It is the method a dancer uses to keep the audience on the edge of their seats, and its effect is closely related to the anticipatory excitement created by a roller coaster poised momentarily at the crest of a hill. (Suzanne Farrell, one of the last of Balanchine's great ballerinas, understood this contrast in dynamics instinctively and was one of its great practitioners.)

Aside from the dramatic and musical benefits inherent in varying one's attack, between fast and slow, sharp and soft, dancing this way also builds great technical strength—principally because it requires complete control of the body. This, I believe, is one of the key reasons why, as a group, the French are probably the finest dancers *sur les pointes* in the world. Nowhere else have I observed such speedy and expressive footwork, such precision, nor such pliability in the feet as they move up and down, on and off *pointe*. To achieve these results with her students, Vaussard uses a variety of methods, including barre exercises in which the ladies move repeatedly from high *demi-pointe* to full *pointe* without ever lowering their heels. In the centre, she may have students execute a *pas marché* exercise slowly, emphasizing control through the foot as they come off *pointe*, then have them repeat the same exercise in a very fast, sharp manner. (Within the 3/4 rhythm of a waltz, her choreography often requires them to take five fast, tiny steps on *pointe* in one count of three beats.) However, it is evident in Vaussard's classes that the development of such agility in the foot does not begin with the study of *pointe* work. It begins with the first *tendu* exercises at the barre.

After *pliés*, her initial *tendu* combination is rather slow, with ample opportunity to feel the foot as it presses or slides into *plié* or stretches into the pointed position. The next exercise is a very fast *tendu* combination that emphasizes bringing the working leg *in* quickly to 5th position. This type of *tendu/dégagé* exercise is also typical of the Balanchine school, and Vaussard admits, "Since working with him, I have always included it." This second *tendu* exercise, however, may include *battements* with the accent out, as well as in, and always involves many weight transfers from one foot to the other. *Pliés* included in this exercise may be drawn out over two counts, then contrasted in the next moment with ones done sharply using only the upbeat.

Vaussard's third *tendu* exercise at the barre is executed at break-neck speed and includes many different kinds of tiny foot articulations: *dégagés* (*tendus jetés*), flex-point ankle (or just toe) movements, fast *pointés* into the floor, *petits passés*, *petits développés* and *raccourcis* (*enveloppés*), *coupés*, and *piqués*. Many of these movements are to develop what Vaussard terms "a small resistance for the foot." Accents are both in and out. I asked her if such speed so early in the barre might not be difficult, even physically stressful, for the students. She seemed surprised at my question. "But I expect my students to arrive fifteen minutes before class to get warmed up," she said. "If I had to warm them up, class would take too long!" She feels that the four exercises (warm-up *tendus* facing the barre, *pliés*, slow *tendus*, and faster *tendus*) that she gives before this very fast one are sufficient preparation. "But," she warns, "one must learn how to move fast without hurting oneself. This type of speedy exercise should not be difficult. You must learn how to do it with ease, to toss it off." She continues: "Always relax tension in the leg in order to work rapidly. Otherwise, you can't do it and it's hard on the legs. So it's the *way* you do a fast exercise that's important." In class, one hears her over and over again admonishing students to "*Lache la jambe!* [Relax the leg!]" In double *rond de jambe en l'air,* for instance, she wants razor-sharp speed, but without tension in the thigh.

Vaussard often demonstrates what she means. "My choreography for one of the *enchaînements* in this year's school performance,"[9] she told me, "was rather jazzy. I had to show my girls what swing style was in order to get them to do it right. Their eyes got very wide watching me," she grinned, "but, you know, the more you know about dancing, the more you can let your legs go—relax them—and the faster you can put your legs out and bring them back in. In *grand battement,* for instance, it's an entire art not to fatigue yourself. The effort must come from the stomach—the body—not the legs. Same with *développé.* And if you're on your legs, on balance, you won't get tired."

She talks often about "antagonistic muscles," beginning with her first warm-up *tendu* exercise facing the barre. "I want them to feel the body solidly, to be aware of their opposing muscles, those they use to go up and those used to go down." This is particularly important in jumping. "The higher you want to go with the body," she says, "the more you must push down as you take off." She remembers that when Aveline taught, he would sometimes sprinkle flour under students' feet before having them execute an *assemblé.* "He wanted to see if we were pushing into the floor, brushing, as we took off," she recalls, smiling.

Vaussard is very specific—as was Balanchine before her—about the positioning of the legs. Presentation of a very turned-out leg is always stressed. "*Croisé de cuisse* [cross the thighs]," she says again and again as students do a series of *passés relevés.* Or on *dégagés (tendus jetés):* "Cross thighs—open thighs!" If she sees that students are losing turn-out or bending their front knee as they close 5th position, she has them repeat the exercise slowly, closing instead in 3rd position, concentrating on keeping the front thigh turned out. Paris Opera Ballet star Isabel Guerin, a former student, remembers that Vaussard "worked my legs like a sculptor."

Frequent, energetic changes from one leg to the other are choreographed into all Vaussard's exercises, as are many changes in body direction: *croisé* to *effacé (ouvert), effacé (ouvert)* to *écarté.* Accents change from in to out. Sometimes she wants the working leg to have a feel of weight, as in a *relevé lent* in an adagio; other times, she wants it light, weightless, as in a series of *grands battements à la seconde* in which the leg is thrown in a small, but high, arch from just slightly in front of the shoulder to slightly in back before it closes 5th position. One of the most beautiful moments in Vaussard's class comes at the very end, when the students execute a *révérence* during which each step they take is preceded by a light, impeccably done *petit battement*, after which the foot and leg are beautifully presented, turned out, in the direction of the next step. This *révérence*, Vaussard says, has been around in the Opera for as long as she can remember.

When coaching her students in jumping *enchaînements*, Vaussard concentrates on rebound, the way one movement propels the dancer into the next. One normally thinks of this as characteristic of the Bournonville School (see p. 368, n. 11), but anyone in the French School will be quick to tell you that the concept originated in Paris. Claude Bessy, director of the Opera School, told me with a touch of annoyance: "All those Danes, Bournonville included, came to receive their training at the Opera in the 1800s. The Bournonville style is really French." Vaussard's jumps, however, more closely resemble Balanchine's than Bournonville's, although the two styles have much in common. Most of her allegro combinations are quite fast, often containing jazzy syncopation. Others are full of exuberant *demi-caractère* movements. She is adamant about control through the foot as one lands from a jump. "*Très souple!* [Very soft!]" she reminds students. One day, on a fast *glissade-jeté* combination, she told them: "Don't jump high. Be softer."

Again, in allegro work, Vaussard wants the footwork very clean. She will stop the class to make a point about how brightly and sharply the foot must be lifted to *cou-de-pied* before a *coupé-assemblé*. However, she sees more than the students' feet as they jump. In an *enchaînement* during which a student was destroying any possibility of elevation through excessive tension in her arms—rigidly pushing them down each time she jumped—Vaussard had the young lady lift her arms, bend them, and place her hands on her shoulders. Then, she had her repeat the combination holding her arms in this position, where it would be impossible for her to use them to help her jump. The student was forced instead to rely on the strength of her legs.

Vaussard used a similar method at the barre. When a student's arm went rigid with tension during a fast *dégagé* exercise, Vaussard made her repeat the exercise with her arm simply hanging, totally limp, at her side. Ease in *port de bras* is as important to Vaussard as accuracy of position. She fills her exercises with arm movements, many of which, in her advanced class, also contain *épaulement* and complete twisting of the torso. She is very fond, for instance, of sweeping the arms in a windmill fashion into 4th arabesque (*arabesque croisée*). Her head positions are less regimented than those, for instance, in the Vaganova (Russian) system, but she often corrects eyes, which she wants well-focused. "Lift your head, lift your head," she'll call out to a student in *penchée arabesque*. "Where are you looking? There—*bien!*" She asks students to look at their hands as they open their arms outward from 5th *en haut*. "*Le bras, la main,*" she coaches in a breathy voice, trying to elicit the correct soft quality of movement from them. As a dancer finishes an adagio, Vaussard tells her to silently command her audience, to think: "Look at me. I'm beautiful!" She advises the young lady to hold the final pose absolutely until the end of the music, with stillness, beauty, and presence. Even students' faces are coached. "*Très important, la bouche!*" she reminds them, asking them to relax their mouths. "As a teacher, you have to notice everything," she told me. "Good eyes are your most important tool."

It is the correcting of many details relating to the feet (how, from the standpoint of dynamics, for instance, one springs up and down through the foot), as well as insistence upon perfect musicality, that, more than anything else, distinguishes Vaussard's classes. I told her I thought fast articulation of the feet was her specialty. "It would be a bit presumptuous of me to think that," she replied modestly. "Balanchine was my inspiration for this, and I hope I adhere to his approach when I choreograph for my students. His choreography and sensitivity to the music led him to speedy footwork. With *Palais de Crystal*, for instance, he did not want to distort the music of Bizet's symphony. He had to find steps that matched the rapid rhythms."

Vaussard remembers with pleasure dancing this ballet: "I was not in *Palais de Crystal* when Balanchine first created it at the Opera, but when it was revived some time later, I was cast as the ballerina in the second—adagio—movement. So I danced it without the opportunity of having him coach me in the role. However, Balanchine arrived in Paris to see the performance and came backstage afterward. 'It's not exactly what I intended,' he told me, 'but I like your version better.'" Vaussard is a humble woman, but she is understandably very pleased with this recollection. "It's the nicest compliment I ever received as a dancer," she told me.

I asked Vaussard about the contemporary ballet world's focus on high extension. "It's important because of today's choreography," she said. "Chauviré, Darsonval, and Fonteyn[10] never had high legs. Before the war,

Christiane
Vaussard during
a private coach-
ing session in a
studio in Paris.

Solange Schwartz and, afterward, Claude Bessy [both *étoiles* at the Opera]
were the first to take the liberty to lift their legs. Aveline did not advocate
this style. Of course, the great 'baby ballerina,' Toumanova, had high extension, as did Balanchine's New York City Ballet star Tanaquil Le Clerq, but
these were natural extensions. As it became desirable for all female dancers
to have high legs, we teachers had to think *how* to help students to do this."
Vaussard concentrates on it, filling her *fondu* and adagio exercises with lots
of *développés* and *grands ronds de jambe*. Never, however, in her advanced
class, are these done in a belabored fashion. (Again, lightness in the legs is
emphasized.) In addition, her barre work always includes a stretching exercise, either foot-in-hand or foot-on-barre, just prior to the final *grands
battements*.

Regardless of current extremes in technique, Vaussard notes that high
extension and speed mean nothing if the body is not correctly placed. "Everything starts from the center," she states emphatically, "from your aware-

ness of your center. When your body's aligned correctly, you can move easily in any direction. Also, when you dance, you have to be comfortable, at ease, in order to be expressive. If the body isn't placed well or is in an uncomfortable position, it will show on your face!" She is obsessed with making sure that her students are on top of their legs and, therefore, on balance. She begins testing them in the first *tendu* exercise after *pliés*, having them do *temps lié* forward and backward, away and toward the barre, frequently changing their weight from one leg to the other. She uses the inside leg at the barre almost as much as the outside one. Often, she asks them to release their hand from the barre to test their balance. Almost constantly, she moves among them, often standing in back of a student and physically, strongly using her hands to lift the dancer up out of her hips.

She is very specific about how the body should be placed over the supporting leg. "The inside of the leg," she states, "must be aligned with the spinal column and the center of the foot." She will also often run her hand in a vertical line from a student's shoulder down to the hip. "*Fil à plomb* [plumbline]," she says as a reminder to the student not to lean sideways. The placement of her students looks very natural. It is especially strong and impressive during balances on *demi-pointe*, of which there are many during Vaussard's class. As they hold a *retiré relevé* position, she tells them to push down into the floor: "The more you push through the ball of the supporting foot, the more your backbone goes up into your head," she says. They stay like statues, unwavering. "*Ah, voilà, mademoiselle*," she nods approvingly at a student who previously had struggled with this balance. Later, she shares a little secret with them as they balance in *attitude devant*: "If you keep that elbow in 1st [5th *en avant*] over your knee, then you'll know you're not leaning back."

Often, I saw Vaussard question students about their mistakes. "When you did that *détourné*, did you feel your popo [backside]?" she asked one young lady. "Did you use it?" When a student let go of the barre and lost her centering over her supporting leg, Vaussard asked her what she had done, forcing the young lady to think about correcting herself. Another time, Vaussard had a student turn sideways to the mirror and repeat a *tombé en avant*. She wanted the girl to see her own back as she transferred her weight forward. Vaussard did not need to say anything. The student's reflection of herself tilting backward was all that was needed for her to correct her own placement.

Obviously, alignment affects one's ability to turn, so Vaussard's well-placed students pirouette very well. Her barre often includes sharp, full *détourné* turns in which the head must snap very fast while the spine is firmly controlled. Sometimes, to force students to control the ending of their pirouettes, Vaussard has them finish *up*, on *demi-pointe*, in 5th position. If students are struggling with turns, Vaussard uses a pirouette combination in which all the turns are done in *cou-de-pied*. "I place the foot around the ankle because sometimes, when one lifts the knee, one throws one's balance off to the side. Also, when you use *cou-de-pied*, you have to use strength in both feet." The exercise is composed of four single pirouettes *en dehors*. It begins in 5th position. The first turn finishes in 1st, the next in 2nd, the third in 4th, and the last in 5th behind. It is then repeated to the other side, and perhaps after that with double turns. Vaussard highly recommends it.

Although Vaussard devotes much time to what she describes as "finding just the right movement so the students will learn," her classes go far beyond the academic. "All exercises at the barre," she remarks, "have to be done as well as possible, but afterwards they have to dance. It's up to them. One variation danced by two different people will produce different results. Two princesses in *Sleeping Beauty* are different. Personality takes a dancer beyond technique."

Aesthetics and artistry are of major concern to Vaussard. To get a young lady who was hanging her head a bit shyly to lift it, Vaussard cleverly urged her: "Push your bun down." In an aside to me she whispered with amusement: "Maybe it will produce the same result as telling her to lift her chin." Vaussard was obviously searching for a new way to give an old correction. Her rapport with students is marvelous. "It may be important for one girl to do an exercise sharply, for another perhaps not so sharply," she told me. "Each student must be treated differently."

In working with young dancers, Vaussard is demanding one moment, sensitive and caring the next. To a child in a private lesson who did an exercise especially well, Vaussard gave a big kiss. One day, when another private student became suddenly tearful, Vaussard rushed over to hug her. "*Ma pauvre cherie* [my poor dear]," she said sympathetically and, putting her arm around the student's shoulder, walked with her for a minute or two around the back of the studio, quietly offering words of encouragement. When a student fails to get something right, a look of consternation crosses Vaussard's face—a mini-cloud. She dives right in to help. "*Pas comme ça* [not like that]," she says, shaking her head a little, then pats the stray part of the student's body into correct alignment. She always tries to stay positive and encouraging. "*Pas mal, pas mal* [not bad, not bad]," she'll say.

Vaussard admits she asks a lot of her students: "I have to push them because they won't be happy if they don't have something to offer. They have to feel good about themselves as dancers. I make them work until they succeed," she says determinedly. "If they are not doing so, then it's my job to figure out why and to find ways to help them." However, she seems instinctively to know when to back off. If, for instance, she has been working intensively with them on their thighs and feet, she will suddenly stop and let them just dance, restricting her comments to such things as breath, *port de bras,* or quality.

Vaussard's interest in her students goes far beyond just teaching them ballet. "I occasionally watch how they behave and dress outside of class, how they speak, their table manners, etc., because one expects an artist to behave in a certain manner." Certainly, Vaussard herself is a fine role model for her students. Physically, she is never less than elegant. Socially, she is gracious, refined, always polite and interested in others. It is lovely to watch how simply and gracefully, albeit quickly, she executes a curtsy to her students at the end of class. "*Merci, mesdemoiselles!*" she says quite sincerely. Above all, with her champagne personality and delightful sense of humor, she seems a thoroughly modern and independent woman. She recalls that her own first teacher, Zambelli, had a great influence on her: "She taught me how to behave with other people in life—not just in dance. She warned me never to say bad things about friends. And," Vaussard remembers smiling, "she told me never to say I was tired. If I did, she said, others would say, 'Oh, she didn't dance well because she was tired!'"

Vaussard, wears three crosses hung loosely on delicate gold chains around her neck. Sometimes entwined with a small rope of pearls, they are almost always visible through the open V-necks of her simply tailored, silk blouses. I asked her about them. "I'm very religious," she told me, "but I don't go to mass except with one of my young private students of whom I'm very fond. She likes to go, so I go with her. We sing together in church and that makes me very happy." She explains that one of her crosses is from her first communion, one was a gift from her best friend, and on the third hangs the wedding ring of her husband, who passed away some years ago. "One of my aunts once asked me," she says smiling, "why I wore all these crosses. 'Haven't you borne enough of them in your life?' she said. So I told her I believed that when people go through a lot, they will rise even higher in the end!"

Vaussard lives on the outskirts of Paris in a spacious apartment on the top floor of a large white manor house set in the middle of a beautifully landscaped yard. Her rooms are filled with antique furniture, silken fabrics, vases of flowers, both dried and fresh, and delicate mementos of her dancing career. The entire place speaks of charm and hospitality. She loves the view of the garden from her windows, and she loves animals. One day, driving home after teaching, she pulled over next to a park near her home. Bustling efficiently, she removed Romy from her lap (where the tiny dog always travels), then took two large bags of bird food from the trunk of her car: "One for the ducks, one for the pigeons." They were waiting for her. She tossed handfuls of seeds to them as only a former ballerina could.

Because of the rigorous selectivity of students admitted to the Paris Opera Ballet School, classes like Vaussard's are filled with an overabundance of talent. Indeed, Vaussard has been the teacher for many of the Opera's current stars. I asked Vaussard if she feels a great sense of responsibility teaching such *wunderkinds*. "No," she told me. "Actually, I feel a greater responsibility with the less talented ones—to try to see that *they* succeed. The others have it all from nature. With them, it's much easier! I don't have to do so much."

I asked her what she remembered about Sylvie Guillem, a phenomenally gifted dancer, now the Paris Opera's biggest international star. "When she arrived at the school, she was very, very thin," Vaussard recalled. "She was very hard-working, took in every word I said. You might say she was possessed with achievement, totally self-involved, and she was always at the top of her class. She lived quite far away from Paris, but she came religiously, every day. She was also a very intelligent girl." Guillem has been quoted in an interview as saying that, of all her teachers at the school, Vaussard was the one who had the greatest impact on her.

Such tributes are not unusual. Often, Vaussard's former students—even stars such as Elizabeth Platel, Isabel Guerin, and Jean-Yves Lormeau—return to the school to take class with her or to seek help with a role on which they are working. Clearly, they continue to have the highest regard for her. Guerin told me: "Mlle Vaussard was my teacher for ten years, from my classes at the conservatory to the time I was elevated to *étoile* at the Opera. I owe her a lot. She is a woman who, in spite of her demanding teaching, loves to give, loves to pass things on. I will be permeated with her lessons until the end of my career—they've become part of me. The most beautiful reward after hours of classes with her is a compliment, a smile. And when you are a star? The presence of Mlle Vaussard in the audience, her joy when she comes to congratulate you, her pride even when she can't prevent herself from pinching your buttocks in order to check whether or not you have an extra hundred grams somewhere—Mlle Vaussard is . . . Mlle Vaussard. There is only one. She is unique!"

Classroom Quotes from Vaussard

After making a dancer take off a chiffon wrap skirt: "I cannot make a dancer I cannot see."

"*Mes enfants,* you are contemporary girls. You must dance like contemporary girls, with the same pizzazz that you do bebop [popular dances]." She demonstrates an improvised jive, bouncing her shoulders up and down, snapping her head. "You must do ballet like that, too—with energy and musicality. You can't be phlegmatic."

"If you take that long closing the leg, the whole step goes to sleep."

"You must have inner joy to be an artist and be able to show it!"

As a warning to teachers about passing their own faults as dancers on to their students: "My teacher, Messr Aveline, always used to say: 'One must teach dance as it should be done—not as one has managed to do it!'"

Order of the Exercises in Vaussard's Class (advanced class, 1½ hours)

BARRE

1. Warm-up tendus facing the barre
2. Demi-pliés, grands pliés, cambrés, and balances on demi-pointe
3. Slow tendus with temps liés
4. Fast tendus
5. Dégagés (tendus jetés) with battements pointés
6. Ronds de jambe à terre
7. Fondus at 90 degrees with grands ronds de jambe
8. Frappés
9. Double frappés with petits battements
10. Développés
11. Fast double ronds de jambe en l'air at 30 degrees
12. Stretches (pied à la main et jambe sur la barre)
13. Grands battements
14. Fast exercise for the feet: pas de cheval à terre facing the barre with fast détournés
15. Fast exercise for the feet: temps levés facing the barre

CENTRE

1. Port de bras
2. Piqués fondus (pas marché sur demi-pointe)
3. Fast tendus en tournant with pirouettes en dehors and en dedans
4. Adagio
5. Pirouettes and grandes pirouettes
6. Petit allegro with jetés portés, assemblés, entrechats quatres
7. Grand allegro with grands jetés, entrechats sixes, and movements en manège
8. Révérence

Note: The following day, all exercises in this class would be executed on pointe, ending with piqué turns, chaînés déboulés, coda combinations en diagonale and en manège, fouettés rond de jambe en tournant, and balances, before the révérence and port de bras.

The Roots of Tradition

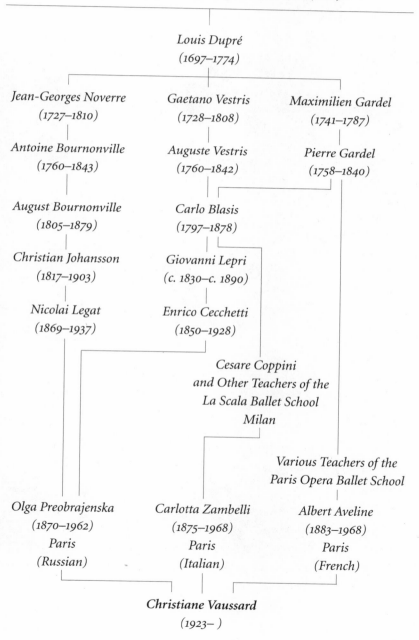

L'Académie Royale de Musique et de Danse (1661)

Louis Dupré
(1697–1774)

Jean-Georges Noverre
(1727–1810)

Gaetano Vestris
(1728–1808)

Maximilien Gardel
(1741–1787)

Antoine Bournonville
(1760–1843)

Auguste Vestris
(1760–1842)

Pierre Gardel
(1758–1840)

August Bournonville
(1805–1879)

Carlo Blasis
(1797–1878)

Christian Johansson
(1817–1903)

Giovanni Lepri
(c. 1830–c. 1890)

Nicolai Legat
(1869–1937)

Enrico Cecchetti
(1850–1928)

Cesare Coppini
and Other Teachers of the
La Scala Ballet School
Milan

Various Teachers of the
Paris Opera Ballet School

Olga Preobrajenska
(1870–1962)
Paris
(Russian)

Carlotta Zambelli
(1875–1968)
Paris
(Italian)

Albert Aveline
(1883–1968)
Paris
(French)

Christiane Vaussard
(1923–)

10 Anne Woolliams

Anne Woolliams demonstrating in class at her school in Zurich in 1991.

*A*nne Woolliams established her international reputation as a teacher and coach during her long tenure with the Stuttgart Ballet. She began her dance career with the Russian Opera and Ballet Company in her native England. There she also appeared in musicals and several films, including *The Red Shoes*. While still in her twenties, she undertook teaching engagements in London, Chicago, and Florence. In 1958 she joined Kurt Jooss as the classical teacher for his school in Essen, Germany. She remained with Jooss, both as a dancer and teacher, for five years until 1963, when John Cranko invited her to join the artistic staff of the newly formed Stuttgart Ballet. In 1964, she and Cranko founded the Stuttgart Ballet School, the first in Germany to offer academic education in combination with dance training. Her close association with Cranko, as company teacher, coach, and assistant director, lasted ten years until his untimely death in 1973. Subsequently, she co-directed the Stuttgart Ballet for three years, before assuming the position of artistic director of the Australian Ballet in Melbourne.

Woolliams spent eleven years (1976–87) in Australia, eight of them as founding dean of dance at the Victorian College for the Arts. Upon her return to Europe in 1987, she was instrumental in setting up the Schweizerische Ballettberufsschule in Zurich, Switzerland. Today, she continues, as she has done for many years, to stage Cranko's ballets around the world. Most recently, she was appointed artistic director of the Vienna State Opera Ballet. She is the recipient of many awards, a frequent member of the jury at international ballet competitions, and the author of a book, numerous articles, and dance reviews.

"Dancing is the torso. The legs must serve it."

Woolliams's reputation as a teacher was well known to me for many years, but it was reading her book *Ballet Studio* (1978) that finally convinced me I must visit her. While writing this chapter, I could not resist including some brief excerpts from it, and I urge interested readers to read all of *Ballet Studio* for themselves. Filled with Woolliams's learned insights, as well as candid photographs of Stuttgart Ballet dancers at work, it is both moving and astute, a major contribution to dance literature. I have long been grateful for the inspiration it provides, and I am now also grateful for the fine memories of the week I spent in Zurich in 1991 watching Woolliams teach. I would also like to extend particular thanks to Shirley McKechnie for allowing me to use material from an interview she conducted with Woolliams in Australia in 1987.

ANNE WOOLLIAMS was taken to her first dancing lesson when she was three and a half. "My mother," she says nostalgically, "probably would have liked to have been a dancer." Woolliams's most vivid recollection of childhood dance classes was that "the teachers would begin combinations by shouting 'And!' and I'd jump like a cat. I always thought they were saying 'Anne' and that I was about to get a correction!" She laughs at the memory. Woolliams strikes one as ageless. Although she is in her sixties, her large, expressive eyes are often filled with wonder. She is a woman full of enthusiasm for life.

By the age of eleven, Woolliams had dedicated herself to dance. Although her native England was in the midst of World War II, she made the risky trip to London twice a week, accompanied by her mother, for ballet lessons. "I never had the perfect ballet body," she recalls. "I wasn't turned out to 180 degrees. My left foot had an instep, but my right one didn't, and, of course, at five feet, seven inches, I was very tall for a ballet dancer, but I was determined." She remembers hearing that Ninette De Valois, director of the Sadler's Wells (later Royal) Ballet, had pronounced the perfect height for a dancer to be five feet, four inches. "Fonteyn, whom I greatly admired, was just that," Woolliams recalls, "and I envied her."[1]

Woolliams's principal teachers during her youth were the well-known British pedagogues Judith Espinosa and Noreen Bush. "Bush," she recalls, "was a martinet—and Espinosa, whom I worked with from ages eleven to fourteen, was a tiny little bird woman. I think I was afraid of my teachers and was thus motivated to work very hard for them." She remembers that Espinosa used to smoke continuously, something that was not uncommon among ballet teachers in those days. "She must have been in her sixties," Woolliams says. "She wore little heels and had a stringy sort of body, like an acrobat. She used to do this little *développé devant* and hold her little stick leg at 90 degrees in front of her while banging on her thigh to show that her leg was absolutely stuck there."

An ambitious student, Woolliams completed her Royal Academy of Dancing (see p. 364, n. 5) Elementary examination at the age of eleven, her Intermediate at twelve, and her Advanced at thirteen, which, she admits, "is quite young." She remembers that her mother made her practice at home and notes: "It's quite difficult for dancers to practice by themselves—I hated it." She also remembers taking piano lessons. "I never could improvise," she recalls, "but I was very rhythmic. We had a lot of exposure to music in our house, not the most highbrow, I'm afraid, but I think I developed a fairly wide appreciation."

During the war, the Woolliams family moved, for safety, from London to her grandparents' farm in the Cotswolds. Finding it difficult to complete correspondence courses from there, Woolliams, at fourteen, regretfully gave up schooling. However, she persuaded her parents to allow her to study dance full-time at the Bush-Davies School just outside London. She remained there for two years. Then, at sixteen—"Too young!" she exclaims—she joined the Russian Opera and Ballet, a group of expatriates from Eastern Europe with whom she toured across wartime England during 1943–44.

At seventeen, Woolliams joined Lydia Kyasht's[2] Ballet de les Jeunesse Anglaise, performing with that troupe for two years until it ran out of money. Kyasht had been in the original cast of Fokine's (see p. 360, n. 6) *Chopiniana* (later retitled *Les Sylphides*). "I always like to think I have an apostolic succession with this ballet because I learned it from Kyasht," Woolliams says.

The dancers who had the strongest influence on Woolliams in her youth were members of the London-based Sadler's Wells Ballet. "I admired artists like Fonteyn, Robert Helpmann, June Brae, Michael Somes, and Pamela May enormously," she says. In addition, she recalls, as a very young ballet student she had seen the famous "baby ballerinas" of the De Basil Ballets Russes. "Baronova, Toumanova, and Riabouchinska were only a few years older than I was," she remembers. "I identified with them, and, of course, hoped one day I would be just like them." She was also much impressed with the great English ballerina Alicia Markova. In *Ballet Studio,* Woolliams writes: "Surely Markova gave us a supreme example of the lightness and speed which beautiful feet can achieve, for how could anyone who saw her as Giselle forget the excitement and beauty of her *entrechats* in the second act of this ballet?"[3] Perhaps it is this memory that drives Woolliams to focus so strongly on *batterie* in her classes.

At nineteen, after the war, Woolliams leapt at the opportunity to join a company called the London Ballet because they were going to India. (She hastens to add that this troupe was not the London Ballet commanded by Antony Tudor.) She admits to a lifelong appetite for travel. She was hired as first soloist and spent the next year entertaining the troops in garrison theaters all over India. The company of twenty-five performed a diverse repertoire—"Certainly not the great, full-length classics!" Woolliams recalls. "They would not have been suitable for a company of our size." With the troupe, she visited Bombay, Calcutta, Madras, Delhi, Darjeeling, Bankok, Rangoon, and Singapore. She even took dance lessons from two renowned classical Indian dance artists, Ram Gopal and Uday Shankar.

In 1948, Woolliams returned to London and acquired a position dancing in a London musical. Obligated to be at the theater only in the evenings, she used the daytime to return to her love of drawing—a skill she inherited from her father, who had always encouraged her ability. For three years, she spent five afternoons a week at the Central School of Arts in London drawing from the nude. "I still love to draw," she says. "My father," she adds, "who was a pilot in the English Royal Air Force, also instilled in me a great love for flying, which I have always associated with dance in a strange way —the weightlessness and soaring movements."

Woolliams remembers post-war London as being alive with dance. Roland Petit's Les Ballets des Champs Elysées was making a big impact. "It was a very exciting, productive, and creative time," she recalls. Characteristically, she attended as many performances as she could. "I've always had a bug which drew me to different sorts of dance," she says. "I've appeared in character, modern, and classical companies, as well as in films and musicals. I think as a dancer I was probably searching for my own medium, and in this search an enormous interest in all kinds of dance was awakened in me." She regrets that dance is inclined "to be bracketed." One of her ambitions, she says, is to instill a very full appreciation of all kinds of dance in her students. "Dance, for me," she states, "is the greatest expression of art through movement and it cannot be confined to one form."[4]

Between 1948–53, Woolliams danced in three London musicals, including *Brigadoon* and *Paint Your Wagon*, as well as the famous ballet film *The Red Shoes*. In between these engagements, she also danced with Alan Carter's St. James Ballet, a splinter group of Sadler's Wells, and at the request of her fellow dancers in this company, at age twenty-three, Woolliams started to teach. "I really resented teaching for years," she admits. "I used to protest to the other dancers that I needed to take class myself!" She does not believe that she is a born pedagogue, although she remembers as a child ranting and raving as she tried to teach her sister and brother. "I only became interested in teaching later," she admits. "I discovered that I got better as a dancer because of my teaching. It is strange how one travels backwards. When you start to teach, you really pass on what you're doing yourself. Then, as you become more experienced, you begin to hear the words of your teachers from long ago, and the training of children—the actual beginnings—becomes more fascinating. I still hear the voices of all my teachers!"

During those formative years as a young teacher, Woolliams came under the influence of the great Russian pedagogue Vera Volkova (see p. 369, n. 12) who, at that time, was giving open classes in London. As Woolliams recalls: "All the dancers from the various companies would come to take her class. I observed them very closely. I don't remember Vera ever giving general corrections to the class. She gave individual corrections, and I was always very interested in her comments." The English ballerina Margot Fonteyn, a great devotee of Volkova's, was often in class. "She had trouble with pirouettes," Woolliams remembers, "and would be in a state of emergency after one and three-quarter turns. I used to look at this great ballerina struggling, and it gave me a kind of hope."

To this day, Woolliams regards Volkova as one of her guiding lights, often quoting her in class. She remembers Volkova saying: "I don't want to see *you* in arabesque. I want to see arabesque!" Volkova was a quiet person, she recalls: "It was her spirit that drove the class." Woolliams remembers that "years later, when I was teaching for Jooss in Essen, we'd invite her to come as a guest teacher. The dancers would all rave about her classes, saying things like 'Now, we understand!' Privately, I'd get a bit hurt. I'd tell Vera, 'But I've been telling them that for ages.' And she was wonderfully gracious. She'd say, 'I know, dear, but it's just a new voice.' And it's true. A new teacher can come in and say something just a bit differently, and suddenly one is enlightened."

"Vera had a Russian accent," Woolliams notes, "which I believe is very effective for teaching. The lack of the article is very direct. It's probably even better to teach in a foreign language. When I first went to Germany and tried to teach in German, I could find only the direct words that I wanted instead of wrapping it all up in some sort of explanation—maybe that's good." Today, after teaching all over the world, Woolliams often mixes languages when teaching. I was amused one day when, after a short explanation in her clipped British-accented English, she used German ("Darlings, nicht vergessen!") to command her students and then began counting the preparation for the next exercise in Russian!

Woolliams remembers Volkova's classes as being enormously well timed. "The rhythm of the class, the speed of it, was very good," she says. "This is something pedagogues don't always learn very well. I mean, they learn about placement and what exercises to do, but they don't learn enough about the tempo of a class. Some exercises must be slow and some fast, and it differs according to the day, as well as to the students. Vera understood this well and always kept us moving and enthused. We used to sweat profusely!"

I asked Woolliams if she could specifically recall in what ways Volkova helped her as a dancer. "She used to correct my arms a lot, my head, and *épaulement*," Woolliams answered. "I think she despaired of my feet, which were never good, and my lack of turn-out. But she was a teacher who understood the possibilities of the body and didn't keep harping on something that wasn't going to be possible. And she always encouraged when she saw improvement."

Woolliams remembers that Volkova definitely had a sense of humor, but could also be enormously aggressive. "Sometimes, just like a dog, she'd get hold of one student and, if the student wasn't doing what she wanted, she'd zero in. If the student started to cry, it made her absolutely livid. 'I won't have anyone crying in my class,' she'd say, 'so the others can all just sit down now!' Of course, the unfortunate student would be reduced to pulp. I don't know if the crying really distressed her, or if she was consciously doing this to build backbone in her students. But I think it really bugged her."

Woolliams's response to a student who is struggling is not quite so extreme. Although she occasionally will shout, "No!" loudly slapping her foot down on the floor and clapping abruptly for the music to stop, she never drills individual students until they fall apart. She watches as they try a correction two or three times; then, if they don't get it, she smiles, encourages them to keep trying, and moves on. She conveys an impression of having faith in the future. However, she notes, she can get desperately irritated by dancers in class. "Sometimes one just really wants to shake them with sheer frustration, especially when they get past the point of really being able to pull themselves together. I suppose it's something within the teacher that identifies with the student. If you've been a dancer yourself, you're inclined to feel yourself within that student's body and, if the body is falling apart, it's a big frustration."

In fact, Woolliams still seems very much a dancer, although she retired as a performer years ago and even hobbles occasionally because of three hip replacement operations. Her lithe body is very alive in class, and she possesses one of the most beautiful *port de bras* I have ever observed. Former students mentioned to me how enthusiastically she used to dance when demonstrating exercises in class. She admits that she herself never much enjoyed barre or centre work. It was the dancey combinations at the end of class that she adored. So, she says, as a teacher she puts a lot of effort into trying to make the more tedious aspects of daily class stimulating. "You have to constantly find new ways to present the old," she says. "I think the evolution of classical technique over so many years has been pretty sound. I don't think you want to fiddle about with it too much, but I think you can always add spontaneity to it . . . make those exercises *live* that one does each day in class . . . because dancers should feel that they're doing them for the first time. In other words, the daily medicine has to have a little bit of sugar coating."[5]

Volkova must have seen the potential for a good teacher in Woolliams, for in 1950, she recommended her for a three-month teaching engagement in Florence with the Maggio Musicale. Ever eager to travel, Woolliams jumped at the chance. It was the first time she had taught seriously and professionally. She was twenty-four years old. She remembers Volkova's parting words of advice: "Prepare your classes and always start the allegro part of class with jumps on two feet."

Woolliams was terribly nervous in Florence. "The French ballerina Zizi Jeanmaire and other European dancers were in the company, and I was just this little English girl in Italy for the first time giving classes." She recalls waking up at 3 A.M. and preparing *enchaînements*. "But it was a good start," she says, "because they liked my classes, and it gave me confidence."

In 1957, she was invited to teach in Chicago for a year. There, at the Allegro School of Ballet in the Fine Arts Building on Michigan Avenue, she remembers dancers like New York City Ballet ballerina Maria Tallchief taking her classes. "I think when one starts to teach," she says, "it's easier to teach professionals. You give them a class you would do yourself, and, providing you exercise them in the way to which they are accustomed, they feel good. And if you have the gift of an 'eye,' you can occasionally, perhaps, tell them things which are helpful, so they think you're a good teacher."[6]

In 1958, Woolliams was invited to Essen to be the classical ballet teacher in the school of the great modern dance choreographer Kurt Jooss.[7] During the five years she spent with Jooss, she both taught and performed with his company. Woolliams remembers being coached by Jooss in one of her favorite roles, the guerrilla girl in his great antiwar ballet, *The Green Table*. "It was enormously exciting," she recalls, "to see him actually showing people how to dance 'Death.' He was like a tank thundering on the floor."

Joining Jooss was a challenging career move for Woolliams. His dancers, she says, had secretly been taking classical ballet classes on the side for years, and "finally, Jooss got round to the idea that maybe it would be good for his dancers to be subjected to this discipline." He recruited Woolliams for the experiment. "It was interesting," she says of her experiences in Essen, "because the ideal that both Jooss and I wanted to produce was, I believe, the same dancer, but we approached it from opposite poles. I would want the dancers to find the perpendicular and then learn how to fall away from it, and Jooss wanted them to fall away from it and arrive at the perpendicular. . . . This is an oversimplification, obviously, but we were starting from two different ends and, in the first years, it made it very difficult for the dancers because our classes were so totally opposed. I remember talking a long time with Jooss about this, because the ideal classical dancer—the ideally *trained* classical dancer—should be able to move in the form of Jooss's technique, and I always like to think I proved this by dancing in his company without his training. I simply had the open-mindedness to want to dance in that style."

During her years with Jooss in Essen, Woolliams had the opportunity to interact with several other great dance figures. "Mary Wigman[8] was still living and around," she recalls. Antony Tudor (see p. 369, n. 3), who was an admirer of Jooss, came to teach a summer course at the school. Woolliams remembers him as "unique—a genius!" She'd seen his choreography years before in London and had admired him tremendously, but it wasn't until Essen that they finally met and became great friends. In 1960, he gave *Lilac Garden* to the Jooss company and rehearsed Anne in the role of An Episode in His Past. Her husband-to-be, Jan Stripling, danced the Man She Must Marry, and Pina Bausch[9] danced Caroline. Stripling credits Tudor with playing Cupid: "Tudor, Anne, and I would be sitting in the backseat of a car, and each time we'd go 'round a curve, he'd lean really hard against me so that I would have to lean too, coming into close body contact with Anne. I think he plotted to start the chemistry going," he says, smiling.

Woolliams and Stripling, a tall, handsome, pipe-smoking, rather intellectual gentleman who is a respected ballet teacher in his own right, were married in 1963. They are a devoted and loving couple. As Stripling puts it, "After all these years, I am her and she is me." Although he is fifteen years her junior, their age difference has never been an issue; they have worked together for more than thirty years, beginning as fellow dancers in the Jooss company. I asked him what changes he'd observed in Woolliams as a teacher over the years. He replied: "Anne had such a temperament in the early days—she's calmer now—but once she flew up from her chair in class and tore her calf muscle showing a *grand jeté*. It was just the will of wanting other people to do what was her image of a particular sequence of movements. It just exploded within her. And she's a toughy, too, so she refused to put that injured leg up. Instead, she hobbled around in one ordinary shoe and one *pointe* shoe—on *pointe!*—because that relieved the pressure on her torn muscle."

Woolliams laughs at that memory. "I'm quieter now," she agrees, "and, of course I don't demonstrate much these days. When the body gives up, one can't. But, actually, I think it's better not to show so much. Better to observe and then try to put yourself 'inside' the body of the student, which as a dancer you can do. Actually, I'm still a very frustrated dancer. I love to be on the stage—I'd love to be an actress."

Woolliams recalls: "When I was sixteen and first in a company, I was the epitome of the Anglo-Saxon virgin, yet I was often cast as a tart. I was always much better in dramatic roles simply because I didn't have all the classical requirements to be a great ballerina. Now, I didn't know anything at all about tarts, but used to act them up as I thought they were. And that's really the joy of being on the stage. You get a release from being yourself."

Stripling says Woolliams's great belief is that energy is generated by one's fantasy. "She feels that unless you are possessed by this fantasy, you cannot convey something to the public. That's why she uses so much imagery when she's teaching." He recalls that Cranko also used imagery to lead people to use their imaginations. Stripling quotes the nineteenth-century theological philosopher John Newman, who said, "What I cannot imagine [i.e., what I do not see in my mind], I don't believe." Stripling continues: "I

Anne Woolliams in class doing port de bras with her students while watching them perform an adagio.

think that's art—to have the power to make one's imagination visible to others."

Woolliams notes that dancers in their teens and twenties are generally less preoccupied with being artists and more with displays of technical virtuosity. "But, then," she feels, "one is most interesting as an artist after thirty." She advises dancers to keep in the back of their minds that their techniques need to last until that age. "Nowadays," she says, "kids are pushed so early. It's important for competition, but I see time and again that at twenty-six they're burnt out mentally and physically—over the top. They've stopped discovering. They've already been there." Woolliams has her own theory about how to counteract this regrettable situation. "If from the beginning of training, one is careful that the magic of dance is not lost, then you know that these dancers will be able to come full circle—from the innocent joy of dancing as a child, through the training and development of the physique, and back to reclaiming that child again—at which point you'll have something really marvelous."

Regrettably, she says, she sees many children who have had the ability to dance drilled out of them. "And later," she adds, "as dancers, when they attempt to choreograph they get so inhibited. The more they know about technique, the more caught up they get in doing it right. They are not prepared to break the rules, so they're not free to become choreographers—and never will be."

To keep children "free" and at the same time disciplined, Woolliams says, is the real challenge of teaching. She told me she was experimenting in Zurich, "and probably being criticized for it because I'm not insisting on certain things too soon. I think young students *have* to dance! And I believe that at the beginning you can't have both things happening at once—technique achievement *and* teaching them to dance. For me, the situation is analogous to a weather vane—the wind can change it, but only from one direction at a time. I believe that the dance instinct inside of young students must be encouraged, then, very slowly, you add the medicine."

This philosophy does not mean Woolliams throws all traditional regimen out the window. In spite of her rather radical thinking, she is a very careful and meticulous teacher. "Actually, I'm afraid of the chaotic," she says, "but I also don't completely trust the systematic. I don't believe you can teach totally by chance, but there is an enormous amount of chance in the arts. I mean, the arrival of a great dancer happens by chance. You can't make one by a system. In fact, I'm becoming more and more dubious. I'm even coming to the conclusion that a bit of so-called 'bad' training may be quite advantageous. As teachers we're all too special with ourselves. We attach too much importance to our training systems, while quite often children who have attended a school that just 'lets them go' have exactly that certain confidence about moving we'd like to cultivate in all dancers."

Woolliams admits that her focus on developing danciness in students may have something to do with what she feels is her weakness as a teacher: "I have a feeling that there are teachers who really excel at making technicians, and I feel really humble about this because I don't feel I can—for several reasons: (1) I'm not sure I have the patience, (2) I'm not sure I'm sufficiently disciplined in myself to keep drilling students over a number of years, and (3) I'm not particularly interested in the prospect. However, as much as I love to dance, and love my students to dance, I realize it's idiotic—amateur really—to say, 'C'mon. Let's all just dance.' If they're going to perform, I'm obligated as their teacher to give them the wherewithal to do so—the strength, technique, and confidence."

I asked Woolliams what advice she'd offer to someone who wanted to teach. "Pedagogy courses are necessary," she answered, "but I do not believe they are sufficient in themselves. You should know something about anatomy, but you learn to teach by teaching." She reflected on her own experiences teaching professional dancers: "If you're working with people who in the evening have really hard things to do, they need a slow, careful class. Whereas, if you're working with corps de ballet dancers who stand on one leg all evening, you really have to make them work hard and fast; otherwise they're not getting any satisfaction out of their dancing. So corps de ballet and soloists need different sorts of classes. I always noticed that when big stars, older dancers such as Margot and Rudi [Fonteyn and Nureyev], took my classes, they worked extremely slowly, feeling all the necessary muscles, so you never had to push them at all. They knew what they were doing. You didn't have to teach them. Whereas, obviously, with students, you're really guiding them, trying to sense what they need. Bodies are all so different—some need stretching, some strengthening, some pushing, some stopping—it's a continual, wonderful challenge to a teacher to try to get the best out of each dancer."

Woolliams also noted that the differences between students are not limited only to physical aspects: "When you teach company class each morning, you're confronted by thirty dancers, none of whom feel the same. Some are tired, some want to 'get at it,' some want to work fast and hard, and some just want to have an easy class. And in some way you've got to get all of them feeling good for their rehearsals that begin an hour and a half later. So you've got to develop sensibilities to what's necessary. Sometimes a class has a general feeling of its own—this wants to be a quiet class—though you're not always aware of it until you get going and the class, in a funny way, takes over. So I'm always very nervous about teaching, especially if I've had a holiday. I always come back and think, well, I've forgotten how to do it. You know, you can prepare a class, but you go in there and sometimes it doesn't work out at all as prepared. Each class has a rhythm and personality of its own, and I've found it's not good to fight it. Unless, of course, it's falling apart."

I asked Woolliams if, considering the fact that at the time she began teaching she was virtually the same age as, perhaps even younger than, many of the dancers she was teaching, she had ever experienced discipline problems. "Well, in the beginning, my colleagues in Carter's company would sometimes argue with me a bit," she replied, "and I did get annoyed." Now, however, with her firmly established reputation, she does not have such problems. "It gets easier to balance being both friend and authority figure as one gets older," she admits. "You're able to be a sort of mother, or even grandmother." She continues: "The authority thing has to happen in the studio because there's a pecking order. So I try to instill in students a respect for anybody who is older or more advanced. Then, when they join a company, they have a proper respect for the soloists. If guests come to our class, my students are expected to ask them if they wish to stand in front." Woolliams says she really doesn't think about being authoritarian. "We're all humans in this together," she says. "If people worry about being authoritarian, it doesn't work. I just expect people to listen to me. I believe authority always has to be benevolent. I don't think you should ever exercise it just to let people know who's boss."

I found Woolliams very down-to-earth and direct in class, a mixture of mock-sternness and friendliness, and never less than an inspiring presence. Her affection for her students is obvious. When a student shows improvement, Woolliams extends her arm for a congratulatory handshake. "But you need to be tough with everybody to a certain extent," she declares. She has definite ideas about discipline: "Dancers don't mind your being tough as long as they don't think you dislike them. Maybe I have an advantage because I really *like* dancers. I don't know why. They can be terribly irritating at times, but they're very special people and they need protection and cherishing. You have to love them, and being tough helps them. My mother taught me that. I remember when I'd complain of not feeling well, she'd say, very matter of factly, 'Well, go to bed then.' There was no conversation. So I'd go to bed, and then, if in an hour or so she hadn't heard from me, she'd come to see how I was doing. She knew that invariably children pretend not to feel well when they want attention, but that this sham does not last, and if I remained longer in bed, it was possible I was really sick. So if a dancer tells me she isn't feeling well in class, I say, 'Sit down.' And I know that if she gets frustrated watching all the others dance, she'll be better tomorrow!"

When John Cranko, the director of the Stuttgart Ballet, invited Woolliams to join his artistic staff in 1963, she had already been teaching professional dancers for many years. It was with the Stuttgart Ballet, however, that her international reputation as a teacher and coach finally solidified.

"I think I wanted to work with a big company again, and I wanted to work with John, who was an old friend," she says. The break with Jooss was difficult, she recalls, "but I think he understood my reasons for leaving." She had come to realize that studying modern and classical ballet simultaneously was tearing the students apart.

"It's a mistake I've made continually in my life," she says. "I've always believed that dancers must be able to achieve both disciplines, but I'm arriving now at the idea that you have to do one before the other. I believe that dancers should be trained, in that they must be given an instrument, and I am convinced that correct classical training, in the right hands, does produce this instrument. I think that modern dance is sometimes more (I don't want to use the word 'intellectual') interesting, and, of course, a lot of choreographers with classical backgrounds are now using this idiom. So I think contemporary dance should possibly be introduced to students at a later age—the physical training, that is. I'm not talking about the opening of the mind. That must be happening all along."[10]

Woolliams acknowledges that most young people readily identify with the magical dreamworld of classical ballet. "There are very few little girls who don't see themselves as Odette or the Sugar Plum Fairy," she says, "but they grow out of these ideas before eventually returning to them. I think one must mature before properly appreciating the skills required to be a good Sugar Plum Fairy, and, during the years in between, a sort of broadening must occur. There comes a time when creative people need the stimulus of modern dance. They really do. Modern dance has been wonderful for classical ballet. It has freed dancers—of all persuasions—to venture into new worlds and expand their chosen medium."[11]

During her ten years with Cranko, Woolliams assumed many responsibilities. "At the beginning I was both giving classes and dancing mime roles, such as Lady Capulet in *Romeo and Juliet*," which I loved. It was a wonderfully rich and creative time. Ballets poured out of John; some were masterpieces and some did not survive, but all sprang from an atmosphere of creativity. Woolliams remembers "living" in the theater: "We didn't consider it work. We were totally on the crest of a wave of creation."[12]

Woolliams remembers that Cranko choreographed ballets very fast. "He would spend an evening with the whole company and choreograph a full ten minutes, which is really a lot. And it would be enormously rough, but I was able to understand what he wanted and do what is known as 'clean it up,' which sounds really impertinent. But, for me, of course, it meant feeling very much part of the creative process."[13] Kathy Bennetts, now a ballet mistress with the Frankfurt Ballet, who danced with the Stuttgart Ballet in those early days, recalls another way in which Woolliams was invaluable in Cranko's company: "I never saw anyone inspire a corps de ballet like Anne Woolliams! She made you feel very important even if all you were doing was standing at the back in a crowd scene throwing an orange. Your part in the scene was *vital* to the ballet. She really meant it and made you believe it, too."

In 1964, Woolliams and Cranko founded the Stuttgart Ballet School. Previously, the only training that had existed in conjunction with the State Opera House in Stuttgart had been a class of dancers who came each afternoon to work in the theater. "John sort of inherited this group," Woolliams recalls. "I thought there were two or three in the class who might be talented, but no demands were being made of them, so I went to John and said I was interested in taking over the class. I was rehearsing the company in the mornings and evenings, but was free in the afternoons. I had a lot of energy in those days!" Woolliams began teaching this class, out of which came two future Stuttgart ballerinas, Birgit Keil and Suzanne Hanke. "And that's really how the school started," she says.

In 1973, Cranko died suddenly and accidentally from the adverse affects of sleep medication on a flight home from America, where the Stuttgart Ballet had just completed a successful tour. His premature death at age forty-six was a tragic, incalculable loss for the dance world. Woolliams remembers being numb. "I don't think any of us believed that it could have happened. It's the only time I've ever experienced that kind of cut-off so suddenly. . . . It was absolutely dreadful."[14]

For the next three years, Woolliams continued to supervise the company as part of a triumvirate of directors that included Cranko's ballerina Marcia Haydée, who later directed the company by herself, and Dieter Graefe, who had been Cranko's companion and to whom Cranko had willed his ballets. In 1974, Glen Tetley joined the troupe as resident choreographer. "We believed," says Woolliams, "that the company was geared as an instrument for choreographers and that we should not rest as a museum for John's ballets." However, after some time, Woolliams says she realized that she and others were so tied to Cranko and so represented "the past" in Tetley's mind that it was difficult for him to assume the leadership role for which he had been hired. Graciously, she began to pull away from her duties within the company and devote more of her time to the school. Then, in 1975, came the invitation to become the artistic director of the Australian Ballet. Perhaps because she no longer felt tied to Stuttgart without Cranko, or perhaps because of the challenge of a position in a new country, she accepted.

Unfortunately, Woolliams's tenure as artistic director of the Australian Ballet lasted only sixteen months. She staged an acclaimed production of *Swan Lake,* as well as Cranko's *Eugene Onegin,* but could not see eye to eye with the administrative director of the company about future repertoire development. Increasingly, as artistic decisions were made with an eye toward the box office, and without her knowledge, she found the situation untenable. She submitted her resignation in 1977. Shortly thereafter, she was offered the position of founding dean of dance at the Victorian College of the Arts. She remained there more than eight years, developing a strong, eclectic academic dance program, which, at the time she established it, was unique in Australia.

In 1987, Woolliams returned to Europe to establish a ballet school in Zurich, where I first met her in 1991. What I noticed immediately was the luminosity of both her skin and her huge, gentle eyes. Her dark gray hair was cropped short in a straight, natural, no-nonsense style. I found her charming and sincere, with a delightful sense of playfulness.

Although never one to dwell upon the past, Woolliams displays two rather sentimental photographs in her school. The first, a framed life-size photo of Pavlova, takes one's breath away. "Magnificent, isn't it?" says Woolliams, smiling. "Nowadays, they don't take photos as softly as that." The picture, which hangs above her desk and which she says she has never seen reproduced elsewhere, was a gift to her from a private collection.[15] "I never saw Pavlova dance," comments Woolliams, "but I was brought up on admiration for her because my mother had been greatly inspired by her performances." Today, seated at her desk with the picture above, Woolliams remarks, clearly delighted: "Now, she watches over me."

The second photograph hangs just outside her office door: a candid picture of two pensive ballerinas in their twenties—Marcia Haydée and Lynn Seymour—resting against a barre. It is lovingly inscribed to Woolliams from both of them. Several other Stuttgart ballerinas who worked with Woolliams during the Cranko years spoke to me of their memories. Birgit Keil, who still dances with the company, recalled: "Anne had a lot of temperament and her enthusiasm was great. In the centre, as we moved, she'd always say, 'You must feel the wind around your ears.' Her class was very alive, and she always kept my interest. I was never bored, and that, to me, is the most important thing about a good teacher. It's rare, too."

Observing Woolliams teach, I was immediately impressed with her vibrant energy. She expects the same of her students. "On the stage," she tells them, "you obviously have to work just under that level of pushing your limits, but in the studio I expect you to really push. Don't be so comfortable. Sweat a bit!" As she later told me: "Of course, some people perspire and some don't, but I feel that if I could just open the pores of the ones who stay so dry, they'd get more juice in their dancing!"

As she teaches, Woolliams constantly uses her hands on her students' bodies, pulling them up by the tops of their ears to get them to lengthen their spines, lifting them out of their hips on their supporting sides, or running her finger along the top of a leg in *tendu* to emphasize that she wants the leg lengthened. As she urges students on, her face has a multitude of expressions; she employs them like flash cards from moment to moment— concern, disapproval, delight, confusion. When she gives a correction, a quick, radiant smile always follows her stern expression.

Clearly, Woolliams is interested in cultivating the intelligent student. Frequently, she will ask questions such as "Why is the arm placed in front in arabesque?" and nod approvingly when a student replies: "Because it corresponds to the line of the lifted back leg." She seems ever cognizant of the fact that many of her students may someday be teachers. In one class, during an adagio exercise at the barre, she put them in pairs. One student did a *développé* and the other held, and manually rotated, the lifted leg during a slow eight-count *grand rond de jambe*. The helper gave verbal corrections throughout the process and then let go at the end, enabling the other dancer to hold the leg momentarily on her own. Then, Woolliams had them exchange places.

Often, to illustrate her point, Woolliams gathers all the students around to observe one student. She will also, like a mother hen, gather them around herself. "Now, come here," she said one day, gleefully rolling up a newspaper salvaged from the studio floor. (She's especially fond of using props.) She rolled the paper into a long, thin cylinder and proceeded to demonstrate the theory of a cantilever. She pressed one end of the roll down firmly on the top of a stool, extending over the edge, and noted that, as a result, the full length of the cylinder stayed suspended out to the side of the stool. She explained that it stayed up because of the downward pressure of her hand on the end on top of the stool. Thus, she demonstrated that in order for a leg extension to stay elevated, it must be firmly held in the hip socket.

She seems to have an endless supply of tricks to help get her point across. She asked a boy who wasn't using the ends of his feet in jumps to sit on the floor and stretch his legs, parallel, in front of him. Then she got on her knees and placed her hand on the floor about two inches in front of his pointed toes. "Now, reach for my hand with your toes," she commanded. He pointed harder. Then, while he maintained the strong arch in his feet, she had him bend and repoint his toes several times, using only the metatarsal joints.

Some of the imagery Woolliams uses can be quite funny. "What are you pointing at God for?" she asked one day when she noticed a girl with her index finger sticking straight upward in 5th position *en haut*. "Curve your fingers!" she begged. She uses a very effective image to make students aware of their front hand in arabesque. "If you go to a manicurist," she tells them, "you put your hand on a cushion and they attend to it. You feel it is beautiful. So when you do an arabesque, place your hand on that imaginary cushion."

More often than not, the trim-figured Woolliams begins the centre work in class with a *port de bras* exercise, the fine points of which she herself demonstrates elegantly, with perfect form. She reminds students: "Your arms must speak, breathe—not just be in a position." To help them limber their upper backs and shoulders, she often starts class by having students stretch their arms above their heads, hands clasped. She also has her female students place their arms behind their backs and clasp their hands at hip level, as if in a handshake. In this position, she has them bend their elbows slightly, then press them together. This stretch, she says, is essential for developing the shoulder flexibility and openness across the upper chest necessary for the *port de bras* in *Swan Lake*.

When teaching, Woolliams talks constantly about how dancers should use their hands. Susan Hanke, a principal dancer with the Stuttgart Ballet and a devoted former student, says she has never forgotten Woolliams's image of "fingers like teardrops dripping down." Hanke also remembers another favorite Woolliams axiom: "The little finger has to be happy. Smile with it. If you drop it, your whole back collapses. Lift it and your whole back lifts." Repeatedly, I watched Woolliams correcting thumbs that were sticking out, wrinkling her nose at the sight, and clucking "Ay, yi, yi" with displeasure. She is also adamant about facial expressions and often passes along the barre lifting up students' bangs and stroking frowns away. "Smile when you're in 5th position," she urges them.

She is quite particular about students' physical attire in class, allowing them nothing on top of their tights and leotards. "Take off all those baggy clothes," she commands. "You've got to *feel* like dancers." Wrinkling her nose, she pulls a string hanging from a girl's leotard sleeve. "What's this?" she asks disapprovingly. "When you come into the studio, you must forget the sloppy contemporary trends of the street. Instead, be special. Take care to look perfect in your grooming—no sags in your tights, no mismatched elastics." One former Stuttgart dancer remembers that Woolliams hated the plastic warm-up pants that so many dancers favor and forbade them in class. "Once," the dancer told me, "a girl came in with them on, and Anne grabbed a pair of scissors, ran over, and began chopping the pants into little pieces *while* the girl was wearing them! Then, she rolled them into a ball and threw them out the window. She could really go off the deep end sometimes. She'd just lose it! But she also had a very soft, sweet side to her."

Woolliams feels strongly that overweight students must not be allowed to camouflage their bodies in class. "You won't really change your shape," she tells one such student, "until you allow yourself to receive it. Don't hide it. Take off your sweatshirt."

There is a great deal of emphasis in Woolliams's classes on developing an awareness of line. "You must see your arabesque in your mind's eye—cut it out in the air before you," Woolliams tells the dancers, "then step into it." She often refers to architecture to make a point. "Don't be Gothic in your 5th *en haut*," she instructs a student whose elbows are sharply bent above her head, making a diamond shape instead of the correct oval. "Know what sort of architecture you are, what shape you're dancing in," she exhorts. "Use your imagination!"

Woolliams's discussion of 5th position *en haut* is not limited to shape alone. "Here is the picture," she says pointing to her face, "and here is the frame," indicating her arm lifted above her head. "What's in the frame must look pleasant, and if you have only half a frame, just one arm up instead of two, the head must still have a sense of being in the frame." She constantly mentions the eyes, both to admonish students who look too often in the mirror, as well as to chide ones who have developed the habit of not using their eyes at all. "If you've got a long line," she tells a tall young lady, "you must have a long look. Look *beyond* the hand."

I was surprised one day to hear Woolliams tell her students to "look with your backs." She explained to me what she meant: "Obviously, a lot of balance is in the eyes, but when the eyes are absolutely plastered forward, you get a rather boring expression. So I'm trying to get them to work *en face* while using 'other eyes,' so to speak, in the back, for fastening onto something behind. It's staring that I object to—that typical expression before a pirouette. If people are really aware, really using their eyes (which is absolutely essential for dancing), then they really know what's around them."

Continually, throughout the class, Woolliams pleads with students, "Live! Be vital." One day, she stopped class to have a short discussion of the words "introvert" and "extrovert." "Tell me what these words mean," she queried the students. "In this *temps lié,* which is the introverted movement and which the extroverted one?" She led the students to understand that there must be a difference in the quality with which they performed the initial *plié,* taking the arms to 1st position with the eyes cast downward (introverted), and the subsequent *piqué en avant* to 5th position, during which they open their arms into a big *croisé* pose and look outward (extroverted).

She is interested in the development of each student's individuality as an artist. In a variations class one day, she allowed each young lady to decide for herself which variation she wished to show. (Then she added that she'd have a look and decide if indeed each had chosen the one most suitable for herself!) To develop their dramatic expressiveness, she again resorted to using a prop. She took a fuzzy leg warmer from the barre, folded it and cradled it in her arms. Then she handed it to the girls, asking them to "talk to the baby." She instructed them to note their expression, as well as the delicacy with which they cradled the bundle and the fact that their shoulders were forward. Then she tossed the leg warmer onto the floor to underline her point about how carelessly they had bashed through a Petipa variation. "You must learn to use your hands and faces more delicately," she coached.

This same class had recently learned Juliet's variation from Cranko's *Romeo and Juliet.* To get these young dancers to use their imaginations and look past the steps, Woolliams asked them to describe who was on the stage with them while they danced the variation (Mother? Father? Tybalt?) and what Juliet felt in relation to each of these people. How, she asked, would Juliet relate her choreography to them? Woolliams remembers how Volkova used to drill students in much the same fashion. "What are you wearing?" the great Russian pedagogue would demand of a dancer about to begin a variation. And when the student answered, "A tutu," Volkova would query further: "And what color is your tutu?"

Stuttgart ballerina Susan Hanke remembers with fondness how Woolliams coached her for her first *Swan Lake:* "She demonstrated how I should use my eyes, my hands, my arms. When I do it now, I always think about her and remember her coaching me. I am forever grateful for the quality and feeling inside that she brought out. She always told me, 'Never do anything that you don't feel inside.'"

Woolliams advocates the study of mime as a way to help prepare students for developing roles. In her book, *Ballet Studio,* she devotes an entire chapter to the subject. It is an impassioned plea for the reinstatement of mime classes in all professional ballet schools. Acting, she notes, is an essential component in "story" ballets, and "on the rare occasions when one is confronted with human emotion portrayed in the grand manner, the impact is colossal" (p. 108). Interestingly, Woolliams views the value of mime in a much broader sense than just preparation for the stage. She writes: "The pure imagination of young children playing 'pretend games' sometimes withers around the age of fourteen and is replaced by the self-conscious gaucheness of teenage behavior. It is a pity that this so often destroys the joy of mimicry and make-believe that can, and should, continue into adult life. Is it also because too much canned entertainment dulls the need for children to create their own worlds of fantasy? Perhaps our scientific age reduces dreams to such a negligible stature that they are considered to be unproductive escapes for the naive or as belonging to the realm of dropouts. If this is really so, we are lost as individuals. However, as long as art flourishes I think there is still hope for us!" (p. 108).

Today's students, she feels, are quite unlike those of her day. "You can't just say, 'Do it like I did,'" she says. "It's a different world out there now, a change that, unfortunately, has had some negative impacts on dance training." She explains: "People today are not as physically tough as we used to be, simply because so much is done for them by pushing buttons. Kids are driven to school now. We used to walk or cycle!"

Woolliams also feels that young people today face a psychological abyss—a multitude of horrors from nuclear holocaust to terrorism to divorce—all of which affect their outlook on life. "And sexual roles are less defined," she notes. "The mystery of sex has been taken away. Men and women don't behave as they used to toward each other. But dancing is sensual. The male and female roles *should* be different."

I asked Woolliams if the staff in her school in Zurich adhered to a syllabus, and she replied that they did. The program is laid out over nine years—three at the beginning level, three intermediate, and three advanced. During the last year, when some of the students' theoretical subjects are dropped, Woolliams encourages them to perform as much as possible, either in the opera house or by taking guest engagements. Unfortunately, she noted, only in Australia did she experience the luxury of watching students complete her entire program. Even in Zurich, students most often come to her school already trained to some degree and at many different levels of technical expertise. This, of course, can be frustrating.

To guide her teachers, she has developed a graph of what is taught and when—how, for instance, a student progresses from learning a simple *assemblé* to an *assemblé en tournant*. "But basically," she told me, "I leave the staff fairly on their own. I just tell them that, in this year, this is what must be achieved—how they do it is their own decision. Some like to get an individual movement really perfect first; others will put it in an *enchaînement* right away. You know, you can only teach if you believe in how you're doing it. If you're teaching a system that's been imposed on you, that doesn't come from your own gut, that's not good.

"If a teacher believes in what she's teaching, it inspires the student to believe in the teacher—and a student's success sometimes can be measured by the amount of this belief. We've all seen young dancers who have terrible physical faults or who have started late, but somewhere inside them is ticking a belief that holds them to the art and pulls them through. It's like a religious belief—a mystic thing. Because dancers endure a constant, demanding regimen of training and practice, there are always times when they suffer self-doubt and despair. Even the best dancers experience this. But your belief in this mystic thing is what keeps you going and permits you to take risks. It gives you courage—even momentary courage. I mean, before you go out onstage, you never know what the performance is going to be like. When you step into arabesque on *pointe*, you don't know if you're going to be on balance or not. But if you do it with belief, you probably will find the equilibrium."

Some dancers, Woolliams says, have this kind of belief even when they are very young. She is always on the lookout for it. "When we audition children," she says, "they are usually very nervous. I call out their names one at a time and ask each to come up to my table to say 'Hello.' Now, the children don't know what is going to happen, but you can almost see by the way they

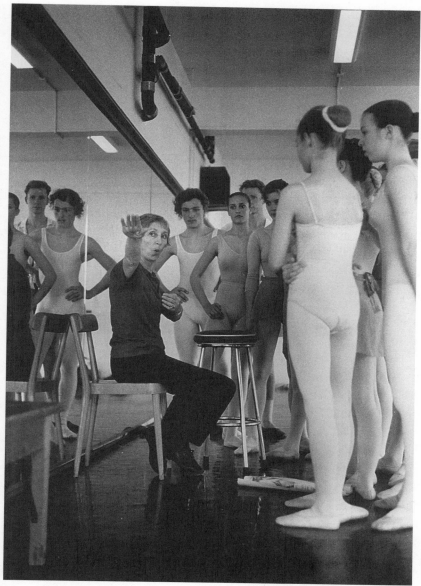

Anne Woolliams speaking to students during class about how to hold the leg in the hip socket.

walk across the floor if they have that kind of secret belief. You can see if they're so inhibited that they'll probably never get over it. Of course, if they come thundering across the floor, that's not good either!" Obviously, Woolliams adds, she also looks for youngsters with the right physical attributes for dance—"because that will make it easier for them. But," she adds wisely, "not always. Having a few faults that you must fight to overcome can be an advantage."

The structure of Woolliams's class is fairly traditional. However, she differs slightly from both the Cecchetti and Vaganova methods (see p. 361, nn. 9, 10) in her placement of *grands battements* at the barre. She inserts them after *ronds de jambe en l'air* and just before *développés* ("to loosen things up a bit"). She is emphatic about how extensions of the leg should be done. "Most students just put their leg up there," she says with disdain, "but that's not it. *Développé* is exactly what it says—the development of the leg. It's the *wonder* of extending it that's important."

A particularly musical teacher, Woolliams uses a variety of rhythms and constantly alternates the tempi at her barre between slow and fast. She has a wonderful chapter in *Ballet Studio* titled "Rhythm and Musicality." Included in it are several tricky combinations that use the music in rather unconventional ways. They are both challenging and fun for the students. "I often do things in canon, so the movement—sometimes with the arms, sometimes with the legs—crosses over the phrase," she says. "It's easy with fives, and it's both a musical, as well as a co-ordination, challenge for the students."

Although especially concerned with getting dancers to move, Woolliams is also very careful about placement. She refers to the hipbones in the pelvis as the "*pas de deux* bones." Thinking from the vantage point of dancers, who most often visualize their alignment from their heads downward (torso on top of hips, on top of legs and feet), she tells students: "If you can have the *pas de deux* bones lifted, and in actual fact, more prominent [as seen from above if you look down] than the thigh muscle, then you're pulled up. As soon as those bones go behind the thigh muscle, you're sitting [i.e., tucking the pelvis]."

Woolliams also has some novel ideas about turn-out. I was interested, for instance, in her method of teaching beginners how to stand correctly in 1st position. She has them stand in a small parallel 2nd position and rotate their heels inward to 1st, as opposed to the much more common manner of having beginners stand in 6th position and rotate their toes outward. Her method, she explains, forces the students to use their inner thigh and rotator muscles under the buttocks to establish the turned out position. "In contrast," she says, "when one rotates the legs outward to 1st from 6th, one contracts the muscles running over the shin bones. This is not beneficial to turn-out."

In teaching turns, Woolliams often focuses on the face. "You must let your eyes govern your head," she tells students. "It's your body that turns away from your head, not your head that turns." As she explained to me: "There are some who can spot without being told. They are always the best turners. But many students have problems when they think about moving their heads. All the muscles in the neck become tense and activated, and, of course, spotting is much better when the head moves easily upon the top of the spine. The only holding one should do is with the eyes."

Woolliams also resorts to an interesting solution to help students who have "lost" their pirouettes. As she writes in the excellent chapter "Pirouettes" in *Ballet Studio:* "In all cases when a turn is not straight and secure, the dancer's confidence must be restored by stopping the practice of the spin and refinding the equilibrium. This can be done by making a small *échappé sauté* into second or fourth position and immediately a *relevé* into the pirouette position, holding the balance on the half-point for as long as possible. It is sometimes necessary to do this for several days before again attempting the turn" (p. 82).

Woolliams is also particularly good at teaching students how to jump. She will have them bounce balls in class to illustrate her theories about jumping. "It's the idea behind the thrust *as it starts* that controls what happens in the air," she tells them. "If you bounce a ball off the ground so that it then hits a wall and returns to you, all the shapes in its trajectory can be altered according to the speed and strength with which you initially throw the ball into the ground." Therefore, she explains, the whole idea about the direction, height, and speed of a jump must be contained in the *plié* with which it begins. If it is, she assures them, the jump will be coordinated. "This is especially true in *pas de deux* work," she notes, "where the coordination you have with a partner is very similar to that which you have with an object you are going to throw."

Woolliams also talks a great deal about how the feet are used in jumps, both in the air and on the floor. "People often 'die' in jumps," she remarks, "because when the heel touches the ground and remains there, the Achilles tendon, if it is short, restricts the *plié*. There is no longer life in the foot. Something stops. The *plié* becomes dead." This is fatal, of course, for *ballon*, as well as other aspects of technique. Even during barre work (which she fills with many slow, generous *pliés*) Woolliams is very specific about how students must bend their knees. Often, she uses her voice to convey the correct dynamic. "Say plee-ay, not puullee-ay," she says to get them to keep their legs vibrant during a slow exercise. To encourage elevation, Woolliams coaches dancers about how to direct their upward thrust: "Don't waste energy opening your legs to 2nd when you *échappé*. Push up with your feet straight down—you'll change the shape of your legs if you work that way!" She is also concerned with aesthetics. "No!" she shouts during a *petit allegro* exercise. "I don't want to see the work in your shoulders. The work is in the feet!" I also found effective her method of emphasizing how one particular jump—a *sissonne fermée de côte*—must travel. She placed a student sideways next to a wall and directed him to *plié* in 5th position. (His bent knee almost touched the wall.) "Now, do the *sissonne*," she commanded. The student had no choice but to actively propel his body sideways, away from the wall, in order to avoid kicking it.

I particularly enjoyed some of the imagery she used about jumping. "Imagine yourself going up through a thick cloud," she told one class, "and at the top bursting through into the sunshine. Then take a look around for as long as possible." In her book, she devotes an entire chapter to *batterie* (jumps during which the legs cross or "beat" in the air), an aspect of allegro work she considers almost a lost art today. She writes that "small beats should accentuate the closings, using the floor as a small drum and bouncing from it quite evenly, but not high" (p. 88).

As my stay with Woolliams in Zurich came to an end, I asked her what she thought made a good teacher. "Chemistry!" she replied without hesitation. "You know, like the old ballerinas. It's just lovely to be near them. But there are also some marvelous teachers who haven't been good dancers at all. They've learned through their own frustrations." She elaborated: "Teachers have to be both visual and rhythmic. They have to have a mixture of confidence and humility. The confidence is important in order to give others confidence—to make students believe in what you're doing. You can't constantly appear to be questioning yourself. This confidence must reveal itself as a belief in dance itself—not as a belief in yourself as a sort of pundit on dance. And if you let this belief in dance take over, it sort of carries everybody along. It's catching! And then you must have humility. It's what keeps you learning. When I watch people's classes (if I don't fall asleep because it can be so soporific!), I'm always saying, 'Oh, that's nice—oh, I must try that.' I know all the years I've been teaching have been teaching me to teach. And I'm sure I haven't learned all about it yet!"

Classroom Quotes from Woolliams

"Turn-out is something a dancer does, not necessarily something he has."

"I believe jumping is 50 percent rhythmic coordination, 25 percent technique and strength, and 25 percent temperament and joy."

"When you dance at a slow tempo, do it with grandeur. Don't creep through the mud."

"You mustn't be nervous in classical dance. It's a very generous art. You must attack a *piqué* before it attacks you!"

"You *cannot* do a preparatory 'breath' opening with the arm if the body is not lifted, if you're not standing up beautifully. It will look like a decoration, like sugar on a cake that doesn't taste good."

During jumps: "Think with your toes!"

"It is ridiculous to think that tap dancing is something inferior to classical ballet. If you're a good tap dancer, you're probably better than a bad Swan Queen."

"When you stand in 5th position, you must feel like you're growing in the rain."

"Dancing is music made visible, song made tangible."

Order of the Exercises in Woolliams's Class (advanced class, 1½ hours)

BARRE

1. Warm-up exercises facing the barre that may include slow tendus, dégagés, various foot stretches, low battements en cloche with a straight leg and in attitude, and grand rond de jambe (low)
2. Pliés and cambrés
3. Tendus with demi-pliés
4. Faster tendus emphasizing articulation of the foot
5. Dégagés
6. Ronds de jambe à terre in combination with fondus at 45 degrees, completed with lifts of the leg to 90 degrees and port de bras
7. Frappés and petits battements
8. Ronds de jambe en l'air
9. Grands battements
10. Développés, including stretches

CENTRE

1. Port de bras with temps lié
2. Single pirouettes in combination with petit battement
3. Adagio
4. Relevés at 90 degrees on one leg
5. Pirouettes using various arm positions
6. Small jumps from two feet (échappés, soubresauts, changements)
7. Small jumps on one foot (temps levés, jetés, assemblés, sissonnes)
8. Petite batterie (brisés, entrechats, brisé télémaque, etc.)
9. Large, traveling, dancey combination with sauts de basque and balancés
10. Grands sautés en manège
11. Grandes pirouettes
12. Port de bras

The Roots of Tradition

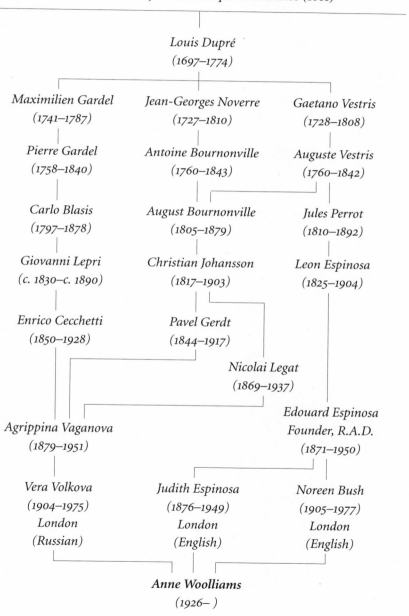

L'Académie Royale de Musique et de Danse (1661)

Louis Dupré
(1697–1774)

Maximilien Gardel   Jean-Georges Noverre   Gaetano Vestris
(1741–1787)   (1727–1810)   (1728–1808)

Pierre Gardel   Antoine Bournonville   Auguste Vestris
(1758–1840)   (1760–1843)   (1760–1842)

Carlo Blasis   August Bournonville   Jules Perrot
(1797–1878)   (1805–1879)   (1810–1892)

Giovanni Lepri   Christian Johansson   Leon Espinosa
(c. 1830–c. 1890)   (1817–1903)   (1825–1904)

Enrico Cecchetti   Pavel Gerdt
(1850–1928)   (1844–1917)

                         Nicolai Legat
                          (1869–1937)

                                                      Edouard Espinosa
Agrippina Vaganova   Founder, R.A.D.
(1879–1951)   (1871–1950)

Vera Volkova   Judith Espinosa   Noreen Bush
(1904–1975)   (1876–1949)   (1905–1977)
London   London   London
(Russian)   (English)   (English)

                    Anne Woolliams
                     (1926–)

Selected Exercises

Ballet exercises from the classes of the teachers profiled in this book appear on the following pages. The musical time signature (e.g., 3/4, 4/4, 6/8) is placed next to the title of each exercise. The musical counts appear on the left side of the page. Musical beats between the counts are indicated through the use of [+] and [-]. Verbal descriptions of the movement using standard French ballet terminology are set to the right of the counts.

In almost all cases, I have employed the French terminology adhered to by the Russian (Vaganova) syllabus. There are, however, some notable exceptions. For instance, in the West, more dancers are familiar with the term "5th en haut" than the less common Russian label for the same pose, "3rd position"; therefore, I chose the more widely used term. In the glossary that follows this chapter, I have listed or pictured other potentially confusing terms— those that have different names in the English, French, or Russian schools. For pictorial clarification of all terms, I refer readers to my book *Classical Ballet Technique.* In centre exercises involving several changes of direction, I have referred to the points of the room using the Russian system as pictured in the glossary. For directions of the leg to the front, side, and back, I have used the abbreviations F, S, and B.

From the Classes of Marika Besobrasova

BARRE WORK

Battements tendus jetés (dégagés) with glissades, 4/4

Besobrasova challenges students to maintain their balance in plié without holding the barre, as well as asking them to transfer their weight via glissades in all directions. This is an excellent exercise to force students, early in the barre work, to take responsibility for their own stability, both in plié and in motion, rather than depending on the barre to support them.

1	Smoothly extend the working leg to 45 degrees devant, executing a plié on the supporting leg.
2–3	Place both arms in 1st position, holding the position above.
4	Close in 5th plié, placing the inside arm on the barre. The outside arm opens to 2nd.
+5	Glissade en avant.
+6	Glissade en arrière.
7+8	Three battements tendus jetés à la seconde.
1–8	Repeat all in reverse.
1–4	Extend the leg à la seconde in plié as above. Close in 5th front plié.
5–6	Glissade de côté away from barre and repeat into the barre.
+	Throw the working leg devant, straightening the support.
7+8	Three battements tendus jetés (dégagés) en cloche (B, F, B).
+	Close briefly in 5th back.
1–8	Repeat the set to the side in reverse.

Battements tendus jetés (dégagé) lent, gentle 4/4, not fast

An exercise like this one (and the similar one above) typically falls third or fourth in Besobrasova's barre. The focus is on maintaining stability without using the barre, not only during the change of weight in the tombé, but also during the difficult unsupported demi-rond. Besobrasova incorporates an exercise such as this one into her barre before introducing any speedy legwork, thus ensuring that her students are consciously and strongly holding the placement of their torsos prior to attempting anything complex or strenuous with their legs.

1	Brush the working leg à la seconde at 45 degrees. *Both* arms lower to 5th en bas.
2	Demi-rond en dedans to 45 degrees devant. The arms lift to 1st.
3	Tombé en avant to the pose 3rd arabesque à terre in plié with the inside arm extended forward.
4	Hold.
5	Soutenu relevé to 5th. Arms to 1st.
6	Release the front leg à la seconde (45 degrees), simultaneously lowering the supporting heel. Open the arms à la seconde and take the barre.
7+8	Close in 5th back and execute two tendus jetés à la seconde (closing F, B).
1–8	Repeat all in reverse.

Battements dégagés (tendus jetés) rapide, 4/4 polka

Begin in 1st position, sideways to the barre.

+1–4	Execute eight fast, light dégagés (tendus jetés) in 1st, alternating directions, with the working leg extended (not closed) on the counts and upbeats indicated: S (+), F (1), S (+), F (2), S (+), F (3), S (+), F (4).
5+6	Three battements dégagés en cloche (B, F, B).
7+8	Three battements dégagés en cloche (F, B, F).
-+1–4	Quickly brush through 1st and open S (+) to reverse the dégagés: B (1), S (+), B (2), S (+), B (3), S (+), B (4).
5–8	Reverse the two sets of dégagés en cloche (F, B, F; B, F, B).
1–8	Plié in pointe tendue 2nd arabesque and slowly fouetté en dehors à terre in plié to pointe tendue devant on the other side (outside arm finishes in 5th en haut).
1–8	Slowly pass the inside (front) leg through 1st plié to finish in the pose 4th arabesque in plié pointe tendue. On the last two counts, close in 5th behind, straightening and coming en face, opening the arabesque arm à la seconde.
1–32	Repeat the entire exercise, starting on the other side.

Petit allegro with temps de cuisse, 4/4 polka, executed quite fast

1–4 Four assemblés over (dessus) en face.

-+-5 Glissade derrière (i.e., to the side toward the back foot without changing the feet), temps de cuisse over.

6–7 Two more temps de cuisse over.

8 Changement.

1–8 Repeat.

Note: Each temps de cuisse is done using the Russian "small pose" (i.e., one arm in low 1st position, the other in 2nd). Besobrasova emphasized that the head must look down, over the elbow, at the foot doing the petit passé each time and that with each sissonne the chest and chin must lift and the eyes look outward en diagonale.

Grande pirouette exercise, 3/4 slow waltz

This is one of Besobrasova's favorite exercises passed down to her from her teachers—a difficult, advanced Cecchetti exercise she remembers Egorova giving in Paris. Many years later, another of Cecchetti's students, an Iranian princess who had studied with Cecchetti in London toward the end of his life, taught Besobrasova the slightly amended version that appears here. (Students of the Cecchetti method will recognize this as his "Quatre Pirouettes en Dedans" described on page 122 of *The Manual.*) Besobrasova remembers the great French dancer Serge Lifar describing the force a dancer feels doing this exercise as being "like what happens when you twist a rope and then release it."

1 Chassé croisé devant, passing through pointe tendue croisée derrière and finishing with the back leg lifted in Russian "big pose" (high 3rd) attitude croisée derrière.

2 Rise in attitude, lifting the downstage arm in reverse to meet the other in 5th en haut.

3 Demi-plié in attitude, leaning forward as the arms lower to 1st position.

+ Allongé the back leg.

4–5 Step backward upstage to finish in pointe tendue croisée devant with the torso twisted so that the back is visible to the audience.

The downstage arm is high in 5th. The other arm is pressed back à la seconde, visible behind the body. The head looks up to the lifted (front) arm.

+ Lunge in a preparatory pose with the arms in low 3rd, *but maintain the twist of the torso upstage.*

6–8 Grande pirouette à la seconde en dedans with the arms in 5th en haut. Finish at 90 degrees in 2nd en face with the arms up.

+1 Passé développé to attitude croisée derrière as in count 1 above.

2–5 Continue exactly as on the counts above.

6–8 Grande pirouette in attitude derrière en dedans, finishing in attitude ouverte (effacée).

1–5 Passé and repeat as above.

6–8 Grande pirouette in 1st arabesque en dedans, finishing at 90 degrees in profile to the audience.

1–5 Passé and repeat as above.

6–8 Pirouette en dedans with the arms in 5th, finishing closing front in 5th plié croisé.

POINTE WORK AT THE BARRE

Piqués and soutenus, 4/4, gentle, sideways to the barre

1–2 Plié, extending the working leg devant. Arm to 1st.

3 Piqué en avant to 5th on pointe. Arm 5th en haut.

4 Sharply lift the back (inside) leg to cou-de-pied derrière. The arm remains up in 5th.

5 Petit développé to the pointe tendue derrière, lowering off pointe into plié on the supporting (outside) leg. The arm extends through 1st to arabesque.

6 Assemblé soutenu relevé to 5th. The arm stays in arabesque.

+7 Petit développé with the front foot to pointe tendue à la seconde, lowering off pointe into plié on the supporting (inside) leg. The arm opens à la seconde.

8 Assemblé soutenu relevé to close 5th behind. The arm lowers en bas.

1–2 Petit développé with the back foot to pose écarté derrière in plié à terre. The arm is in 5th en haut.

3–4	Soutenu en tournant en dehors (full turn, changing the feet). The arm closes to 1st.
5–6	Petit développé with the front foot to pose écarté devant in plié à terre, raising the arm to 5th en haut.
7–8	Soutenu en tournant en dedans (full turn, changing the feet). The arm closes to 1st.
1–16	Reverse the entire exercise.

Pointés and petit passés, 2/4, coda, sideways to the barre

+1---	Sharply petit développé à la seconde and execute four tiny, fast pointés.
2	Close in 5th behind.
3–8	Repeat three times more, alternating the closings.
1–4	Two petits passés relevés in two counts each, holding the foot at ankle level each time, closing in back and in front.
5–7	Three petits passés relevés.
8	Pointe tendue derrière.
1–3	Three tendus jetés (dégagés) en cloche (F, B, F), the last to relevé 45 degrees devant.
4	Hold.
5–8	Reverse the dégagés en cloche and relevé.
1–6	Twelve fast dégagés en cloche (off pointe, finishing derrière).
7–8	Plié in the pose 2nd arabesque à terre.

Petits battements with ballottés sautés, 4/4

+	Petit développé to plié pointe tendue ouverte (effacée) devant.
1–3	Relevé petit battement battu in ouverte (effacée) devant.
4	Petit développé to plié pointe tendue ouverte (effacée) devant.
5–6	Ballotté sauté over (dessus) en tournant with a half-turn toward the barre, finishing on the other side in plié pointe tendue ouverte (effacée) devant.
7–8	Repeat the ballotté sauté with a half-turn, finishing on the first side.
1–7	Relevé, petits battements serrés en face.
8	Plié 2nd arabesque à terre.
1–16	Reverse the entire exercise.

Emboîtés sautés sur les pointes, 2/4, coda

1   From 5th plié, jump onto pointe on the outside foot, bringing the inside foot cou-de-pied derrière.

2–4   Execute three emboîtés sautés in cou-de-pied derrière, jumping from point to point in plié without coming down.

5   Emboîté to plié on the flat foot, lifting the inside foot to cou-de-pied derrière.

6   Relevé with a half-turn toward the barre, bringing the back foot to cou-de-pied devant.

7–8   Hold in cou-de-pied devant. Close 5th plié on count 8.

1–8   Repeat all, beginning on the other side.

Do the entire exercise eight times in sequence, alternating sides.

⌣∴∾ *From the Classes of Willam Christensen*

BARRE WORK

Gargouillades with ronds de jambe en l'air, 4/4

In this exercise, Christensen combines a traveling jump, away from and back to the barre, with a standard barre movement.

+1   From 5th, quickly brush the working leg à la seconde at 30 degrees, executing a single rond de jambe en l'air en dehors on the upbeat and closing behind in 5th on the count.

2–4   Repeat with rond de jambe en dedans, and again en dehors and en dedans.

+5   Gargouillade away from the barre, lifting the arms to 5th on the jump and finishing in 5th plié with the arms in open 5th high.

6   Hold the pose.

7–8   Repeat the gargouillade, traveling towards the barre with the same port de bras and holding the pose in plié on count 8.

Pierre Vladimirov's grand battement, 4/4

Christensen was an admirer of the great Russian expatriate teacher Pierre Vladimirov, whom he often observed teaching at Balanchine's School of American Ballet in New York City in the 1950s. This is one of his favorite exercises, which he finds useful as a preparation for the Bournonville grand pas de basque at 90 degrees.

1–3 Standing with one's back to the barre, execute 3 grands battements devant (accent down), finishing the last one in demi-plié in 5th.

++4 Jump, throwing the front leg up in grand battement devant, and exchange the legs at the top of the jump in the manner of a large hitchkick (jeté passé devant at 90 degrees). Finish in 5th plié with the other leg front.

Execute four times, alternating legs.

Note: This exercise was also executed in reverse, facing the barre with grands battements derrière, as well as in 2nd, sideways to the barre, with a half-turn en l'air during the hitchkick. (In 2nd, the jump occurs as the first battement comes down so that the second battement of the jeté passé is executed on the other side. The turn is away from the barre.)

CENTRE WORK

Exercise for turning out the knee in pirouettes, 6/8 jig

1–8 Execute four échappés relevés à la seconde in two counts each with épaulement, arms in 2nd allongée, executing the initial demi-plié on count 1.

1 Demi-plié in 5th.

2 Single pirouette en dehors with the arms in 1st.

3 Plié in the retiré position, opening the arms à la seconde and pressing the lifted knee back with the hand of the leading arm.

4 Single pirouette en dehors, maintaining the arms in this position, pushing the lifted knee back during the turn.

5 Demi-plié en face in the same pose.

6 Single pirouette en dehors as above.

7 Demi-plié en face as above.

8 Double pirouette en dehors, closing both arms to 1st position.

1 Close behind in demi-plié in 5th in preparation to begin entire combination again.

2–16 Repeat as above on the other side.

Italian petit allegro, 2/4

The folk-dance-style paddle steps in this lovely enchaînement are related to those seen in Slavic character dance. They were also a favorite of Balanchine, who often used them in his choreography.

1+2 Execute three changements en face, finishing the last one in 4th position demi-plié in preparation for pirouettes en dehors.

3–4 Pirouettes en dehors, finishing behind in 5th position.

+5 Execute a petit jeté derrière, throwing the back leg out in écarté towards the downstage corner and emphasizing the elevation (suspension in the air). The arms are thrown outward to 2nd and the body is inclined downstage with the upstage arm higher than the downstage arm on the finish of the jump.

+6–8 Execute six paddle steps (i.e., coupé-tombés, staying in plié on the balls of the feet with the ankles crossed in 5th position croisé), pumping diagonally upstage, character dance style, gradually bringing the downstage arm in from 2nd across the body with the palm down.

+ Coupé under with a quarter-turn en dehors, simultaneously executing a tiny développé ouvert (effacé) devant with the front leg.

1+2 Tombé diagonally downstage into 1st arabesque and execute two hops in arabesque plié at 90 degrees.

++3 Quickly twist the body en face, sharply bringing the back leg forward into a low écarté devant position and pas de bourrée en tournant en dedans to croisé as preparation for the next count.

++4 Execute a low Bournonville pas de basque en l'air, finishing with pas de bourrée en tournant en dedans to croisé.

5–8 Coupé under and repeat the hops in arabesque, the pas de bourrée turn, and the pas de basque on the same downstage diagonale and finish the combination with a chassé en avant to croisé, finishing in B+, the arms executing a half port de bras to demi-seconde, palms up.

Petit allegro with pas couru and cabriole, 4/4

Begin in the upstage corner 6 in B+ croisé on the right leg.

++1	Coupé under, turning the body one-quarter en dehors to face the downstage diagonale, and execute a widely traveled pas couru (three steps: ouvert, croisé, ouvert) along the diagonal toward pt. 2, arms extended in 2nd, finishing in 5th plié with the right foot in front, the body inclined downstage, arms in 2nd allongée (palms down, with the upstage arm higher than the downstage one).
2	Entrechat trois derrière.
3	Coupé under, inclining the body downstage.
4	Jeté battu derrière, changing the body en l'air to finish inclined upstage. (The downstage arm in 2nd allongée is now the high arm.)
5–8	Repeat counts 1–4, traveling downstage on the same diagonal.
1	Execute a half-turn to the right with a tombé onto the back (right) foot, turning to face the upstage corner you came from, leaning into the turn and bending the arms into low 3rd position with the head turned over the elbow of the downstage arm in 1st.
2	Cabriole in 1st arabesque, turning (half) to the right to face the downstage corner on the jump.
+3–4	Coupé under to repeat the tombé en tournant and the cabriole in the same manner as above on the same diagonal.
5–6	Coupé under and tombé ouvert (effacé) downstage into pas de bourrée under to 4th position croisé plié in preparation for pirouettes en dehors.
7–8	Pirouettes en dehors, finishing in a wide 4th position lunge croisé.

Grand jeté exercise for men, 2/4

Executed traveling diagonally downstage from the upstage corner 6. Begin in 5th position croisé, right foot front.

1–4	Execute four emboîtés sautés in cou-de-pied devant, each with a half-turn, traveling diagonally downstage to pt. 2.
5	Grand jeté en avant in 1st arabesque toward pt. 2, landing on the right leg.
6	Coupé under, turning (three-eighths) upstage, finishing with the right foot sur le cou-de-pied devant, arms in 1st, facing pt. 5.
7	Repeat the grand jeté upstage to pt. 6.

8   Coupé under, turning downstage (one-quarter), finishing in plié croisé cou-de-pied devant, bringing the arms to low 3rd preparatory pose to begin entire sequence once again.

POINTE WORK IN THE CENTRE

Enchaînement with pirouettes, 3/4, a soft, slow waltz

Christensen asked his dancers to try to move seamlessly through this exercise, emphasizing a soft rolling through the foot to come off pointe.

Preparation: Stand upstage (pt. 6) in croisé B+ on left leg.

1–2   Take two soft steps (off pointe) diagonally downstage, ouvert (right leg) and croisé (left leg), with the arms in demi-seconde, palms down.

++3   Glissade précipitée de côté (in the direction of the right foot without changing feet) and grand battement relevé à la seconde en face with the right leg. The arms lift through 1st and open to a high 2nd position.

+4   Passé, staying on pointe, and close the right leg softly in front in 5th position plié, arms bending into low 3rd position (right arm in 1st), inclining the body over the arm to the right with the head turned looking over the elbow.

++   Glissade précipitée de côté (toward the left foot without change).

5   Piqué de côté onto the left foot, bringing the right to retiré devant. Arms stay in the same low 3rd ("small pose") position as in count 4.

+   Close in front in demi-plié 5th softly.

6   Relevé passé the front leg.

+   Close in back in 5th plié, changing the arms to the other "small pose" (left arm in 1st).

7   Execute a single pirouette en dehors from 5th (lifting the left foot), keeping the arms in low 3rd position (left arm in 1st), but turning the palms to face the floor. During the turn the body inclines sideways toward the lifted (passé) leg and the head looks over the leading shoulder (i.e., do not spot).

8   Finish the turn, taking the passé leg back into a wide lunge 4th croisé, opening the upstage arm to the side (downstage arm is already in 2nd) as the body inclines downstage to finish in the pose écartée derrière allongée (palms to floor).

1	With the back (left) leg, piqué en avant in profile to 1st arabesque at 90 degrees (to pt. 7).
2	Failli croisé with right leg.
3–4	Walk to the left in a small circle upstage, finishing in the pose pointe tendue croisée devant (standing on the right foot facing pt. 2), arms in 3rd low (left in 1st).
+5	Turning the body to the left, lift the left foot at ankle height and pass it to the back through cou-de-pied to finish in a 4th croisé lunge pose, opening the arm across the body to 2nd and finishing in ecartée allongée, leaning downstage (as above).
+6	Step back onto the left leg, turning the body to the right while executing another small passé to the back with the right leg to finish in a preparatory lunge croisé for pirouettes en dedans.
7	Relevé on the left leg, executing a grande pirouette en dedans in attitude derrière, arms in 3rd high ("big pose").
8	Failli croisé to B+, finishing on the right leg.

↶∶↝ From the Classes of Janina Cunovas

BARRE WORK

Battements dégagés (tendus jetés), 4/4, very staccato

1–2	Two dégagés (tendus jetés) devant.
+	Brush (dégagé) devant.
3	Flick (*flic*) into fully pointed (not wrapped) cou-de-pied devant.
4	Close 5th.
5–6	Two dégagés (tendus jetés) devant.
+7+	Brush devant (+) and execute two battements pointés (7+).
8	Close 5th.
1–4	Four dégagés (tendus jetés) à la seconde, finishing the last in demi-plié 5th, closing in front.
5–8	Relevé passé. Hold. Close 5th in back on the last count.
1–16	Repeat all in reverse.
1–32	Repeat all again both ways. Sustain balance at the end.

Battements frappés, 4/4, bright and quick

Preparation: Brush à la seconde to 25 degrees in 2 counts.

1+2	Three frappés à la seconde.
3+4	Repeat.
5–6	Two double frappés à la seconde.
7–8	Flick (*flic*) to relevé passé, arm to 1st. Hold (8).
1–2	Hold on balance.
3–4	Slowly développé the leg à la seconde at 45 degrees, opening the arms to 2nd, maintaining balance on demi-pointe.
5–6	Hold.
7	Close in 5th demi-plié, arms lowering to 5th en bas.
8	Preparation à la seconde to repeat (or remain in 5th when exercise finishes).

CENTRE WORK

Port de bras for beginners, 3/4 adagio

Stand en face in 1st position, arms in 5th en bas.

1–2	Lift one arm to 5th en haut (accent up on count 1) and open it to 2nd. The eyes follow the hand throughout.
3–4	Repeat with the other arm.
5–6	Demi-plié, simultaneously lifting one arm in reverse (en dedans) to 5th en haut, turning the head and tilting it forward slightly to look under the elbow.
7–8	Straighten knees, opening arm to 2nd. The eyes follow the hand while the head straightens and inclines slightly back over the shoulder.
+	The arms lower to 5th en bas.
1	Tendu devant with the arms lifting to 1st position.
2	Close foot to 1st.
3	Tendu to 2nd, opening arms to 2nd.
4	Close foot to 1st.
5–6	Tendu derrière and close 1st. The arms remain in 2nd.
+	Allongé the arms.
7	Demi-plié in 1st, lowering the arms to 5th en bas.
8	Straighten with arms in 5th en bas.
1–16	Repeat all to the other side.

1–32	Repeat all with the tendus beginning to the back, with arms as follows:
	Tendu derrière—arms in 1st
	Tendu à la seconde—arms in 5th en haut
	Tendu devant—arms in 2nd

Small adagio, 3/4, slowly

Begin in 5th position croisé, right foot front.

1	Step en avant in croisé (to pt. 8), simultaneously doing a half port de bras gesture with the right (downstage) arm.
2	Continuing in the same direction, repeat the step and port de bras with the other arm and leg.
3	Continuing in the same direction, step croisé to pointe tendue croisée derrière, turning palms to the floor in 2nd position.
4	Reverse both arms to finish in 4th position with the upstage arm high.
5–6	Temps lié en arrière through 4th position demi-plié to finish in pointe tendue croisée devant. The arms change through 2nd position to the other 4th position with the downstage arm high. The body leans upstage to the side as this port de bras happens.
7–8	Pass the leg through 1st position to pointe tendue ouverte (effacée) derrière. The arms pass through 1st position and extend into the pose 1st arabesque. (Body is facing pt. 8.)
1–4	Lift the leg to 90 degrees and hold in 1st arabesque.
5	Plié, holding the leg at 90 degrees.
6	Pas de bourrée under (dessous) to 5th position croisé, lowering the arms to 5th en bas. Finish facing pt. 8.
7–8	Rise in 5th croisé, lifting the arms to 5th en haut.
1–4	Turn the body ouvert (to pt. 2) and lift the leg (relevé lent) to 90 degrees ouvert (effacé) devant with the arms in high 3rd in opposition (Russian "big pose"). Hold.
5–8	Slowly lower the leg, passing it through 1st position and lifting it in back in Russian 3rd arabesque (2nd arabesque croisée facing pt. 2).
1–2	Plié arabesque and pas de bourrée under to finish facing the other croisé (pt. 8) in 5th en demi-pointe, arms in 1st.
3–4	Battement the front leg croisé devant en demi-pointe, arms in 2nd. Tombé into a preparatory lunge position for pirouettes en dedans.

5–6	Pirouettes en dedans, finishing in 5th croisé in front in demi-plié, facing pt. 2, arms demi-seconde.
7–8	Straighten legs while arms allongé and lower to 5th en bas.
1–32	Repeat all to the other side.

Port de bras/adagio with run, 3/4 waltz

It is typical of Cunovas to use walks and runs with port de bras to get students moving, especially in lower-level classes where so much of the work is static. The students enjoy feeling as if they are dancing. However, this exercise is not as easy as it looks; walking and running in the classical ballet manner are difficult to master. Both, as Cunovas knows well, require much practice.

Begin in B+ croisé in upstage corner 6.

1–4	Execute four walks (ouvert, croisé, ouvert, croisé) downstage toward pt. 2. The arms swing back and forth, across the body in low 3rd position (Russian "small pose") in opposition, changing with each step (upstage on the first, downstage on the next, and so forth).
5–6	Run to pt. 2, pressing the arms slightly behind the body in demi-seconde.
7–8	Step onto the right leg, facing pt. 2 in the pose 1st arabesque.
1–3	Lift the leg to 90 degrees and hold in 1st arabesque.
4–6	Plié in arabesque and pas de bourrée under to 5th plié croisé.
7–8	Using the back (right) foot, change directions, stepping through to pointe tendue croisée derrière on the right, facing pt. 8. The arms execute a half port de bras.
1–16	Repeat all to the other side.

Sissonnes fermées with balancés, 3/4 waltz

Start in B+ croisé in upstage corner 6, standing on the left leg.

| + | Coupé under with a quarter-turn to the right, extending the left leg downstage to pt. 2 in écarté, back to the audience. |
| 1 | Tombé downstage onto the left leg into balancé de côté (body facing pt. 4), swinging arms downstage across the body in low 3rd position (Russian "small pose" with the right arm in 1st). |

2	Balancé de côté onto the right leg, facing pt. 6 and changing the arms across the body to the other low 3rd position.
3	Step upstage on the left leg to face pt. 6, standing in pointe tendue ouverte (effacée) derrière, arms in high 3rd (Russian "big pose"), downstage (right) arm high.
4	Hold the pose.
5–6	Execute two balancés de côté (to the right, then left), traveling backward downstage to pt. 2 (body facing pt. 6). The arms exchange twice overhead in the "big poses."
7–8	Turn downstage (to the right) and step into 1st arabesque à terre, facing pt. 2. Close behind into 5th demi-plié, facing pt. 2, right foot front.
1	Sissonne fermée en avant in 1st arabesque to pt. 2.
+2	Stretch the knees and demi-plié again.
3–4	Repeat the sissonne and the stretch-plié.
5–7	Three sissonnes fermées en avant to pt. 2, bringing the back (left) arm down, through, and up to the pose Cecchetti 3rd arabesque (Russian arabesque à deux bras). The arm moves smoothly and continuously through all three counts. The first two sissonnes close in 5th behind. The last closes in front (passing quickly through 1st) to finish in 5th croisé plié.
8	Straighten the legs in 5th, lowering the arms to 5th en bas.

Port de bras for hand movements, gentle adagio

Cunovas gives this exercise immediately preceding the révérence. It is characteristic of her to insert somewhere in her class "free-form" movements such as these, which are designed to make students more aware of the expressiveness of their arms and hands.

Stand in B+ en face with the arms dropped naturally at the sides of the body.

+	Invert one hand so that the palm faces away from the body (thumb to the back). The arm is rotated inward so that the point of the elbow faces outward away from the body.
1	Lift the rotated arm diagonally forward to demi-seconde height with palm facing up.
2	Turn the hand so the palm is up (i.e., rotate the arm in the opposite direction so that the point of the elbow now faces the floor), fingers gesturing to the downstage corner.

3–4 Turn the hand so the palm faces the floor and lower the arm softly.

5–8 Repeat with the other arm.

1 Bend the elbow, lifting the arm across the chest, palm facing the audience, thumb down.

2 Press the hand outward en diagonale toward the downstage corner ("pushing the air"), stretching the arm.

+ Turn the hand so the palm is up.

3–4 Turn the hand so that the palm faces the floor and lower the arm softly.

5–8 Repeat with the other arm.

1–8 Repeat the first set of eight, but on the hand rotations lift the arm all the way up sideways (approximately to the height of open 5th, instead of demi-seconde).

1 Lift both arms overhead in the manner of the "flapping" port de bras from *Swan Lake* (top of wrist leads upward, palms begin facing the floor; at the top they face out away from body).

2 Open the arms outward, pressing them down on both sides of the body (wrists lead, fingers trail upward, elbows slightly press back).

3–4 Repeat the flap up and down.

5–8 Repeat the flaps up and down with one step forward on each movement (total of four steps, each to B+).

❧ *From the Classes of Gabriela Taub-Darvash*

BARRE WORK

Battements tendus in 1st position, 3/4, gently, not too fast

In this and subsequent barre exercises, notice how Darvash—rather than having students stand for long periods of time on a straight supporting leg—challenges the dancers to maintain their placement over their supporting leg while repeatedly bending and straightening it.

1 Pointe tendue devant, simultaneously executing a demi-plié on the supporting leg.

2	Straighten the supporting leg, simultaneously flexing the working foot and bringing the leg in, knee bent, to the position cou-de-pied devant with the foot fully flexed.
3–4	Petit développé (pointing the foot) to pointe tendue à la seconde on plié. Then straighten, bringing the foot inward to flexed cou-de-pied devant.
5	Petit développé (pointing the foot) to pointe tendue devant (no plié).
6	Demi-rond en dehors to the side.
7	Close 1st position demi-plié, lowering the arm to 5th en bas (Russian "preparatory position").
8	Relevé in 1st, lifting the arm to 5th en haut (Russian 3rd position).
1	Demi-plié in 1st, lowering the arm to 1st.
2	Pointe tendue à la seconde, opening the arm to 2nd.
+	Close 1st.
3–7	Five tendus à la seconde, closing in 1st. All are accented out on the count.
8	Close in back in 5th.
1–16	Execute the entire exercise in reverse.

Ronds de jambe à terre, 3/4 waltz, not too fast

1–2	Two ronds de jambe en dehors.
+3	Double rond de jambe en dehors.
+	Fondu sur le cou-de-pied derrière.
4	Extend derrière at 45 degrees, straightening supporting leg.
5–8	Repeat.
1–4	Repeat.
+5	Pass the leg through 1st to pointe tendue devant en plié and immediately soutenu relevé to 5th.
6	Hold.
+7	Plié 5th and pointe tendue à la seconde.
8	Close 1st.
1–16	Execute the entire exercise in reverse.

Note: Darvash concludes this exercise with various cambrés and grands ronds de jambe at 90 degrees.

Battements fondus with fouettés at 90 degrees, 3/4 waltz

1–2	Fondu relevé à la seconde at 45 degrees.
3–4	Lower into 2nd position demi-plié and temps lié away from the barre, finishing with the inside leg pointed in 2nd.
5	Demi-plié in 2nd position.
6	Relevé passé on the inside leg (transferring the weight back to the barre).
7	Plié développé devant at 90 degrees.
8	Relevé fouetté en dedans with a half-turn (turning toward the barre), finishing in arabesque.
1	Pass the leg through 1st to finish at 90 degrees devant en plié (inside leg is lifted).
2	Relevé fouetté en dedans (turning outward away from the barre), finishing in 2nd arabesque.
3	Hold en relevé.
4	Close to 5th behind en relevé.
5–6	Fondu relevé devant at 45 degrees with the inside leg.
7	Lower in plié to pointe tendue devant.
8	Soutenu relevé to 5th.
1–16	Execute the entire exercise in reverse.

Grands battements, 3/4, brisk, strongly accented mazurka

Notice the lovely musicality of this combination, as well as the departure from the customary practice of having the battements accented (i.e., close in 5th) on the count.

1+	Grand battement devant (accent up on the count, lowering on +).
-2+	Close 5th ("ah") and pointe tendue devant (2). Hold ("and").
-	Sharply fondu cou-de-pied devant.
3–4	From fondu cou-de-pied, grand battement devant and close 5th.
5–8	Repeat à la seconde.
1–8	Repeat in reverse.

Note: Each count above equals three beats (i.e., one, and, ah, two, and, ah, etc.).

CENTRE WORK

Battements tendus with temps liés and fouettés à terre, 3/4, evenly

This is typical of Darvash's first exercise in the centre. In it, she employs temps liés and pirouettes with the tendus, but also prepares students, with the quarter-turn pivots, for the mechanical coordination they will use later in class in grandes pirouettes devant en dehors and arabesque en dedans.

Begin standing in 5th croisé, arms in 2nd, facing pt. 8.

1   Pointe tendue écartée devant with the front leg.

2   Demi-plié in 2nd. The upstage (left) arm curves into 1st, the downstage one stays in 2nd.

+3   Temps lié onto the downstage (right) leg with a quarter-turn en dehors to finish with the left leg in pointe tendue devant, facing pt. 6. The arms exchange places across the body to finish with the right in 1st, left in 2nd.

4   Close 5th, facing pt. 6, arms in 2nd.

5–8   Repeat all again, but begin with the *back* leg pointing to écarté, plié in 2nd, temps lié onto the right leg turning left, and finish with the left pointed in front, facing pt. 4. Close front.

1–3   Repeat all again exactly as above (counts 5–7), finishing facing pt. 2 with the left in pointe tendue croisée devant.

4   Transfer the weight forward into demi-plié in 4th preparation croisé for pirouettes en dehors.

5–6   Pirouettes en dehors finished in lunge croisé, facing pt. 2.

7   Soutenu relevé 5th croisé, facing pt. 2, arms in 5th en haut.

8   Lower, opening arms à la seconde.

Immediately reverse:

1–2   Point back (right) foot écarté derrière. Plié in 2nd position with upstage (right) arm curving to 1st.

+3   Fouetté en dedans one-quarter (turning upstage) to finish with the left leg in pointe tendue derrière, facing pt. 4. The arms exchange places across the body through 1st.

4   Close 5th behind.

5–8   Repeat, continuing to turn in the same direction (R), but begin by using the *front* foot to pointe tendue écarté.

1–4   Repeat exactly as above in counts 5–8 (closing 5th behind on 8).

5–6   Pointe tendue (right) croisée devant and lunge in preparatory pose for pirouettes en dedans facing pt. 8.

7–8   Pirouettes en dedans, finishing closing the left leg in front in 5th croisé facing pt. 2.

1–32   Repeat the entire exercise, starting to the other side.

Pirouettes, 3/4 waltz

1   Plié in 5th croisé preparatory pose for pirouettes en dehors facing pt. 8.

2   Single pirouette en dehors with the arms in 5th en haut.

3   Finish in plié développé écarté devant at 45 degrees with the downstage (right) arm in 5th en haut, the upstage arm in 2nd (i.e., Russian "big pose").

4   Pas de bourrée under to finish in preparatory lunge croisé for pirouettes en dedans facing pt. 8.

5–6   Single pirouette en dedans; finish in plié, taking the lifted leg back into Russian 3rd arabesque plié at 90 degrees (croisé, facing pt. 8).

+7   Temps lié en arrière to finish pointe tendue croisée devant.

8   Fondu cou-de-pied devant in croisé, facing pt. 8 with the downstage arm in 1st, upstage in 2nd.

1–2   Relevé développé écarté devant (120 degrees). Tombé downstage to pt. 2.

3–4   Pas de bourrée under, turning to finish in 4th croisé plié facing pt. 2 in preparation for pirouettes en dehors.

5–6   Grandes pirouettes en dehors en attitude derrière with the arms in 5th en haut. Finish in attitude plié in croisé with the arms in 2nd.

7–8   Temps lié en arrière to finish pointe tendue (left leg) croisée devant. Close 5th croisé, facing pt. 2.

Emboîtés sautés (lower intermediate-level class), 4/4 polka

Start in 5th position en face, right foot front.

1   Echappé sauté to 2nd en face.

2   From 2nd, sauté and land with the right foot cou-de-pied derrière.

3–4   Two emboîtés sautés, exchanging the feet in cou-de-pied derrière turning in place upstage to the right and finishing facing pt. 6.

5	Temps levé, turning (one-eighth) to face pt. 8 and bringing the back (right) leg forward by means of a petit développé to finish in pointe tendue croisée devant.
6–8	Three emboîtés sautés, changing the feet in pointe tendue devant (ouvert, croisé, ouvert) facing pt. 8. (These are done very terre à terre—with tiny hops.)
1	From the pointe tendue ouverte (effacée) devant position, jump, lifting the front leg and executing a fouetté sauté en dedans (quarter-turn) to the right to finish facing pt. 2 in arabesque effacée at 90 degrees on the right leg with the arms in Russian "big pose" allongée with the downstage (left) arm high.
2	Emboîté sauté onto the left leg into cou-de-pied croisé derrière facing pt. 2.
3–4	Execute two emboîtés sautés in place (facing pt. 2) in cou-de-pied derrière (ouvert, croisé).
+5	Petit développé through with the back (right) leg and piqué (on count 5) diagonally downstage, bringing the downstage (left) foot in front to finish in 5th croisé on the demi-pointe. The arms pass through 1st to finish in Russian "big pose," right arm high.
6–7	Hold the pose in croisé facing pt. 2.
8	Plié (as preparation to begin all on the other side). Arms in 5th en bas.

Batterie, 4/4 polka in character dance style with strongly accented upbeat on each count

The Moiseyev Dance Company was performing in New York City when Darvash gave this exercise in class. The two coupé-jetés de côté in the middle of the combination were inspired by a Moldavian folk dance step she saw in the performance.

1–4	Glissade derrière (i.e., to the side, toward the back foot, without changing the feet) followed by three petits jetés battus derrière.
5–8	Repeat on the other side.
+1	Coupé under and jeté élancé (jeté porté) de côté toward the front leg, bringing the back foot sharply to cou-de-pied derrière.
+2	Repeat the coupé-jeté.
+3	Pas de bourrée under.

| 4 | Brisé en avant diagonally downstage. |
| 5–8 | Four brisés en avant. |

Sissonnes fermées with fouettés ronds de jambe en tournant, 3/4 brisk, light waltz

Begin in 5th croisé, facing pt. 8.

1–2	Two sissonnes fermées in Russian 3rd arabesque to pt. 8.
3	Sissonne fermée de côté over (dessus) in écarté with quarter-turn en dehors to finish facing pt. 2.
4	Entrechat quatre in croisé.
5	Sissonne fermée changée under (dessous) de côté en tournant (quarter-turn to left toward the back foot), traveling downstage to pt. 2 in écarté derrière (facing pt. 8). Arms are in Russian "small pose" with the right in 1st, left in 2nd.
6–7	Two sissonnes fermées de côté in the same pose, traveling in the same direction as above, both closing the left foot behind.
8	Entrechat quatre in croisé, facing pt. 8.
1	Passé relevé with the front foot, turning one-quarter en dehors to face pt. 2.
2	Lower into 4th croisé preparatory plié for turns en dehors.
+3–6	Pirouettes en dehors to the right on the upbeat (+) as preparation for four consecutive relevé turns (fouettés ronds de jambe en tournant for the ladies; relevé turns à la seconde at 90 degrees en dehors for the men) on counts 3–6.
7–8	Pull in to finish the sequence of turns with pirouettes en dehors completed in lunge croisé.

Grand allegro, 3/4, big waltz

Begin in the pose B+ croisé on the left leg in the upstage corner, pt. 6.

+1	Coupé under, tombé (onto left leg) croisé, brushing back (right) leg forward into grand battement sauté effacé devant (Russian "big pose" arms, left high), traveling diagonally downstage to pt. 2.
2	Tombé onto the right leg and repeat sauté battement, brushing the other leg to croisé devant.
+	Tombé croisé.

3–4+ Two grands jetés développés ("split" jetés) with the arms in arabesque à deux bras, traveling downstage to pt. 2. After the first jeté, execute a failli (tombé croisé devant). After the second, bring the back leg through by means of a low développé to croisé devant as preparation for the following piqué.

5 Piqué to pt. 2 in Russian 3rd arabesque on the left leg.

6+ Execute two steps, turning upstage to right to face pt. 6.

7–8 Tombé onto the right leg and execute a grand fouetté sauté en dedans (half-turn) to finish facing pt. 2 in arabesque ouverte.

+1 With a tiny hop, développé the back leg through into piqué Russian 3rd arabesque to pt. 2.

2+ Execute two steps, turning upstage to right to face pt. 6.

3–4 Tombé onto the right leg and grand jeté entrelacé (tour jeté) to finish on left in arabesque croisée facing pt. 2.

+ Coupé under, turning one-quarter en dehors to left to face pt. 8.

5–6 Two pas de basques en avant à terre to pt. 8, using the poses croisée and ouverte (effacée) devant, arms in arabesque in opposition with the front arm reaching low toward the front foot with épaulement each time.

+7–8 Tombé downstage onto left leg and step across into double piqué turn en dehors on right, finishing placing the left leg back into a lunge croisé facing pt. 8.

Port de bras for the end of class, 3/4 adagio

1–4 In 2nd position en face, cambré forward.

5–8 Leaning over, turn the legs parallel, grabbing behind the ankles, plié, then stretch legs, pulling the head to the knees.

1–4 Turn out, then recover upright with the arms in 5th.

5–8 Backbend, lowering the arms to 1st and turning the head to look over one shoulder. Recover, opening arms to 2nd.

1–4 Cambré to the side with the arms in 4th and recover.

5–8 Repeat, bending to the other side.

1–4 Plié in 2nd and pirouette en dehors, closing behind in 5th.

5–8 Repeat the pirouette to the other side.

Extra music: Bows to the pianist.

⌣∶⋍ *From the Classes of David Howard*

BARRE WORK

Pas de cheval, 3/4

Howard typically places a pas de cheval exercise between the dégagés (tendus jetés) and ronds de jambe à terre. He uses this movement because the "up and over" leg action is in opposition to the "under and out" action in tendus and dégagés. Interestingly, he asks students to imagine all battements as circular movements, rather than straight "out and in" ones.

1   Pointe tendue devant.
2   Plié in the extended position.
3   Close 5th, staying in plié.
4–5   Pointe tendue devant, stretching supporting leg. Close 5th on count 5.
+6–8   Four pas de cheval devant, all with accent "in" on the count.
1–24   Repeat one set each to the S, B, and S again.
Execute on the other side, then repeat both sides faster.

Fondus with port de bras, 3/4 adagio

Howard uses many port de bras in his barre exercises. Often, as here, he will insert separate movements for the arms and torso either before or after the legwork. Such port de bras are beneficial for loosening tension in the back. They also provide students with an extra opportunity to practice moving through the classical arm positions.

Stand in 5th, both arms in 5th en bas.
1–2   Reverse the arms, lifting through 2nd to 5th en haut.
3–4   Holding the arms in 5th, demi-plié in 5th and straighten.
5   Twist the torso toward the barre, arms in 5th.
6   Still standing in 5th, open both arms outward to shoulder height, palms up.
+7   Exchange the arms in a windmill fashion (i.e., the front arm lifts through 5th en haut and opens to the back while the other arm passes down through 5th en bas and lifts forward). Finish with the arms in 1st arabesque. (Stationary stance in 5th is held.)
+8   Windmill the arms once more, this time finishing in 4th arabesque, still standing in 5th.

1–2	Battement fondu devant, lifting the arm to 5th en haut.
3–4	Battement fondu à la seconde, arm to 5th en haut.
5–6	Battement fondu relevé derrière, arm to arabesque.
7–8	Hold and close back in 5th on count 8.
1–8	Repeat port de bras as in first eight counts, but instead of twisting toward the barre, twist out, away from the barre.
1–8	Reverse the fondus as above.
1–8	Cambré en rond both toward and away from the barre.
1–4	Développé into 4th arabesque penchée (inside leg lifted), facing diagonally into barre.
5–8	Recover and rise in attitude croisée derrière.
1–8	Hold balance in attitude.

Grands battements en cloche and ronds de jambe en l'air, 4/4

This exercise demonstrates how Howard incorporates more than one type of step into a single exercise. Note the changes in rhythm.

1–8	Seven grands battements en cloche. Close 5th front.
+	Brush leg à la seconde to 45 degrees.
1+2	Three ronds de jambe en l'air en dehors with the last one finishing in plié. (Accent out.)
3+4	Repeat three ronds as above.
5+6	Repeat again.
++7	Three petits battements (cou-de-pied B, F, B).
8	Close 5th behind.
1–16	Repeat all in reverse.

Piqués and relevés, 4/4, mellow

This is one of the final exercises in Howard's barre, and one to which he attaches great importance because it emphasizes the contrast in dynamics between a sharp piqué and a soft rolling down through the foot. He notes that when lowering, the knee and ankle must release slightly before the heel touches the floor.

Begin facing the barre.

1	Piqué sideways sharply into a position with one leg lifted à la seconde at 30 degrees.

2   Fondu smoothly, rolling down through the supporting foot, bending the lifted leg to finish sur le cou-de-pied derrière.

3–4   Repeat the piqué and fondu to the other side.

5–6   Repeat to the first side.

7   From the cou-de-pied, relevé to arabesque at 45 degrees.

8   Close back in 5th on demi-pointe.

Execute four times, alternating sides (twice slowly, twice a bit faster).

CENTRE WORK

Adagio/port de bras, 3/4

1–2   Chassé en avant to pointe tendue croisée derrière, arms in high 3rd ("big pose"), downstage arm high.

3–4   Temps lié en arrière through 4th plié to pointe tendue croisée devant, arms changing to other "big pose." Look up to the top hand.

5–8   Repeat the temps liés en avant and en arrière through 4th plié, changing the arms as above each time.

+   Passé the front leg, turning en dehors one-quarter to the other downstage diagonal.

1–2   From passé, pointe tendue croisée derrière, arms open to "big pose," upstage arm high.

3–4   Taking the arms to 3rd arabesque (Russian), slide into a deep lunge in croisé, back flat, head lowered with ear aligned with front arm.

+   Recover from lunge.

5–8   Port de bras cambré en rond (begin upstage) with temps lié en arrière through 4th plié to finish pointe tendue croisée devant. Close 5th on count 8.

1–2   Fondu développé croisé devant, "big pose" arms in opposition (upstage arm high).

3–4   Lower the leg en cloche and lift to 1st arabesque.

5–6   Step backwards en arrière diagonally upstage, bringing the other (front) foot behind (using a rond de jambe en dehors) into pose B+ croisé, while lifting the arms through 1st into 4th position, downstage arm high.

7–8   Cambré to the side (downstage) in this pose with a slight inclination backward.

1–2   Taking the back foot forward, step downstage into 1st arabesque on the diagonal.

3–6   Tour lent (promenade) en dedans one complete rotation. Plié in arabesque at the end.

++7   Pas de bourrée under to 5th on demi-pointe.

8   Demi-plié 5th croisé, arms en bas.

Repeat to the other side immediately.

Tendus and pirouettes, 4/4 polka, light but not too fast

This is typical of the second exercise in Howard's centre work. It is interesting to note the influence of Balanchine's choreography in the last eight counts. Howard asks students to get into the pirouette quickly on count 5 and to really suspend it. It is this turn, more than anything that precedes it in the combination, that is the focal point—the main technical problem—of the exercise. This is a very clear example of Howard's method of constructing short exercises, usually designed around one difficult movement, that are then repeated several times in succession. Thus, students have many opportunities to tackle and, hopefully, master the difficulty.

1–2   Two tendus croisé devant, arms in "small pose" in opposition.

+3   One tendu en cloche from croisé devant to effacé derrière, changing arms to the other "small pose."

4   Close 5th back.

5–8   Repeat all with the same leg in reverse from effacé derrière to croisé devant, closing 5th front.

1–2   Turning one-quarter en dehors toward the front foot, quickly tombé ouvert (effacé) diagonally downstage into a fast pas de bourrée under, finishing *up* in 5th croisé on demi-pointe.

3–++   Turning one-quarter en dehors toward the other downstage diagonal, repeat the tombé-pas de bourrée to the other side, finishing up in 5th.

4   Plié 5th en face in the preparatory pose for pirouettes.

5   Single sustained pirouette en dehors, arms in 5th en haut.

6   At the end of the turn, temps lié en arrière into 4th plié croisé, lowering the arms down though 1st position.

7   Stretch into pointe tendue croisée devant, arms opening from 5th en bas to 2nd, palms down.

8   Close 5th front croisé.

Execute four times, alternating sides.

Relevés développés and grands fouettés relevés, 3/4 grand waltz

This is a difficult exercise that Howard gave in a women's company class at American Ballet Theatre. Some of the dancers did it on pointe.

Begin in B+ croisé, standing on the left leg.

++ Glissade précipitée de côté toward the back (right) foot, without change, traveling diagonally downstage to pt. 2.

1 Relevé développé écarté devant on the left leg (right lifted).

2 Failli to croisé.

+3-4 Turning the body upstage to the left, step out onto the left leg (count 3) to pt. 6 and brush the right leg through 1st position plié forward to pt. 6 into grand relevé fouetté en dedans (half-turn), finishing on count 4 in 4th arabesque penchée on flat (left) foot, facing pt. 2.

+ Coupé under, bringing the body upright and turning one-quarter en dehors into the following ballonnés.

5–6 Two ballonnés relevés ouvert (effacé) devant, accent up on count, traveling to pt. 8. Arms in "small pose" opposition on the first relevé, "big pose" on the second one.

7–8 Tombé ouvert (effacé) downstage onto the left leg to pt. 8 into a fast pas de bourrée under, finished up in 5th on demi-pointe, right foot front.

Execute four times, alternating sides.

Pirouettes, 3/4 waltz

This is a wonderful, dancey combination into which Howard has built a very specific challenge: The piqué to the side in attitude must be done on balance if the preparation for the pirouette and, therefore, the pirouette itself that immediately follow are to be executed successfully. Thus, throughout this flowing exercise, the dancer's placement must be carefully controlled. This is a perfect example of Howard's philosophy that it is the exercises that should teach the dancer, rather than lots of verbal explanation.

Begin in B+ croisé, standing on the left leg:

++ Glissade précipitée en avant, traveling diagonally downstage to pt. 2.

1 Piqué 1st arabesque diagonally downstage on the right leg.

2 Failli to croisé.

3–4   With the back (right) leg, tombé to the side into a balancé en tournant, turning upstage (to the left) and finishing facing downstage in B+ croisé on the left leg, arms in 4th with the downstage (left) one en haut, the other (right) en bas.

5   Piqué de côté to pt. 3 onto the back (right) foot, bringing the other leg into attitude croisée derrière (90 degrees), arms in "big pose," downstage (right) arm en haut.

6   Lower into a 4th croisé lunge.

+7   With the back (left) leg, tombé en avant diagonally downstage to pt. 8 into an open lunge and step across onto the right leg, executing a piqué turn en dehors to the left.

8   Finish taking the retiré (left) leg back to end in a lunge croisé facing pt. 8.

Repeat the entire combination to the other side immediately. Then repeat both sides again.

Pirouettes with piqués turns en dehors, 3/4 waltz

This is an advanced exercise that incorporates a difficult transition from piqué arabesque into piqué turn en dehors.

1   Piqué 1st arabesque diagonally downstage. Plié on the third beat, simultaneously bringing the back leg forward through 1st position to step into the turn en dehors.

2   Piqué turn en dehors (single or double). Plié on third beat, extending the lifted leg ouvert (effacé) devant as preparation for repeating the arabesque.

3–4   Repeat the first two counts on the same downstage diagonal.

5–6   Tombé ouvert (effacé) devant into pas de bourrée under into 4th plié preparation croisé.

7–8   Pirouettes en dehors finished in 4th lunge croisé.

Pirouettes in attitude derrière en dehors, 2/4 tango

This exercise followed one with balancés done to a waltz. Howard, in asking for a tango here, was obviously seeking musical variety. However, this choice of music also made this exercise seem dynamically stronger, more deliberately accented (especially on the upbeat preceding the attitude turns) than it would have been if it were accompanied by a waltz.

Begin in B+ croisé on the left leg.

1–2   Tombé ouvert (effacé) devant diagonally downstage onto the right leg to pt. 2 and pas de bourrée under, finished in 4th plié preparation croisé.

3–4   Pirouettes en dehors to the right, finished in lunge croisé facing pt. 2.

5   Fouetté en dehors à terre, turning three-quarters toward the back leg and finishing in "big pose" pointe tendue croisée devant facing the other downstage diagonal (pt. 8).

6   Tombé croisé onto the right leg, bringing the downstage arm forward into 4th arabesque.

+   With the back (left) leg, tombé de côté, traveling toward pt. 7 (body en face), opening the arms à la seconde into the following pirouettes.

7   Grandes pirouettes attitude derrière en dehors (relevé on left, lifting right leg) with arms in 5th en haut.

8   Lower into lunge croisé, facing pt. 2, opening arms à la seconde.

+   Quickly coupé under, turning body ouvert (effacé) to pt. 8.

1–8   Repeat immediately to the other side.

Temps levés and pirouettes, 2/4 gallop or polka

The challenge in this deceptively simple, delightfully rhythmic exercise is to make the transitions between the steps seamless. The last plié of each step must be used as the preparation for the next; thus the last changement is the preparation for the pirouettes en dehors. And the finish of that turn is the preparation for the final pirouettes en dedans.

1+2   Three changements en face.

3+4   Repeat.

5   Single pirouette en dehors from 5th.

6   Finish the turn with a tombé en avant ouvert (effacé) to a preparatory 4th lunge.

7+8   Double pirouette en dedans, finishing in 5th croisé (closing front on count 8).

Continue in a series coming downstage, alternating sides.

Petits jetés with grand jeté, ballonné, and brisé, 4/4 polka, fast and light

1   Glissade de côté without change toward the back foot.

2   Petit jeté derrière onto the back foot.

3–4   Coupé under, ballonné ouvert (effacé) devant.

5   Grand jeté en avant in 1st arabesque diagonally downstage.

6   Pas de bourrée under.

7   With the back foot, petit jeté derrière battu.

8   Brisé en avant.

Execute four times, alternating sides.

Petits jetés with cabriole, fast 3/4 polka

Howard builds speedy transitional footwork into this exercise by putting five steps into two counts (+5+-6).

1   Glissade de côté toward the back foot without change.

2   Petit jeté battu derrière.

3–4   Repeat to the other side.

+   With the back leg coming forward, cabriole ouverte in the pose ouverte (effacée) devant.

5+-6   Tombé ouvert (effacé) into pas de bourrée under, traveling diagonally downstage.

+7   Turning the body one-quarter en dehors toward the front foot, glissade backward diagonally upstage (en arrière) ouvert (effacé).

8   Petit jeté derrière coming en face.

Execute four times, alternating sides.

Assemblés portés and brisés, 3/4 polonaise

This is a heavier allegro exercise, demanding leg power, in which the first three jumps rebound directly into each other. Notice the way the first part of the combination emphasizes elevation, while the second part works into and along the floor.

1   Failli sauté croisé, traveling diagonally downstage.

2   Assemblé porté over (dessus) in écarté devant on the same diagonal with the arms in ecartée allongée.

3   Grand échappé sauté en face to 2nd.

4   Pas de bourrée under, still traveling downstage on the same diagonal.

5–6   Two brisés en avant, traveling diagonally downstage.

Execute four times, alternating sides.

↷∿ From the Classes of Larry Long

BARRE WORK

Battements tendus jetés (dégagés), 4/4

This is a brisk exercise for the articulation of the foot. As is typical, Long constructs the movement first with holds, then with increased speed.

+1   One tendu jeté (dégagé) devant, accent "in" on the count.

+   Petit retiré devant to cou-de-pied level.

2–3   Hold in cou-de-pied.

4   Close 5th.

5–8   Repeat all as above.

1–2   One tendu jeté devant followed by one petit retiré devant closing 5th.

3–4   Repeat tendu jeté and petit retiré devant.

5–7   Three tendus jetés devant, last closing in demi-plié.

8   Stretch the knees.

1–16   Repeat all à la seconde.

1–16   Repeat all derrière.

1–16   Repeat all à la seconde.

Ronds de jambe à terre, 3/4 light waltz

Long's barre work includes many opportunities for repeatedly going down and up on one's supporting leg while keeping the other extended. This plié-straighten action demands a subtle shift in placement in order to maintain one's balance over the supporting side. It also provides an excellent warm-up for the thigh muscles, which must repeatedly stretch and contract as the leg bends then straightens.

1	Plié pointe tendue devant.
2	Stretch in pointe tendue.
3	Plié again.
++4	Demi-rond en dehors to the side and close 5th front.
5–8	Repeat à la seconde with demi-rond to the back.
1–8	Repeat all in reverse.
1+	Pointe tendue plié devant and rond de jambe en dehors, straightening to the back.
2–8	Immediately pass the leg forward through 1st into seven ronds de jambe à terre en dehors.
1	Grand battement en cloche devant. Arm in 5th en haut.
2–4	Passé développé to arabesque with full port de bras en dehors from 5th en haut to 2nd arabesque.
5–8	Repeat battement passé développé as above. Close back.
1–32	Repeat entire exercise in reverse.
1–8	Cambré forward and back in 5th.
1–8	Cambré forward and back in 4th.
+1	Plié pointe tendue devant and rond de jambe en dehors to the back, straightening.
2–8	Lunge and cambré all the way down, recover half-way up, and backbend.
1	Lift the back leg to arabesque at 90 degrees, straightening supporting leg.
2–3	Grand rond de jambe en dedans to devant 90 degrees.
4	Close 5th plié in front.
5–8	Lift the leg devant and grand rond de jambe en dehors at 90 degrees. Close back.

Vera Volkova's frappé, 4/4

This is one of the exercises Long remembers and treasures from the classes of Vera Volkova, who taught in Chicago when the Royal Danish Ballet toured there in 1959. Long followed this exercise with a waltz, during which he did fondus-développés en croix at 120 degrees with the same flex-point foot action as in the exercise below.

Begin by brushing the working leg à la seconde to 45 degrees with the foot strongly flexed at the ankle (i.e., not pointed).

1   Bend the leg into cou-de-pied devant, keeping the foot flexed.

+2   Point the foot while smoothly opening the leg à la seconde by means of a développé at 45 degrees. (The movement has a pulled, sinuous quality.)

3–4   Repeat, bringing the flexed foot to cou-de-pied devant and petit développé devant as above.

5–6   Two frappés devant.

7+8   Three frappés devant.

1–8   Flex the foot and repeat the entire combination à la seconde. (The first développé is devant, the second is à la seconde.)

1–8   Repeat all derrière. (The first développé is à la seconde, the second is derrière.)

1–7   Seven double frappés à la seconde en relevé.

8   Soutenu en tournant en dedans (half-turn).

1–32   Repeat all on the other side.

1–32   Repeat all with fondu as the leg comes to cou-de-pied and relevé as it développés. On the double frappés à la seconde, do the first four on relevé, then the next four lowering to plié pointe tendue à la seconde each time the leg opens.

Frappés, 4/4

This exercise includes a novel way to change sides at the barre mid-exercise.

1–4   Four frappés à la seconde.

+5–8   Coupé over into four frappés derrière with the inside leg.

+1–4   Coupé under into four frappés devant with the outside leg.

+   Coupé over, turning one-quarter to face the barre.

5–7   Three frappés à la seconde (with the other foot), facing the barre.

8   One-quarter-turn en dehors, bringing the working foot flexed to cou-de-pied devant while executing a fondu on the supporting leg.

1–8   Repeat all on the other side.

1–16   Repeat both ways.

Pause, then repeat all with relevé. The frappés facing the barre become doubles frappés.

Ronds de jambe en l'air, 3/4

Here, at the end of the series of ronds de jambe, Long has the students momentarily travel away from the barre. Thus, by introducing danciness into a static exercise, he succeeds in breaking the tension of rond de jambe en l'air (an exercise most dancers find taxing), and manages to find an unusual way for the dancers to turn to the other side without disrupting the flow of the combination.

1–4	Lifting the arm to 5th en haut, brush the working leg to the side and execute two ronds de jambe en l'air en dehors. Close back in 5th, closing the arm to 5th en bas.
5–8	Reverse.
1–8	Repeat both ways on relevé.
1–8	Repeat both ways on relevé with double ronds de jambe.
1++2+	Sissonne-tombée en avant diagonally forward, away from the barre, followed by a pas de bourrée under (still traveling away from the barre) with the last step of the pas de bourrée becoming a contretemps with a half-turn (rond de jambe the back leg en dedans and jump onto it, finishing with the other leg in cou-de-pied derrière facing diagonally toward the barre on the other side).
+3++4	Bring the back foot forward from cou-de-pied derrière, past the ankle, and execute a tombé en avant (count 3) diagonally toward the barre, followed by a quick pas de bourrée under, traveling to the barre with the last (third) step being a piqué arabesque (count 4) at 90 degrees, diagonally to the barre, both hands on the barre. (Inside leg is lifted.)
5–7	Release both hands from the barre and balance in arabesque croisée.
8	Close 5th back, turning the body en face (sideways to the barre) ready to begin the other side.
1–32	Repeat all to the other side immediately.

Grands battements, 2/4 march

This is an example of how Long changes the dancers from one supporting leg to the other within combinations.

1	Grand battement devant with the arm in 5th en haut.

2	Lower the leg, passing it to the back through 1st to a wide 4th position lunge (front leg in plié, back leg straight, heels on the floor).
3–4	Grand battement en cloche devant (straightening the supporting leg) and close in 5th front.
5–8	Repeat all.
1	With the inside leg, grand battement derrière, arm in arabesque.
2	Lower the leg, passing it forward through 1st to finish in plié pointe tendue devant with the arm lifting to 5th en haut.
3–4	Grand battement en cloche derrière (straightening support) and close in 5th back.
5–8	Repeat all.
1–8	Four grands battements à la seconde in two counts each, closing in 5th B, F, B, F.
1–8	Relevé in 5th, arms in 5th en haut. Hold and half-turn to the other side.
1–32	Repeat all on the other side immediately.

CENTRE WORK

Pirouettes en dehors, 3/4 upbeat waltz

This is another exercise culled from Long's experience with the Danish School. He learned it from Henning Kronstam but believes it originated with Volkova. The swinging motion of the arms and leg en cloche provides just the right impetus into the turns. Long tells students to "go for the rhythm" and emphasizes that there must be no stopping in the poses. Instead, the arms should swing, in a rather free-form fashion, loosely and easily from one pose to the other, while the leg moves en cloche, without pausing in the extended positions. He highly recommends this exercise for helping students who are having difficulty turning.

1–2	One tendu croisé devant. Arms in "small pose" in opposition.
3–4	One tendu croisé devant, finishing in demi-plié.
5–8	Repeat with the other leg in 4th arabesque.
1	One-quarter-turn en dehors to pointe tendue ouverte (effacée) devant, arms in "small pose" in opposition.
2	Without pausing, pass the leg en cloche to pointe tendue derrière through 1st. Simultaneously, the arms swing into 3rd arabesque.

3–4	Without pausing, repeat the swings en cloche devant and derrière with the leg and arms moving as described above.
+	Demi-plié in 4th preparation for pirouettes.
5–8	Pirouettes en dehors finished in 5th.

Execute four times, alternating sides.

Bournonville-style temps lié and jeté, 4/4 polka

This lovely, light terre à terre combination, with its many quick transfers of weight, is more difficult than it appears. Long asked students to "stay up there" in the petit jeté—that is, to sustain it by getting off the ground quickly and staying in the air as long as possible.

1	Using a petit développé, temps lié en avant en face to pointe tendue derrière. Arms do a half port de bras with the head turned toward the front foot.
2	Close 5th behind, lowering arms to 5th en bas.
3+	Repeat temps lié and close.
4	Sharply brush the back foot à la seconde, simultaneously executing a plié on the supporting leg.
++5	With the front foot, pas de bourrée over.
++6	Pas de bourrée under to 5th plié.
+	Petit jeté (high!) derrière (dessus).
7	Step upstage in écarté toward the back leg, finishing in the pose pointe tendue écartée devant with arms in écartée allongée.
8	Close the downstage leg in 5th front croisé, arms lowering 5th en bas.
1–8	Repeat all on the other side.
1–16	Repeat all with petit jeté battu.

Small jumps, tendus jetés, and pirouettes, 4/4 polka, light and bouncy

This exercise shows how effectively Long combines several different movements into one combination. In the class, this was the transitional exercise between centre work and petit allegro.

1–4	Four tendus jetés (dégagés) à la seconde en face with the same leg (under, over, under, over).
5–6	Two changements.
+	Sissonne simple devant.

7	Coupé over.
8	Assemblé over in écarté devant, finishing in 5th plié croisé.
1	One-eighth turn en dehors toward the front foot to pose pointe tendue ouverte (effacée) devant, arms in "big pose" (downstage in 5th en haut, upstage in 2nd).
2	Hold the pose.
3–4	Tombé ouvert (effacé) and pas de bourrée under en avant to 5th.
5–8	Pointe tendue croisée devant, tombé into preparatory lunge and pirouettes en dedans, finishing in 5th croisé. Do the combination four times, alternating sides.

Petit allegro with changes in direction, 4/4 polka

This exercise includes several sharp changes in body direction and, rhythmically, is in the style of Bournonville.

Begin in 5th position croisé, right foot front.

1–3	Three entrechats quatres in croisé, facing pt. 8.
4	Entrechat trois derrière, coming en face.
5	Glissade de côté toward the back (right) foot without change en face.
6	Gargouillade volée (Cecchetti method), finishing in pointe tendue ouverte (effacée) devant, facing pt. 8.
7	Tombé ouvert (effacé) en avant.
+8	Coupé under with the back foot into assemblé under, changing the hips during the assemblé to finish in 5th plié ouvert (effacé) facing pt. 2 (right foot front).
+1	Temps levé chassé (through 4th plié) en avant ouvert (effacé) toward pt. 2.
+2	Coupé under, assemblé devant ouvert (effacé), finishing in 5th facing pt. 2 (right foot front).
+3	Temps levé chassé upstage in écarté toward pt. 4 with the right foot leading.
+4	Coupé under, assemblé under in écarté to finish 5th croisé, facing pt. 2.
5	Echappé sauté to 4th plié croisé, facing pt. 2.
6	Jump, executing a three-quarter tour en l'air, turning the body upstage toward the back foot, finishing on the left leg with the right in cou-de-pied croisé devant facing pt. 8.

7   Tombé croisé en avant to pt. 8.

8   Assemblé over, turning the body écarté devant, finishing in 5th plié croisé (left foot front), facing pt. 2.

Batterie, 4/4 fast polka

This is a difficult, advanced exercise that demands the upper body be held well-lifted off the legs.

Begin in 5th position croisé, facing pt. 2.

1   Brisé volé devant downstage to pt. 2, finishing in a low attitude croisée devant.

+2   Coupé over, coupé under (dessus, dessous), using cou-de-pied positions.

3+4 Reverse (still facing pt. 2).

5   Turn upstage to the right and step on the right foot toward pt. 4.

6   Facing pt. 4, bring the back (left) leg through into a grand battement fouetté sauté en dedans with a half-turn, finishing in 4th arabesque, facing pt. 8.

7   Glissade en arrière in 4th arabesque.

8   Cabriole fermée in 4th arabesque.

Execute four times, alternating sides.

POINTE WORK AT THE BARRE

Piqués and pas de bourrée, 3/4

Begin facing the barre in 5th.

+1   In one fast, smooth movement, plié pointe tendue devant and immediately rond de jambe the leg en dehors to the back into B+, while simultaneously straightening the supporting leg.

+   Plié on the support while lightly pressing down on the arch of the back foot in B+.

2   Straighten in B+.

+3   Repeat the press and straighten.

4   Petit développé the back leg à la seconde at 30 degrees with plié.

5   Piqué de côté onto the extending leg, bringing the other to cou-de-pied derrière.

6   Roll down through the foot into fondu cou-de-pied derrière.

7+8   Pas de bourrée piqué under to 5th.

Execute four times, alternating sides.

Echappés relevés, 2/4 brisk gallop

Notice how rhythmically specific Long is about the petit développé preparation for the piqué onto pointe. He is always particular about the articulation of the foot prior to stepping on pointe.

Begin facing the barre in 5th.

1–8   Four échappés changées relevés à la seconde, evenly in two counts each.

1   Sous-sus.

+   On pointe, release the back foot sharply to cou-de-pied derrière.

2   Plié développé à la seconde at 30 degrees with the back foot.

3–5   Two piqués de côté, each to retiré devant with coupé over and well-articulated petit développé on count 4 in between.

6   Coupé over to cou-de-pied derrière.

7–8   Coupé under into assemblé (sauté) under, finishing in 5th plié.

Execute four times, alternating sides.

POINTE WORK IN THE CENTRE

Pointe pirouettes, 2/4 gallop

1   Tombé ouvert (effacé) devant as preparation for pirouettes.

2–3   Two pirouettes en dedans.

4   Close 5th croisé devant plié.

5   Relevé détourné, turning (seven-eighths) toward the back foot to finish en face.

6–7   Hold 5th on pointe en face.

8   Coupé under with petit développé devant.

1–3   Bourrée en avant en face.

4   Finish in 4th plié preparation. (Bring the back foot forward into 4th.)

5–8   Pirouettes en dehors, finishing with coupé under into petit développé ouvert (effacé) devant to begin other side.

Execute four times, alternating sides.

✌:∿ From the Classes of Larisa Sklyanskaya

BARRE WORK

Battements tendus jetés (dégagés), 6/8

This is an excellent exercise for developing correct placement and stability on the supporting leg because students are periodically required to release their hands from the barre.

1–3	Three tendus jetés (dégagés) devant with the outside arm in 1st position.
4	Hold in 5th position with *both* arms in 1st position.
5–7	Repeat the three tendus jetés with both arms in 1st.
8	Hold, placing the inside hand back on the barre and lifting the outside arm to 5th position en haut.
1–3	Three tendus jetés à la seconde with one arm in 5th (close F, B, F).
4	Lift the other arm to 5th.
5–7	Three tendus jetés à la seconde with both arms in 5th (close B, F, B).
8	Hold, lowering the outside arm to 1st and placing the inside hand on the barre.
1–16	Repeat all, starting with tendus jetés derrière.

Petits battements, 4/4 coda, even, not fast

This exercise, from a men's class, is an example of how pirouettes can be inserted into barre work. Note how Sklyanskaya has the students establish (i.e., feel) their balance on relevé on one leg (in the pose in which the turn will finish) *before* doing the first turn. Note also that plenty of time is allowed at the end of each turn for the student to firmly reestablish his aplomb in case the pirouette has been shaky.

1–4	Four even petits battements (B, F, B, F) in the wrapped cou-de-pied position.
5	Tombé-coupé over to cou-de-pied derrière in fondu.
6	Temps levé sauté in cou-de-pied derrière.
+7	Coupé piqué under with a low (30 degrees), fast développé 2nd.
8	Bring the foot to fully pointed (i.e., not wrapped) cou-de-pied devant on relevé.

1–2	Execute a single temps relevé en tournant (see note below) en dehors to 2nd.
3–4	Hold in 2nd on relevé at 45 degrees.
5–8	Repeat with double turn and hold as above on counts 3–4.
1–16	Reverse all.

Note: Temps relevé en tournant is a whipping turn unique to the Russian syllabus. For a detailed description, see Warren, *Classical Ballet Technique,* p. 156.

Stretches, adagio

This stretching exercise was done at the end of the barre in a men's class.

Begin facing the barre with one leg placed on it à la seconde.

1–2	Demi-plié.
3–4	Rise.
5–8	Repeat.
1–4	Cambré side over the leg on the barre, arm overhead, and recover.
5–8	Cambré side away from the leg and recover.
1–4	Slide sideways along the barre into a split and recover.
5–8	Push in the other direction into hip and recover.
1	Lift leg to 90 degrees off the barre.
2	Bend the leg to retiré derrière, toe at knee level.
3–4	Backbend in retiré derrière and recover.
5–8	Développé derrière, hold and close 5th in back.

CENTRE WORK

Battements tendus, 4/4

Sklyanskaya gave this exercise in a men's class. Her use of 1½ musical phrases (i.e., 24 counts instead of the more usual 32) is intentional, and something she does whenever an exercise is difficult in order to avoid overworking the legs, particularly if the exercise will be immediately repeated to the other side.

Begin in 5th position croisé, right foot front.

1–2	Two tendus ouvert (effacé) devant, closing 5th on the count, facing pt. 2, using Russian "small pose" arms in opposition.
+3	Petit développé to pointe tendue ouverte (effacée) devant in plié.

4	Demi-rond en dehors to écarté derrière, straightening support. The downstage arm opens to 2nd while the upstage arm lifts in reverse to 5th en haut.
5–6	Close in 5th back and execute one tendu over.
+7	Petit développé to pointe tendue écartée derrière in plié.
8	Demi-rond en dehors to Russian 3rd arabesque à terre.
1–2	Close 5th and execute one tendu croisé derrière. Arms remain in 3rd arabesque.
+3	Petit développé to pointe tendue croisée derrière in plié. Arms curve into "small pose" (upstage arm in 1st).
4	Fouetté en dehors à terre (three-eighths turn) to face pt. 5 (looking upstage, facing away from the audience) in pointe tendue à la seconde.
5	Close 5th in front.
6–7	With the right leg, execute two tendus à la seconde en tournant by quarter-turns (closing B, F) to finish en face in preparatory 5th position plié.
8	Double pirouette en dehors, arms in 5th high.
+	Close 5th in front.
1+2	Three tendus jetés (dégagés) side (closing B, F, B) with the front (right) leg.
3+4	Repeat tendus jetés with the other leg.
+5–6	Pointe tendue à la seconde with the front leg and plié preparation in 2nd.
7–8	Pirouettes en dehors, closing 5th behind.

Repeat immediately to the other side.

Balancés and pirouettes, 3/4

This is a lovely traveling combination with turns.

Begin in 2nd arabesque à terre on the upstage leg, facing pt. 6.

1	Turn downstage and, stepping onto the right leg, execute pas de basque en avant, traveling diagonally downstage toward pt. 2. As the left leg comes forward to croisé, the arms lift to Russian "big pose" croisé devant, with eyes looking under the downstage arm.
2	Balancé en tournant (one half-turn), opening arms into 2nd arabesque.
3–4	Continue turning downstage and piqué soutenu turn en dedans to

pt. 2, finishing with passé to 4th position croisé plié preparation for pirouettes en dehors, facing pt. 2.

5–8 Grandes pirouettes attitude derrière en dehors and hold the plié attitude croisée at the end, facing pt. 2.

1–2 Coupé under into two balancés de côté executed diagonally (i.e., in écarté) facing pt. 2. The first travels downstage, the second upstage.

3–4 Piqué downstage to pt. 8, executing a soutenu turn en dedans to 5th croisé.

5–6 Tombé into chaînés downstage to pt. 8.

7–8 Coupé under, turning upstage (one-quarter) and piqué soutenu turn en dedans to pt. 6. Finish facing upstage corner (pt. 6), stepping into the pose 2nd arabesque à terre (ready to repeat the entire combination).

Petit allegro, 4/4 rag

1–2 Petit jeté battu derrière and temps levé in cou-de-pied derrière.

3–4 Petit jeté derrière and coupé under.

5–6 Two ballonnés sautés ouvert (effacé) devant, traveling diagonally downstage.

7 Grand jeté en avant in 1st arabesque diagonally downstage.

8 Pas de bourrée under.

Repeat to the other side immediately and continue in sequence.

TWO EXERCISES REMEMBERED FROM THE CLASSES OF MARINA SEMYONOVA

Semyonova, one of the greatest pedagogues in Bolshoi Ballet history, was Sklyanskaya's teacher for many years. I asked if there were any exercises from Semyonova's classes that Sklyanskaya perhaps occasionally used today in her own classes. She showed me the two below, both very challenging and for advanced dancers only.

Grandes pirouettes, 3/4

Begin in 5th croisé and, as a preparation in two counts, execute a grand temps relevé en dehors—i.e., fondu retiré devant en face, extend the leg forward (staying in plié) into attitude devant, then sharply relevé with demi-rond en dehors to 2nd at 90 degrees (straightening the working leg), and continue the rond de jambe en dehors to finish in plié attitude croisée derrière.

1–2   Lower the back leg to the floor, settling into a wide lunge croisé, and execute grand port de bras en rond, finishing in the preparatory pose for pirouettes en dedans.

3–4   Grande pirouette en dedans in attitude derrière, finishing in plié attitude ouverte (effacée) derrière.

+   Relevé in attitude, turning one-quarter en dehors and finishing in croisé.

5–6   Repeat counts 1–2 above.

7–8   Grande pirouette en dedans in 1st arabesque, finishing in plié arabesque ouverte (effacée).

+   Repeat the relevé en dehors, bending the knee to attitude croisée as above.

1–2   Repeat counts 1–2 above.

3–4   Grande pirouette en dedans à la seconde, finishing en face in plié.

+   Repeat the relevé en dehors, bending the leg and taking it back into attitude croisée as above.

5–6   Lower into lunge croisé preparation for en dedans turns.

7–8   Pirouettes en dedans (initiated with dégagé à la seconde) and finish in 5th position croisé.

Medium allegro with sissonnes battues, 4/4

1   Sissonne développé ouverte à la seconde en face with the front leg.

+2   Ballonné battu under (i.e., beat front, back).

3   Assemblé croisé derrière.

4   Entrechat quatre in croisé.

5   Sissonne fermée battue en avant croisé in 3rd arabesque.

6   Sissonne fermée battue en arrière croisé (Russian "small pose" arms, upstage arm in 1st).

7   Sissonne fermée battue de côté en face, traveling toward the front leg, using an entrechat quatre beat, closing in back after landing. Change the arms to the other "small pose."

8   Sissonne fermée battue de côté en face, using an entrechat quatre beat, traveling in the opposite direction (i.e., toward the back foot), and closing in front. Again, change the arms to the other "small pose."

Immediately repeat to the other side.

ᴖ᠂ᴖ From the Classes of Alexander Ursuliak

BARRE WORK

Battements tendus, 4/4, not fast

This exercise shows how Ursuliak incorporates changes in port de bras into simple barre exercises, and how he uses fouettés à terre to change sides.

1–2	Tendu devant. Arm in 2nd.
3–4	Tendu devant. Arm allongé and lower to 5th en bas.
5–6	Tendu derrière (inside leg). Arm in 2nd arabesque.
7–8	Tendu derrière again. Arm curve to 1st as leg closes.
1–8	Repeat all.
1–2	Tendu à la seconde under (dessous). Arm in 2nd.
3–4	Tendu over (dessus). Arm allongés with body inclined slightly back, head and eyes turned to hand.
5–8	Repeat tendus under and over with same arm positions as above.
1–3	Three tendus à la seconde in 1st, closing on the count, lowering the arm en bas.
+4	Execute a petit développé à terre with a half-turn en dehors (away from the barre), finishing on the other side in pointe tendue croisée devant in fondu, facing diagonally away from the barre. Arm in 1st, body inclined slightly forward over arm.
5	Pass the leg through 1st, turning diagonally toward the barre and straightening to finish in 4th arabesque (arabesque croisée) à terre.
6–8	Hold and close behind in 5th on count 8.

Repeat all to the other side. Repeat all faster on both sides.

Battements tendus, 4/4, fast

This exercise develops stability on the supporting leg while descending into plié, staying in plié, and straightening out of it, all while the other (working) leg remains raised at 45 degrees.

1–6	Two tendus devant, two side (closing F, B), two derrière—all with the outside leg.
+7	Plié (fondu) as the front (inside) leg executes a petit développé to pointe tendue devant. Arm lifts to 5th en haut.
8	Close to 5th, staying in plié.

1–2	Repeat petit développé devant to 45 degrees, staying in plié.
+	Close 5th plié.
3	Repeat the petit développé to 45 degrees, staying in plié.
4	Hold.
5–7	Slowly straighten the supporting leg, maintaining the 45 degree extension to the front.
8	Close 5th.

Repeat all in reverse.

Battements tendus jetés (dégagés), 4/4

This exercise followed the one above and illustrates how Ursuliak provides a new technical challenge based on the same theme. Now, the dancers practice petit développé on demi-pointe, reversing the pattern of the exercise they've just done.

1+2	Three tendus jetés (dégagés) devant.
3+4	Three tendus jetés à la seconde (closing B, F, B).
5+6	Three tendus jetés derrière.
7–8	Relevé, executing a petit développé devant with the inside leg to 45 degrees.
1–2	Close 5th on demi-pointe and repeat the petit développé devant.
+3	Close 5th and repeat the petit développé, still staying on demi-pointe.
4	Hold.
5–7	Slowly plié on the supporting leg, lowering the heel while maintaining the working leg at 45 degrees.
8	Close 5th, straightening the supporting leg.

Reverse all. Repeat all.

Ronds de jambe à terre en tournant, 3/4

As illustrated in this exercise, Ursuliak often incorporates changes of direction into his barre exercises, a methodology which forces students to make frequent, subtle balance adjustments in order to maintain stability over the supporting leg.

Begin facing the barre in 1st position, both hands on the barre.

| 1 | Pointe tendue devant. |

+2	Rond de jambe en dehors, finishing pointe tendue devant.
+3	Repeat the rond, finishing in plié pointe tendue devant.
+4	One rond with quarter-turn en dehors, finishing sideways to the barre with the working leg pointed derrière.
5–7	Three ronds en dehors with the last one finished in plié pointe tendue devant.
+8	Straightening the supporting leg, execute one rond en dehors with half-turn to finish with the working (inside) leg pointed derrière.
1	Battement en cloche to 90 degrees devant with the inside leg.
2–4	Passé développé to plié arabesque.
5	Straightening the supporting leg, turn the body en dehors (quarter-turn) toward the lifted leg, while maintaining it at 90 degrees (i.e., grand fouetté en dehors). Finish facing the barre with the lifted leg à la seconde.
6	Hold.
7–8	Lower the leg to pointe tendue à la seconde. Close 1st.
1–16	Repeat all with the other leg.
1–8	Facing the barre, cambré to the side in plié pointe tendue à la seconde.
1–8	Straighten the supporting leg, while placing the other leg in retiré derrière. In this position, cambré back.
1–16	Repeat the cambrés on the other leg.

Repeat the entire rond de jambe exercise in reverse, beginning with the back to the barre.

Battements fondus, 4/4, slow and even

This is an example of an uncomplicated, yet challenging exercise.

1–2	Fondu devant at 45 degrees.
3	Demi-rond en dehors to 2nd.
4	Demi-rond en dedans to devant.
5–6	Fondu relevé à la seconde.
+	Demi-rond en dedans to devant with plié.
7	Relevé sharply with demi-rond en dehors to 2nd.
8	Close 5th front on demi-pointe, executing a quick half-turn toward the barre to finish on the other side.
1–8	Repeat all on the other side.
1–16	Repeat all in reverse on both sides.

CENTRE WORK

Traveling adagio, 3/4

This is a particularly lovely combination with several changes in épaulement. Included are two challenging moments of balance on demi-pointe.

Begin in 5th croisé, right leg front.

1   Sissonne-tombée ouvert (effacé) en avant onto the right leg, turning diagonally downstage to pt. 2 (left arm in 5th en haut, right in 2nd).

++2   Pas de bourrée under, turning on the third step of the pas de bourrée to finish in 4th demi-plié ouvert with the left leg front, facing the opposite downstage corner (pt. 8). During the movement, the left arm opens to 2nd while the right arm comes across the body to 1st to finish in Russian "small pose" with the torso inclined slightly forward.

3   Brush the front (left) leg through 1st into relevé attitude ouverte (effacée) derrière, while simultaneously turning the body en dedans one-quarter to face downstage pt. 2. Left arm lifts to 5th en haut, right arm opens to 2nd.

4   Allongé arms and leg in arabesque on relevé.

+   Close behind in 5th on demi-pointe.

5   Coupé under, finishing in a low fondu attitude ouverte (effacée) devant on the downstage (left) leg, facing pt. 2. Arms in 1st.

6–7   Relevé grand rond de jambe en dehors on the left leg, straightening the right leg as it travels around to finish in 3rd arabesque (arabesque croisée) on relevé.

8   Close behind in 5th croisé on demi-pointe.

+   Execute a quick plié in 5th as preparation to repeat the exercise.

1–8   Repeat the entire combination to the other side.

Arabesque and attitude turns, 3/4 lilting waltz

1–2   Two balancés de côté en face, to the right, then left, with the arms swinging across the body in Russian "small poses."

3   Tombé relevé onto the right leg in 1st arabesque facing pt. 4.

4   Plié-relevé, turning en dedans in arabesque to pt. 6.

5   Plié-relevé, continue turning en dedans in arabesque to pt. 2.

Selected Exercises—Ursuliak

6	Tombé backward onto the left leg.
7	Brush the other (right) leg backward through 1st position to the back and relevé into a single or double grande pirouette en dehors in attitude derrière. Left arm is in 5th, right in 2nd.
8	At the end of the turn, maintain the balance on relevé, then bring the back (right) leg through by means of a low développé à la seconde in preparation for tombé to begin the entire exercise again.

Bournonville-style allegro, 2/4 gallop

1	Begin with right foot front. Echappé sauté en face to 2nd.
++2	Pas de bourrée under traveling to the right, staying up on demi-pointe and going directly into the following courus.
+++3+++	A series of Bournonville courus (little bourrées on demi-pointe with knees relaxed), traveling sideways, left foot in front.
4	Close 5th plié, left foot front.
5–8	Repeat all the other way.
1	Ballotté sauté under to finish ouvert (effacé) devant.
2	Ballotté sauté over to finish ouvert (effacé) derrière.
+3	Coupé, ballonné under in écarté derrière.
++4	Pas de bourrée en tournant dessous to finish in a lunge croisée preparation for pirouettes en dedans, facing pt. 8.
5–8	Pirouettes en dedans, closing left front to finish in 5th croisé.

Medium allegro cabrioles, 3/4 waltz

1	Tombé onto the right leg into cabriole ouverte in 1st arabesque, facing pt. 3.
2–3	Chassé, turning the body downstage, traveling toward pt. 7 and tombé onto the left leg into cabriole ouverte in 1st arabesque, facing pt. 7.
4	Hop, bringing the back leg through to the front by means of a low passé and turning the body downstage en dehors.
5	Tombé de côté onto the right leg, traveling to pt. 3 (with the body facing en face).
+6	Coupé under and execute a ballonné under, finishing in croisé.
+	Sauté en tournant (one turn) en dehors in cou-de-pied devant.
7	Tombé en avant in croisé toward pt. 8.

8   Assemblé par terre, drawing the back leg into 5th and traveling en
      avant in croisé to pt. 8.
Bring the back leg through to the front in order to repeat the entire combination to the other side.

Batterie, 4/4

This was the final exercise in one class and presented the students with the
challenge of going from a quick series of jumps into a sustained balance on
relevé.

1–3   Three entrechats quatres in croisé.
4   Entrechat trois derrière to croisé.
+5   Close 5th plié and relevé immediately into attitude croisée devant at
      90 degrees with the arms in demi-seconde allongée.
6–7   Allongé the attitude leg while staying on balance on demi-pointe.
8   Close 5th plié.
Repeat three more times, alternating sides.

∿∴∿ From the Classes of Christiane Vaussard

BARRE WORK

Battements tendus with temps lié, 4/4 fast polka

This exercise stresses change of weight from one leg to the other in two different ways.

1–4   Four tendus devant.
5–6   Chassé en avant through plié in 4th position to finish up on a
      straight outside leg with the inside leg pointe tendue derrière.
+7   Temps lié en arrière through 4th position plié to finish with the
      outside leg pointe tendue devant.
8   Close 5th.
1–16 Repeat the entire combination to the side and to the back. (The

inside hand releases from the barre on the chassé à la seconde.) Do not close on the last count, but remain in pointe tendue derrière.

1–2	Execute a two-count battement tendu en cloche en avant through 1st position plié to finish pointe tendue devant on a straight supporting leg.
3–4	Reverse the battement tendu en cloche as above.
5–6	Repeat the battement tendu en cloche to the front as above.
7–8	Soutenu half-turn to the other side.
1–32	Repeat all on the other side immediately.

Dégagés with pointés and petits développés, 4/4 polka, medium tempo

This exercise is one of many that Vaussard uses to develop the sharp, quick foot articulation that is one of the major focuses of her class.

1	Brush the working (outside) leg devant to 30 degrees, while simultaneously rising sharply to demi-pointe on the supporting leg.
2	Close to 5th, lowering from demi-pointe.
3 +++	Dégagé devant and execute three quick pointés devant.
4	Close 5th.
5	Petit développé devant sharply to 30 degrees.
6	Close 5th.
+	Brush devant sharply.
7	Raccourci the foot inward to fully pointed (not wrapped) cou-de-pied devant.
8	Close 5th.
1–16	Repeat the entire combination to the side and to the back.
1–2	With the inside leg, execute two dégagés (tendus jetés) à la seconde, closing both in 1st position.
3+4	Three dégagés as above.
5–8	Seven dégagés as above.
1–2	With the outside leg, execute two dégagés en cloche (F, B).
3+4	Three dégagés en cloche as above (F, B, F).
5–6	Two dégagés en cloche (B, F).
7+8	Two dégagés en cloche (B, F) and close 1st on count 8.
1–2	With the outside leg, execute two dégagés à la seconde, closing 1st.
3+4	Three dégagés as above.
5–8	Seven dégagés as above.

Ronds de jambe à terre, 3/4 waltz

Again Vaussard demonstrates how to prevent barre work from becoming static by including temps liés after the sets of ronds de jambe. Also note the fact that the ronds are repeated with sequential relevés, a difficult, strength-building challenge. The exercise finishes with a lovely, flowing set of cambrés.

1–2	Two ronds de jambe à terre en dehors.
3+4	Three ronds as above.
+5	Single rond, finishing with a chassé through 1st plié into a temps lié en avant through 4th plié, finishing on a straight outside leg with the inside leg pointe tendue derrière.
+6	Using the inside leg, execute another chassé through 1st into 4th and temps lié en avant to pointe tendue derrière (outside leg).
+7	Plié 4th and temps lié en arrière to pointe tendue devant (inside leg).
+8	With the inside leg, chassé through 1st into 4th plié and temps lié en arrière to pointe tendue devant (outside leg).
1–8	Reverse all.
1–16	Repeat all with relevé. Each rond de jambe is done at 30 degrees with its own individual relevé from 1st flat (i.e., no plié), and each temps lié finishes on relevé with the working leg lifted to 45 degrees.
1+2	Battement devant and passé développé derrière at 45 degrees.
3+4	Repeat battement passé développé as above at 45 degrees.
5–7	Repeat battement passé développé at 90 degrees.
8	Pass the working foot forward through 1st position to pointe tendue devant.
1–8	Reverse all the battements passés développés.

Port de bras:

1	Pointe tendue devant, arm in 2nd.
2	Cambré forward, taking the arm en bas, then to 1st.
3–4	Plié on both legs in 4th position at the bottom of the cambré and temps lié en avant, straightening to pointe tendue derrière (inside leg) with the arm lifting to 5th en haut.
5–8	Backbend in pointe tendue derrière. Recover with the arm in 2nd and close the foot to 5th behind.
+1	Petit développé with the inside (back) foot to finish in plié pointe

tendue derrière. The arm comes across the body to 1st, the head inclines to the barre.

2–3 Holding this position in plié, cambré away from the barre en rond into a backbend. The arm opens side and curves in reverse to 5th en haut.

4 Recover in pointe tendue derrière on a straight supporting leg with the arm lifting directly to 5th en haut (i.e., come straight up from the backbend without completing the cambré en rond by bending to the barre).

+5 Coupé under with petit développé to pointe tendue plié devant. The arm begins to lower to 1st and the body to bend forward.

6–8 Complete the cambré forward, holding the pose pointe tendue plié devant while bringing the arm from front to back along the side of the body, to finish extended high in back of the shoulder above the head. As the arm finishes its sweep upward to the allongée position, the torso twists outward away from the barre and the head turns to look up at the hand. Hold the pose.

Battements fondus, 2/4 tango

In her advanced class, Vaussard does fondus at three levels: 45, 90, and 120 degrees. "Fondus," she says, "are most difficult at 90 degrees, but the exercise is mostly to develop deep plié, as well as for bringing the leg back in while maintaining balance. In my fondu combinations, we practice many different ways of using the working leg while passing it from one position to another." In the exercise below, extension is stressed. Therefore, this exercise really acts as the first of two adagios at the barre.

1–2 Relevé lent ouvert (effacé) devant on flat foot.

3–4 Plié on the support (fondu), bending the working leg to retiré at 90 degrees.

5–6 Relevé développé ouvert (effacé) devant.

7–8 Hold balance.

1–8 Coupé over, turning diagonally toward the barre, and repeat with the inside leg in croisé derrière.

1–8 Coupé under and repeat en face à la seconde, finishing with both arms in 5th en haut on the balance.

1–2 Demi-rond en dedans on relevé to devant (full height of extension).

3–4	Grand rond de jambe en dehors to arabesque.
5–6	Demi-rond en dedans to 2nd.
7–8	Hold balance in 2nd.

Battements frappés, 4/4, fast

This exercise includes both an interesting change in dynamics (drawn out versus sharp) and the challenge of performing sequential relevés on the supporting leg. Vaussard always uses a flexed ankle in cou-de-pied for her brushed frappés on flat foot.

1–2	With resistance, dégagé the working leg devant, taking both counts to do so and pressing strongly into the floor on the outward brushing movement.
3–4	Two frappés devant (using ankle flexation with each).
+	Close 5th quickly.
5–8	Repeat to the side.
1–4	Repeat to the back.
5–8	One frappé en croix (B, S, F, S).
1–16	Reverse all.
1	Relevé, bringing the leg sharply to cou-de-pied wrapped.
+	Beat the working foot to cou-de-pied derrière, simultaneously executing a plié on the supporting leg.
2	Frappé relevé sharply to the side.
3–4	Repeat the double frappé with relevé-plié-relevé as above.
5–8	Four frappés to the side, staying up on demi-pointe.
1–8	Repeat the double frappés and four on demi-pointe as above.
1–16	Sixteen frappés to the side with the accent "in" (alternating wrapped cou-de-pied devant and cou-de-pied derrière).

Double ronds de jambe en l'air with détournés, 4/4 polka

This is a quick, difficult exercise for developing equilibrium in fast turns. Vaussard notes that it is "for speed and for tightening everything up." She also notes that the timing of turning the head is very important. "In turns, the head must turn immediately—your shoulders, too. Some teachers say 'leave your head,' but the best turners always turn their heads immediately."

++	One fast, low double rond de jambe en l'air en dehors.
1	Close back in 5th plié.
+	Détourné relevé one full turn (toward the back foot), changing feet.
2	Lower into 5th position.
3–4	Repeat all.
5	Pointe tendue à la seconde.
6–7	Hold the position.
8	Close 5th behind.
1–8	Reverse the entire exercise.

Grands battements, 2/4 march

This is an advanced exercise. The battements are high, light, and fast. The difficulty is increased when it is repeated with relevé.

1	Grand battement devant with the accent down on the count.
2	Grand battement, throwing the leg from the front in a high arch en dehors to 2nd and closing 5th in back.
3	Grand battement à la seconde, closing in 5th front.
4	Grand battement, throwing the leg in a high arch from 2nd to arabesque and closing 5th in back.
5–8	Reverse all.
1–8	Repeat all, but with a relevé from flat foot (i.e., no plié) on each grand battement.

FAST FOOTWORK EXERCISES

TO CONCLUDE THE BARRE

Vaussard always ends her barre work with two or three exercises that stress tiny, fast, very articulate movements of the feet. Often, small terre à terre jumps are included. The exercises are done either with or without pointe shoes. It was these exercises, so characteristic of the French School, that left the greatest impression on me. I had not seen them elsewhere. I recommend them highly. Below are several examples.

Petits développés-raccourcis, 6/8, very fast

Begin facing the barre.

+1+2   Execute a sharp, low petit développé devant that ends with a battement pointé, which immediately rebounds into a low, sharp
raccourci returning to cou-de-pied devant (fully pointed). Close 5th.

3–4   Repeat to the side.

5–6   Repeat to the back.

+7   Execute one double petit battement (F, B), strongly accented to the
back.

8   Close 5th behind.

1–8   Repeat in reverse with the same foot.

Repeat all with the other leg.

Glissades and ballottés, 6/8, fast and sharp

To better understand the various directions into which the body turns during this exercise, think of pt. 1 as being directly in front of the dancers as
they stand facing the barre, ready to begin the exercise.

Begin facing the barre.

1–2   Two glissades changées de côté (fast, hardly traveling, both initiated
toward the front foot).

3   Glissade croisée (to the barre) en avant to pt. 8.

4   Glissade croisée (away from the barre) en arrière.

5   Ballotté under (very small jump) with quarter-turn to finish plié
pointe tendue ouverte (effacée) devant (to the barre, facing pt. 2).

6   Ballotté over to plié pointe tendue ouverte (effacée) derrière.

7   Ballotté under (dessous) in 2nd en face to pointe tendue à la seconde
in plié.

8   Close behind in 5th, staying in plié.

1–8   Repeat all to the other side.

Temps de cuisse, 6/8

Begin facing the barre.

+1–2   Temps de cuisse over, Italian-style (with dégagé).

+3–4   Repeat other side.

+5   Pointe tendue à la seconde and demi-plié in 2nd position.

6   Execute a royale (changement battu) to close.

+7–8   Repeat the tendu, plié, and royale with the other leg.

| 1–8 | Repeat all. |
| 1–16 | Reverse all. |

Pas de cheval sautés, 4/4, fast

Begin facing the barre

++1	Execute a low petit développé devant followed by one pointé.
+2	Raccourci to cou-de-pied devant fully pointed (not wrapped) and close 5th.
3–4	Repeat.
5–8	Four pas de cheval sautés devant, very low and fast. The accent is "in" to 5th plié on the count. The foot is very articulate and seems to stroke the floor with each pas de cheval.
1–8	Repeat à la seconde.
1–8	Repeat derrière.
1–8	Plié 4th preparation (facing the barre) and execute a pirouette en dehors. Hold the finish of the turn. Close behind.
1–32	Repeat all with the other leg.

Temps levés, 4/4, light and quick

Begin facing the barre.

1–2	Two changements.
3–4	Echappé sauté changé.
+5	Echappé en tournant (i.e., changement en tournant one full turn toward back foot, finishing in 2nd plié, facing the barre).
6	Jump to close in front in 5th.
7	Changement.
8	Entrechat quatre.
1–8	Repeat on the other side.

Echappés battus, 4/4, fast

Begin facing the barre.

1	Echappé sauté to 4th plié croisé.
+2	Jump, beating the legs into 5th and open again to land in 4th plié.
+3	Repeat the jump with battu, but open the legs to land in 2nd plié en face. (Turn one-eighth in the jump.)
+4	Battu in, beating front-back (royale) to finish in 5th.
5–6	Echappé sauté to 4th croisé and back to 5th croisé.

+7   Détourné relevé three-quarter-turn toward the back foot to finish in croisé 5th plié.

+8   Repeat the détourné relevé turning in the other direction.

1–8   Repeat all on the other side.

Assemblés, 2/4 gallop

Begin facing the barre.

1–2   Assemblé under, pressing into the plié on count 2.

3–4   Two assemblés (over, under).

5–6   Two assemblés under.

7–8   Two assemblés over.

1–8   Repeat all on the other side.

1–16   Repeat all with sissonnes fermées de côté instead of assemblés.

1–32   Repeat all with battu.

CENTRE WORK

Pas marché, 4/4, stately, not fast

This transfer-of-weight exercise, which tests stability on one leg while the other développés both in and out, began the centre work in one class. Vaussard had the students keep their arms in 1st position throughout the entire exercise, presumably so that they could not use them to stabilize their balance. Thus they were forced to concentrate on correct placement of the torso over the legs. The following day, Vaussard had the students repeat the exercise on pointe—a considerable challenge!

Prepare in pointe tendue croisée derrière.

+   Petit passé développé from back to front to finish in ouvert (effacé) devant plié at 30 degrees. Arms in 1st.

1+2   Step onto the front leg and, with the back one, petit passé développé to the front to finish in croisé devant plié at 30 degrees.

3   Raccourci the front leg into fully pointed cou-de-pied devant, while simultaneously straightening the supporting leg.

4   Plié, extending the leg (petit développé) croisé devant.

5–8   Repeat counts 1–4, traveling en avant along the same downstage diagonal. Begin by stepping onto the croisé leg, bringing the back leg through to finish in effacé devant plié.

1–4 Repeat the entire combination again.
5 Bring the extended front leg to cou-de-pied croisé devant, straightening support.
6–7 Lift the leg to retiré devant at 90 degrees and passé en tournant slowly en dedans on flat foot to finish retiré derrière in croisé, facing the other downstage diagonal.
8 Pointe tendue croisée derrière.
Repeat the entire combination to the other side.

Battements tendus with fast changes of direction, 4/4

Begin in 5th croisé, right foot front, facing pt. 8.
1 Pointe tendue écartée devant.
+ Twist (fouetté en dehors one quarter-turn) to ouvert (effacé) devant. (Face pt. 2.)
2 Close 5th in front.
3–4 Tendu ouvert (effacé) devant with plié as the leg extends, then straighten the support as it closes 5th.
5 Pointe tendue ouverte (effacée) devant.
+ Demi-plié in 4th.
6 Temps lié en avant, while bringing the back leg around to pointe tendue croisée devant by means of a rond de jambe à terre en dedans, simultaneously straightening the supporting leg.
7 Close 5th croisé facing pt. 2.
+8 Using the front (downstage) leg, tendu écarté derrière with a quarter-turn en dehors to face pt. 8 and close in back in croisé.
1 Tendu ouvert (effacé) devant with a quarter-turn en dehors to face pt. 2.
2 Tendu derrière with the other leg with a quarter-turn en dedans to face pt. 4.
3–4 Two tendus under, each with a quarter-turn continuing to turn in same direction. Face pt. 6, then pt. 8.
+5 Relevé détourné three-quarter-turn toward the *back* foot to finish in croisé, facing pt. 2.
6 Release the back leg into plié 4th preparation croisé for pirouettes.
7–8 Pirouettes en dehors with the foot in retiré back, finishing in lunge croisé, facing pt. 2.

Adagio with grands ronds de jambe, 4/4

Visually, this exercise is exquisite. The dancer, by repeated twists upstage, gives as much importance to poses seen from behind as to those seen from the front. Vaussard particularly stressed how beautifully students must articulate the petit développé step into the arabesque à terre pose from which each set of développés begins.

Preparation: Using a petit développé devant, step downstage onto the right leg into the pose 2nd arabesque à terre to pt. 2.

+1   Using a petit développé passé with the left leg, turn half en dehors and step diagonally upstage to the pose 2nd arabesque à terre on the left leg, facing pt. 6.

2   Brush the right leg through 1st and lift it devant to 90 degrees, facing pt. 6. The arms lift to 5th en haut.

3–4   Slowly fouetté en dedans at 90 degrees to finish in 3rd (croisé) arabesque, facing pt. 2, opening the left arm to 2nd, and keeping the right arm in 5th en haut.

5–6   Passé the right leg through to développé plié ouvert (effacé) devant. The arms change with full port de bras through 1st to finish with the left high in 5th, the right in 2nd.

7–8   Grand rond de jambe en dehors to croisé, straightening the supporting leg, and finishing in 3rd arabesque croisée.

+1   Bending the lifted leg, passé en tournant one quarter en dehors and développé devant at 45 degrees to finish stepping into the pose 2nd arabesque à terre on the right leg, facing pt. 4.

2–8   Repeat the entire combination on the other side as above, but at the end of the grand rond de jambe en dehors, without pausing, grand fouetté en dehors (half-turn) to finish facing upstage pt. 4 with the left leg lifted devant.

+1   Step onto the left (downstage) leg into the pose 2nd arabesque à terre, facing upstage pt. 4.

2   Brush the back (right) leg through to devant at 90 degrees, arms in 5th en haut.

3–4   Slowly grand fouetté en dedans at 90 degrees to finish in 2nd arabesque, facing downstage pt. 8.

5–6   Passé the right leg through to finish développé plié croisé devant, facing pt. 8.

7–8	Grand rond de jambe en dehors to 2nd arabesque, straightening supporting leg.
+1	Passé en tournant half-turn en dehors and développé the right leg devant at 45 degrees to finish stepping upstage to pt. 4 into 2nd arabesque à terre on the right leg.
2	Brush the left leg through to lift devant, facing pt. 4. Arms to 5th.
3–4	Slowly grand fouetté en dedans at 90 degrees to arabesque croisée, left arm in 5th, right in 2nd.
5–6	Passé the left leg through to finish développé plié ouvert (effacé) devant at 90 degrees, changing the arms with full port de bras to finish with the right in 5th en haut, left in 2nd.
7–8	Grand rond de jambe en dehors to 3rd arabesque croisée, straightening the supporting leg.

To begin all on the other side: Passé the back (left) leg through to step downstage to pt. 8 in the pose 2nd arabesque à terre.

Cabrioles, 4/4, jazzy polka

This exercise is light and brilliant and includes, as do most of Vaussard's combinations, quick changes of body direction, as well as movement across the floor.

1–2	Coupé under, cabriole ouverte croisée devant.
3–4	Coupé over, cabriole ouverte à la seconde en face with the back foot.
5–6	Coupé over, cabriole ouverte croisée derrière.
+7	Close behind in 5th plié and quickly détourné relevé three-quarters to back foot to finish 5th croisé.
+8	Changement.
1–8	Repeat all on the other side.
1–4	Four ballottés à terre: ouvert (effacé) devant, derrière, devant, derrière. Pick up both feet on each jump and use petits développés on the extensions.
+5–6	Coupé under and do two chassés en avant ouvert (effacé), traveling diagonally downstage.
7–8	Tombé ouvert (effacé), pas de bourrée under to croisé 5th plié.
1–8	Repeat the ballottés and chassés to the other side.

Repeat all in reverse.

Assemblés soutenus, 4/4

This exercise is done in a very fast, brilliant manner. The series of four assemblés staying on pointe must be very staccato, with the extension of the leg strongly accented out each time.

Begin facing the barre in croisé.

1–4	Two assemblés soutenus relevés croisé devant in two counts each.
+	Flick (*flic*) the back foot to cou-de-pied derrière.
5+6+7+8+	Coupé under into four assemblés soutenus devant, *staying up on pointe* (i.e., the plié each time is on pointe, too). Each time, the leg extends on the count, closes on the upbeat. Each assemblé turns one-sixteenth en dehors so that at the end of the series of four, the dancer has completed a quarter-turn, finishing with the body ouvert (effacé) to the barre.
1-+-	Bourrée de côté toward the front leg.
2	Flick the back leg to cou-de-pied derrière.
3-+-	Bourrée de côté toward the back leg.
4	Flick the front leg to cou-de-pied devant.
5-+-	Bourrée de côté toward the front leg.
6	Flick the back leg to cou-de-pied derrière.
7+8	Pas de bourrée under.

Piqués et fouettés at 90 degrees, 4/4

Begin facing the barre.

1	Piqué sideways and flick (*flic*) the other foot through 5th on pointe to cou-de-pied devant.
2	Plié développé 45 degrees à la seconde.
3–4	Repeat the other way.
5–6	Piqué sideways in the first direction and flick the foot into a full développé 90 degrees à la seconde.
+	Fouetté one-quarter-turn en dedans to arabesque, staying on pointe.
7	Fouetté one-quarter-turn en dehors back to 2nd, facing the barre and staying on pointe.

+-8   Pas de bourrée over.

1–8   Repeat all on the other side.

Ronds de jambe en l'air relevé, 4/4, not too fast

In this exercise, Vaussard emphasized the difference in dynamics between the first sharp coupé-piqué and the drawn-out plié développé ("With resistance!") that follows. The exercise finishes with one of her typically lovely changes of direction: ouvert (effacé) front through en face to ouvert (effacé) back.

Preparation: Facing the barre in B+, petit développé the back leg à la seconde to 30 degrees in plié.

1   Coupé-piqué over, drawing the leg straight into 5th in front on pointe, lifting the back leg to cou-de-pied derrière.

2   Développé-fondu the back leg à la seconde at 30 degrees.

3–4   Relevé double rond en l'air en dedans, finishing in plié at 30 degrees.

5–8   Repeat all on the other side.

1–4   Repeat all on the first side.

5   Relevé cou-de-pied devant, turning the body one-eighth en dehors into ouvert (effacé), facing diagonally into the barre.

+   Fondu, extending the leg ouvert (effacé) devant 30 degrees.

6   Relevé grand rond de jambe en dehors, turning the body (one-quarter) away from the leg to finish in ouvert (effacé) derrière and bringing the working leg immediately into cou-de-pied derrière.

7   Hold.

8   With the cou-de-pied (back) leg, développé plié 30 degrees to the side, turning en face.

1–16   Repeat all on the other side.

✌:∽ From the Classes of Anne Woolliams

Woolliams wishes to emphasize to the reader that she has certain misgivings about sharing the exercises below out of the context of a complete class. It is her strong belief that the shape of each enchaînement must be influenced by what has been practiced before it, as well as by what will follow. In addition, she feels that the construction of exercises should reflect daily variables, such as the weather (which can affect dancers' bodies). Finally, she notes the difficulty of communicating the movement quality of an enchaînement simply through counts and the written word. She fears that without knowledge of the original musical accompaniment, readers may easily mistranslate an exercise. Unfortunately, when this happens, it may bear little resemblance to the original.

BARRE WORK

Ronds de jambe à terre, 3/4 slow waltz

In this exercise, Woolliams uses a head roll to relieve tension in the neck. The combination is also a coordination challenge because the head must circle smoothly at the same time as the working leg inscribes the ronds de jambe. Such use of the head is common in the study of contemporary (modern) dance, but is somewhat of a departure from the norm in ballet barre work, where the head is generally maintained upright in various set positions.

1–4	Four ronds de jambe à terre en dehors while simultaneously executing one full head roll. (Begin by dropping the chin forward, then rolling the head toward the barre and around to the back.) Finish the ronds in pointe tendue derrière.
5	Grand battement en cloche to 90 degrees devant.
6	Fondu, bending the working leg to attitude devant.
7	Straighten both legs.
8	Lower the working leg to pointe tendue devant.
1–8	Reverse all.
1–7	Grand battement passé développé from front to back, finishing in plié with the lifted leg at 90 degrees.

8	Lower the leg, bringing it through 1st to finish pointe tendue devant while simultaneously straightening the supporting leg.
1–8	Reverse the grand battement passé développé.
1–32	Reverse the entire exercise.
1–8	Cambré forward and back in 5th.
1–8	Cambré forward and back in 5th on demi-pointe. For the backbend, lift the back foot and hold in cou-de-pied derrière.
1–16	Hold a balance on demi-pointe in cou-de-pied derrière.

Battements frappés, 5/4, briskly

This exercise, set to a 5/4 rhythm, is a wonderful challenge, requiring both musicality and coordination. Students will initially find it difficult, but will master it with practice. It provides a nice break from the usual diet of ballet class accompaniment in 2/4 and 3/4.

Preparation: Pointe tendue à la seconde.

1	Demi-plié on the supporting leg, bringing the working leg into cou-de-pied devant with the foot sharply flexed at the ankle.
2	Frappé à la seconde, stretching the supporting leg.
3–4	Repeat (cou-de-pied derrière with plié, frappé straightening).
5	Repeat count 1.
1	Frappé à la seconde *in plié.*
2	Return sharply to flexed cou-de-pied, *straightening* the supporting leg.
3–4	Repeat (frappé in plié, straightening on return).
5	Frappe à la seconde *without* plié.

Execute four times on flat foot, followed by four with relevé (each time the supporting leg straightens).

Pirouettes on pointe, 3/4 polonaise (slow)

This is an excellent preparatory exercise for pas de deux work when the same movement—a pirouette begun and finished on pointe without an initial relevé—will be repeated with a partner. (For purposes of clarity, this exercise has been notated the way dancers would count it—by beats, rather than bars. Count: 1 2 3, 4 5 6 / 1 2 3, 4 5 6 / etc.)

Begin facing the barre in 5th.

| +1 | Relevé in 5th (sous-sus). |

2	Remain on pointe in 5th.
3	Lift the front foot under the knee of the supporting leg (retiré devant).
4	Exchange weight quickly, lifting the back leg to retiré behind the supporting knee, staying on pointe.
5	Repeat, lifting the front leg to retiré devant.
6	Place the front foot in 5th on pointe.
1 2 3	Bourrée in place.
4	Retiré the front leg devant.
5 6	Hold in retiré devant.
1 2 3	Développé the leg à la seconde at 45 degrees.
4	Pull in with a single pirouette en dehors, placing the foot in back of the supporting knee.
5 6	Hold in retiré derrière on pointe, facing the barre.
1 2 3	Développé derrière at 45 degrees.
4 5	Hold in arabesque.
6	Close in 5th behind in demi-plié.

Repeat all to the other side.

CENTRE WORK

Adagio, 3/4

This lovely adagio both begins and ends with the dancers running.

Begin in the upstage corner (pt. 6), standing in B+ croisé on the left leg, with the arms demi-seconde, facing pt. 2.

1	With the upstage (right) leg, step diagonally en avant toward the downstage corner (pt. 2).
2	Run diagonally downstage.
3	Assemblé over to 5th croisé (right foot front), arms in écartée devant allongée.
4	Relevé in 5th, arms in 1st (5th en avant).
5	Plié in 5th in the preparatory pose for pirouettes en dehors.
+6	Pirouettes en dehors with the arms in 5th en haut.
7–8	Finish the turns in arabesque croisée (3rd arabesque) in plié at 90 degrees and hold.
1–2	Execute six tiny hops in arabesque plié, turning en dehors to complete one full circle that finishes in croisé.

3–4   Relevé, executing a half-turn en dehors in arabesque, finishing with a quick fouetté en dehors to plié effacé (ouvert) devant at 90 degrees, facing pt. 2.

5–6   Straighten the supporting leg while lowering the working leg through 1st position and lifting it to arabesque croisée. Finish in plié.

7–8   Pas de bourrée en tournant to 5th croisé.

1–2   Développé écarté derrière with the back (left) leg.

3   Fondu in cou-de-pied derrière, leaning downstage over the supporting leg with the arms in 4th position (downstage arm in 1st, upstage in 5th en haut).

4   Pas de bourrée en tournant en dehors to finish in a preparatory lunge croisé, facing pt. 2.

5–8   Two sequential grands fouettés relevés en tournant en dedans on the left leg, each beginning with grand battement développé à la seconde and finishing in attitude croisée derrière.

1–3   Fondu in attitude croisée and passé-développé the back leg through to effacé (ouvert) devant.

4   Piqué 1st arabesque en diagonale downstage to pt. 2.

5–8   Failli to croisé and run in a circle upstage to pose facing downstage in B+ croisé on the right leg in the opposite upstage corner (pt. 4) from which the adagio began.

Execute the entire adagio to the other side.

Relevés at 90 degrees, 3/4 mazurka

This is a difficult, advanced, strength-building exercise, an excellent preparation for grandes pirouettes and grands fouettés relevés. Throughout this exercise, the rhythm for each bar is relevé on 1, hold on 2, fondu on 3.

+1   Plié-relevé retiré devant en face, arms in 1st.

+2   Plié-relevé (on one leg) with a quarter-turn en dehors, simultaneously executing a développé devant at 90 degrees. Arms remain in 1st.

+3   Plié-relevé with a quarter-turn en dehors, simultaneously executing a passé développé à la seconde. Arms open à la seconde.

+4   Plié-relevé with a three-eighths turn en dehors, simultaneously pressing the lifted leg en dehors into attitude derrière and finishing in Russian "big pose" effacé derrière (attitude ouverte) with the downstage arm in 5th en haut, the other in 2nd.

+5	Plié-relevé with a quarter-turn en dehors in attitude, but finish with the lifted leg stretched in arabesque croisée (Russian 3rd arabesque).
+6	Plié-relevé in arabesque croisée.
7	Close behind with a plié.
8	Sous-sus in 5th croisé, arms en haut, and hold.

Traveling allegro with saut de basque, 3/4 Spanish waltz

This lovely, dancey combination is typical of Woolliams.

Begin in B+ croisé on the left leg in the upstage corner pt. 6 and travel diagonally downstage toward pt. 2 (Cecchetti corners 3 and 1).

1	Step-tombé onto the right leg, traveling diagonally upstage toward pt. 4 and temps levé in arabesque effacée (ouverte), arms across the body in arabesque à deux bras (Cecchetti 3rd arabesque).
2	Failli (chassé passé croisé), traveling toward pt. 2, with arms in 1st.
+3	Coupé dessous (under) and repeat the temps levé in arabesque à deux bras on the downstage (left) leg, arms changing across the body to corner pt. 8.
4+	Failli (chassé passé ouvert) and coupé dessous (under), arms in preparatory "small pose" (Cecchetti 4th en avant), upstage arm rounded in front of body.
5	Step ouvert diagonally downstage to pt. 2 on the right leg into a saut de basque, arms to 1st.
6	Repeat the step ouvert and saut de basque, continuing to travel toward pt. 2.
+7–8	Step ouvert (+) and, bringing the back (left) leg forward (failli), immediately tombé-sauté (7++) in retiré croisé derrière (right leg lifted). The downstage (left) arm is lifted in 5th, head looking under at the audience, while the upstage arm is in 2nd. (The rhythm for the tombé-sauté is syncopated: tombé on 7, spend the two beats after count 7 in the air, then land on 8.)
++	Quickly execute the first two steps of a pas de bourrée under while turning (half) upstage.
1–8	Tombé onto the right leg and repeat the entire combination, traveling upstage diagonally toward the original corner, pt. 6.

Glossary

The terms listed here are often used to mean different things to different teachers. For complete, detailed, pictorial descriptions of all French terms and individual movements described in the exercises, please refer to my comprehensive reference text *Classical Ballet Technique* (University of South Florida Press, 1989).

A la seconde Using the working leg to the side.

B+ Balanchine's term for the pose *attitude derrière à terre.*

Cambré A bend of the body.

Coupé A change of weight from one leg to the other through 5th position.

De côté Traveling to the side.

Dégagé Same as *battement tendu jeté.*

Derrière Using the back leg in a backward direction.

Détourné A *relevé* turn in 5th position in which the feet exchange places. It is always initiated toward the back foot.

Devant Using the front leg in a forward direction.

Effacé(e) Same as *ouvert(e)* when used to indicate an open directional pose of the body, such as *effacé devant.*

En arrière Traveling backward.

En avant Traveling forward.

En croix In a cross; refers to the pattern of the working leg when it executes a series of *battements* to the front, side, back, and side again.

Enveloppé The action of bringing the foot and lower leg from an open, extended position inward by bending the knee to finish in the position *sur le cou-de-pied* or *retiré*.

In opposition Refers to the relationship between the working leg and an opposite arm lifted in either 1st position or 5th *en haut*. For instance, if the right leg is lifted in attitude, the left arm would be lifted in 5th (or 1st) to form attitude in opposition.

Ninety (90) degrees Indicates that the lifted height of the working leg is at least hip level or at the full height of extension.

Over Dessus.

Plié Used interchangeably to mean either a *plié* on both feet or on one leg (sometimes called a *fondu*).

Pointé Same as *battement piqué;* the pointed toe of the working leg quickly taps and rebounds off the floor.

Pointe tendue The *position* of the working leg stretched outward with pointed foot in any direction, as opposed to the term *tendu*, which is used to indicate the action of both extending and closing the leg.

Raccourci Same as *enveloppé*.

Relevé lent A slow lifting of the working leg, either straight or bent in attitude, from 5th position or *pointe tendue* usually to 90 degrees or higher.

Rond A short term for *rond de jambe à terre* or *en l'air*.

Soutenu Closing the working leg to 5th from an open position. *Soutenu* may be done to 5th flat or 5th *relevé*, with or without a turn (i.e., *soutenu en tournant*).

Temps lié A change of weight from one leg to the other that moves through an open position (2nd or 4th) in any direction.

Tendu jeté Same as *battement dégagé*.

Tour lent Same as promenade. A slow rotation on one leg on flat foot with the other held at 90 degrees.

Under Dessous.

POINTS OF THE ROOM
(RUSSIAN SYSTEM)

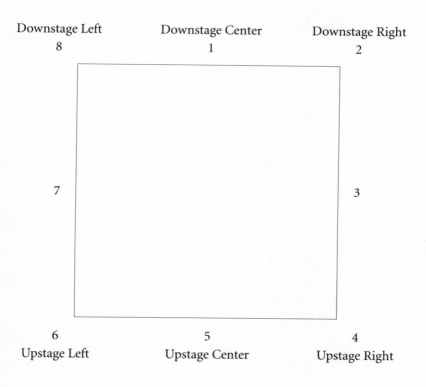

Downstage Left   Downstage Center   Downstage Right

8   1   2

7   3

6   5   4

Upstage Left   Upstage Center   Upstage Right

1st position

2nd position

4th position

5th position en bas
(also preparatory position)

5th position en haut

Russian "big pose"
(also 3rd en haut)

Russian "small pose"
(also 3rd low)

Ecarté devant allongée

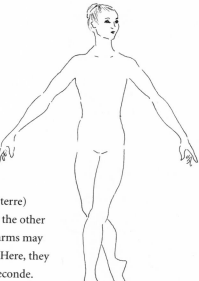

B+ (also attitude à terre)
A pose on one leg with the other
placed behind it. The arms may
be held in any position. Here, they
are shown in demi-seconde.

THE ARABESQUES

1st arabesque

2nd arabesque

3rd arabesque

4th arabesque

Arabesque à deux bras
(also Cecchetti 3rd arabesque)

Notes

Chapter 1. Marika Besobrasova

1. Sergei Pavlovich Diaghilev (1872–1929) was a Russian impresario who is generally credited with effecting the complete reformation of the European ballet scene in the early 1900s. He is considered the single greatest influence on the development of twentieth-century contemporary ballet. A man of remarkable artistic taste and vision, he brought together leading dancers, composers, and artists of his day to create works for his famous troupe, the Ballets Russes. The company triumphed at its Paris debut in 1909 and continued to enjoy wide critical acclaim across Europe until Diaghilev's untimely death in Venice in 1929. Among the artists he commissioned to work with him were the choreographer George Balanchine (then virtually unknown) and the composer Igor Stravinsky, as well as such luminaries as Picasso, Braque, Matisse, Bakst, Benois, Prokofiev, Ravel, Debussy, and Poulenc and the great dancers and/or choreographers Nijinsky, Pavlova, Karsavina, Fokine, Spessivtzeva, Danilova, Massine, Dolin, and Lifar.

2. Although Besobrasova first gave ballet lessons in Monte Carlo in 1939, she did not officially open a school there until 1949. Her current school, the Académie de Danse Classique, a much larger enterprise where students board and receive ballet and other dance-related classes, opened in 1974.

3. George Balanchine (1904–83) is generally considered the most significant neoclassic ballet choreographer of the twentieth century. Born in St. Petersburg, he trained at the Petrograd Ballet School, where he first began making dances. He performed briefly with GATOB before touring Europe with his own small company. In 1924, he accepted Diaghilev's invitation to join the Ballets Russes, where he was soon appointed chief choreographer and for whom he created such enduring works as *Apollo* and *Prodigal Son*. It was at this time that he began his lifelong creative relationship with Stravinsky. Balanchine moved to the United States in 1933 and stayed to build what became the New York City Ballet and its associated school, the School of American Ballet. Over a period of fifty years, he choreographed more than four hundred works, most of them for his own com-

pany. Among these are such masterpieces as *Serenade, The Four Tempera-ments,* and *Agon.*

4. Julie Sedova (1880–1969) was a Russian dancer and teacher. She was trained at the Imperial Ballet Academy, and danced at the Maryinsky from 1898 to 1916, during which time she also made guest appearances in Europe. She left Russia after the Revolution, settling in Nice, where she maintained a school for many years, teaching a number of famous French dancers including Golovine and Skibine.

5. In 1932, three years after Diaghilev's death, René Blum and Colonel de Basil founded the Ballets Russes de Monte Carlo, a company designed to be the successor to Diaghilev's famous troupe. Both Balanchine and Massine choreographed for the new company, which enjoyed much international success. However, in 1936, Blum and De Basil quarreled, severing their relationship. As a result, two new companies were founded. De Basil named his the Ballets Russes du Colonel de Basil. Blum's was called the Ballets de Monte Carlo and briefly employed Mikhail Fokine as chief choreographer. Subsequently, Blum sold this company to an American enterprise, the World Art Company. In 1938 it moved its base of operations to the United States. At that time, Léonide Massine was appointed artistic director and replaced Fokine as chief choreographer. Because the company retained the name "Monte Carlo" in its title, it was obligated to return to perform in Monaco each year. With the onset of World War II, however, the troupe was unable to make the trip across the Atlantic. Thereafter, it was known as the Ballets Russes de Monte Carlo until it finally ceased performing in the United States in 1963. See also p. 363, n. 3.

6. Mikhail Fokine (1880–1942), a Russian dancer and choreographer, was a graduate of the Imperial Ballet Academy in St. Petersburg and a soloist at the Maryinsky Theatre. He began teaching in 1902 and choreographing in 1905. He was engaged as principal choreographer for the Diaghilev Ballets Russes in 1909. Among his most famous works for this troupe were *Scheherazade, Petrouchka,* and *Le Spectre de la Rose.* His 1907 ballet, *Chopiniana* (later retitled *Les Sylphides*), was the first plotless, one-act ballet ever created. It paved the way for the so-called "abstract," neoclassic ballets that became so prevalent in twentieth-century ballet choreography. To this day it remains a popular inclusion in the repertoires of many major ballet companies. In 1923, Fokine settled in New York, where he remained until his death.

7. Lubov Egorova (1880–1972) was a ballerina with the Maryinsky Theatre in Russia in the early 1900s. Later, she danced with Diaghilev's company in Paris. She moved to France in 1918 and opened her ballet school in Paris in 1923. In 1937, she founded Les Ballets de la Jeunesse.

8. Victor Gzovsky (1902–1974) was a Russian dancer who began teaching at a very early age. He moved to Berlin in 1924. Subsequently, he was appointed ballet master of several major European companies, including the Berlin State Opera (1925), the Markova-Dolin Ballet (1937), the Paris Opera (1945), the Ballets des Champs-Elysées (1946–48), the Munich State Opera (1950–52), Dusseldorf State Opera (1964–67), and the Hamburg Opera (1967–73). For many years, beginning in 1938, he worked mainly as a private teacher in Paris. He was one of the most internationally respected pedagogues of his generation.

9. Enrico Cecchetti (1850–1928) was an Italian dancer and ballet master, but is best remembered as a teacher. He studied with Carlo Blasis's student Giovanni Lepri in Florence, debuted at La Scala in 1879, and toured Europe as a guest *premier danseur*. In 1890, he was appointed second ballet master at the Imperial Ballet in St. Petersburg. He also danced with the company and created the roles of Carabosse and the Blue Bird in Petipa's *Sleeping Beauty*. From 1892 to 1901, Cecchetti taught at the school attached to the Maryinsky Theatre, where his classes were responsible for a significant improvement in the technical standard. He was revered as a teacher by many famous dancers, including Pavlova, Nijinsky, Egorova, Kschessinska, Karsavina, and Fokine. In 1910, Diaghilev engaged him as the teacher for the Ballets Russes. Later in life, Cecchetti ran a school in London and from 1925 to 1928 was in charge of the La Scala ballet school in Milan. His method was originally preserved by the Cecchetti Society (London, 1922) which was later incorporated under the Imperial Society of Teachers of Dancing and the Cecchetti Council of America. To this day, certified teachers throughout the world follow his methodology.

10. Agrippina Vaganova (1879–1951) was a Russian dancer and teacher who is best remembered for her pioneering work in establishing the world-famous Soviet ballet syllabus. She studied at the Imperial Ballet Academy, joined the Maryinsky Theatre in 1897, and was appointed ballerina in 1915. During the 1920s, she became the most famous teacher at the Petrograd State Choreographic School (later the Leningrad Choreographic School, which was renamed the Vaganova Choreographic School in her honor in 1957). During this time she gradually developed her pedagogic system, which became the basis for ballet education throughout the USSR and Eastern bloc countries. She is considered one of the most important pedagogues in ballet history. The renowned virtuosity of twentieth-century Russian ballet dancers is directly attributable to the system she created.

11. Rudolf Nureyev (1938–1993), a legendary Russian dancer, was trained at the Vaganova School in Leningrad, danced as a soloist with the Kirov

Ballet, and skyrocketed to fame after defecting to the West in 1961. A truly international star, Nureyev performed with every major Western ballet company, staged many full-length classical ballets, and spent several years as director of the Paris Opera Ballet.

12. French ballerina Violette Verdy (1933–) studied with Rousanne and Gzovsky and made her debut with Roland Petit's Ballets des Champs-Elysées in 1945. She performed as ballerina at La Scala in Milan, appeared with the London Festival Ballet in 1955 and with American Ballet Theatre in 1957. In 1958, at the invitation of George Balanchine, she joined the New York City Ballet and has been closely associated with this company ever since. Balanchine created many roles for her in ballets such as *Liebeslieder Waltzes, Jewels*, and *Tchaikovsky Pas de Deux*. In 1977, she became the first woman in history to be appointed artistic director of the Paris Opera Ballet. Later, she directed the Boston Ballet. In 1992, at the invitation of Claude Bessy, she spent several weeks as a guest teacher at the Paris Opera Ballet School. Today, Verdy is much in demand internationally as a guest teacher and choreographer and continues to be associated with the New York City Ballet as a consultant.

13. Besobrasova uses a Grundig reel-to-reel deck and has installed an excellent speaker system in the studio.

14. Léonide Massine (1895–1979) was a Russian-American dancer, choreographer, ballet master and teacher. He graduated from the Bolshoi School in 1912 and danced with that company before joining Diaghilev's Ballets Russes in 1914. Diaghilev was instrumental in guiding his career as a choreographer. After Diaghilev's death, Massine continued to work in various roles (choreographer, ballet master, artistic director) with the Ballets Russes de Monte Carlo. He is principally remembered for his success in comic character roles of his own creation and as the originator of the symphonic ballet. He staged many of his works internationally, among the most famous of which were *Le Tricorne, Parade*, and *Gaîté Parisienne*.

15. Mathilda Kschessinska (1872–1971) was the reigning ballerina of the Maryinsky Theatre in St.Petersburg in the late 1800s. A virtuoso technician, she was the only dancer other than Pierina Legnani to be officially awarded the title Prima Ballerina Assoluta (1893). She left Russia after the Revolution and, in 1929, established a school in Paris, where she continued to teach for almost forty years.

Chapter 2. Willam Christensen

1. Stefano Mascagno (dates unknown) was born in Italy. He studied with his father, Ernesto, and with Aniello Ammaturo at the San Carlo Theatre in Naples, where he made his debut. He danced in Russia in 1897 and at La Scala in 1899. After touring Europe, the United States, and South America, he settled in New York in 1915, opening a school that existed for twenty years. He retired to Los Angeles.

Chapter 3. Janina Cunovas

1. Anatole Oboukhoff (1896–1962), a Russian *danseur noble*, was considered one of the greatest dancers of his time. He graduated from the Imperial Ballet Academy in St. Petersburg and danced with the Maryinsky Theatre, where he was appointed soloist in 1917. He left the Soviet Union in 1920, danced in Bucharest, South America, London, and with the Ballets Russes de Monte Carlo in the late 1930s. In 1940, he settled in New York City, where he taught at Balanchine's School of American Ballet for more than twenty years.
2. Vera Nemtchinova (1899–1984), wife of Anatole Oboukhoff, was a Russian dancer and teacher. She joined Diaghilev's Ballets Russes in 1915 and became a principal dancer in 1924. Among the companies with which she performed after Diaghilev's death were the Mordkin Ballet, Teatro Colon Ballet, Markova-Dolin Ballet, Kaunas Opera Ballet, and Ballets Russes de Monte Carlo. After retiring as a dancer, she settled with her husband in New York, where she remained a prominent teacher for many years.
3. René Blum (1878–1942) was a French ballet impresario. After Diaghilev's death, he was appointed the ballet director of the Monte Carlo Opera. He was instrumental in creating the Ballets Russes de Monte Carlo, which he managed from 1932 to 1934, then directed until 1936. After breaking off his partnership with the company's impresario, Colonel de Basil, Blum founded his own René Blum Ballets de Monte Carlo, which enjoyed great success with Fokine, and later Massine, as its chief choreographers. An exceptionally cultured man, Blum is credited with preserving much of the Diaghilev repertoire. He was deported during the Nazi occupation of France and died in Auschwitz in 1942. See also p. 360, n. 5.
4. Asaf Messerer (1903–1992) was a Soviet dancer, ballet master, and teacher. He studied with Mordkin and Gorsky at the Bolshoi Ballet School in Moscow. After graduating in 1921, he became one of the company's most popular principal dancers and continued to perform until 1954. He began

teaching in 1923 at the Bolshoi School and in 1942 was put in charge of the *classe de perfection*. He taught company classes for the Bolshoi, where among his students was his niece, prima ballerina Maya Plisetskaya. He was internationally revered as one of the finest teachers of the twentieth century.

5. England's Royal Academy of Dancing was originally created in 1920 as the Association of Operatic Dancing in Great Britain. Its founders included Adeline Genée, Tamara Karsavina, Phyllis Bedells, Edouard Espinosa, and Philip Richardson. The Association received its Royal Charter and present name in 1936. Its mission is to further the cause of artistic dancing, primarily classical ballet, and to support the improvement of dance teaching standards. Annual examinations are held internationally for dancers and teachers. The Academy also awards scholarships and sponsors a number of educational lectures, courses, conferences, and so forth.

6. Edouard Borovansky (1902–1959) was a Czech dancer and choreographer. He studied in Prague and became *premieur danseur* of the Prague National Theatre Ballet. After dancing with the Ballets Russes de Colonel de Basil from 1932 to 1939, he settled in Australia. Staging both the classics and his own contemporary choreography, he became one of the pioneer forces in the development of ballet there. In 1940, he opened a school in Melbourne from which arose the Borovansky Ballet in 1942. Its first professional season was in 1944. After his death, many of his dancers were absorbed into the newly formed Australian Ballet (founded in 1962).

Chapter 4. Gabriela Taub-Darvash

1. GITIS is the Russian abbreviation for Gosudarstvenny Institut Teatralnovo Iskusstva, also called the Moscow Lunacharsky State Institute for Theatre Arts. It began as a school for actors in 1878, then added faculty to teach criticism and history (1930), choreography (1946), and dance pedagogy (1958). Today, degrees are offered in acting, musical theater, directing for theater, dance pedagogy, theater criticism, and choreography and directing. GITIS graduates in dance pedagogy have undergone a rigorous five-year program, are trained to teach all levels of the Russian syllabus in ballet and character, and have studied all related subjects such as dance history, music, choreography, and anatomy. Considerable prestige is attached to receipt of a GITIS degree.

2. Leonid Lavrovsky (1905–1967) directed the Bolshoi Ballet from 1944 to 1956 and again from 1960 to 1964. He was trained in St. Petersburg, was a leading dancer with GATOB (predecessor of the Kirov Ballet) in the 1920s, and eventually became one of Russia's most important choreographers. He is

best known for creating the first ballet production of Prokofiev's *Romeo and Juliet* in 1940 for the Kirov Ballet.

3. Galina Ulanova (1910–) is the most revered Russian prima ballerina of the twentieth century. She was trained in St. Petersburg, first by her mother, Maria Romanova, and later by Vaganova at the Petrograd State Ballet School. She danced first with GATOB (predecessor of the Kirov Ballet), then joined the Bolshoi in 1944. A radiant, lyrical dancer who was considered one of the great dance actresses of her time, Ulanova created the role of Juliet in the first production of *Romeo and Juliet* in 1940. During the 1950s, she toured the world as the Bolshoi's biggest star, developing an international following. Ulanova retired from the stage in 1962 and now coaches young ballerinas at the Bolshoi.

4. In the United States, 1-900 telephone numbers provide information services ranging from weather reports to horoscopes.

5. Marina Semyonova (1908–) is a Russian teacher of great fame. For decades she has been a leading teacher at the Bolshoi Ballet, as well as a highly respected professor at GITIS, the university for teacher training in Moscow (see note 1). In her youth, she was a member of Vaganova's first class at the newly formed post–Russian Revolution school on Rossi Street, the Leningrad Choreographic Academy. She became Vaganova's most famous pupil. After graduating in 1925, she became one of the leading Russian ballerinas of her time, dancing first with GATOB (predecessor to the Kirov Ballet) from 1925 to 1930, then later becoming prima ballerina of the Bolshoi (1930–52). Although she was the first Soviet ballerina to dance *Giselle* at the Paris Opera (with Lifar in 1935), she remained little known in the West. Semyonova's methodology is discussed in detail in this book by Larisa Sklyanskaya (chapter 7), who was her student at the Bolshoi for many years.

6. Darvash is referring here to turns from the standard ballet curriculum, but notes that dancers eventually must be able to turn in any unusual, crooked pose that may be required by a choreographer.

7. Anna Kisselgoff, Review of Darvash Concert Series, *New York Times*, 15 June 1984, C3.

8. For years, Campbell's Soup advertisements showed American children, lips pressed together, above the slogan "Mmmm, mmm good!"

Chapter 5. David Howard

1. George Goncharov (1904–1954) was a Russian dancer, choreographer, and teacher who received his training in St. Petersburg. He danced briefly with a small troupe in Russia before settling in Shanghai, where he maintained

a company and ballet school in the 1920s and 1930s. He moved to London in 1945, taught for the Sadler's Wells Ballet School, and eventually took over the school of his close friend, the great Russian teacher Vera Volkova.

2. Tamara Karsavina (1885–1978) was a ballerina of the Russian Imperial Ballet in the early 1900s and one of the leading members of Diaghilev's Ballets Russes. She graduated from the Imperial Ballet Academy in St. Petersburg, where she studied under several illustrious teachers including Cecchetti and Johansson. Among the many ballets created for her were *Les Sylphides, Spectre de la Rose,* and *Petrouchka.* After marrying an English diplomat, she moved to London in 1918, thereafter devoting many years of her life to British ballet. She was well known as a mime teacher, an advisor for revivals of Diaghilev productions, and instrumental in the development of the Royal Academy of Dancing.

3. Adeline Genée (1878–1970) was a Danish-trained ballerina who became a star of London's music-hall ballets at the beginning of the twentieth century. She settled in England and devoted herself in retirement to fostering the development of British ballet. She was a founder of the Royal Academy of Dancing and, in 1930, proposed a system of medal awards to recognize talented dancers. For more than fifty years, these bronze, silver, and gold medals—which include substantial cash awards—have been presented to highly talented young dancers, many of whom have gone on to enjoy distinguished careers. Entrants, who must have completed the Royal Academy of Dancing Advanced or Solo Seal exams at the level of Highly Commended or Honours, come from around the world to compete.

4. Raymond Franchetti (1921–) is a well known French teacher who studied with Ricaux, Egorova, and Preobrajenska. He made his dancing debut with Kyasht's Ballet de la Jeunesse Anglaise in 1937, then continued his career with the Ballets de Monte Carlo and the Paris Opera Ballet, where he was particularly admired in character roles. He has taught for the Opera school and for the Royal Ballet School and company in London, and he has also maintained his own studio in Paris for many years.

5. Maria Fay (1928–) was born in Hungary, where she trained in ballet (Soviet-method), character, and modern dance. She then joined the Budapest State Theatre Ballet Company, where she became a leading dancer and choreographer. After immigrating to England in 1956, she opened her now highly reputed London ballet studio. She also taught ballet and character classes for many years at both the Royal Ballet School and the Royal Academy of Dancing, for whom she has also written syllabi and created educational videos. In addition, she has worked as teacher, coach and choreographer with major international companies.

6. Rebekah Harkness (1915–1982) was an American composer and philanthro-

pist who studied music with Boulanger and dance with Fokine. In 1961, she established the Harkness Foundation, through which she provided financial support for the ballet companies of Robbins, Joffrey, and others. She founded her own company, the Harkness Ballet, in 1964 and her school, the Harkness House for the Ballet Arts, in New York in 1965.

Chapter 6. Larry Long

1. "White Russian" is the term used to describe those Russians who voluntarily exiled themselves from Russia after the 1917 Revolution. They settled mainly in Europe and the United States. Many were members of the former Russian aristocracy and retained a strong loyalty to the czar. They were fervent anti-communists.
2. Maria "Alexandra" Baldina (1885–1977) was born in St. Petersburg, Russia. She studied at the St. Petersburg Theatre School and graduated into the Maryinsky Company. Shortly thereafter, she moved to Moscow, where she became a ballerina at the Bolshoi. Baldina created the Prelude in Fokine's *Les Sylphides* with Diaghilev's Ballets Russes in Paris in 1909. After leaving Diaghilev, she settled first in England, then later immigrated to southern California, where her husband, Theodore Kosloff, had established a ballet school.
3. Nana Gollner (1920–1980) was an American ballerina who danced with De Basil's Ballets Russes in 1935–36, with Blum's Ballets de Monte Carlo in 1936–37, as prima ballerina with the Original Ballet Russe in 1941–43, and with Ballet Theatre (now American Ballet Theatre) in 1943–45. In 1947, she was guest ballerina with London's International Ballet, where she was the first American ballerina to dance a complete four-act *Swan Lake*. She performed extensively with her Danish-trained husband, Paul Petroff (1908–1981), with whom she ran a ballet school in California.
4. After the phenomenal success of the Diaghilev Ballets Russes in Paris in 1909, ballet fans showed little interest in dancers of other nationalities. Therefore, it was common for Western dancers to adopt Russian-sounding names. These were considered more glamorous and provided non-Russian dancers with an automatic theatrical pedigree.
5. Ruth Page (1899–1991), an American ballerina, began her career as a dancer with Pavlova's company. She performed with Diaghilev's Ballets Russes and the Metropolitan Opera in New York. She enjoyed considerable success as a choreographer, especially for the many operas she turned into ballets. She started as a director with the Page-Stone Ballet (later the Chicago Ballet Company), which was the first American company to tour South America. In 1953, she formed Ruth Page's Chicago Opera Ballet, with whom Rudolf

Nureyev made his American debut. After twelve years, this company evolved into Ruth Page's International Ballet. She published two books on dance and was also involved as choreographer in numerous television and film projects.

6. Dolores Lipinski (1936–), who is associate director of the Page Foundation School in Chicago, was a ballerina with Page's company when she and Long met. She received her training from the famous Chicago teachers Bentley Stone and Walter Camryn. In addition to dancing for eighteen years in all of Ruth Page's companies and projects, Lipinski also appeared as a principal dancer with Frederic Franklin's National Ballet of Washington.

7. Alicia Alonso (1921–) is a Cuban prima ballerina who, since 1959, has directed the National Ballet of Cuba. She studied in Havana, at the School of American Ballet in New York, and with Vera Volkova. In the 1940s she appeared in Broadway musicals and with Ballet Theatre in New York, as well as with her own company, the Ballets Alicia Alonso in Cuba. During the 1950s, prior to Castro's rise to power, Alonso frequently appeared in the United States either with American Ballet Theatre or in productions she staged herself using both Cuban and American dancers. After the Cuban revolution, she established her now famous National Ballet school and company in Havana.

8. Valentina Pereyaslavec (1907–) is a Russian-American dancer and teacher. She graduated from the Bolshoi School in 1926 and danced with companies in Kharkov, Sverdlovsk, and Lvov. She studied teaching with Vaganova in Leningrad and became her assistant. During World War II she was deported by the Germans from Lvov to Leipzig as a factory worker. She immigrated to America in 1949, where she first taught in Philadelphia. From 1951 to 1980, she taught at the School of American Ballet Theatre in New York, establishing an international reputation for herself as a teacher.

9. William Dollar (1907–1986) was an American dancer, choreographer, and teacher. He studied with Fokine, Mordkin, Balanchine, Vladimirov, and Volinine. He danced with and was ballet master for several American and European companies in the 1930s and 1940s, but was most highly regarded as a teacher.

10. Gelsey Kirkland, with Greg Lawrence, *Dancing in My Grave* (Garden City, N.Y.: Doubleday, 1986).

11. August Bournonville (1805–1879) was a Danish dancer, choreographer, and director of the Royal Danish Ballet, with whom he was closely associated for almost fifty years. With his keen sense of theater and his high technical standard of dancing (imported from years of study and performance in Paris), he greatly elevated the artistic standards of the Danish

company. His best known ballets, *La Sylphide* and *Napoli,* are still performed around the world. Much of his choreography began in his classes, giving rise to what today is referred to as the "Bournonville School" or "Bournonville technique"—a light, lively, charming style. He is particularly credited with elevating the role of the male ballet dancer after its considerable decline during the era of the Romantic ballet.

12. Vera Volkova (1904–1975) was one of the most revered ballet pedagogues of the twentieth century. Among her students were many of the most famous post–World War II dancers, including Margot Fonteyn. Volkova was born in St. Petersburg and studied with Romanova (Ulanova's mother) at Volynsky's Russian Choreographic School, a private school where Vaganova first taught. She danced at GATOB (as the Kirov Ballet was then known), then left Russia to tour China and Japan with George Goncharov's company in the 1920s. She settled in Shanghai in 1929, then moved to London in 1936, where she taught for the Sadler's Wells Ballet and its school (1943–50). She was soon recognized as the leading Western authority on the Russian training method. In 1943, she opened her famous private studio in London. In 1951, at the invitation of Harald Lander, she moved to Denmark, where she spent the remaining years of her life as both company teacher and artistic advisor to the Royal Danish Ballet. She also frequently worked as a guest teacher for companies abroad. Volkova was a major influence on another teacher in this book, Anne Woolliams, whose memories of her are included in chapter 10. Were she living today, she would most certainly have been included in this book.

Chapter 7. Larisa Sklyanskaya

1. Nina Ulanova (dates unknown) was the head of the Estonian Ballet Company from 1965 to 1987. She is well known in Germany, where she worked at the Palucca School.

2. Yelisaveta Gerdt (1891–1975) was an outstanding dancer and teacher. Among her most famous students are Plisetskaya, Struchkova, and Maximova. Gerdt studied with her father, Pavel Gerdt, and Mikhail Fokine. She graduated from the Imperial Russian Ballet School in 1908 and was appointed ballerina at the Maryinsky in 1919. From 1935 to 1970, she was one of the top teachers at the Bolshoi. Choreographer George Balanchine frequently referred to her as the dancer who, in his youth, most influenced the direction of his pure dance aesthetic. He is quoted as saying: "I wanted to be like her."

3. Antony Tudor (1908–1987) was a well-known British choreographer who began his career with the Ballet Rambert, for whom he created his famous

Jardin aux Lilas in 1936. He moved to New York City in 1939 and, in subsequent years, created several works as resident choreographer for American Ballet Theatre, among them *Pillar of Fire* and *Dim Lustre*. He was a master at expressing psychological nuance through movement and is considered one of the foremost choreographers of the twentieth century. Tudor was also well known as a teacher and worked during the 1950s and 1960s at both the Metropolitan Opera Ballet School and the Juilliard School.

4. Martha Graham (1894–1991) was a brilliant, world-acclaimed American modern dancer and choreographer. A great innovator, she created a revolutionary new dance language, the Graham technique, and is generally credited with being the "mother" of American modern dance. A tempestuous and egocentric personality, Graham began her career as a dancer with Denishawn in the early 1900s. In 1927, she founded her own New York City–based school of contemporary dance and, soon after, her company, for which, over a period of some sixty years, she created more than 160 works.

5. Mikhail Baryshnikov and Vladimir Vasiliev are two of the greatest male dancers Russia has ever produced. Since his 1974 defection, Baryshnikov's stellar reputation has been well established in the West. However, Vasiliev, a longtime star of the Bolshoi, is less well known to American audiences. Sklyanskaya clearly idolizes him and often shows films of his dancing to her students. Speaking about him, she says: "His unlimited technical abilities and amazing talent as an actor make him unparalleled in many roles he created—and would probably make Nijinsky uncomfortable!"

6. Sklyanskaya is alluding to the fact that much of what we know about Nijinsky was written by his adoring wife, Romola, who is believed to have seriously diminished the historical veracity of his biography and diaries with heavy, selective editing.

Chapter 8. Alexander Ursuliak

1. Harald Lander (1905–1971) was a distinguished character dancer, ballet master, and choreographer with the Royal Danish Ballet.

Chapter 9. Christiane Vaussard

1. Carlotta Zambelli (1875–1968) was a renowned teacher at the Paris Opera, where she was addressed as "Grande Mademoiselle." In addition to teaching company classes for top-level soloists and stars, she also directed the Opera school (1920–35). Zambelli, along with her assistant, Albert Aveline,

is generally credited with reviving the Paris Opera Ballet School after a hundred-year period of decline, during which this institution produced few dancers of note. In addition to her work at the Opera, she also maintained her own private studio where she gave classes in the evening. Her work as a teacher followed an illustrious career as the leading Parisian ballerina at the turn of the century. Zambelli trained at the La Scala School in Milan, made her Paris Opera debut in 1894, and, in 1901, was the last foreign ballerina to dance at the St. Petersburg Maryinsky Theatre.

2. In 1987, the school moved to its own modern, custom-designed complex in Nanterre on the outskirts of Paris. Thereafter, the conditions under which the Opera's students trained improved considerably. The new facility, with both dormitories and academic school attached to ten large dance studios and a lovely in-house theater, allowed expansion of both curriculum and student body. For the first time in its history, it became possible for the Opera to recruit and easily house talented youngsters from outside Paris, thus vastly increasing its pool of talent. Today, the Paris Opera Ballet School is certainly the most deluxe, and arguably the best, professional ballet academy in the world.

3. Olga Preobrajenska (1870–1962) was one of the most famous and respected ballet teachers in Paris for almost forty years. She was born and trained in St. Petersburg at the Imperial Ballet Academy. In 1900, she was made prima ballerina of the Imperial Ballet, with whom she appeared in approximately seven hundred performances. She left Russia in 1921 and taught in several places across Europe before settling in Paris in 1923. She retired from teaching at age ninety, two years before her death.

4. Leo Staats (1877–1952) was a famed French dancer, choreographer, and teacher. He joined the Paris Opera Ballet in 1893 and went on to become Zambelli's partner. He was ballet master at the Opera from 1907 until 1936 and also maintained his own private school. He choreographed many ballets, as well as staging productions of the classics. It was Staats who, in 1926, conceived the Défilé du Corps de Ballet, which is now a tradition of the company.

5. For the *Concours*, the dancers in each of the ranks (*Quadrille, Coryphée, Sujet*, etc.) are assigned an obligatory solo by rank. In addition, each dancer performs a second variation of his or her own choice. The solos are danced all day, one after the other, on the bare opera house stage to piano accompaniment in front of an illustrious twelve-member jury that includes members of the Opera's artistic staff, star dancers past and present, as well as three non–Paris Opera persons, usually company directors or well-known dancers from elsewhere in France or Europe. The dancers wear simple practice attire (everyone the same) for the obligatory solos,

but may wear costumes for the solos of choice. The audience, attending by invitation only, consists of company staff members, dancers from the company and their families, former Paris Opera dancers, and students and teachers from the school—in short, an artist's nightmare: an entire audience filled with people able to knowledgeably critique what they are watching! No applause is allowed. The occasion is regarded most seriously. The tension both onstage and off is palpable. At the end of the day, the jury ranks the dancers 1–6 in each rank. If, subsequently, someone leaves or retires from the company, their position will be offered to the highest-ranking dancer in the next rank below.

6. Alexandra Balashova (1887–1979) was a ballerina with the Bolshoi Ballet, which she joined in 1905. She settled in Paris in the 1920s, where she continued to dance at the Opera. She opened her own school in Paris in 1931.

7. Serge Lifar (1905–1986) was the most famous *premier danseur* of the Paris Opera Ballet in the first half of the twentieth century. He was born in Kiev, Ukraine, and joined Diaghilev's Ballets Russes in 1923, where he soon rose to stardom. He directed the Paris Opera Ballet from 1929 to 1945, choreographing many ballets and returning the company to the world-class stature it had not enjoyed since the 1800s. He is generally considered the architect of modern French ballet.

8. In 1947, George Balanchine, founder of the New York City Ballet, and arguably the greatest ballet choreographer of the twentieth century, spent one season as guest ballet master at the Paris Opera. During that time, he staged his ballets *Serenade, Apollo, Le Baiser de la Fée,* as well as creating a new work, *Le Palais de Crystal,* which later, restaged for his own company, was retitled *Symphony in C.* Set to the Bizet music after which it was eventually named, this ballet, conceived in Paris, became one of his most famous and enduring works. Balanchine had great fondness for French dancers, as well as for Paris, where he had enjoyed his first major choreographic successes with the Diaghilev Ballets Russes in the 1920s.

9. In late fall every year, the Paris Opera Ballet School presents its students to the public in an all-day performance at the opera house called *La Porte Ouverte* (The Open Door). Each of the twelve classes in the school (six male, six female) gives a well-rehearsed demonstration of classroom exercises, choreographed by their teacher. They perform in practice clothes on a stage set only with barres and a piano. Their teachers, voices amplified, appear onstage with them. The occasion offers a delicious peek at up-and-coming talent and is very popular with the Parisian public. There are two performances, both usually sold-out. In the spring, the school again per-

forms at the Opera, but this time in fully produced repertoire, both classical and contemporary. In the summer, the students tour abroad in a mixed program containing both demonstrations of classwork and repertoire.

10. Yvette Chauviré, Lysette Darsonval (both French), and Margot Fonteyn (English) were prima ballerinas at the height of their careers from 1940 to 1960.

Chapter 10. Anne Woolliams

1. Dame Margot Fonteyn (1919–1990) was the most famous English ballerina of the twentieth century. She received her early training in Shanghai with George Goncharov and in London with Astafieva and at the Sadler's Wells School. A protégée of Dame Ninette de Valois, Fonteyn made her debut with the Vic-Wells Ballet in 1934. Rising quickly to stardom, she went on to become the highest-ranked dancer of the Sadler's Wells, and later, the Royal Ballet, where she was made Prima Ballerina Assoluta in 1979. Frederick Ashton created many roles for her and she danced all the major classics. During the 1960s, her partnership with Rudolf Nureyev became legendary. She was noted for her exquisite line, musicality, and remarkable interpretive qualities in dramatic roles. She became president of the Royal Academy of Dancing in 1954, a post she held while continuing to perform around the world for many years thereafter.

2. Lydia Kyasht (1885–1959) was a Russian ballerina, trained at the St. Petersburg Imperial Ballet School under Gerdt. She became a soloist at the Maryinsky Theatre, but went to London in 1908, where she succeeded Adeline Genée as leading ballerina at the Empire Theatre. She also toured with Diaghilev's company. She taught for many years in Cirencester and London, where she had her own company in the 1940s.

3. (New York: Mereweather, 1978), p. 90; hereafter cited parenthetically in text.

4. Interview by Shirley McKechnie, Melbourne, Australia, 1987.

5. Ibid.

6. Ibid.

7. Kurt Jooss (1901–1979) was a German dancer, choreographer, and teacher who was the first major choreographer to attempt a synthesis of classical ballet and modern dance techniques. For his company, the Folkwang Tanzbuhne, he created many works, among them his famous *The Green Table*. Forced by the Nazis to leave Germany in 1933, he resettled his company in England. Ballets Jooss toured internationally for many years

before disbanding in 1947. Jooss went on to stage works in Chile and Germany. He reestablished his Folkwang school and company in Essen in 1949.

8. Mary Wigman (1886–1973), a German dancer, choreographer and teacher, rose to fame after World War I. The stark, emotional works she created and danced were in direct contrast to the decorative prettiness of ballet. She was a student of Dalcroze and, later, of Rudolph von Laban, who, in the early 1900s, developed a dance form called Ausdrucktanz, or expressive dance. Wigman, who eventually became Laban's assistant, was one of the greatest practitioners of German expressionist dance. (Laban is best remembered today as a movement theorist and inventor of the system of dance notation known as Labanotation.)

9. Pina Bausch (1940–), a German dancer and choreographer, was trained in Germany and America. Since 1973, she has directed the Wuppertal Dance Theatre and is considered the leading choreographer of avant-garde dance theater in Germany.

10. Interview by McKechnie.

11. Ibid.

12. Ibid.

13. Ibid.

14. Ibid.

15. The Serge Leslie and Doris Niles Collection of ballet books went up for sale in 1971. It was purchased by the State of Wurtemberg at Cranko's request. Today this collection rests in the public library in Stuttgart. At the time the negotiations took place, Cranko and Woolliams were each presented with a gift by the owners from the collection. Hers was the picture of Pavlova. The Stuttgart Ballet School was given an exquisite bronze statue of a dancing figure, which still stands in the school's lobby.

Bibliography

Barzel, Ann. "European Dance Teachers in the United States." *Dance* (April–June 1944): 56–100.

Beaumont, Cyril. *A Miscellany for Dancers*. New York: Dance Horizons, 1981.

———, and Stanislas Idzikowski. *A Manual of The Theory and Practice of Classical Theatrical Dancing*. London: C. W. Beaumont, 1977.

Blasis, Carlos. *An Elementary Treatise upon the Theory and Practice of the Art of Dancing*. Milan, 1820. Rev. ed. New York: Dover, 1968.

Eglevsky, Andre, and John Gregory. *Nicholas Legat*. New York: Dance Horizons, 1977.

Gale, Joseph. *Behind Barres*. New York: Dance Horizons, 1980.

Grant, Gail. *Technical Manual and Dictionary of Classical Ballet*. New York: Dover, 1982.

Gregory, John. *The Legat Saga*. London: Javog, 1992.

Guest, Ivor. "Carlotta Zambelli." Part 1. *Dance* (February 1974): 51–66.

———. "Carlotta Zambelli." Part 2. *Dance* (March 1974): 43–58.

Gullette, Margaret Morganroth, ed. *The Art and Craft of Teaching*. Cambridge, Mass.: Harvard University Press, 1984.

Hammond, Sandra Noll. *Ballet: Beyond the Basics*. Palo Alto, Calif.: Mayfield, 1982.

Hering, Doris. "America Meets Vera Volkova." *Dance* (September 1959): 36–38, 71, 88–89.

Highet, Gilbert. *The Art of Teaching*. New York: Vintage, 1955.

Kahn, Albert E. *Days with Ulanova*. New York: Simon and Shuster, 1962.

Karsavina, Tamara. "My Partners at the Maryinsky." *The Dancing Times* (December 1966): 143.

Kisselgoff, Anna. "For Balanchine, Her Dancing Was a Path to the Future." *New York Times*, 10 October 1993.

Koegler, Horst. *The Concise Oxford Dictionary of Ballet*. New York: Oxford University Press, 1987.

Kostrovitskaya, V., and A. Pisarev. *School of Classical Dance*. Moscow: Progress Publishers, 1978.

Lawson, Joan. *A History of Ballet and Its Makers*. London: Dance Books, 1976.

Lifar, Serge. *Lifar on Classical Ballet.* London: Allan Wingate, 1951.

Messerer, Asaf. *Classes in Classical Ballet.* Garden City, N.Y.: Doubleday, 1975.

Moore, Lillian. *Echoes of American Ballet.* New York: Dance Horizons, 1976.

Morris, Michael. *Madame Valentino.* New York: Abbeville, 1991.

Petipa, Marius. *Russian Ballet Master: The Memoirs of Marius Petipa.* Edited by Lillian Moore. London: Dance Books, 1958.

Shook, Karel. *Elements of Classical Ballet Technique.* New York: Dance Horizons, 1977.

Tarasov, Nikolai Ivanovich. *Ballet Technique for the Male Dancer.* Garden City, N.Y.: Doubleday, 1985.

Terry, Walter. *The King's Ballet Master.* New York: Dodd, Mead, 1979.

Vaganova, Agrippina. *Basic Principles of Classical Ballet.* New York: Dover, 1969.

Warren, Gretchen Ward. *Classical Ballet Technique.* Gainesville, Fla.: University of South Florida Press, 1989.

Woolliams, Anne. *Ballet Studio.* New York: Mereweather, 1978.

———. Interview by Shirley McKechnie. Melbourne, Australia, 1987.

Index

Beethoven, Ludwig van, 46
Béjart, Maurice, 206; company of, 112
Bennetts, Kathy, 215, 217, 220, 223, 267
Benois, Alexander, 359
Berlin State Opera, 361
Besobrasova, Marika, 12–43, 201, 215;
advanced classes of, 31, 35–36, 42; and
Aga Khan, 21–22; on anatomy, 27, 30;
on arabesque, 29; on artistry,
development of, 38–39; and Ballets de
Cannes, 13, 21; biographical profile of,
13; birthplace of, 18; on breathing, use
of, 20, 31, 32; Casa Mia, 13, 14, 16, 24,
38; class structure of, 33–34; classroom
quotes by, 41; and combining aspects
of Russian and French schools, 36;
dog of, 14, 19; and WW II, 21–22; early
education of, 19; and Egorova, 22; on
flic-flac, 26; floor exercises of, 28; on
the foot, 36, 38; graded examinations
of, 26; influenced by *Inner Game of
Tennis*, 37; on hands, 17–18; languages
spoken by, 19, 37; on leaving Russia,
19; and musical accompaniment for
classes, 32–33, 34; on musicality, 34–35,
39; order of exercises in class of, 42;
pedagogical lineage of, 43; on placement, 29; *pointe* classes of, 36; relaxation classes of, 31–32; school of, 13, 23,
24, 359; selected exercises of, 284–89;
seminars of, 26–27, 28; syllabus of, 25–
26; teaching young children, 39; uncle
of, 21–22; on using hands to correct
students, 27–28, 40; on use of muscles,
28, 29; on verbal corrections in class,
30–31; and yoga, 31–32
Bessy, Claude, 242, 244, 362
Bizet, Georges, 243, 372
Blasis, Carlo, 43, 61, 77, 109, 139, 169, 199,
227, 251, 281, 361
Bluebell Girls (Paris), 111, 116
Blum, René, 13, 360, 363; Ballets de
Monte Carlo, 13, 19; and Jean Babilée,
21; and Lithuanian Ballet Company,
66
Bolshoi Ballet, 83, 174, 175, 176, 177, 180,
182, 184, 185, 229, 365, 367, 369, 372;
school of, 362, 363, 364, 368

Borovansky Ballet, 364
Borovansky, Edouard, 364; school of, 63,
68–69
Borrer, Cosima, 70, 71, 74
Boston Ballet, 362
Boulanger, Nadia, 367
Bournonville, Antoine, 43, 61, 77, 109,
169, 199, 227, 251, 281
Bournonville, August, 43, 61, 77, 109, 169,
199, 227, 251, 281, 320, 321, 333, 368;
technique (school) of, 8, 152, 153, 164,
221, 242, 369
Brae, June, 255
Braque, Georges, 359
Brigadoon, 257
Broadway Dance Centre, 85
Bruhn, Erik, 26, 133, 155, 206
Budapest State Theater Ballet, 366
Burns, George, 48
Bush, Noreen, 254, 281
Bush-Davies School, 255

California, University of, 143
Campbell's Soup (advertisements), 105,
365
Camryn, Walter, 368
Carousel, 202
Carroll, Elizabeth, 17, 38
Carter, Alan, 257
Carter, Jack, 204
Cecchetti Council of America, 361
Cecchetti, Enrico, 22–23, 43, 52, 61, 77,
109, 125, 139, 155, 169, 199, 204, 227, 237,
251, 276, 281, 286, 321, 361, 366
Cecchetti Society, 361
Central School of Arts (London), 256
Cesbron, Mauricette, 231
Chapman, Wes, 111, 127
Charlesworth, Terri, 64
Charrat, Janine, 21
Chauviré, Yvette, 233, 243, 373
Chicago Opera Ballet, 141, 146, 147, 150
Chicago Opera House, 152
Chopiniana, 53, 360. See also *Sylphides,
Les*
Christensen, Harold, 45
Christensen, Lew, 45, 46, 54
Christensen, Moses, 51

Johnson, Robert Henry, 187–88, 190
Jooss, Kurt, 253, 257, 260, 266, 373
Juilliard School, 112, 370

Kansas, University of, 149
Karsavina, Tamara, 114, 143, 359, 361, 364, 366
Kaunas Opera Ballet, 363
Kaye, Danny, 116
Kaye, Nora, 150
Keil, Birgit, 267, 268–69
Kennedy, John F., 223
Kiaksht, Georgiy, 66, 77
King, Martin Luther, 223
Kirkland, Gelsey, 111, 119, 120, 151, 368
Kirov Ballet (Leningrad), 52, 79, 151, 176, 361, 364, 365, 369; school of, 83, 178; training style of, 85
Kisselgoff, Anna, 365
Kistler, Darci, 111
Klavin, Robert, 203, 227
Klekovic, Patricia, 146
Kneeland, Joanna, 113, 118
Knight, Marian, 114, 119, 139
Kolomeyka (Ukrainian dance), 202
Kolpakova, Irina, 70
Kostrovitskaya, Vera, 178
Kosloff, Theodore, 169, 367
Kovach, Nora, 83
Krishnamurti, 223
Kronstam, Henning, 153, 319
Kschessinska, Mathilde, 40, 361, 362
Kurvitz, Nina, 178, 179, 199
Kyasht, Lydia, 255, 366, 373
Kylian, Jiri, 206

Laban, Rudolph von, 373
Lady of the Burlesque, 135
Lander, Harald, 205, 369, 370
Larsen, Nils Bjorn, 150, 153
La Scala, 361, 362, 363; school of, 361, 371
Lavrovsky, Leonid, 83, 109, 177, 364
Lavrovsky, Mikhail, 179
Le Clerq, Tanaquil, 244
Legat, Nicolai, 43, 61, 77, 109, 169, 199, 227, 281
Legnani, Pierina, 362
Leningrad Choreographic Academy, 365
Lenzi, Sabrina, 30

Lepri, Giovanni, 43, 61, 77, 109, 139, 169, 199, 227, 251, 281, 361
Les Grands Ballets Canadiens, 151
Leslie, Serge, and Doris Niles Collection, 374
Liebeslieder Waltzes, 362
Lifar, Serge, 229, 236, 286, 359, 365, 372
Lilac Garden (Jardin aux lilas), 260, 370
Linder, Eric, 114, 127
Lindhart, Katja, 169
Linley Wilson School, 68
Lipinski, Dolores, 146, 147, 148, 151, 159, 368
Lithuanian State Ballet, 63, 66; state choreographic academy of, 65
Little Humpbacked Horse, The, 177
Little Me, 111, 117
London Ballet, 256
London Palladium, 111, 115, 116, 135
Long, Larry, 140–169; analogies used by, 158–159; barre work structure of, 150, 162, 163; biographical profile of, 141; on class content, 151–52; on class theme, 148; classroom quotes by, 167; combinations of, 154–61; dance career of, 146, 147; demonstrating by, in class, 161–62; development of, as teacher, 146, 148, 149–50, 151–52, 153; on extension, 163–64; family history of, 142, 144; gymnastic background of, 142; and humor in class, 160; interaction of, with students, 160; on jumping, 164–65; on men's technique, changes in, 155–56; on mirrors in class, 157; musicality of, 142, 154–155; order of exercises in class of, 168; pedagogical lineage of, 169; on personality of dancer, 157–58; on placement, 163; on plié, 162; on pointe work, 165–66; on port de bras, 162; on reading, 159; reminisces about famous dancers, 150; selected exercises of, 315–23; on teacher as inspirer, 166; teachers of, 143, 144, 145–46, 156; on tour en l'air, 164; on turning, 143, 164
Lopokov (Leningrad teacher), 66
Lormeau, Jean-Yves, 248
Louis XIV of France, 4